Motion Picture Empire

VARIETY

"DON JUAN"   LOS ANGELES, CALIF., WEDNESDAY, OCTOBER 27, 1926   VITAPHONE

VITAPHONE THRILLS L. A.

REMARKABLE FIRST NIGHT CROWD ACCLAIMS VITAPHONE

Critical Audience of Celebrities and General Public Thrills at Introduction of New Instrument—Vitaphone Called "Great Invention"

Vitaphone made its initial bow to the Pacific Coast tonight in the most brilliant premiere ever staged at Grauman's Egyptian theatre, where Sid Grauman, Warner Brothers and the Vitaphone corporation introduced this startling discovery as a prelude to John Barrymore in "Don Juan".

Celebrities of the films, including stars, directors, and producers, along with the socially elite, and those prominent in the business and professional life of the city, comprised one of the most representative first-night audiences ever collected for a premiere.

Not only did Vitaphone thrill the sophisticated audience of first-nighters, but also it added another laurel of pioneering to Sid Grauman, who now introduces to Western theatre fans the most revolutionary development the screen world has yet seen.

True, it was a slightly incredulous audience that passed through the doors at 8:15 o'clock. So much has been talked and written about sound and pictures that many were openly skeptical. But it was those who came doubtingly that passed out later warmest in their enthusiastic praise of a new art that, as Will H. Hays said in his opening address, "is the beginning of a new era in music and pictures."

The unanimous verdict was that all the superlatives that have been used to exploit the Vitaphone have not been enough. Vitaphone is the greatest invention the world of music and pictures has yet known, and "Don Juan" from start to finish is a great production. Vitaphone is reviewed elsewhere in this paper.

Crowds began to pour into the forecourt of the Egyptian as early as 7:45 o'clock, and one by one as the celebrities arrived they were introduced over the loudspeaker. Powerful arc lamps played across the sky in gorgeous arcs and illuminated the outdoor loyer more brilliantly

(Continued on Page 2)

NEXT MENJOU PICTURE

Adolphe Menjou is to be starred in "With Their Eyes Open" which is being adapted from the Saturday Evening Post story of A. A. E. Wylie by Julian Josephson for F. P. L. Luther Reed will arrive here about Dec. 15 to direct the picture. Alice Joyce will play the feminine lead.

SCORING THIRD PICTURE

Vitaphone Corporation is now scoring the third picture for Warner Bros., John Barrymore in "Manon Lescaut" with Dolores Costello.

Vincent Lopez and his band have also been signed as a Vitaphone attraction. This booking is believed to be pregnant with possibilities concerning the future of bands in vaudeville.

Numerous other stars of the musical comedy, operatic and vaudeville world will be signed up by the Vitaphone corporation in the near future, and all of them will be heard on Vitaphone programs throughout the land.

WARNER BROS. ROAD SHOWS AS UNITS

"Don Juan" First to Go Out with Vitaphone Presentation

All of Warner Bros. road shows are to be sent out as a unit, according to information given out at the Warner Bros. studios here. In addition to the Vitaphone-"Don Juan" combination now at Grauman's Egyptian, similar units are being presented in New York, Chicago, St. Louis and Atlantic City. Preparations are now under way to launch unit productions in Boston, Philadelphia and other important key centres, with similar towns to follow.

All of the road shows will have a Vitaphone presentation, and it is planned to play all key cities before the picture is released generally, thus giving the exhibitors the advantage of general country-wide advertising.

"Don Juan" will have the same Vitaphone presentation on the road as it is having in Hollywood, or as near to it as possible. This means that the key cities will hear Giovanni Martinelli, Anna Case, Mischa Elman, the New York Philharmonic Orchestra, etc., or artists of equal importance.

Blase First-Nighters Get A Taste of Something New and Really Worth While—Perfect Synchronization of Sound and Motion Causes Spectators to Gasp—'Sid' Grauman Praised On All Sides For His Master Stroke of Showmanship.

IT REPLACES PROLOGUE

By ARTHUR UNGAR

Well folks they went and did it at Grauman's Egyptian tonight! They put on something which Hollywood has been hearing about but never had the chance to hear. It was nothing more than that uncanny device—the Vitaphone. It was presented in conjunction with John Barrymore's sensational cinema, "Don Juan," and held everybody among the lucky 1,800 in the house spellbound and thrilled them as they have never been before. New history was made in Hollywood picture annals and it looks as though if anyone wants to keep abreast of the times when showing de luxe pictures they will have to get that Warner Brother's Vitaphone attachment. That will spell sure success and long runs, as "Don Juan" with the new device appliance operating in conjunction with it is sure to remain on Hollywood Boulevard until the Lenten season comes around.

Those hard-boiled picture people who have been waiting to see what this thing was all about, were shown and shown aplenty. That gang of skeptics who sit on the side lines and say "It must have been an accident," when something good on pictures or presentations have been achieved, did not have chips on their shoulders tonight. They just let their eyes bulge out of their heads and their ears strain as they never did before. They heard and saw and not once did they have an opportunity to assert themselves in a facetious manner. They found that the Warner Boys—Harry M., Jack L, Sam and Albert—had pulled a ten strike which marks a new turning point in the history of the motion picture and theatre entertainment.

Many thousands have already seen "Don Juan" during the eight-week sojourn at Grauman's in conjunction with the Sid Grauman master prolog. These same people

(Continued on Page 3)

JUST CURIOUS

A woman stepped up to the box office of the Egyptian Theatre a few days before the opening of "Don Juan" and Vitaphone, and asked the treasurer:

"Is Vitaphone a new kind of refrigeration?"

NEW ERA IN PICTURES, SAYS HAYS OF THE VITAPHONE

M. P. Czar First Man to Address Public Through New Device—Welcomes Synchronized Music as Big Advance in Industry—Sees Great Possibilities

Predicting that the Vitaphone will revolutionize the motion picture and musical worlds of the future, Will H. Hays, president of the Motion Picture Producers and Distributors' association, welcomed the instrument to the industry at Grauman's Egyptian theatre tonight, when it made its Western premiere in conjunction with John Barrymore in "Don Juan". Mr. Hays spoke through the Vitaphone, and his voice registered as clearly as though he were present in person.

It was the only demonstration of the synchronization of the speaking voice during the evening, the rest of the program consisting of vocalists and instrumentalists. Mr. Hays said:

"My friends.

"No story was written for the screen is as dramatic as the story of the screen itself.

"Tonight we write another chapter in that story.

"Far, indeed, have we advanced from that few seconds of shadow of a serpentine dancer thirty years ago when the motion picture was born—to this public demonstration of the Vitaphone synchronizing the reproduction of sound with the reproduction of action.

"The future of motion pictures is as far flung as all the tomorrows, rendering greater and still greater service as the chief amusement of the majority of all our people and the sole amusement of millions and millions, exercising an immeasurable influence as a living, breathing thing on the ideas and ideals, the customs and costumes, the hopes and ambitions of countless men, women and children.

"In the presentation of these pictures, music plays an invaluable part. The motion picture is a most potent factor in the development of

(Continued on Page 8)

ACKNOWLEDGE THANKS

In an aftermath of the sensation and thrill which came in the Pacific coast premiere of Vitaphone with John Barrymore in "Don Juan" at Grauman's Egyptian Theatre tonight, a most significant note was reached by the Warner Bros. Pictures, Inc., when they extended their thanks for the unusual aid given them by the Metropolitan Opera Company and the Victor Talking Machine Company in the selection of Mischa Elman, Marion Talley and Giovanni Martinelli to be the first world-famous artists to appear on the Vitaphone.

SELL OUT FOR OPENING OF VITAPHONE

Music Lovers Crowd Grauman's Egyptian to Hear First Performance

Motion picture crowds in the past have been much the same for all premiere picture showings in Los Angeles and Hollywood. They have been easily distinguishable from the first-night audiences at legitimate attractions. They have been made up largely of stars, directors, film executives and exhibitors.

It remained for Warner Brothers to spring as great a novelty with their opening crowd at Grauman's Egyptian tonight as they did with their Vitaphone, which was having its premiere in connection with the road show attraction, John Barrymore in "Don Juan."

Not in the history of Los Angeles' legitimate or picture openings has such a cosmopolitan gathering been on hand as was present tonight. It was made up not of those professional applauders whose presence is considered necessary to help put some shows over. It was not a gathering exclusively of film folk. Film executives were there in good-

(Continued on Page 4)

BATHING BEAUTY SCORNED $300 NOW SIGNS AT $85

Toronto, Oct. 26.

Jean Ford Tolmie, "Miss Toronto" at Atlantic City beauty pageant, has signed two theatrical contracts. The first is for one week at $30 in the Uptown (pictures), the second for 30 weeks at $85 in "Captain Al Plunkett's Revue," a musical piece now in rehearsal.

Before going to Atlantic City Miss Tolmie was offered $300 a week for two weeks at Loew's. She said it was not enough, but being an also ran in Jersey made a difference. Donald Goody, newspaper man, is her manager.

Motion Picture Empire

Gertrude Jobes

ARCHON BOOKS
Hamden, Connecticut
1966

Library of Congress Catalog Card Number: 66-14715

Printed in the United States of America

To

Rose and Walter Oertly

Programme *First Programme of the Talking Picture*

WARNER BROS. *Present*

VITAPHONE

AND

JOHN BARRYMORE
in "Don Juan"

VITAPHONE PRELUDE

Hon. Will H. Hays
President of Motion Picture Producers and Distribution of America welcomes Vitaphone.

The New York Philharmonic Orchestra
107 Concert Musicians.
Henry Hadley conducting. Overture from "TANNHAUSER," Wagner.

Roy Smeck
in "HIS PASTIMES."

Anna Case
"LA FIESTA," supported by the Cansinos and Metropolitan Opera Company chorus. Accompanied by the Vitaphone Symphony Orchestra, Herman Heller conducting.

Mischa Elman
Josef Bonime, accompanist
"HUMORESQUE," Dvorak.

Giovanni Martinelli
By arrangement with the Metropolitan Opera Company.
Vesti la Giubba, from "I PAGLIACCI," Leoncavallo.
Accompanied by the New York Philharmonic Orchestra.

Intermission Ten Minutes
Program subject to change without Notice

Incidental music to the above numbers played by members of the New York Philharmonic Orchestra, Herman Heller conducting.

WARNER BROS. *Present*

JOHN BARRYMORE *in* "Don Juan"

With Mary Astor
Directed by Alan Crosland
Adapted by Bess Meredyth

Musical score by Major Edward Bowes, David Mendoza and Dr. William Axt. Played on the Vitaphone by the New York Philharmonic Orchestra.

THE CAST

Characters	Players
DON JUAN	John Barrymore
Adriana Della Varnese	Mary Astor
Pedrillo	Willard Louis
Lucretia Borgia	Estelle Taylor
Rena (Adriana's maid)	Helena Costello
Maia (Lucretia's maid)	Myrna Loy
Beatrice	Jane Winton
Leandro	John Roche
Trusia	Inez Marlowe
Don Juan (5 years old)	Yvonne Day
Don Juan (10 years old)	Phillipe de Lacy
Hunchback	John George
Murderer of Jose	Helen D'Algy
Count Borgia	Warner Oland
Donati	Montagu Love
Duke Della Varnese	Josef Swickard
Imperia	Lionel Braham
Marquis Rinaldo	Phyllis Haver
Marquise Rinaldo	Nigel de Brulier
	Hedda Hopper

A Warner Bros. Production

Licensed by New York State Motion Picture Commission—No. 145607
Presentation directed by Herman Heller
The entire program produced and presented under the personal supervision of
S. L. Warner

Warner Bros. Pictures, Inc., and The Vitaphone Corporation take this occasion to thank the Metropolitan Opera Company and the Victor Talking Machine Company for the great assistance rendered by them in connection with selecting the artists for this unusual musical program.

Mischa Elman and Giovanni Martinelli appear by courtesy of the Victor Talking Machine Co.

The New York Philharmonic Orchestra records exclusively for the Brunswick-Balke-Collender Company, makers of Brunswick records. Mr. Elman was accompanied upon a Steinway piano.

Contents

List of Illustrations

(Illustrations, which are grouped by general subjects, appear in the order of listing.)

Introduction

Only now, as i think about those who in some way helped me with this history, do I realize how many years ago this work was begun. I no longer remember the exact date, which was somewhere in the middle '40's. During that period Dan Michalove and I had luncheon together every Friday in the Barbizon Plaza dining room. We had known each other quite a long while, dating back to the days when we had both been on the staff at Warner Brothers, he as assistant to Albert Warner, I as secretary to George Skouras. In the early '40's he was owner of a chain of southern theatres as well as the right hand, or left hand, or both hands, of first Sidney Kent, then of Spyros Skouras, presidents of Fox Film Corporation. I was next door on the staff of Hearst-Metrotone News (the newsreel, News Of The Day). Quite naturally our conversations often turned to the industry. One day I asked him why cavalcades of express companies, of territorial settlements, of so many adventures were produced, but never a cavalcade of the exciting film industry.

"It is too involved, too complex," he answered.

"Nonsense," I scoffed, "histories of the world have been written."

He laughed. "The world isn't as complicated as the film business. I guess the truth is we don't dare tell on one another."

"It can't be as bad as that," I said smugly, convinced I knew much of what was to be known.

Again he laughed. "You think you can write; let me see what you can do with the industry."

That afternoon I began my research in the Encyclopaedia Britannica that stood behind my desk. As my research, periodically interrupted by my Dictionary of Mythology, Folklore and Symbols and other writings, progressed through books, almanacs, magazines, newspapers published in widely separated sections of the country, and court records, I realized how little I actually knew of people with whom I had been closely connected. Item after item amazed me.

I am sorry that Mr. Michalove has not lived to see published this work in which he had great, if amused, interest. Others too have helped me in one way or another, and to them I offer my thanks here. They are Mrs. Rose Oertly, Mrs. Augusta Cantor, Mr. Charles Werner, Mr. Sidney Mattison, librarians at the New York Public Library and the Library of Congress, as well as members of the staff of the Attorney General's Office, where situations that had taken place in the courts were checked.

The photographs were kindly supplied by Columbia Pictures Corp., Metro-Goldwyn-Mayer, Inc., Motion Picture Producers and Distributors of America, Inc., Radio City Music Hall, Paramount Pictures, Inc., The Strong Electric Corporation, United Artists Corp., Variety, and Warner Bros. Pictures, Inc.

G. J.

Book One, Part One

A Trust is Formed

(1000 BC to 1908)

Edison's First Antagonist

ONE DAY IN THE YEAR OF 1881 a self-conscious youth, William Kennedy Laurie Dickson, stood before Thomas Alva Edison, recited his qualifications, and said he had left his home in England solely because his heart was set on finding a place, any place, in the shop of the world's most renowned inventor. Dickson's awkward eloquence was rewarded; he became Mr. Edison's apprentice.

For eight years master and apprentice worked harmoniously until October 6, 1889 when Dickson tightened the last screw in a wooden cabinet almost four feet high called a Kinetoscope. Dickson threaded the device with a celluloid strip of action photographs of the factory comedian, Fred Ott, one of the mechanics at the plant. When Edison placed his forehead against the metal eye-shade to peer into the glass opening in the top of the cabinet Dickson had misgivings. He had ample cause for apprehension. Edison had wanted action pictures merely to provide illustrations for his sound recordings hoping that the sales appeal of the phonograph, patented by him in 1887, might be enhanced. Dickson had other ideas. With entertaining pictures he hoped to influence 'The Chief' to market action pictures independently. What if 'The Chief' were not amused by the snuff-induced sneeze of a would-be comic?

Spontaneous hearty laughter broke through Dickson's pent-up fears. Years of arduous work had passed their trial; a dream had became a reality. Dickson's plans could be set in motion; the factory could be enlarged; production would go forward on an extensive scale; experienced actors would be employed; agents could handle distribution. With laughter in his voice, Edison said, "Scrap it."

Edison had enjoyed the pictures. Yes, shows photographed by the

3

Kinetograph camera for the peep-box, or Kinetoscope, were amusing. Just because they made him laugh Edison decided against them. They could not possibly have commercial value; a man felt sheepish looking at such tomfoolery through a small hole.

For eight years neither setbacks nor problems, neither long working hours nor repeated failures, had disturbed their unity of purpose. Their friendship had been cemented by the respect and admiration each bore the other. Now, in a moment, divergent commercial outlooks created a rupture. The one saw vast possibilities in the future of action pictures, the other only a meaningless toy.

Dickson, who felt that Edison had not the right to scrap the machines without consulting him, brooded over the situation. But he had not the means to carry on alone or the courage to remind Edison that he was co-inventor and entitled to a voice in any disposition made of the machines.

Edison was too busy to notice the dejected, sulking Dickson. The project itself was forgotten when the mails brought in a report which indicated that on January 21, 1889, before the Kinetoscope and its mate, the Kinetograph, had been shelved, William Friese-Greene, an English photographer, had applied in London for a patent on the Kinematograph, a living picture camera.* A great deal of publicity attended Friese-Greene, who was hailed the inventor of living or action pictures.

The publicity, Dickson hoped, would impel Edison to act. It did. Edison flew into a rage. He accused Friese-Greene, his first of many antagonists in the picture field, of appropriating principles of the Kinetograph. Edison felt his invention should not be tampered with by anyone; his decision should be final. That his rights remained unprotected by patents or that Friese-Greene had begun experiments in 1885 was of no consequence as far as Edison was concerned.

Anger did not penetrate Edison's stubbornness. Two years passed before a friend induced him to file specifications with the United States Patent Office. To do this was to throw money away, but Edison could not resist the argument to place himself on record as the inventor of action pictures. However, he flatly refused to apply for patents abroad. No sense to throw more money away on a device that never could be more than a penny-catcher. Thus the Kinetograph camera and the Kinetoscope peep-box, over which two men had dreamed and sweated, labored and laughed, rusted.

---

*Friese-Greene began his experiments on single camera photography in 1885.

Friese-Greene did not share Edison's point of view. He exhibited his model to a group of bankers and solicited their support. They were not interested in an arcade novelty. Friese-Greene regarded them as fools and appealed to friends. When here too he was refused aid, he gathered what cash he could, walked out of his flourishing photography business, and travelled across England as an itinerant showman, ballyhooing little skits that could be seen through a small hole. Friese-Greene's enthusiasm had no effect on Edison who, in turn, looked upon his English rival as a fool. Indeed, as the years rolled by, Edison might have repeated time and again, "I told you so."

The Englishman, like many who followed, engaged in a losing battle all the way. In time he went bankrupt and was condemned to debtor's prison. To meet his obligations, the machine along with other possessions was sold at public auction. Who bought it or whether it ever were put to any use is not known.

Misfortune did not deter Friese-Greene. Upon his release from prison he resumed his experiments and devoted the rest of his life to action pictures. His acquaintances called him eccentric; his business associates considered him a bad risk. In 1921, when a committee of English producers met to decide the future of British films, no one thought to invite the aged Friese-Greene. That he was ignored did not keep him away. Without friend or follower he had resolutely clung to hopes born thirty-odd years before. Long riled by the sluggish procrastinations of English manufacturers, he sprang to his feet at the meeting and upbraided his listeners for their dilatory attitude toward a great opportunity. He implored them not to forsake the field in favor of American producers then dominating the industry. The excitement proved too much for him. In the midst of his plea he succumbed to a heart attack. The cause he fought for died with him, and a rare chance slipped through the fingers of the English.

A search of the dead man's pockets for his name and address disclosed only a few coins . . . his entire estate. Friese-Greene, humble, deserted, resolute, to whom the world is indebted for the commercial birth of the motion picture, thus came to an end.

Edison, mighty, esteemed, authoritative, who had no faith in living pictures and who considered them one of his follies, eventually reaped a fortune from them.

Edison Changes His Mind

In 1893, FIVE YEARS AFTER THE KINETOSCOPE had been cast aside, Thomas R. Lombard, a gramophone dealer, dropped into Edison's Menlo Park, New Jersey plant to place an order. He wandered around, poking his head under black sheets and dusty oilcloths to glimpse at the many curious devices which were always a source of fascination. His inquisitiveness led him to the Kinetoscope, and when he looked through the lens that magnified the complicated mechanism of the box, he asked a factory hand, "What's the idea of the glass covered key-hole?"

"To see the pictures."

"What pictures?"

The story of the birth and burial of the Kinetoscope was related to Lombard, who was amazed that Edison failed to see commercial potentialities in pictures that moved. A high-pressure salesman, Lombard promised Edison to dispose of machines as fast as they could be made. Disarmed by the outsider's enthusiasm, Edison disinterred the Kinetoscope; at the same time he issued instructions to "keep production costs down." His instructions were followed implicitly. As a result, the stage, a three-walled shed covered with tar paper which revolved so the players always faced the sunlight, was set up in the factory yard at a cost of $637.67. It wabbled and swayed on its base and was called Black Maria.

No attempt was made to tell a story. Films were a mere record of action, a man dressing, a couple waltzing, a child at play. With these jerky little pictures, Lombard set out to fulfil his impulsive promise. His first customers were the Holland Brothers, caterers to the frivolous and sportive. On April 6, 1894, they opened a Kineto-scope Parlor at 1155 Broadway in New York City, where Annabelle the Dancer and other daring celluloid performers might be seen through a *glass-covered key hole.* A coin in the slot started the fifty feet of film on a spool bank. The subject ran for about a quarter of a minute.

That amusement seekers would soon tire of peeking into a box to look at inane pictures Edison had not a doubt. His fear was that the novelty would bore a fickle public before he had a chance to realize on his investment. Apparently his fears were justified. Living pictures arrived unheralded. Theatrical pages completely ignored the debut of the most fascinating form of entertainment the world has ever known, an entertainment that reflects thousands of years of effort, despite the fact that the Kinetogram, an Edison catalogue, carried a picture which was identified as "Thomas A. Edison, to whom the world owes the moving picture idea."

Except for those who toyed with the idea, few realized the centuries of research, experiment, and heartache that went into the achievement. The slow, timeless processes that lead to the gradual unfolding of any mechanical contrivance were never more clearly illustrated than in the evolution of the camera.

Three thousand years ago lenses were ground in Assyria. For what purpose they were used never has been determined. Euclid (300 B.C.) projected images through small apertures. In the first century Nero used a crude lens to heighten his enjoyment of the brutal combat of gladiators in the arena. Ptolemy in Egypt solved astronomical mysteries that greatly assisted later scholars in their works on optics. In China, India, and Persia, mathematicians, philosophers, and astronomers pursued the study of light. Right up through the ages scholars and scientists strove to harness the rays of the sun. Steadily they labored until early in the 19th Century, when the first fixed photograph appeared.

The only person known to have seen this photograph was Charles Chevalier, a Paris optician. One day in 1825, a poorly dressed lad stood staring at the merchandise on display in the optician's window. At last he walked into the shop and inquired the cost of a Camera Obscura, a box that reflected light. The price was more than the young man could afford, but the crestfallen youth could not tear himself away from this paradise of lenses, levers, gears, shutters, and diaphragms. He lingered to talk with Chevalier and withdrew from his waistcoat a sharp, clear view of the city of Paris. The merchant did not realize the importance of the image and permitted the boy to repocket his picture and step from the shop into obscurity.

Eight years more passed before the general public saw a fixed photograph; sixty-odd years passed before motion and photography were successfully combined.*

Although ignored by *Billboard* and other theatrical papers, peepbox shows at Holland Brothers prospered. Above the rumble of horsecars and hansom cabs, a barker, normally given to exaggeration, shouted to the pleasure bent on Broadway in the middle-nineties, "Step right inside, ladies and gentlemen, step right inside. See the greatest invention of all time, Edison's Kinetoscope of living pictures."

---

*In October, 1935, a two-reeler called "Diaphanous" (one reel depicting the Minnesota Massacre of 1862, the other a general newsreel) was shown. According to the New York Times, it had been produced in 1870, was the first motion picture ever made, and was shown extensively in opera houses and theatres in the United States in the seventies. The author has no further evidence that a motion picture had been publicly exhibited before 1894. Still figures on a revolving disc, that gave an illusion of motion, were projected on a screen as early as 1853, and in 1870 Heyl's Phasmatrope employed a shutter and intermittent movement.

Edison Dawdles

KINETOSCOPE PARLORS APPEARED IN CHICAGO, Richmond, Cleveland, Dallas, San Francisco, Atlantic City, New Orleans, St. Louis, and Coney Island. Across the country amusement arcades and shooting galleries installed peep-boxes as an extra attraction. Itinerant showmen traveled from village to village putting on shows in van and tent. Medicine venders enticed the gullible with outdoor performances. Even so, Edison remained skeptical.

Notwithstanding Edison's skepticism, two adventurous youths left the United States and opened a combination phonograph and Kinetoscope parlor in London. Their business prospered and, in need of additional machines, they commissioned Robert Paul, a young English instrument mechanic, to build them. At the Patents Office Paul discovered Edison's failure to protect his rights abroad. Temptation was great; Paul succumbed. He patented in England in October of 1895 a machine identical to the Kinetoscope, sold it widely, and ordered Edison's pictures for his programs.

The many inventions attributed to Edison had made him world famous. Legends circulated about him. It was said he worked sixteen to twenty hours each day; that he never slept more than three or four hours a night, often merely lying down for a short nap on the leather sofa that stood amid the grotesque contraptions in his shop. For hours at a time he exchanged stories with travelling salesmen, laughing at their coarse jokes until his body shook and his hearty guffaws resounded throughout the factory. Although weaknesses as well as eccentricities were attributed to his genius, he came to be looked upon as a god-like character. Men travelled half way around

9

the earth to consult him; homage and respect became his due; his
word was tantamount to the law. That Paul dared to defraud him
was incredible. Edison could not quite believe that Paul had disregarded priority rights. Edison's attorneys were more realistic;
they threatened to sue. Paul kept on building and selling peep-boxes.

Paul was not alone. Like the opening of a gold-field with its mad
rush of prospectors impatient to exploit the wealth of rich lodes,
countless speculators bought, built, or stole a magic box. Competitive cabinets flooded the English market.

On an errand for a Paris friend, Charles Pathé arrived in London
to find the amusement center agog over peep-shows. Wherever he
went, jobbers solicited exhibitors, exhibitors sought desirable show-
room locations, and seamstress, clerk and student stretched their
necks to see each new release. Pathé, whose life until this time had
been composed of lengthy periods of leisure interspersed with odd
jobs, became fired with ambition. With living pictures in a Paul
cabinet, accompanied by music on an Edison talking machine,
the debonair Frenchman turned side-show artist attached to fairs
and circuses in his native land. Under his breath Pathé cursed parsi-
monious villagers who left him to starve. In desperation he cried
out, "Enter as my guest! Travel at my expense around the City of
New York. Feel the cool breezes of an American beach. See the beautiful, daring dancer, Annabelle."

Naive rural folk took him at his word. They swarmed into his
tent and Pathé showed them the unbelievable — pictures in motion.
When Pathé called to departing audiences, "A fair reward for the
showman! A fair reward for the showman!" coppers and silver
poured into his upturned hat.

The transition from dilettante to entrepreneur transformed Pathé.
In place of shiftless, easy-going airs, feigned when he wished to cloak
days of forced economy, a reserved, dignified demeanor seemed
more fitting, especially when profits from the traveling show enabled
him to become proprietor of a London amusement parlor.

Although Edison did not believe in the future of living pictures
and refused to spend a penny to promote them, he denied anyone
else the right to profit from his labors, and shortly after Pathé
opened his London place, Edison cancelled all shipments of pictures
to Paul. Where threats had failed to keep Paul from duplicating
the Kinetoscope, Edison was sure a lack of program changes would

not. He underestimated Paul, who immediately set out to call on his customers.

At the Pathé establishment, while the proprietor adjusted earphones to the head of a little boy who had deposited a coin to hear:

Two apples for a penny,
Very nice strawberries,
Peaches, plums and cherries,
Taste before you buy

Paul asked for time. He would produce pictures of his own make; he already had leased a factory for this purpose.

The news that his picture supply would be temporarily halted seemed neither to surprise nor upset Pathé. Casually he assured Paul that he still had the talking machines and bagatelles, but as soon as he was able to arrange his affairs, without informing Paul, Pathé set out for France. There, in the shadow of the ancient castle at Vincennes, he and his brothers each invested the equivalent of $500 and established the firm of Pathé Freres. A proud and haughty chanticleer proclaimed the arrival of Pathé productions. For years its silent call resounded in Edison's healthy ear. In time its silent call carried over the earth.

Paul was just as annoyed as Edison by what he considered Pathe's perfidy, but he reacted differently. The added competition impelled him to concentrate greater effort to retain and, in instances, regain customers. His pictures as a result were more interesting and covered a wider range of subjects than those made at the Edison factory. Upon their release, American as well as English exhibitors eagerly sought them. Into first place he soared in what now promised to be a thriving business. Once he was securely established, Paul helped found the Kinematograph Manufacturers Association, an organization designed to protect manufacturers against those who considered it smart business tactics to adopt the brain children of others as their tools.

An influx of foreign pictures created a furor at Edison's plant, with much talk of how the Chief had been outwitted and speculation about what he would do. He did nothing. Still convinced that living pictures would die an early natural death, Edison was unwilling to become involved in activities that might divert him from things he considered worthy of his genius. Again he spoke of destroying Black Maria; again Dickson pleaded for the invention on which he had staked his future. Edison consented only to fill orders as they came in; he wanted no efforts made to open new accounts.

The gulf between Edison and Dickson widened. Dickson felt Edison stood in the way of his future. Edison could not understand Dickson's rabid interest in a picayune device that appealed to adventurers, gamblers, charlatans, chislers, and mountebanks. So many items of importance were produced at the plant: the incandescent lamp, the carbon transmitter, the speaking machine. Inconceivable that a man should focus his hopes on senseless pictures. He called his one-time apprentice mad when Dickson said that someday he hoped to make a fortune by throwing pictures on a screen for the entertainment of a number of people at one showing.

The Latham Boys
Put Their Father To Work

DICKSON WENT ABOUT IN CONSTANT TREPIDATION lest Edison discontinue manufacturing living pictures. To bolster trade he took a personal interest in the sales department. Here he met Grey and Otway Latham, two West Virginians, who operated an amusement parlor in New York City. In discussions together they treated the future, especially the radical changes that would take place when pictures were enlarged so that several people might view them at one showing. Like Dickson, they foresaw a tremendous development in the industry. Common hopes fanned the friendship. Dickson confided his disappointment in Edison. Grey and Otway listened sympathetically and convinced Dickson that their father, Woodville Latham, who formerly had lectured on chemistry and engineering at the University of West Virginia, had the experience and knowledge necessary to transfer living pictures onto a screen.

Several years before, the brothers had insisted their father's abilities were wasted in the poorly paid job of a university professor when clever speculation in wheat, rye, or grain might make the family millionaires. A fortune was to be made in stocks, bonds, land, oil, steel. Persuasive arguments and glowing descriptions of the romance and adventure in building an industrial empire proved irresistible to the professor. One important factor none of the family had considered was that great ventures were beyond their means, and their meager savings went into real estate. The properties were sold at a loss.

After the real estate project they opened a drug store. That too failed. A series of small enterprises followed. One undertaking after

13

another collapsed. As each venture crashed their capital shrank. With the last remaining dollars, Grey and Otway prevailed upon their father to let them try their luck in New York. On Broadway they wandered into an arcade to play the throwball games and saw living pictures, something that transcended the dull routines of an ordinary commercial undertaking and did not require a large investment.

Their father was less fortunate. He had found no niche into which he fitted. After leaving the university he drifted from one thing to another, uncertain of his aims or desires, groping for a reason for existence. Yet, when this mad-cap pair approached him in connection with the motion picture idea, Woodville Latham, with paternal affection, forgot the anguish and hardship he had endured because of these pampered youths and thought only of how fortunate he was to have sons to provide an occupation in keeping with his talents. Of course he could build a projector! Was he not a skilled chemist and engineer!

With funds provided by the amusement parlor, work started on the projection machine early in the fall of 1894. Through their acquaintance with Dickson, the Lathams counted on the cooperation of Menlo Park. But, to the myriad of arguments, logical and fanciful, Edison turned his deaf ear.

Lack of assistance did not dampen Woodville Latham's ardour. Day and night he labored and in the spring of 1895 with the Latham Loop freed living pictures from the narrow confines of the peep-box. Late in April of 1895, the Lathams opened to the public a show of motion pictures projected on a screen in a darkened corner of their amusement parlor at 156 Broadway in New York City. Innocent of salesmanship and blind to name appeal, Latham encumbered his device with the high-sounding appellation, Pantoptikon.

The projector perfected, Dickson approached Edison again. Once Edison saw a demonstration of the Pantoptikon, which had been built to carry Kinetograph pictures, he might be won over. Edison simply flew into a rage. He had no commercial interest in living pictures. But he had his rights! Woodville Latham, he said, had appropriated ideas embodied in the Kinetoscope, had infringed on Edison patents. Friendship with the Lathams caused Dickson to be regarded with suspicion at the Edison plant. This coupled with Dickson's resentment of Edison's attitude further strained the breach between the two men. Dickson had little choice; he cast his lot with the Lathams, who sold their amusement parlor that they might concentrate on the Pantoptikon.

That Dickson had made a mistake was not long in coming to light. The Lathams were not business men. The father was kindly and scholarly; the boys glib and shiftless, always seeking easy money ventures. They talked of great things and accomplished little. This irritated Dickson, who had been trained on long hours and hard work. He blamed his partners for everything that went wrong. They were poor salesmen because they failed to convince showmen of the uselessness of waiting for Edison to produce a projection machine. They were weaklings because they failed to induce showmen, fearful that Edison would refuse to supply them with pictures, to install the Latham device. They were numskulls because they failed to stir the imagination of showmen with the name "Pantoptikon." In time Dickson blamed them for the loss of his job at Edison's. Dickson reached a point where he could hardly talk civilly to the happy-go-lucky West Virginians and their indulgent, adoring father. Late in 1895 he arranged a short holiday and took a train for Canastota, New York. There he called on Henry Norton Marvin and Hermann Casler, two men with whom he had worked at Edison's, and who now ran a shop of their own where they repaired broken down machinery. They were steady and hard working. Dickson understood them better than he did the irresponsible, capricious Lathams. Although he hoped he might tie up with them, he feared they might offer sales resistance to a proposition, and pretended to be visiting in the vicinity.

When they asked, "How is business?" Dickson answered evasively, "There's a great future for living pictures." He went on to say that in time theatres would show nothing else, that the spoken stage would die because better dramas would be shown on the screen at a fraction of the price of admission.

Marvin agreed and said further he wished Dickson were not already committed to others. Dickson did not miss his cue; he confessed that the Lathams were too flighty, too shiftless, they lacked the stuff of which success is made.

The three men agreed to pool their savings; even so they had not enough to organize a company. Marvin approached a friend in the novelty toy business by the name of Koopman, who not only

was ready to gamble on a new idea, but who had financial connections. Koopman joined the venture as a silent partner, and on
his recommendation the Empire Trust Company capitalized a new
corporation, the American Mutoscope Company.

Edison Is Left Behind

Assisted by Casler, Dickson designed the Mutoscope; Marvin took charge of the administrative and sales departments. To help meet expenses while showmen slowly awoke to the entertainment value of life size pictures, the partners marketed a miniature device or peep-box.

In an effort to avoid a conflict with Edison, who controlled a patent that prevented anyone from shooting pictures on a perforated strip, Dickson and Casler modeled their machine to carry an unperforated film broader than Edison's. That the strip might be rewound on a projection machine, a special contraption clicked away punching holes in the film as it left the camera, and small particles of negative spread about the floor. To avoid infringement on still another patent, a small kerosene lamp was attached to the base of the camera. Tubes carried fumes and smoke up through a small chimney at the top. The heat of the lamp kept the film strips from being affected by static but did not save the cameraman from choking and coughing, and the confusion, odors, and noise in the little machine shop at Canastota were like those of a voodoo's workroom.

Their projector was neither rented nor sold; instead machine, film, and operator went into a vaudeville theatre as an act. The first booking was at Hammerstein's Music Hall, New York City, in November of 1896. After that showing orders arrived faster than they could be filled at the Mutoscope plant. Edison, who would not tolerate a repetition of the English affair on this side of the ocean, especially by former employees, brought suit. His desire to restrain others from entering the field was not based on monetary reasons alone. He still believed that living pictures were doomed to an early death, but his vanity was hurt by having others engage in the manufacture of living pictures without his permission, a permission he gave to no one.

The demand for peep-boxes became so great, Edison was forced to turn distribution over to a company equipped to handle a nation-wide business, and appointed Frank R. Gammon and Norman C. Raff, sales agents, with offices in New York City, his special representatives. Their first request was for life-size pictures. Edison pointed out that life-size pictures were cloudy, unsteady, that they irritated the eyes, people dubbed them "flickers," that they never would be more than a mere curiosity. He pointed to the fate of the Lathams. A Pantoptikon sold only here and there, and shortly after Dickson broke with the Lathams, the Ansco Company, a large photographic supply house, offered Woodville Latham a small sum for all rights to his patents, and he gladly closed the deal.

Thus Woodville Latham had scratched with all his might at the portals of an epoch-making event and barely left a mark. Tired, heartsick, he faced the future. Everything was gone—even his sons. Their turbulent careers had been cut short by death. Otway died as the result of an appendectomy. Grey was mysteriously slain, probably by street rowdies who ransacked his pockets and tossed his body into a gutter. The father, left to carry on alone, eked out a scanty income from odd jobs.

Though Edison pointed to failures, though he called those who persisted fools, though he argued that living pictures were destined to die, he was powerless to stunt their growth.

The brothers Lumière, Louis and August, manufacturers of photographic equipment at Lyon, France, coordinated ideas embodied in various machines and developed the Cinématographe, a camera, film printing device, and projector, all in one. This was an improvement over the Edison and other cameras and had a tremendous influence on the popularization of moving pictures. The Kinetograph weighed almost a ton and, consequently, was confined to the Edison back yard. The Lumières, with characteristic French imagination, recognized the world as a stage. They constructed the Cinématographe so it might be transported anywhere. Around the globe it went to take pictures of strange scenes and odd people, and to show in remote places pictures taken in France.

On March 28, 1895, the Lumières held a private screening of a picture of lunch hour at their factory, and on December 28, 1895,

opened to Parisians in the unpretentious basement of the Grand Café
on the Boulevard des Capucines a performance of several subjects.
The pictures although genre or topical were not localized as were
the pictures of competitors.

Edison maintained that the principles of the Lumière machine
were his. Inasmuch as he had failed to protect the Kinetoscope with
foreign patents, he was unable to do anything about it.

Paul, not to be outdone by the Lumières, rearranged his machine
to throw life-size pictures on a screen. So did Pathé.

Leon Gaumont, a French manufacturer of photographic supplies,
purchased the patent rights of a motion picture camera from one
George Demeny. Gaumont considered silent pictures inadequate and
with a phonograph gave a voice to his screen characters.

Cinematographers opened plants in Germany, Denmark, and Italy.
Reports of new factories reached the Edison plant with alarming frequency. Of all who scorned the claims of Edison, only one was inspired with a sense of aesthetic creation, a puppet master named
George Méliès. He was so enthralled by the pictures at the Grand
Café, he offered the Lumières his entire fortune for their invention.
The Lumières chuckled with gratification, but warned Méliès against
foolishly throwing money away. Méliès could not be restrained;
he was determined to express himself through this new and glorious
medium. Abandoning his puppet shows he went in search of a
camera. From the moment his deft fingers closed on a crank he
created all sorts of feats. He made things vanish before the audience,
he introduced metamorphosis, simultaneous dual roles, multiple ex-
posure, stop-motion scenes, and many other tricks. But greater
than his mastery of the mechanical uses of the camera was his
ability to apply it as a medium for dramatic expression. In 1896,
Méliès produced on a screen "A Trip To The Moon" and other
fantastic stories.

Edison no longer could close his eyes to the course of events.
He had been left behind; without life-size pictures his position was
hopeless. When the Pantoptikon had been shown to him he had
berated Woodville Latham for infringement. The Mutoscope and
the Cinématographe, he contended, were copies of the Kinetograph.
As each new machine appeared he accused its builder of encroaching
on Edison discoveries. And yet, at Menlo Park no apparatus was
capable of throwing life-size pictures onto a screen.

Edison's Vitascope

EDISON'S TURN ABOUT FOUND HIS SALES AGENTS, Gammon and Raff, prepared. They were prepared because two youths had not been able to stand together through adversity.

For two years Francis C. Jenkins, a government stenographer with an inventive turn of mind, experimented with a projection machine. To acquire technical knowledge to improve his device, Jenkins enrolled at a night school for engineers at Washington, D.C. Still unable to overcome faults in his primitive design, he took Thomas Armat, a fellow student into his confidence. Together they perfected the machine.

With youthful enthusiasm they demonstrated their projector at the Cotton States Exposition at Atlanta in 1895. Their display was a sensation; overtures and propositions were made to them. As they basked in the first flush of success a fire broke out; everything they had been able to scrape together and more had gone into that device. There it lay, a worthless, smoldering mass; their hopes and dreams consumed in a blaze. The offers and bids disappeared with the smoke. Despair and discouragement led to quarrels and the inventors parted.

In December of the same year, Jenkins read a paper before the Franklin Institute describing his invention. Armat showed a model to the Edison agents. The following spring Jenkins borrowed some money and exhibited pictures on the boardwalk at Atlantic City. His show was successful enough, but he remained short of cash because whatever he took in went toward paying his debts. Even worse than Jenkin's monetary troubles were the boasts of Armat that the idea was his; that Jenkins had stolen it. Lawsuits followed. Jenkins (in the nineteen twenties hailed as the father of television), completely disillusioned, agreed to an out-of-court settlement in which he received $2,500, advanced by Gammon and Raff, and Armat walked off with all rights to the device.

This machine Gammon and Raff recommended to Edison. At first it sold under the label Edison Vitascope-Armat design. Later Armat's name was dropped. Edison's reputation as an inventor inspired confidence. Latham, the Lumières, and others attracted only a limited audience. The Edison trade mark was an Open Sesame to success.

On April 23, 1896, as soon as the Edison Vitascope was ready, Koster and Bial, a vaudeville theatre on Herald Square in New York City, added motion pictures as a regular feature to their variety bill. They appeared at Keith houses a short time later. Before long, no vaudeville program was complete without them, and with projection came censorship, brought on by the pictures "The Kiss," in which May Irwin was booked as star, and "Delorita's Passion Dance," the names of the pictures rather than the subjects inspiring censorship.

Subjects usually were simple, a motor car puffing and choking, a contingent of troops on parade, a trolley proceeding through traffic. Notwithstanding, the magic of the screen intrigued an amusement-hungry public. Men, who hesitated taking their families to hear the vulgar jokes of the variety stage, brought their wives and daughters to see this remarkable curiosity. The mechanical wonder was the attraction and it was enough to draw large crowds.

As theatre after theatre installed projectors and clamored for pictures, Edison forgot his early contempt. He enlarged his plant and displayed an interest in production. No matter how fast he expanded he could not keep pace with demands. By fair means or foul, other producers sought to break Edison's hold. They bribed and wheedled vaudeville and arcade managers to run their pictures. Wherever they appeared, Edison slapped down an injunction. One lawsuit after another was filed against competitors, whose machines Edison called undependable as well as illegal. Some theatres preferred foreign subjects; others tired of taking orders from Edison. Yet, most feared to take a stand against one so powerful. Dissension and animosity prevailed. The result — chaos. Inane pictures, pictures that Edison deemed trivial and insignificant led to a debacle that might ruin all engaged in making them.

A Wild Scramble

IN THE MIDST OF THEIR EARLY STRUGGLE TO GAIN A FOOTHOLD, motion pictures were entered as an exhibit at a bazaar for the underprivileged of Paris. On May 4, 1897, the opening day, diplomats, socialites and officials, all eager to prove their compassion for the poor, crowded the barnlike exhibition hall. Late in the afternoon, the place bustling with shoppers and sightseers, someone shrieked, "Au feu! Au feu!"

Before the startled crowd realized what had happened, flames burst from the cinematograph booth and quickly ignited the building of dry wood. Exits were few and all on one side. Terror stricken, the crowd rushed for them pushing and tearing at each other, forming impassable barricades. Clothes were torn off in the scramble; some were left completely nude. Many were crushed and trampled. Wind carried the flames toward the surging, fighting mob. Women with dresses afire ran about, bewildered and deranged, crazed by fear and pain, setting others ablaze. Rescuers burned their hands and faces in heroic efforts to extinguish the flames. Suffocation overcame many as they struggled to find a way out. Workers were trapped in their stalls. So rapidly did the fire spread through the flimsy structure that a whole row of victims perished in their seats.

Outside, horrified passers-by stood petrified, unable to aid those trapped. The agonized screams and groans of the doomed mingled with the creaking of crumbling wood. Posts supporting the ceiling gave way; the roof collapsed. In twenty minutes the building was reduced to ashes. One hundred and eighty lay dead in the charred ruins.

Motion picture men were stunned. They feared the public might come to look upon cinema shows as fire-traps.

Newspapers blared the names of the dead, the Duchesse d'Alcençon, sister of the Empress of Austria, General Meunier, Viscountess Marie Bonneval, Marquise des Maison, Baronne St. Didier, Countess d'Humolstein. Whispers spread abroad that men had beaten their way out with canes; duels were fought over accusations of cowardice. For weeks echoes, sad and cruel, retold the tragedy. The origin of the fire was mentioned cursorily. An investigating committee blamed the cinematograph operator for carelessness in lighting a match near the ether used in the machine. Where newspapers dealt with the causes of the disaster they harped upon the negligence of lawmakers who permitted a wooden building without sufficient exits to be used as a public auditorium. For weeks, exhibitors stood outside their theatres and in loud, animated voices described their shows and recounted the precautions they had taken against fire.

On May 26, 1897, about three weeks after the tragedy, the *New York Times* ran an editorial unreservedly praising pictures of the Corbett-Fitzsimmons prize fight. Through the medium, the editors pointed out, all men might see a boxing match, not only those in the city where the bout was held.

In Chicago, on June 2nd of the same year, two contestants in a cycle road race claimed first place. The referee of the race said to reporters who questioned him, "To assist us in securing fairness, we shall have a private view of the Kinetoscope pictures some evening this week and then we shall probably be able to place each rider at the finish." This was the birth of the photo-finish of races.

Lively and interesting news items were drawn from the industry's infinite supply of surprises and problems. Exhibitors, tying in with the publicity, ran small cards in theatrical columns and retired inside to manage their show rooms. George Méliès, who showed his pictures at the Théâtre Robert Houdin in Paris, set a precedent by advertising daily. Lumière and Méliès established sales agencies in the United States. Marvin added Biograph (Life-pictures) to his company's name, because it better described his product, and as Biograph the corporation became famous. Although synchronization was not always perfectly timed, Gaumont established a regular weekly showing of sound pictures.

Careless of Edison's claims, opportunists swamped the industry to seize riches that lay hidden in the camera. James Stuart Blackton, who had tried his hand at many jobs including drawing, acting, and news gathering, called on Edison in his role of reporter. During the interview Edison spoke of his most recent invention, the Kinetoscope, and let Blackton examine it. At his lodgings Blackton told a fellow roomer and friend, Albert Smith, an unemployed magician with mechanical leanings, what he had seen. Together they induced William (Pop) Rock, who ran a Harlem pool parlor, to finance them in the purchase of a second-hand Edison projector. By replacing a part here and a part there the three transformed the machine into the Vitagraph camera.

A minstrel show manager in Chicago, William Selig, copied the Lumière machine and was the first to produce an animal feature. The Lumières had never patented their device because they did not wish to make their secret a matter of public record. They believed the precaution of placing God-fearing operators under oath never to divulge its mechanism would protect them.

George K. Spoor, a Chicago theatrical agent and brother-in-law of Billy Sunday, the world's most publicized evangelist, opened his purse to Edwin Hill Amet. Amet had a crude device with which Spoor hoped to produce superior pictures.

Rivals sprang up on all sides. Factories were situated in bizarre places. The electric bulb was not powerful enough to permit interior shooting. Sets, therefore, were erected outdoors, frequently on the roof of a tall building to avoid incongruous backgrounds. But the backdrop quivered in the breeze and as a result walls of a room zigzagged crazily or a forest staggered. At times the curtain blew high and admitted into pictures flashes of the city which were not in the shooting script. Even death scenes were not free of laughs. Many a corpse struggled with his shroud to keep the wind from carrying it away. Staircases, poorly constructed to save time and expense, shook and sagged under an actor's weight. Chimney smoke choked the cast, smudge spots soiled the costumes. Often a sudden shower ended the day's screening altogether.

Actors, if such they might be called, were a motley lot. The bookkeeper was summoned from her accounts to pose as a mother feeding her gurgling baby. Innocent bystanders were utilized for walk-on bits, the neighborhood searched for types, the park and the saloon combed for idlers, whose pay consisted of a good meal or a stiff

drink. Stenographers were employed with the understanding they
would double in pictures when necessary. Partners, in a valiant
effort to keep their units running at a profit, doffed their coats and
rolled up their shirt sleeves to crank the camera, direct the players
or develop film. Everyone was called upon and was expected to do
his bit.

Although competition stimulated sales and induced greater activity at his plant, Edison, honored as the electrical wizard of his
generation and one of the great inventors of all time, was irritated
that anyone should cut into his pie. As soon as one company was
under way, he started suit, but like a small boy pitted against the
neighborhood, when one adversary was floored, another leaped at
him.

Sigmund Lubin too was in the fight. For years, this witty, smiling
Polish immigrant trudged through small Pennsylvania towns. With
a huge sack weighing heavily on his shoulders, he beguiled tight-
fisted Quakers to detect flaws in his stock of eyeglasses, utensils, and
other wares. Although he invariably received more than his goods
were worth, villagers enjoyed matching their wits against his. In
time he opened an optical supply store in Philadelphia. There,
through the sale of lenses and cameras, he met the disconsolate
Francis C. Jenkins. They grew friendly and Lubin arranged to finance Jenkin's design for an improved camera. On one occasion a
young chap drifted into Lubin's shop looking for work. He was a
general handyman and Lubin gave him odd jobs about the place.
The second day of his employment a customer came in to purchase
a motion picture machine. After talking to his customer for a few
minutes, Lubin called to his handyman.

"How long have you been here?" he asked.

"Two days."

"Here's a man who has been here only two days. You will see
how well he runs our machine. It is so simple even a child can run
it." Whereupon Lubin asked the handyman to give the demonstration.

Try as he might, the handyman could not make the film stay
on the sprocket. He sweated and stammered. He cleared his throat
in embarrassment. His hands trembled and loose film wound around
his fingers. He looked the fool that Lubin called him.

Lubin, colored a sickly red, ordered the handyman from the

room. When the customer left, Lubin walked into the factory and
noticed the handyman putting on his hat and coat. "Where are you
going?" he called.

"You fired me, didn't you?"

"No."

"You called me a fool. Certainly you don't want a fool to work
for you."

"My boy, that man was a fool. He would not understand if I
told him the film always comes off unless it has a coat of moist
glue to make it stick. What does he know about such things? I show
him the machine. If the film stays on I sell it to him. If the glue dries
and the film comes off, I call you a fool and sell him from the
catalogue. You are a good actor. You must always say you have
been here only two days."

The buffoonery as well as the challenge to the imagination attracted many to the field, including Enoch J. Rector, who for a
time had been associated with the Lathams in their arcade. Charles
H. Webster, sales representative of Gammon and Raff, and Edward
Kuhn, who formerly had been a mechanic at the Edison plant,
became partners in a device. Small fry all, but strong enough to
stir up a legal tempest. Edison surrounded himself with lawyers.
Gammon and Raff, dissatisfied with the treatment they received,
started suits of their own. Armat, incensed when Edison dropped
his name from the Vitascope, engaged counsel to protect his interests.
Each newcomer in turn sought legal advice.

How some obtained the necessary apparatus is still a mystery,
but piracy flourished without qualms or conscience. Most speculated
that fortunes might be made and corporations dissolved before litigation could be pushed through the crowded calendars of the courts.
A get-rich-quick mania whipped the scramble. No one believed the
foundation was being laid for a mighty industrial empire. They were
not planning for tomorrow; they hoped to capitalize on a passing
fad. Ethics were spurned. Agents brazenly advertised any performance
as Vitascope's. Vitascope representatives retaliated by bribing mechanics, operating competitive devices, to spoil the show. At the
Edison plant another machine was built to sell in competition to the
Vitascope, because on the Vitascope, commissions had to be paid
to Gammon and Raff, royalties to Armat.

In 1897, Rector paid a large sum for the rights and photographed the Corbett-Fitzsimmons fight on 11,000 feet of film. Lubin engaged two actors and, using a newspaper review of the event as his working synopsis, reproduced the match, blow by blow. Whenever a picture was a success it was copied. Some went as far as to buy pictures of other producers and sell duplicates printed from them under another title. This practice became so common it was casually nicknamed *duping*.

All watched and sparred in these short preliminary bouts without an inkling of the great battles to follow. The combatants were oblivious of the future, the turbulent, frenetic future, they were molding. There was no hint that doors were opening to riches greater than a rajah's, splendor greater than a mogul's, power greater than a pharaoh's. In spite of ruthless competition, streaked film, and crudely photographed scenes, the industry prospered. A curious public went to see pictures in beer gardens, in tents, in stores, arcades and vaudeville houses. No one noticed whether pictures were good or bad. To see the wonder of the age was enough.

Then, at the turn of the 20th Century, without warning, Edison's early prophecy came true. Audiences lost interest in the novelty. Variety houses turned back to vaudeville and used film merely as a *filler-in* between shows. Actually, films were booked as insurance. In 1900, the White Rats, an actors' association, called a strike. Performers walked off the stage in the middle of the show and the cinema provided the only means with which to keep theatres open. The common practice was to flash a picture on the screen at the end of each performance. When a theatre was crowded, over-zealous managers put on a *chaser* before completing the vaudeville bill. Unthinkingly, a great part of the audience left, only to discover on rereading the program outside that management had cheated them. Here and there a beer garden continued to show movies. The exhilarating effects of the beverage moved the drinkers to be amused by immature blurry pictures. Arcade owners, who had partitioned their space to accommodate screen showings, could not lure customers into the darkened sections. So cool had the public turned, it became mindful of pickpockets infesting the dark, dirty showrooms and uninterested in the unimaginative offerings. The lusty infant industry died aborning.

Resurrection

THE INDUSTRY'S LIFE HAD BEEN SO BRIEF, it had had no chance to outgrow the grotesque, incommodious factories of its suckling years. Crude as they were, the unorthodox production methods were not the stumbling blocks. Producers, with no standard for comparison, knew no better. Although means of production were inadequate, poor tools never kept an artist from producing a masterpiece. The problem was of another nature — manufacturers had failed to discern they had ideas, not merchandise, for sale. Audiences, unintrigued by the quality or length of film raw stock became indifferent to the uniqueness of a mechanical contrivance. In an era of great industrial strides, curiosity shifted from one machine to another — the horseless buggy, the telephone, the gramophone, automatic farm appliances. Countless inventions created more leisure for the masses and, with more leisure, a longing for fun, but the endless repetition of artless subjects, such as two old cronies at chess, poking a stick at gold fish, or the wild chase of fire engines, could not fill the void.

The world was on the verge of great industrial changes, sleepy villages were bursting into active commercial centers; tragedy and comedy could be read in the daily newspapers; expeditions were penetrating uncharted jungles and frozen wastes; wars were being fought, and libraries were stocked with exciting literature, but motion picture producers were unable to find subjects vital enough to kindle public interest.

Neither were producers concerned about beauty or logic. Edison, with the greatest control, preferred to devote his time to inventions

28

he valued more. He had consistently refused to go to any trouble or expense to produce pictures. He never made an attempt to release a drama or to tell a story. He made new films only after repeated urgings by Gammon and Raff, his disgruntled agents.

At all studios, pictures were released as shot. Cutting and retakes were unthought of. Only exceptional subjects, such as prize fights, were allowed to run over fifty feet. When a cameraman discovered his strip was running low, he speeded up his cast and slowed down his crank to get in the entire subject, creating characters that dashed madly about or gesticulated wildly in scenes which called for slow, calm action. Monstrosities were released, just as long as they brought in the customary ten to eleven cents a foot.

In addition to a loss of income caused by the lack of talent and ideas, each factory suffered a bad case of jitters brought on by Dyer and Dyer, who, as Edison's attorneys, attached equipment, real estate, bank accounts, whatever was to be had. Individual mechanics who had built cameras or projectors, small distributors, and others, who were unable to cope with Edison's onslaught, disappeared. Rector and Webster & Kuhn were among the first to bolt their doors. With the Lumière apparatus as the basis for his machine, Selig was surprised to find himself an Edison target. Nevertheless, he too was caught.

The brothers Lumière, whose machine had been purloined and whose pictures had been copied, were themselves victims of Edison's litigiousness. They actually were pushed off the American continent, and their representatives made an escape that embodied all the elements of melodrama. The Frenchmen, their arms laden with prints they were determined to save, and with subpoenas close on their heels, jumped into a small boat and floated around outer New York Bay, beyond the jurisdiction of the United States Supreme Court, until a European bound liner picked them up and carried them back to France. So heated had the fight become, Louis and August Lumière, with a sense of relief, retired from the production of pictures and confined themselves to the manufacture of the apparatus.

Although the scruples of Rock, Smith and Blackton might not have borne close scrutiny, they were likeable fellows, and their personalities as much as the impetus of public curiosity had helped their company to become one of the leaders in the field. The business suited their temperaments. Beating a competitor or getting *an exclusive* thrilled them. When public interest waned, they redoubled their efforts to overcome the apathy. With staged scenes they exaggerated current events to make them exciting. They sent camera crews into remote sections of Mexico and South America to produce interesting travelogs. But poor business trapped them on one side; the power of an injunction on the other. Although their situation was desperate, the owners of Vitagraph refused to regard it as hopeless. They worked out a deal whereby they agreed to let the Edison Company distribute Vitagraph's entire line of pictures on a royalty basis. In a dead market what difference that Rock, Smith and Blackton had sacrificed their independence?

With alarm, Sigmund Lubin watched the swift progress of Edison's attorneys, Dyer and Dyer. He had duped pictures, copied ideas, infringed on patents, and had no reason to hope for arbitration. In a position too precarious for a fight, he gathered his profits and fled to Europe.

In Los Angeles, Thomas L. Tally, a young cowboy who had deserted the wide open spaces to closet himself in a musty arcade, ruefully watched the industry expire. While films were the rage he partitioned most of his arcade to accommodate movie audiences and, through insistent plugging and ballyhoo, built a substantial clientele. Obstinately he showed pictures after others admitted defeat, but the shortage and poor entertainment value of most films released forced him to the wall.

The down grade caught Sam and Albert Warner too. However, they took their loss philosophically. Hard luck was part of their normal existence. Poverty had pervaded their childhood. Their father, a Polish cobbler who had migrated to the United States, was so poor that Sam left home while still a boy to stoke coal on an Erie Railroad train. In swift succession he passed from one job to another. At sixteen he was an accomplished jack of many trades. That summer he obtained work in an amusement park in Ohio. Albert, meanwhile, found employment with a meat packer. When the amusement park closed for the winter, Sam paid Albert a visit and raved about the wonder he had seen — Edison's Kinetoscope. He spoke of the tremendous crowds attracted by motion pictures, and the brothers, as one, decided their future.

The Warner partnership began with the purchase of a second hand

projector, a purchase made possible when Sam pawned a watch he
had received as a gift from his father on his thirteenth birthday.
Unable to afford a supply of films that would provide a change of
program, they travelled from town to town through Pennsylvania,
showing pictures in stores, churches, and schools, wherever they
might lease space to raise a screen. Hardly had they embarked on
their daring venture than the tide turned. After a long day, shouting
through a megaphone at the door of some makeshift theatre to coax
patrons to enter, cranking a squeaky decrepit projector, or eagerly
fingering each nickel as it passed into their hands, Sam and Albert
would return to their room at night weary and fatigued, but not
discouraged. As they cogitated ways to keep ahead of the sheriff
during this trying period, they developed a finesse that served them
well in later years. Aware of the retrogression in the industry, they
did not think of quitting because they had no place to turn. Any
business would present the same problem of juggling finances. Although they had no doubt that their future in motion pictures was
doomed, they were determined to stick it out as long as they might
last.

Soon after the Mutoscope was ready, Henry Marvin sent Dickson
abroad to sell the device in his native land — a move made for two
reasons. First, it absented Dickson, whom Marvin felt might not be
a combatant equal to Edison in the courts, from the American
scene. Second, it dissociated Dickson's name from the construction
of the Biograph camera for which Casler was given full credit. As
constructed, the Biograph device required an expert to run it. This
limited the market to vaudeville houses that treated the package
booking of machine, film, and operator as an act. When business
flourished, a market restricted to vaudeville houses made little difference; enough theatre managers were willing to pay to run a
machine that filled their seats, and the Biograph Company became
second in size to Edison. Once business turned sour, this policy
made Biograph's position hopeless, so hopeless, the Edison suit
against Marvin and his associates seemed pointless.

The public was not aware of the evolution of the motion picture
camera or concerned about it. Why shouldn't it have sprung from
the world famous Edison plant as a jack rabbit springs from a magician's silk hat! Without public support and with all odds against
him, Marvin, who resented Edison's claims to all-embracing rights,

decided on a fight to the finish.

Selig took heart from Marvin's stand and released his stock of pictures. However, the frigid response from his customers made him wonder if his efforts to revive an interest in pictures were worthwhile.

Ever alert, Pathé followed the course of events in the United States and thought he might snatch business from vanquished Edison foes. He suffered from the delusion that his pictures were superior in subject matter to those of his American competitors. Pathé applied every conceivable sales ruse; his films, nevertheless, met with a spiritless response. The venture appeared to be foolhardy.

Though these insurgents possessed the determination and courage to carry on, there was little point in doing so, and no new releases appeared on the market. To get a new print of an old subject was difficult.

Dyer and Dyer had successfully gagged competition. The victorious Edison controlled a worthless market. Not even the intense acrimony which outlived production interested the public. Edwin Porter, a cameraman at Menlo Park, wondered how soon he would be out of a job. With little to do around the factory he occupied his time studying films of various producers. He discovered the effectiveness of closeups, used in Germany as early as 1898, of the dissolve, cut-ins, montage effects, etc. Mainly he was impressed by the technical superiority, mechanical tricks, and dramatic treatment of George Méliès. In fact the only pictures in demand during this period were the fantasies and fairy tales produced by Méliès, who designed elaborate settings, dressed his characters for their parts, and constantly introduced unusual photographic effects. Porter compared Méliès' films with contemporary productions, which falsified spot news or depicted the ridiculous antics of Happy Hooligan, Foxy Grandpa or other comic strip heroes, and finally realized that a lack of suspense or dramatic interest had lost public support for the industry.

Unlike Méliès, who found an outlet for his imagination in weird and sentimental stories, Porter was vigorous and realistic. He added a heroic rescue sequence to some discarded film of a fire stored in the Edison vaults, dramatized the events by cutting and rearranging the scenes, inserted a love interest, and in 1903 released a theme that long had been a hit on the spoken stage, "The Life Of An

American Fireman."

Barkers had something new to shout; theatre owners had something new to advertise — a thriller. Sordid adventure reawakened American audiences. The tense excitement aroused by this picture inspired the making of others. Porter chanced "The Great Train Robbery" and films more daring. Appeal to human emotions through sensationalism was illustrated.

Kinetoscope Phonograph and Graphophone Arcade. San Francisco, Calif. c1899.

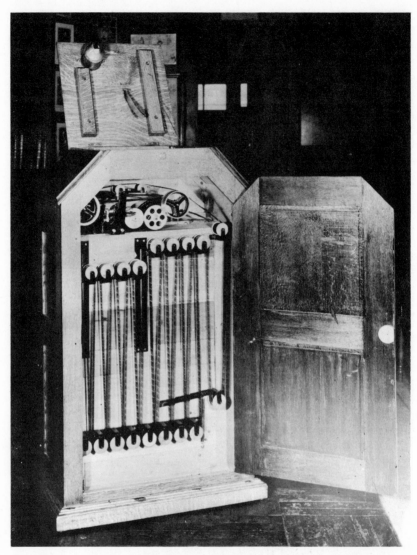

The Edison Kinetoscope.
First demonstrated on October 6, 1889 at West Orange, N. J.

Paul's Theatregraph devised in October 1895.
Demonstrated at London Royal Institute February 28, 1896. Employed a hand-fed arc lamp.

Power's Peerlescope Projector made by Nicholas Power in New York City in 1902. Equipped with a gas light and belt driven directly from the rim of the crankwheel. Film that passed through the projector dropped into a cloth bag.

Phantoscope invented by C. Francis Jenkins.

In a collection at Franklin Institute in Philadelphia. Photographed by Gladys Muller.

Ed DuPar and Willard Van Engen shooting from an early sound booth. This was used for the filming of the JAZZ SINGER in 1927. This sound booth kept the outside mike from picking up the camera noises.

The Projection Department of the Radio City Music Hall, the world's largest theatre. Images are thrown from the front of the playhouse to the huge plastic screen, a distance of 190 feet, with perfect visibility for the patrons from every part of the 6,200-seat theatre. Ben Olevsky left, is Chief Projectionist.

The fabulous control board in the wings of Radio City Music Hall's great stage from which the many mechanical wonders of the stage (hydraulic elevator platforms, orchestra pit elevator, revolving stage and contour curtain) are electrically operated. As shown here is John Jackson, director of stage operations, giving instructions by phone to technicians high in the flies. At left in the photo are loudspeakers, back-stage PAX call system equipment and rows of lights which indicate when dressing rooms are occupied.

Progress

IF PORTER THOUGHT HE MIGHT HOLD THE FIELD UNCHALLENGED, he was mistaken. Activity at the Edison plant provoked rivalry. An urge to save investments and jobs spread like a plague. Actuated by laws of self-preservation, wits became sharper. Turmoil, cunning, greed — each took its place in the new scheme of things, and the sagacity and tenacity of man were demonstrated once again.

In an attempt to avoid a hit and miss policy, Marvin engaged an author to write breath-taking skits and a director to keep actors from strutting pompously in the foreground and to guide them into a display of emotions seemly for the screen. Since prudence had not saved him from the wrath of Edison, he modified the Biograph to carry thirty-five millimeter films, standard size for all other projectors. This cut down the cost of blank stock and extended his market.

The wealth of story material in the adventures of men leading lonely lives on ranches, in mining settlements, or lumber camps, and the austere beauty of their surroundings, had inspired William Selig when he traveled through the west during his days as a minstrel. Now, they provided him with plots and settings for *westerns*. He went into a California wilderness to make his pictures for two reasons. The first, to take himself as far as possible from the annoyance of subpoenas. Watchmen stood guard, and when a stranger appeared in the neighborhood, the equipment was hidden or rushed over the Mexican border. The second reason was to get natural backgrounds for his films, which were dramatizations of stories in which pioneers, cowboys, and Indians rode, ran, and fought. Selig

34

gave the words "moving pictures" new significance — from movement of pictures on a reel to movement in pictures.

George Spoor returned to the scene. The result was Essanay, fabricated from the initials of the last names of Spoor and his partner, G. M. Anderson, famous on the screen as Bronco Billy. An imitation of Selig's cowboy and Indian thrillers started Essanay on its way.

In 1905, Samuel Long, a business executive, Francis Marion, a newspaper man, and George Kleine invested a total of $600 and unfurled the Kalem banner in the Edison stronghold — New Jersey. Kleine was a seasoned veteran in the field. From his father he had inherited a stereopticon views business, the oldest such factory in the United States. To this he added a film department and became the American representative for Gaumont, Warwick, and other European producers. The chance of acquiring some of the business lost by firms that had dropped from the field tempted him to go into the manufacturing end. His entry was accompanied by an outburst of invectives. He called Edison unfair, rapacious, belligerent; he publicized widely Edison's attempts to monopolize the industry; he blamed Edison for the slack. At the same time he turned to prospective customers with flattery and extravagant promises. He used the names of popular novels and plays as titles for his pictures, keeping to the story only if he were so inclined. When Kleine was sued by the estate of the novelist Lew Wallace for an infraction of copyright in the filming of "Ben Hur," he berated the heirs for lack of gratitude in failing to appreciate the publicity derived from the photoplay. The court however awarded the Wallace heirs $25,000. In spite of lawsuits, the business tactics of Kleine were profitable. Three years after Kalem was organized the company reported a profit of $500 weekly.

As old competitors stepped up production, life abroad became monotonous for Lubin. Nothing was as exhilarating as a match with an equal combatant, so jovial moon-faced Lubin sailed for Philadelphia. An old army game, something for nothing, was the simple expedient by which he reestablished himself. Each subscriber to Lubin's film service received a premium, a Victor Talking Machine, complete with horn and sound box.

Commitments to Edison, submitted to in a moment of weakness, just slipped the minds of Rock, Smith, and Blackton. News, that it might be presented without delay, was synthesized from newspaper reports, often melodramatically unconvincing. Stage successes were pushed into work for the screen. Even at the height of their enthusiasm they took precaution and credited a copyright owner on the picture's main title in exchange for permission to use the material free of charge. (In 1954, a former trans-Atlantic flyer was paid $1,000,000 for the right to produce his biography as a film.) Thus Vitagraph avoided the lawsuits that Kalen encountered.

The names of great personalities of the Parisian stage appeared in the Pathe' list of characters. Famous romances were adopted by his French competitors. Italy held the spotlight with historic pageants and costumed spectacles. In England the trend was less ambitious. The early English lead, once held by Paul, Warwick, and Urban, had been lost, but by, imitating heroic American films and sentimental French love scenes, these firms were carried along by the swelling tide.

All producers increased their incomes by selling footage at the end of a story to an industrial advertiser. The footage so used was called an "Educational Feature." Among the titles of these disguised advertisements were: "The Making of Money," "Fishing at Gloucester, Mass.," "The Wonders of the International Harvester," "The Magic in a Golf Ball."

Studios replaced old factories, no longer adequate to house the stage, executive offices, developing rooms, and storage space required for the ever increasing supply of costumes, scenery, furniture, and props. Poorly financed producers, unable to bear high rentals, remodelled vacant barns and stables to serve them. Rococo or austere, large or small, the new quarters swarmed with excitement. Doors opened and slammed from morning until well into the night as an endless stream of costume designers, scenic artists, and electricians scurried in and out. Rasping screeches announced the property man as he pushed furniture around the set. A piano played to inspire actors with the proper emotions. Directors megaphoned their orders. Chief executives, unwilling to fall into the background, yelled above the hubbub.

Notwithstanding internal disagreements and incessant commotion this reckless industry won the serious consideration of large and well established commercial institutions. Nationally known express agencies bid for its business. Railroads rearranged schedules to facilitate film shipments. Automobile salesmen demonstrated the advantage of the motor car over the bicycle for local deliveries. Telegraph wires buzzed with orders and instructions. Advertising agents presented sensational promotional schemes.

As the industry forged ahead, its troubles increased. Actors presented the greatest problem. Heretofore film performers mended their wardrobes, repaired the scenery, helped with the props, or assisted at other odd jobs. Stars of the speaking stage would not condescend to do this; except as a lark or for some extraordinary picture, they refused to appear in films. They looked upon the movie as upon a poor relative. Supporting players hesitated to accept film engagements for fear prejudice against the movies might jeopardize their stage future. Antipathy became so great, procuring an actress often became impossible, and men had to be dressed to impersonate female characters. The only actors consistently available were *turtles** unwilling to admit defeat and thankful for the $50 weekly paid to leads or the $20 or $25 paid for minor roles.

To fill the need for stories, writing competitions were held. The average prize was $10 or $15; sometimes as much as $25 was paid for a single scenario. News reporters, although they regarded it as a prostitution of their talents, entered these contests. Dogging celebrities, flattering a debutante, exposing dire slum conditions, or tracking down a fugitive brought a meager reward, not more than $30 or $35 weekly from the Fourth Estate. Crudely written tales, often recitals of exciting professional adventures that required a mere hour or two to jot down, or dramatized versions of items that appeared in the *New York Herald's* "Personal Column," increased their earnings to upwards of $100 a week.

The chase scene became a *must* is practically every film. Slapstick comedies and melodramas were turned out by the score. Studios put themselves on a schedule of a picture a day. One thing was obvious, bankers and other monied interests were not deeply involved in the financial obligations of these early producers, as comedies and tragedies alike treated problems of social significance: the cruelty of poverty, the curse of drink, the seduction of an innocent working girl by her employer, the ruthlessness involved in the struggle for success, the temptation to steal. All were over-sentimentalized. Nevertheless, they revitalized the industry.

---

*Those who had no measure of success, the laggards.

As better cameras made steadier pictures, films were lengthened and releases ran from 150 to 400 feet. The invention of the mercury vapour lamp made the shooting of indoor pictures possible. Subtitles, first introduced by Pathé, were added so that a raconteur no longer was required to inflame or depress the audience with exciting or melancholy interpretations as each scene was flashed on the screen. Some theatres, desiring a realistic effect, disregarded the titles and placed an actor behind the curtain to work sound effects or talk for characters in the film.

Tom Tally, encouraged by the activity, tore out his toy rifles, mechanical gypsy fortune-teller, and bagatelle games. His arcade was transformed into an "Electric Theatre for Moving Pictures" exclusively, admission ten cents for evening performances, five cents for matinees.

Movie houses began to appear in all principal American cities. In 1904, Archie L. Sheppard, a theatrical booking agent, sent road shows, composed of a projectionist, machine, and films, on tour through the eastern states.

With the revival, Harry Warner sold his bicycle and shoe repair shop and threw his lot in with his brothers. The capital he brought into the business enabled them to open the Cascade Theatre at New Castle, Pennsylvania. Jack, the baby brother, when not engaged in sweeping the rubbish or running errands, sang popular songs in an off-key tenor to pep up the show.

John P. Harris and his brother-in-law, Harry Davis, theatre owners with property in western Pennsylvania, saw appeal for the less fortunate in the heart-rending stories of the poor and the ludicrous involvements of the average man. In 1905, they tore out the front of one of their stores in McKeesport, set an entrance back several yards to effect a theatre lobby, draped the interior with cast-off decorations of an operatic production, installed ninety-six straight-back chairs and a piano, and opened a "Nickelodeon", that is a picture house with an admission of five cents. From eight each morning until midnight, a steady flow of miners and farmers came to be entertained.

Arcades transformed into little theatres and presented twenty-minute shows. Enterprising men with small capital blacked the windows of vacant stores, installed a hundred or two (not more than two hundred ninety-nine, as three hundred seats legally constituted a theatre) cheap spindle-back wooden chairs or benches (sometimes rented from the town undertaker or caterer), an out-of-tune piano or a phonograph with records that were scratched, hung out a sign reading, "Nickelette" or "Nickelodeon", and were in the movie business. Posters, advertising the shows, were pasted on barns, outhouses, or other buildings in the surrounding countryside. Frequently theatre owners did the work themselves. Local bakers and other shopkeepers who displayed programs or window cards were paid with ducats (passes).

One firm, the Superior Film Company of Toledo, Ohio, made a fortune by selling completely furnished theatres on the installment plan to would-be operators. Pop Lubin sold stamped-metal fronts for permanent theatres and lithograph fronts to transient operators. Thus he opened the way for pre-fabricated homes and the mass production of building panels, such as those that were used in 1953 to enclose the twenty-six stories of the skyscraper at 99 Park Avenue, New York City, in six and one-half days.

An impoverished Kentuckian scandalized his neighbors by transforming his Louisville mansion into a picture palace operated by one man. The front hall became the lobby; the parlor made a luxurious auditorium. Tickets were sold by the proprietor, himself, who also acted as barker. When enough tickets had been sold to fill the parlor, the box office, a decorated dry goods case, was closed. The cashier then took his place as doorman and usher by turn. When everyone was seated he locked the door and gave his attention to a rickety projection machine. As he ground the crank, he gave an improvised lecture, calling attention to unusual items in the film. After the picture he announced, "Ladies and gentlemen, I have a colored porter here who can do a monologue or a contortion act to wind up the performance. Which do you prefer?"

Ice cream parlors, skating rinks, beer gardens ran films as an added attraction. At Vincennes, Indiana, a church was converted into a motion picture palace. At a Hudson Bay post on the Skeena River, two weeks' journey from Vancouver, a dank storage cellar, dug in the side of a hill, resounded with the appreciation of men who were saved from losing contact with the outside world as they sat on crates and barrels to look at pictures imported from the United States. The United States Navy itself voted appropriations for the production of films to lure the youth of the nation with scenes of adventures to be had at sea. These pictures were circulated free to theatres, which ran them in lieu of a travelogue or newsreel.

No Main Street was complete without its nickel show. One thousand sprang into existence in 1906, and within three years between eight thousand and ten thousand were established in the United States. By 1914, the United States alone had twenty thousand motion picture houses representing an investment of $5,000,000,000. Most were *grinds* offering continuous performances. A few were deluxe, that is, a curtain was closed for almost a minute after the showing of the feature to indicate the end of one performance and the beginning of another. As a week-end attraction, some shows added *flesh* (vaudeville), frequently composed of *pluggers* sent out free-of-charge by music publishers to plug their songs. An exhibitor in an extravagant mood engaged a *ten-percenter* (theatrical agency talent). The rush for motion picture theatre licenses afforded vast opportunities; a deputy chief in charge of the New York City bureau grew rich.

Quiet and peace passed from daily life. Talking machines blasted away in front of theatoriums, playing a song, telling a humorous story, or announcing the day's attraction. But more than likely the low price of admission itself filled the house. Five reels for five cents made it possible for a poor man to take his family out for a good time.

A fever called progress spread. With pitifully small aspirations, entrepreneurs sought divers ways to prove themselves showmen and incidentally to increase their intake. Theatres throbbed with touching, romantic ballads, illustrated on the screen for audiences who joined in the choruses. Beauty contests created envied belles. Amateur nights brought out local talent. Occasionally colored or pronouncing pictures (pictures accompanied by a talking machine) were introduced. A baby-checking system was inaugurated. Prize contest puzzle slides were shown. On souvenir days, dishes, pencils, fans, mirrors, or other articles were given away. One theatre owner installed two projectors that he might run his show for an hour and a half without intermission. In some instances, the player piano was supplemented by two extra pieces in the hope that louder music would drown the screeching and scraping of a noisy projection machine. Painted slides reminded the housewife to stop at the bakers for steaming hot buns, or contributed to the self-consciousness of the well-dressed *gent* in the back row when he compared the shabby straw hat under his seat with the handsome panama advertised on the screen. Sidewalks were littered with leaflets that described current and coming attractions. Exhibitors sought as social contacts local hotel clerks, teachers, and ministers, and pointed out to their friends the entertainment, educational, or moral value of the movies. And there an exhibitor's mission in life ended.

The poet Nicholas Vachel Lindsay relates that he went to see Julia Ward Howe's "Battle Hymn of the Republic." A huge banner announced "The Battle Hymn of the Republic by Harriet Beecher Stowe." Hour after hour the proprietor's daughter played "In the Shade of the Old Apple Tree" as accompaniment to the picture. When Mr. Lindsay asked why she did not play and sing the "Battle Hymn," she replied that she "just could not find it."

Hilarious laughter often was provoked by attractions not on the program, such as an off-stage dog fight or a cat chase accompanied by hysterical shrieks when a feline lost its way in swishy skirts. These riotous performers entered when the door was left ajar to admit a little fresh air by someone overcome by perspiration odors. The heliotrope sprays, purchased at an expenditure of fifty cents a gallon, were unable to sweeten the air.

Floors were not graded so, of necessity, cards were flashed that carried the plea, "Lady, there's someone behind you. Kindly remove your picture bonnet." This method of communication between management and audience proved so satisfactory, no show was complete without, "Please do not stamp your feet. The floor may cave in." "Intoxicated patrons are not desired." "Do not spit on the floor." "It is raining outside." "The baby in the brown carriage is crying."

Store theatres replaced corner hangouts. Frequently programs changed twice a day to keep up with the demand. But whether they changed daily or twice daily, the dirty, stuffy showrooms had plenty of customers for the peanuts, popcorn, candy, and soda, peddled in the aisles during performances. Children, particularly, were fascinated by the movies and stayed to see the same picture over and over, presenting quite a problem. When the situation got out of control, late checks were issued, different colors for different hours. At the conclusion of each show lights were flashed, and all patrons were requested to produce their stubs. Unless a thorough search was made under the seats and in the lavatories, attendants never were sure some culprit had not remained.

However, youngsters were not always a nuisance, especially little boys, who felt important when they were of assistance. In some theatres illuminating gas was stored in a bag. A breakdown in the automatic attachment was a common occurrence. Until it was repaired, the easiest way to obtain the needed pressure was to have someone sit on the bag. If a call were broadcast for a volunteer, a wild rush of tiny feet scampered down the aisle. Managers were not always fair to their young patrons either. When a theatre became overly crowded, the manager yanked a group of children from their chairs and sent them to play in the basement until seats were available in the auditorium. But that was an era in which children were expected to be seen and not heard!

Archie Sheppard, feeling the pulse of the business, converted the Manhattan Theatre on Greeley Square, New York City, into a five-and-dime house, taking the five cent movie public into a rococo palace, just as he had elevated motion picture road shows from tents and vans to the shelter of a solid structure.

Lubin erected elaborate theatres in Philadelphia, Richmond, Norfolk, Cincinnati, Baltimore, and other cities, with a balcony to accommodate the five-cent audiences and an orchestra for those paying higher admissions. When he leased a theatre at the unheard-of rental of $50,000 yearly, his competitors laughed at his insanity, sure that bankruptcy would be the result. Nevertheless his magnificent circuit spread through Pennsylvania and Virginia, and prospered.

In Europe, as in the United States, exhibitors bought pictures outright. Stacks of discarded films, that had been run over and over until they no longer attracted an audience, piled high in storage vaults. As junk, they were practically valueless. In 1904, three assistants at Méliès' Paris plant (Michaux, Assix, and Lallement), impressed by the waste, bought the output of various producers and leased pictures for short runs.

Harry J. Miles and his brother Herbert, free-lance *photycrafters* or *mug-artists,* sold their talents for cash, gold dust, or nuggets in Alaska. With the capital thus acquired they moved to San Francisco, where they introduced an arrangement similar to the one in Paris, and called it a film exchange. The word *exchange* was a carry over from the days when exhibitors made a practice of exchanging with one another films bought outright. Doubtful of how this revolutionary plan might be received, the Miles brothers were afraid to invest in office space and transacted their first deals from their furnished room.

The Warners quickly recognized the opportunities of an exchange man, or jobber, who obtained for each rental one quarter of the purchase price. The Cascade Theatre was sold and the Duquesnes Amusement and Supply Company came into existence. Richard Rowland and James B. Clarke of the Pittsburgh Calcium Light Company, suppliers of theatre equipment, introduced a film rental department. Harry Davis likewise turned to distribution. Montgomery Ward & Company listed motion pictures in their famous mail order catalogue. By 1908, over one hundred exchanges had been established in thirty-five principal American cities, handling distribution on states right arrangement, that is each jobber purchased pictures with the understanding he might rent them only in states agreed upon in the deal.

The rental of pictures became so widespread, the New Era Film Service, headed by Harry Randall, was capitalized by the sale of securities on the open market. Thus was the general public initiated into the film business.

And through all the progress, Dyer and Dyer quietly, efficiently gathered valuable evidence.

The Moving Picture
Trust Is Formed

THE ESTABLISHMENT OF FILM EXCHANGES CREATED A NEW PROBLEM, the question of runs or who should exhibit a picture first. Attempts were made to regulate prices according to size, location, and run of a house but, if a customer hesitated, film salesmen took no chances and quickly slashed their prices. At exchanges, bookers were easily tempted to switch bookings. Owners, themselves, did not refuse a higher price for a picture that had been committed only a few minutes before. On the other hand, once a film had been delivered, no one had scruples about limiting its use. It might be leased for one house, but that did not prevent private arrangements for a fee with a friend or even a competitor. Each theatre timed the show at a different hour, and a boy provided with a bicycle transported the pictures from place to place, a practice termed "bicycling." In addition, exhibitors were indifferent to the condition in which a film was returned. Pictures frequently went back badly torn or scratched.

Producers forced their apparatus into theatres by refusing to sell pictures for use in competitive devices. Often these machines were so poorly constructed they fell apart as the projectionist ran a film. Solder melted, screws dropped out, or parts broke, and in the middle of a reel the screen went black. Audiences screamed, whistled, clapped their hands, and stamped their feet, but the projection machine simply would not work.

As manufacturers, large and small, were devoid of public financing, producers asked for substantial deposits from distributors and exhibitors before putting a story on film. Often the pictures failed

44

to appear and down payments did not find their way back home.

Most producers lacked confidence in their own judgment or were reluctant to hazard a guess. Those who displayed brilliance or courage confronted a maddening dilemma. Trusted assistants frequently turned out to be spies. As a result, rare flights of imagination became trite in a monotonous succession of productions with similar plot and setting before the original picture was released. This habit of producing types of stories in cycles became accepted practice and, in 1941, seriously embarrassed several producers. Isolationists in Congress cited a chain of successful anti-Nazi pictures, and forced top movie executives to prove they were not warmongers. In 1905, one man actually sold shares in a company formed for the purpose of duping the pictures of others, and made $40,000 before he was stopped by the Film Theft Committee, one of the first of vigilante committees periodically formed within the industry. *Toadies* also played a part; they obtained employment at a rival factory, where they ruined negatives or pieced scenes from different pictures on a reel and released them as one story, held back deliveries, misdirected shipments, and stirred up mischief in any way possible. Shipping clerks accepted bribes to get pictures off a day or two before bulk deliveries were made, and thus gave artful distributors the jump on competitors.

Exhibitors, too far from exchanges to make selections in person and compelled to rely on exchangemen, who vouchsafed "No favoritism shown", never were sure what they might receive. The prints mailed to them were spotted, streaked, broken, frequently so poorly mended, many pictures were without continuity. Sometimes old films were reshipped with new titles and advertising matter. These were sent to reach the theatre just in time for its first show, so that the exhibitor remained in ignorance of the deception until he saw the picture on his screen.

Small companies unable to stand the violent competition bobbed in and out of business. In their coming and going they made a desperate effort to survive and contributed to the wild and intemperate dealings.

The puny esteem manufacturers held for their own product was reflected in advertisements which offered, "Films For Rent — New Goods, Good Service,"or "60,000 Feet at Genuine Bargain Prices." Few mentioned pictorial effects or dramatic treatment. Even at the present time, to quote Arthur Mayer, "Exhibitors have always been allergic to anything artistic and their most damning description of a film is that it is 'artistic'. The mere mention of the word in their presence can often make them break out with occupational hives and invectives."

Méliès, disgusted with the lack of aesthetic quality and the absolute indifference that marked the average release, grew frantic when his pictures were duped. To protect himself against thievery he conspicuously printed a trade mark in each scene. Other producers, profiting by his lead, did likewise. Pathé relied on his faithful rooster. An Indian Head stamped Essanay films. American Biograph used its initials. Neither this nor anything else curbed the practice. Audiences were ignorant of production policies and exhibitors were unconcerned as long as the price was right.

To add to the confusion, retail merchants crusaded against motion picture shows. They complained that theatoriums increased the rental values of stores and at the same time lowered the character of a street with continual noise and ballyhoo. In Philadelphia, Washington, and other cities, legal proceedings were instituted, which claimed that movie houses disturbed the peace and created a public nuisance.

As if to emphasize its propensities, a horrible disaster again struck the industry. At Rhode's Opera House in Boyerton, Pennsylvania, a religious pageant presented by the St. John Lutheran Church was held in conjunction with a showing of motion pictures on January 13, 1908. Seats were placed in the aisles to accommodate the overflow. Standees filled all available corners. In the middle of a picture a muffled blast escaped from the projection booth. The film disappeared from the screen, and the motion picture operator presented himself to request everyone to remain calm and leave the theatre, quickly and quietly, as an oxygen tank had exploded.

The audience leaped to its feet; helter-skelter, it pushed in all directions. People pressed into one another. Groups were wedged against pillars and walls. Loose seats were turned over and obstructed the passageways. A church member backstage, waiting to appear in the revue, raised the curtain and fled. As he crossed the kerosene footlights, he tripped over one of the lanterns and set the oil reserve ablaze. All reason left the mob. In a body, it rushed to the main staircase, completely overlooking a fire escape surrounding the auditorium. The frenzied mass stumbled down the steps and, the doors at the base, opening inward, closed.

Brave men and women tried to smother the fire or at least keep it under control. The brick building was well constructed. Quick action on the part of the fire department might have saved it. But the firemen had been celebrating and, almost without exception, were in a drunken stupor. In their intoxication, they engaged in tiffs and brawls on the street while two hundred of their townfolk perished inside.

This time the newspapers were destitute of pity. Since the Paris fire, they had come to hate motion pictures, fearful of the loss of a reading public and its effect on advertising rates. Theatoriums were called fire traps, cheap filthy dens of sedition, where the young were led away from church to a life of crime and sin. A common mechanical defect provided cartoon material. Rewind spools, if slightly awry, would not pick up film, and the distraught projectionist on an undersized platform, cranking away to keep the picture moving, let the loose film fall to the floor. Various artists caricatured this scene with the projectionist slipping off his platform while the film floated around like confetti, tickling a bald pate or startling a woman when an end trickled into her blouse!

But the movies had made their mark. Nothing could supplant them. The populace refused to be bullied by the newspapers. Did not the law require theatres to have adequate exits in case of fire and prohibit the showing of films in any building used as a residence? Where else might a boy take a girl for five cents? Where else might a poor man entertain his family? Where else might a populace bored with itself while away the hours?

Theatrical magazines, taking cognizance of public predilection, ran a digest of each film as it was issued. Some went so far as to criticize productions. One picture provoked, "Someone developed a morbid brain condition. The film occupies two minutes in running. Since it requires so short a time, it may as well have been left undone." Another critic wrote, "This picture is not funny to anyone over twelve years of age." The cry even in those early days was, "Too much trash supplied. There is room for improvement." But at the rate nickels piled up on the cashier's ledge, the public obviously was not as analytical as professional reviewers.

However bad, movies now commanded printed space. Items of screen gossip crept into periodicals formerly devoted exclusively to the spoken drama. *Variety* ran a column devoted to film information. Periodicals and papers for the trade were set in motion. Established corporations circulated catalogues which ran a digest of their movies and gave helpful hints to exchangemen and exhibitors. Useful promotional ideas were adopted. Phonograph companies expanded their libraries of sound effect records and the squeals of a pig accompanied the picture, "A Day At The Stockyards". Advertising material was supplied with feature releases. A collection of stills which supposedly illustrated scenes from films accompanied each shipment for lobby display. The lithograph sheets which announced a film on Richelieu had the men of the French court dressed in swallow tails, black pants, stiff white shirt, starched collars, and high silk hats, perfect attire for a party early in this century. The Morgan Lithograph Company advertised, "Send us $5 and we will express you 100 fine assorted lithographs suitable for any subject, western life, classic, rural, wild animal, romantic." In an attempt to rewoo variety houses, the standard reel length was fixed at one thousand feet, as one thousand feet took about the same time to run as the average vaudeville skit.

And early in 1906, when all were making huge profits, Edison gave the word and Dyer and Dyer instituted legal action against William Selig. Although Selig had copied the Lumière device, the court adjudged Selig guilty of infringement. Sigmund Lubin, Essanay, Pathé Frères, The Kalem Company, George Méliès, and the Vitagraph Company of America, as well as the Selig-Polyscope Company, paid Edison royalties for the right to engage in the production of motion pictures.

Biograph alone remained obdurate. If Marvin had altered his opinion, his hands were tied, bound by a policy that satisfied a bank. His was no longer the last word. The loose practices of motion picture people had made The Empire Trust Company uneasy. The bank did not like impetuous decisions and untested policies, so Jeremiah J. Kennedy, from a Board of Director's chair, directed Marvin. With years of experience as boss engineer to a construction crew behind him, Kennedy did not shrink from a fight; more important he knew how to wage one. He waded through old records for arguments that might carry weight in the courts. He recalled Dickson to tell his story. He offered Armat, who had been frozen out of the Edison Company, a $3,000,000 option for his patents.

This option Kennedy never exercised, but it made Armat a ready ally. For $2,500 all rights to the Latham Loop were purchased from the Ansco Company, and the personal testimony of Woodville Latham was obtained by endowing the broken man with a thirty dollar weekly pension.

Thus fortified, Biograph became the aggressor in a fight against Edison and his licensees. The Edison group laughed. "The whole thing is a joke, especially the Latham patent," they said. While they laughed, a Biograph witness took the witness stand and introduced a strange shade of the past. Under his supervision, a machine was constructed in the courtroom according to the specifications of a patent granted on January 10, 1888 to one Louis Augustine Le Prince. The device was barely known. It never had appeared on the market because on September 16, 1890, before Le Prince had a chance to manufacture it, he vanished from a train bound for Spain, where, financed by British capitalists, he was to photograph a bull fight. Rumors were spread that he had met foul play at the hands of men who had reasons to fear his accomplishments, but no one has ever proved what had happened to him.

George Kleine, who subscribed $5,000 for an Edison license and sold cameras he purchased in England to *outlaw* producers, did not like this turn of events. He invited to luncheon the top executives of Edison, Biograph, Vitagraph, Essanay, Kalem, Lubin, Selig, Pathe, and Méliès — the companies possessing the machinery, equipment, patents and vision necessary to the efficient administration of the film business. Present were such diverse personalities as the deaf Thomas Edison, loud-voiced Pop Rock, plodding Albert Smith, flamboyant James Stuart Blackton, serious Henry Marvin, the bank executive Jeremiah J. Kennedy, laughing Sigmund Lubin, pompous William Selig, glib George Spoor, and dapper representatives of the French firms.

After eating heartily Kleine rose. He patted his globular midsection and breathed in deeply. With a broad cordial smile he addressed his guests, "I enjoy a good meal, gentlemen." He smiled and went on, "When I asked you to join me here I said I had something important to discuss. Well, first consider what any of us can gain if Edison loses to Biograph. And then I want to ask, isn't it better to pay royalty and restrict the field than to break Edison's claims and open the industry to anyone? Patent rights will protect us against accusations of violation the Sherman Anti-Trust Law."

The argument carried. Edison lost no prestige; he was ac-knowledged the inventor of the motion picture camera, and received royalties besides. In turn, he paid tribute to those present by saying this was the first combination he ever got into that treated him fairly. Allowing incidental concessions to Biograph and holders of certain patents, the nine factories accepted the plan, and formed the Motion Picture Patents Company on December 18, 1908. The Patents Company thereupon released an advertisement which stated, "This company has for its grand object purification and elevation of the moving picture show."

The Trust Is Smashed

(1908 to 1914)

Opportunity Is The Keynote Of Business

O NE MORNING A STEADY STREAM OF MEN poured into the gaily decorated lobby of the Imperial Hotel in New York City. Good wishes passed from one to another; many paused to chat. Italian, Greek, and Jewish accents mingled until they became indistinguishable. The slow studied speech of westerners awed quick-tongued easterners. Boisterous laughter drifted from the staircase, where four or five middle-aged men stopped to tell jokes and stories. The corridors reveberated with hilarity and high spirits. A holiday mood was evident. The day was New Year's, 1909. More than that, an armistice was about to be celebrated. The newly formed Motion Picture Patents Company had called a meeting to mark the end of the bickering and strife that had torn at the industry since its inception.

Except for an occasional remark in which a hint of cynicism or pessimism might be detected, nothing indicated that the former pants-pressers, brick-layers, pedlars, telegraph operators, cowboys and waiters, who loitered about the carpeted halls, had just emerged from a 20-year war. They were expensively clothed and obviously well fed. Their manner of dress expressed a reckless devil-may-care spirit. Sleek black bowlers tilted at rakish angles. Fawn-colored spats set off suits with broad shoulders. Heavy gold watch chains dangled against corpulent paunches. Large diamond rings glittered in the light. Almost everyone wore a flashy stick pin. For all the foppery and ostentation, a convincing air of prosperity pervaded the lobby.

Mainly the men spoke of their experiences and exchanged ideas. One related the adventures of thirty-one year old J. D. Williams, who left a good job at Parkersburg, West Virginia, to open the first store show in British Columbia. From there he moved on to Australia, where backed by George T. Eaton, a cattle man, he opened forty theatres in two years. He applied tricks he had learned in the carnival business, and set up a Malayan honey bear, a kangaroo, and other animals in a cage outside the theatre to attract customers.

Another told of the success of a man on Grand Street in New York City, who specialized in outlandish contests. On one occasion, he offered twenty-eight prizes to ladies only with the stipulation that the winners don their gifts on the stage. The winners failed to cooperate; the lucky numbers drew stays! A Scranton, Pa., exhibitor had the whole town plugging his shows at practically no cost. To the man, woman, or child who sold the most tickets for him he gave five dollars each week.

The mood was cheerful when the meeting was called. Patiently the chairman waited for the men to settle. Opening phrases penetrated minds still foggy from jokes and hilarity. Quizzical glances darted across the aisles. As the speeches progressed, diplomatic as they were, the import of the meeting was comprehended. Regulations worked out by Jeremiah J. Kennedy, who had wrested leadership from Kleine, came as a staggering blow. The merging of interests instead of harmoniously adjusting disputes to the satisfaction of all merely shifted the methods of Edison to a combine. The aggregate of power had been transferred.

Edison, glad to be rid of details that hindered him from exploring new fields, seldom interfered with the policies of Kennedy, who frankly stated, "In making a success of a thing you cannot be too particular about your methods. This is good business."

In several instances, Kleine, in whose mind the Trust had been conceived and who thought of himself as the natural leader of the group, opposed Kennedy. Along with others, he discovered it was "cooperate or else." Besides the Trust for six exchanges, four in the United States and two in Canada, paid Kleine $338,000, of which fifty per cent represented the value of films, equipment, and other inventory items, and fifty per cent represented good will.

Unprepared to meet the strength of Kennedy, small businessmen held their tongues. Those who aspired to enter the manufacturing end experienced a quick defeat. No one outside the combine might build, sell, or use a camera legally for the purpose of producing motion pictures. Jobbers were informed that only those who had obtained a Motion Picture Patents Company license might have a state's right to pictures of any of the nine organized companies. One clause in the contract stipulated that the jobber agreed not to distribute the films of *outlaw* producers. Eight thousand odd motion picture theatre owners throughout the United States were ordered to subscribe two dollars weekly for each theatre for the right to use the projection apparatus bought or rented from one or another of the Trust concerns.

The two dollar subscription was to be accepted or declined according to the whim of the Patents Group. A jobber was forbidden to service a theatre, "until he had ascertained whether the exhibitor had paid his license fee," and the jobber was to collect these royalties, "to facilitate collection for the convenience of exhibitors and rental exchanges." Thus the Motion Picture Patents Company saved the expense of bookkeepers to carry these numberless small accounts. Subscriptions accounted for almost a million dollars a year.

A notice was circulated prohibiting anyone but the Motion Picture Patents Company to export film to insular possessions of the United States, and demanded that exchanges:

> "must furnish the Company a complete list of all theatres serviced by them, together with size, location, and details of film service;
> "return all film to the manufacturer at the expiration of six months, whether or not a profit had been earned;
> "shall not order less than $2500 worth of film each month for each branch office, payable weekly,"

concluding:

> "The whole agreement may be terminated by The Motion Picture Patents Company by giving notice two weeks in advance of its intention."

Those present had no time to analyze all the implications, but the meeting broke up in a funereal mood. Adieux were short. All left without lingering to talk, fearful how emissaries of the Patents Company, mingling in the crowd, might interpret their comments.

The Symbols
Dollars And Cents

BEFORE ANYONE RECOVERED FROM THE SHOCKS received at the meeting, the meeting attended so expectantly, the evidence that some facts had been withheld was apparent. The Eastman Kodak Company had been guaranteed enough business to win its consent not to supply raw stock to anyone outside the Motion Picture Patents Company. Film salesmen had orders to confiscate projectors loaded with so called Independent pictures. Exhibitors and distributors were notified fines would be imposed on anyone who infracted the rules. One western film renter was penalized $5,000 for an alleged violation of his contract; he had sold films to a travelling road show unlicensed by the Trust. This obviously was not the only instance of punishment administered without court adjudication, as *Views and Film Index*, the Trust paper, titled the editorial which related the incident, "Another $5,000 Fine."

One hundred dollar fines against exchangemen for placing films on the market before release date became commonplace. The Trust threatened to close exchanges and theatres that dealt in unorthodox film or in any way challenged its conditions. Soon expulsions were reported.

Sleuths, disguised as messengers, delivery clerks, or salesmen, invaded theatres and exchanges. Raids were made on small factories that kept alive by purchasing foreign cameras, removing the inferior works, and refilling the boxes with more efficient American mechanisms bought second hand. Acid was thrown on their films; their equipment destroyed. If a *fugitive* cameraman were caught shooting, strong-armed rowdies plundered or despoiled his apparatus and often, for the fun of it, beat up the cameraman in the bargain. Sometimes injunctions were obtained in an attempt to legally restrain these companies from operating, but more often this was vetoed as too slow a procedure.

An inquiry held in Chicago revealed that the Board of Examiners had been bribed to see that operators' licenses were issued only to projectionists faithful to the Trust. Further, the head of the Board sold motion picture machines and supplies on the side, and was president and business manager of a projectionist's union that catered to personnel directors of The Motion Picture Patents Company.

Cautiously one Independent spoke to another. Feeble mutterings were uttered of ingratitude on the part of those who had been supported through battles against Edison. Within weeks expressions became bolder. From muffled grumblings a seething of resentment and indignation spread, and Independents called a meeting in Chicago on January 26, 1909. One speaker offered encouragement with the reminder:

> "Most of you know that sometime ago the same movement along different lines was taken by the Edison Company, who said it would close up every 5¢ theatre that did not take films from them and took out injunctions against a good many theatres. This resulted in a movement among local exhibitors which forced the Company to finally give up its fight, or, as it did, buy out the concerns which the Independents supported. In its fight, the Edison Company soon found out it had not enough strength in its patents. None of the patents owned today by the combined manufacturers are strong enough to sustain a victory in the United States Supreme Court."

The next day in Detroit, Independents of Michigan, Ohio, and Indiana, passed a resolution:

> "To arrange as a body for an adequate film service at reasonable prices and to see that none of our members is discriminated against or imposed upon."

The Southwestern Motion Picture Association gathered at Little Rock, Arkansas, on February 1, 1909, to hear a prophetic speech:

> "The $2 a week license fee assessed by the Motion Picture Patents Company for the privilege of using licensed films is in all probability only the first and possibly the least one of the many requirements that are to follow after this little appetizer has been consumed."

Uneducated men became inspired orators. All over the country individuals banded together and grew fearless. With vows to fight until injustice had been crushed, meetings were adjourned.

Back at their desks, with no one around to inspire them, small business men grew thoughtful. Many rationalized, "the Motion Picture Patents Company's promise to limit the issuance of new licenses will hold down competition."

Multifarious problems besides those caused by internal altercations assailed avowed revolutionists. Certain health officers, who could not be reached by patronage, insisted on a monthly inspection to see that theatres were properly cleaned and aired, that sufficient space was allotted for each spectator. Where vaudeville was part of the program, separate dressing rooms were demanded for male and female actors. Many cities had under discussion the moral aspects of permitting Nickelodeons to remain open on Sundays. Child welfare organizations campaigned against the admission of children unaccompanied by an adult. Fires occurred with alarming frequency and caused Mayor George B. McClellan to revoke all motion picture licenses in New York City, pending an investigation by civil authorities to ascertain what improvements would be necessary to provide protection for theatre patrons.

The symbols, dollars and cents, swayed the balance. Owners of cheaply constructed theatoriums, in a desire to avoid expenditures they considered nonsensical, sought the protective wings of those who demonstrated a knack to soar above restrictions. All arguments over the justification of license fees ended. Two dollar bills poured into the coffers of the triumphant Patents Company.

W. N. Rubel
And William Fox

THE WEAKNESS OF THE EXHIBITORS SADDENED W. N. RUBEL, head of the Chicago Film Exchange, and he continued to point out to showmen that the license agreement not only robbed them of independence but "imposes a tax on you from $100 to $500 or more yearly for the privilege of using your own machine, for which you have already paid full price." He implored theatres to give independent and foreign producers not affiliated with the Patents Group a chance. Charles O. Baumann was willing to support him, but Rubel turned down all of Baumann's offers. Baumann, who had chosen the risk of defying a trust in preference to the uncertainty of the turf, was secretly backed in his traffic in unlicensed film by Adam Kessel, also a former bookmaker, whose activities at the race track had been terminated by law.

In his search for someone to crusade with him, Rubel approached William Fox. Fox was known to be a fearless fighter; his thunderous voice had routed many foes for early in life he had learned its strength. Fox was not more than seven when penury at home drove him on a door-to-door canvas with stove blacking prepared in their squalid tenement kitchen by his father, Michael Fried, an Hungarian immigrant. According to William's mood, householders were coaxed or shamed into a purchase. The child's persistance was inescapable. Mature men and women were embarrassed to admit a tiny tot had outwitted them and, as an apology for weakness, characterized him as precocious or cute. William cared not what he was called; he knew only that he browbeat his elders. But, without realizing it, those days left their scars. He seldom smiled, and his dark eyes were marked by pathos and bewilderment.

At nine came his first contest with the law. He tried to dodge the policeman but his legs were too short. The courtroom frightened him into keeping his mouth shut. That battle was lost. A magistrate warned him to cease peddling lozenges along the docks without a license. He was careful not to repeat the mistake when, on rainy nights, waving an umbrella longer than himself, he ran up to well-dressed pedestrians unprotected from the storm calling, "Wauk ya ta tha el fer a nickel! Whatdaya say, mista? "

An ingratiating voice helped dispose of his basket of souvenirs and sandwiches at parades and conventions. Sundays he hawked peanuts and balloons in the park. Before he was twelve, he decided on a trade and talked a sweatshop proprietor into giving him a job. Eleven hours a day he cut linings for men's suits.

Even at home, his life was a succession of action and noise. One child after another was born until there were thirteen. The children ran through the sunless flat in wild confusion. Everyone shouted to be heard. In the hubbub his mother hustled about washing thread-bare clothes, scrubbing splintered wooden floors, or stitching fancy slippers to help feed the ever-growing family.

William accepted worn shoes stuffed with cardboard as a matter of course. He saw nothing unusual in the fact that a boy as young and frail as he contributed to the family upkeep. School and play were for the rich; such luxuries had no place in the life of the poor. William was not presumptuous enough to desire things beyond his station, but, as malnutrition and disease snatched the life of six of his young brothers and sisters the idea of providing for those who remained obsessed him. With a boyhood chum, Cliff Gordon, later famous as a comedian, he appeared as a clodhopper in cheap vaude-ville houses. He jumped from one thing to another, no job was too menial, as long as he worked. By the time he was 24, his name Americanized, he had $1,600 in the bank, proceeds from the sale of a cloth-shrinking and second-hand clothing shop he had operated in partnership with one Sol Brill, a young man like himself who had run the gamut of hard times.

The year was 1903. Amusement parlors with an aisle of peep-boxes were the rage. An establishment on Broadway, Brooklyn, owned by James Stuart Blackton was brought to his attention. The arcade was always crowded, and when William asked why Blackton wanted to sell it, he was told, "The Vitagraph factory is expanding rapidly. Mr. Blackton can't afford to give the arcade any time. As a Vitagraph partner he is a very rich man; this place is a drop in the bucket to him." To Fox, who regarded men of wealth as men of honor, the excuse seemed reasonable, and he convinced Brill to keep their partnership intact. Their first lesson in the ethics of the film business came with the transfer of ownership. Upon receipt of the keys they became aware that an officer of one of the great producing units had peopled the hall with professional plants. Brill cried about the money he stood to lose until Fox did not know which annoyed him more — the perfidy or the whimpering. Fox had ideas for improving the place, but Brill's unwillingness to gamble further handicapped him, so he arranged to take over his partner's share.

For hours at a time Fox stood outside the arcade, his arcade, counting passersby, scrutinizing the entrance, surveying the wall space available for advertising. He turned the second floor into a movie theatre, but the home-loving people of Brooklyn were not curious. They walked past his one-sheets without reading them; they barely noticed the large banners strung across the front of the building. Fox engaged a magician as a come-on. Part of the act was performed in the street. Those who had gathered were then invited to see absolutely free the completion of the trick upstairs in the movie theatre. Skeptics drifted away; the trusting few were well rewarded. Not only was the promise fulfilled but pictures were flashed on a screen. In this manner, Fox introduced motion pictures which, in their day, had served as a hooker for itinerant medicine venders. Word spread about the marvel. For a full week shows were gratis. When admission was charged, Fox had to call in police reserves to control the mob.

Every time he passed a vacant store his eyes ran from the foundation to the roof and a mental image transformed the place into a Fox Amusement Palace. Two friends who had followed his career agreed to finance him, but before signing an agreement a clause was inserted that F-O-X was to be conspicuously displayed at the entrance of each theatre. A conversion of dingy, grimy stores into crude motion picture houses made the Fox name a by-word in thickly populated areas. In time the name was daubed all over metropolitan New York.

The rapid increase in store shows attracted apostles of reform. Newspapers, more fearful than ever of a potential rival, picked up

the denunciations, and editorials proclaimed that in these sordid re-
sorts youth were taught to steal, girls encouraged to lead a way-
ward life and unmentionable escapades of men condoned. The birth
of deformed and feeble-minded children was blamed on the movies.
Evangelists, citing *teasers,* the term by which the immature, inartistic
love stories of the period were known, preached passionate sermons
condemning these modern vice decoys. Angel and sinner were summoned back to the fold. Lawyers, taking advantage of the attacks,
sought leniency for guilty clients with the plea, "He was corrupted
by the movies."

Fox met the challenge. He renovated and decorated his houses,
displayed program cards, installed regulation theatre chairs, employed ushers to guide patrons to empty seats and otherwise provided for their comfort. He contended that, instead of demoralizing
the nation, motion pictures brought the average man to the theatre
in the company of his family and kept him out of a saloon, that
boys now congregated in Nickelodeons instead of on street corners,
and that young folk were provided with an evening's fun for a few
cents. He booked Carrie Nation, violent foe of hard liquor, to speak
from his stage on her favorite topic. Carrie Nation also was opposed
to smoking and would not come to terms with Fox until he agreed
not to smoke. True to his promise, Fox never picked up a cigar,
a great source of pleasure to him, during the life of the Carrie
Nation booking.

The attacks continued. Fox always had been overbearing and
cantankerous. Narrow-minded disapprobation that cut into his revenue made him worse. The corporation, as a unit, was his obsession.
He did not pretend that anyone in the organization interested him
as an individual. His rare smiles disappeared entirely, and a constant scowl darkened his normally sallow skin. A mustache, evidence
of his growing prosperity and importance, gave him a sinister
appearance. His fiery temper was loosed upon all, associates as well
as meanest clerk. When he entered the office everyone trembled.
Rarely did anyone answer him. Even his partners feared him. One
day he went too far. Anxious to get out of a business that was
under constant outside pressure as well as to be relieved of Fox,
they indicated a desire to sell their shares. Fox bought them out.

A stride in pictures or perhaps a risqué flavor provoked by vil-
ification inflamed public interest. Whatever the reason, Fox added
house after house to his chain. Established theatoriums were ab-

sorbed and remodeled, new houses were built. And at each construction job, Fox, who never wholly trusted anyone, could be seen in a white sweater prowling about the place at night to see what had been accomplished during the day. He wore white to attest his prosperity and a sweater to supply warmth to his crippled left arm, an arm which forever bound him to the tragedies of his childhood.

In those bleak years of his youth when a nickel bought so many things, he refused to waste one on carfare. Instead he transported himself about the city on the back of a horse-drawn vehicle. One day a delivery wagon, onto which he had hitched, lurched and he fell off. His arm broke as he hit the cobble stones. Michael Fried rushed his son to the best doctor he could afford. The doctor removed the elbow joint to heal the break and left the boy's arm permanently disabled.

The diligence and economy of Fox were proverbial. Even his infirmity did not restrain him. On every project Fox prodded the workers, climbed the scaffolding to check construction, and carefully examined the second-hand bricks that went into the rear of his structures. Although his sedulousness and parsimony were the butt of many jokes, these very characteristics impelled bankers to consider him an excellent risk, and "Fox is building another small-timer," became a commonplace remark. But on one occasion at least he was outsmarted. Shortly after he had built the Riverside with 1,900 seats in New York City, the man who owned the adjoining lot built a theatre and pointed out to Fox that he would be wise to buy the property rather than let it fall into a competitor's hands. Thus, two Fox houses stood side by side.

Fox noticed that his orders were not always filled by the exchanges to which they were sent. On investigation he learned that many exchanges could not handle all the business they received and passed surplus orders on to friendly competitors. With little loss of time, he invaded the distribution field with Greater New York Film Rental Company. Free advertising posters baited customers.

When Rubel approached this man who had fought almost every inch of his way, Fox admitted he did not care to jeopardize his position and frankly said, "At first I thought the Patents people had a hell of a nerve, and I told them so, as you know. But I've had a tough climb. My business is good, and I don't want to do anything that will hurt it. I can meet the demands. Why should I upset the applecart?"

Adolph Zukor
Lacks What It Takes

IF HE WERE TO SUCCEED, RUBEL NEEDED EFFECTIVE SUPPORT. Someone suggested Adolph Zukor, treasurer of the Loew chain of variety houses. Rubel rejected the suggestion because he said, "Zukor lacks what it takes."

Little was known of Marcus Loew's diminutive partner. Grave and silent, he remained in the background. The death of his parents when he was a small child left him untalkative, and his reserve cast a cloak over ambitious tendencies. At sixteen he indicated his boredom as an apprentice in a general store, and the simple people of Ricse, Hungary, wondered what ailed the boy. Their wonderment turned to speechlessness when this shy undersized youth boarded a third-class coach for the German coast.

There, with forty dollars sewed in the lining of his suit, he left on the Steamer *Russia* for New York. The filth and stench of the steerage nauseated him. For seventeen days he tossed in his bunk without removing his clothes, unable to retain food. His face turned green and his hands grew lifeless, but he never uttered a word of complaint. To fellow passengers he was an enigma. They could not understand his utter lack of self-commiseration. He seemed to be dying. Nevertheless when he spoke, he spoke of the future, although he had no set plan and no idea what he would do in America.

Adolph disembarked on Bowling Green in the autumn of 1888. No one greeted him, but homesickness and lonesomeness were alien to him. He stood transfixed before cold, grey buildings six to twelve stories high along lower Broadway. Tiny, weighing less than 100 pounds, the insignificant boy in his wrinkled, untidy suit was a ludicrous sight as he gaped at examples of industrial progress in America. However, he was oblivious to everything but his intense desire to become an integral part of all he saw. A kinship existed between him and the sight he viewed.

Prospects for the young immigrant were bleak. He had no trade and was unable to speak English. *Landsleit* in the city's Hungarian section were not too cordial. They feared this undersized boy might be a burden. But the somber, perplexing Adolph depended on no one. He learned his way about the city and went in search of work, any sort of work.

An upholsterer took one look at his size and offered him $2 a week. Adolph accepted, and no matter how unreasonable the demands of his employer, he fulfilled them. His employer had no mercy; each night Adolph returned to his room, too exhausted to move. The laborious tasks did not discourage him. What offended him was the impracticability of paying three dollars for room and board on a two dollar weekly salary.

Before his forty dollars were spent, Adolph looked for other work. A fur manufacturer doubled his salary and acquired an alert, steady, industrious porter. Here, Adolph believed, lay his destiny. Closely he observed the furriers and learned the trade. In three years he commanded the expert's salary of eight dollars a week.

Time was precious; not a minute was to be wasted. In the slack season Adolph bottled imported wine. His evenings were spent at Ridley's Department Store, where he wrapped packages to increase his earnings by fifty cents daily, or at night school to overcome difficulties imposed upon him by his ignorance of the English language. During a decade of rigid abstinence, in which Zukor regarded expenditures for any form of amusement an unnecessary extravagance, Le Prince, Edison, Friese-Greene and others perfected an entertainment device which eventually provided Adolph Zukor with a fortune and industrial position beyond his wildest fancies. Seeking success as a furrier, the advent of peep shows was meaningless to him. As arcades opened and prospered he bent lower and lower over a sewing machine, seaming furs. Silently, persistently, he labored. Late into each night he worked, designing and cutting fur neckpieces from odd pelts.

The fantastic tales related by co-workers of fortunes to be made in the west kindled the insatiable desires hidden behind his immobile mask. With a bundle of furs he left New York. On the way westward he transacted a sale here and a sale there so that by the time he reached Chicago he had to replenish his stock. In that muddy, disorganized city, he traded with Morris Kohn, also an Hungarian. "Why go west?" Kohn asked, "The big money's in the east. With your experience in New York and my stock we ought to get together."

The unsuspecting Zukor was invited to Kohn's home for dinner. Present was a niece of whom Kohn was very fond. She related exciting stories of her early life on a South Dakota farm, worked by her parents under a government land grant. Zukor made frequent calls to hear how her mother baked bread every Friday and gave the Indians a share as a peace offering, and how her uncle entered the fur business through trading with the redskins. After the adventure stories came a friendly game of pinochle over a glass of *schnapps* or wine with a piece of home-baked sponge cake. The vivacious niece, prompted by her mother, settled the question of the combine. She settled other questions as well! Wedding bells rang and Kohn and Company came into existence.

Things developed as the uncle predicted. Adolph invented a fur clasp that brought the company into prominence. In a few years Kohn and Company took its place at the top in the New York fur market. Zukor was a well-to-do man, although a stranger meeting him for the first time might not suspect it. He was no different than the bashful immigrant of fifteen years before except for the scent of raw skins that hovered about him. He had had no spectacular rise to wealth or magic formula for success. Hard work, care in buying, and rigid economy formed the axiom he followed. He remained a slave to his business and worked into early morning hours on scarfs, collars, and fur novelties.

So life might have continued if in 1903, a relative, Max Goldstein, had not asked for a loan of $3,000 for a third interest in a penny arcade that Mitchell Mark and a fellow named Wagner, who had a similar place in Buffalo, planned to open. Zukor's habit of letting his eyes roam from the speaker made Goldstein uneasy. And everytime Zukor's glance rested on his needle-pricked fingers, Goldstein was compelled to compare his own smooth, white hands. Whether or not Zukor did it intentionally, Goldstein could not tell. When Zukor finally spoke, Goldstein was relieved to hear him say, "I am willing to talk it over with Kohn, although it sounds silly to me."

Something had to be done for Goldstein; unless he were set where he could make a livelihood his relatives would not be free of their charge. He was poorly trained and to investigate a proposition that interested him seemed advisable. The result was the formation of a partnership, Mark, Wagner, Goldstein, Kohn, and Zukor. Business began in a penny arcade on South Union Square in New York City. The arcade followed the usual pattern, bagatelles, mechanical fortune-tellers, throw-ball games, a line of peep-boxes, and a barker who collected crowds with the challenge, "I'll guess your weight within three pounds."

Kohn, fascinated by the excitement about the arcade, became active in its affairs. Zukor remained to manage the fur factory. Marcus Loew, a friendly competitor in the fur business, was hurt that his friends failed to include him in their new enterprise. To bring Loew into the group a second amusement emporium was opened uptown.

Money poured in. The balance sheets were incredible. Stooping over a work table in a fur shop suddenly lost its allure. Zukor wanted a voice in the business on Union Square. Inasmuch as Kohn and Company could not exist without him, the fur shop was closed. Zukor, bolstered by Loew, was eager to expand before the field became over-crowded with newcomers. More conservative members of the firm wanted to take it easy; they did not want to reinvest all their profits until the Kinetoscope, the arcade's main attraction, proved itself more than a fad. In the heated arguments, Zukor and Loew were eased out of the company.

With hardly a second thought Loew opened a ten to thirty cent vaudeville house and adopted the common procedure of showing action pictures. Zukor was not so decisive. The circumstances that determined the affairs at the arcade had made him thoughtful. In 1905, he had about $200,000 cash and was vacillating between one proposition and another when he heard that William A. Brady, lately turned from fight promoter to theatrical manager, had bought eastern rights to Hale's Tours. These were show places designed to provide the audience with a sensation of travelling along through scenic wonders flashed on a screen. The entrance imitated the observation platform of a pullman car, and instead of a ticket chopper, a *conductor* passed among the *passengers* to collect fares. The seats, on springs, rocked from side to side to effect a moving train. So realistic was the impression, several cases of car sickness were reported.

The originality of the Tours appealed to Zukor. Inarticulate, in broken English, he approached Brady, who at first insisted he was not interested in a partner. However, as the conversation progressed, the sound sense and keen business insight of his extraordinary caller became apparent. Besides, as a legitimate stage manager, the Broadwayite was a bit apologetic about having his name connected with motion pictures, which were still, in some quarters, looked upon with disdain and contempt. Before Zukor and Brady parted Zukor owned a part of the Tours.

Their novelty theatre could not accommodate the crowds that sought admittance. Zukor's speculative instinct was awakened. Brady proved as great a gambler. They opened houses in Newark, Boston, and Pittsburgh, only to discover the unusualness of the place rather than the beauty of panoramic views attracted patrons. After three or four visits, people rarely returned. Brady wanted to close the theatres and write off his losses. Not so Zukor. Brady, ashamed of his association with this ugly-duckling branch of the theatre, especially since it lost money, allowed Zukor to manage the Tours in his own way.

The seats were fastened to keep them from swaying, the theatre fronts were altered to look like those of any other store show and story pictures were added to the programs. Audiences that had become bored by scenes of grandeur did not come back. In desperation Zukor invested in small-time vaudeville. He engaged the cheapest acts he could find, but he struggled along for two years before he could inform his partner the theatres had pulled out of the red. Meanwhile he and Loew discovered an advantage in booking acts together. When Zukor could not induce Brady to invest further in these cheap combination vaudeville and motion picture houses, he affiliated with Loew. Their company was called Loew's Incorporated. Loew, lively and jolly, characterized as a good fellow, was elected president; the less social Zukor remained in the background.

Small wonder that Rubel, searching for an influential dynamic personality to support him, should not petition Adolph Zukor. His talents as a leader and organizer were still latent. His acumen, his aplomb, his profundity escaped notice. Nothing indicated he would some day be the undisputed leader in the field and leave an indelible impression on the motion picture industry. Probably some good genius restrained Rubel from calling upon him. A call would have been that much time wasted. Zukor pretended he had no interest in the contest. Without agitating himself over the merits or demerits of subscription fees, he quietly went about expanding his circuit. No one ever knew the close tabs Zukor kept on events. On the rare occasions he spoke of the situation, he spoke with philosophical dispassion as if he were a detached observer.

Carl Laemmle
Of The White Front

PASSING OVER ZUKOR, RUBEL APPROACHED CARL LAEMMLE. Like
thousands of other immigrants, Laemmle had known years of
hardship, drifting from one job to another. His climb had been slow;
pennies had been saved from small wages. He had no outstanding
qualities to recommend him. His appearance and personality were
poor. Five feet in height, he barely attracted notice. When he did,
it was because of his smile, which gave him a rather silly expression.
Diligence and conscientiousness were his only obvious characteristics.

Potential employers were unimpressed by the slow undersized
boy. Often the circumstances controlling his life were so discouraging
since that day in 1884, when he landed in New York, he thought
of returning to his native village of Laupheim in South Germany.
For ten years he swept floors, ran errands, catered to an inebriate,
kept books, and even fed pigs on an Iowa farm. Not until his
wife's uncle, Samuel Stein, made him a clothing salesman in a shop
at Kenosha, Wisconsin, had he felt satisfied with his lot. A promotion
to the management of Stein's Oskosh store was the realization of
a life's ambition. The commonplace customs of the mid-western city
suited his placid temperament. Each morning he pedaled to work
on a bicycle. As he rode along he contemplated the duties that lay
before him, and he experienced a sensation of achievement and
importance. His imagination never roamed beyond the existing
sphere of his intimate circle or questioned the security of his position. When his request for an increase in salary culminated in
his discharge, he was shocked. His shackles were broken, but he
did not see it this way. All he could think of was how, for ten years,

he had shifted from one job to another hardly earning subsistence.

In this frame of mind he arrived in Chicago early in 1906 to consult Robert H. Cochrane, who had ably directed the advertising of the clothing shop, and with whom he had corresponded in a friendly vein. Cochrane took one look at his conservative small-town friend and advised him to invest his $2,500 fortune in a five and dime store. While Laemmle roamed the Chicago streets looking for a suitable site, he observed the attendance at motion picture theatres. Cochrane almost fell from his chair when this meek, faltering man announced he had purchased a house on Milwaukee Avenue. How could a yokel run a theatre in Chicago! Even a movie theatre! With misgivings Cochrane agreed to help him.

One thing Cochrane knew, and that was how to capitalize on a man's personality. At his suggestion the building's exterior was painted white to impress the neighborhood with its cleanliness. The White Front it was called. Regulation uncomfortable wooden chairs were installed. A fourteen-year old boy, Samuel Katz, the son of a neighborhood barber, strummed a cheap piano, and here began an amazing career. Up the street in another nickel show, Abe Balaban, a seventeen-year old youth tried to steal Sammy's following with a repertoire of heart-break ballads. For months Abe made life miserable for Sammy, but Sammy banged away until the keys almost broke and came through triumphant.

Within two months Laemmle had enough money to open another house. The new place was called The Family Theatre to give it an air of respectability. And respectable it was. His competitors might be tempted by the extra revenue of Men's Day, with saucy pictures for men only, when no women were admitted except those lacking in decorum and slim enough for a disguise of male attire, but not the owner of The Family Theatre.

Service at the exchanges went from bad to worse. Laemmle wrote letter after letter complaining; he never received an answer. When he called on one offender he learned why. The man was sitting behind a desk littered with a great stack of mail. The distributor opened each envelope, peered in, removed checks and orders, and without reading the correspondence tossed all letters into a huge wastebasket. "Don't you read your mail?" Laemmle enquired. "I haven't time. They're mostly complaints. Why should I annoy myself."

On October 1, 1906, Carl Laemmle organized his own exchange. This time Cochrane invested $2,500, the amount with which Laemmle had started, and acquired a tenth interest in the business.

Thrifty and precise, Laemmle did not trust strangers with his precious merchandise. He, personally, supervised deliveries and sales. After each booking he examined all prints. Salesmen received strict instructions to be as straightforward as was expedient, not to promise more than was absolutely necessary to close a deal, and, under all circumstances, to remain pleasant and well-mannered. Prospective customers were invited to view pictures in a demonstration room. Matrixes and copy accompanied each shipment to encourage theatres to advertise in local papers. A month's free film service was effective bait in tempting the installation of his machine. The Laemmle Service came to be known for its honesty, its courtesy, and its generosity. But to more than any other factor, its success must be attributed to the defiant, biting humor of Cochrane. He plagued vaudeville houses for showing films that were fit to be used only as chasers and frankly boasted, "Until I (meaning Laemmle) entered the field, the film folk were sound asleep." By magnifying the honesty, courtesy, and generosity of the Laemmle Film Service, Cochrane gave lustre to the chary, plodding, meticulous habits of his partner. The wariness of Laemmle was paraded as strength, Laemmle's smile was well exploited. Cochrane nicknamed him Uncle Carl, and the smile of Uncle Carl was trained to win the confidence of those about him.

Like others, Carl Laemmle listened to Rubel. After a talk with Cochrane, he praised Rubel for his fearlessness and pluck, and then said, "Sorry, I'm all out for the Motion Picture Patents Company. I maintain it should have a chance to prove what it can and will do." Except for a pitifully few adherents, who had everything to gain and nothing to lose by championing his cause, Rubel stood alone.

The Little Giant Of Kenosha

WITH SATANIC SATISFACTION, Jeremiah J. Kennedy watched Rubel's vain attempts to awaken others to the seriousness of their plight. Within a few weeks the voice of Rubel died out. Would-be revolutionists thus reduced, Kennedy concentrated on matters of importance. Under the cloak of modesty he sacrificed his name to that of the Patents Company, and thus was protected from personal criticism.

From raw stock manufacturers the Patents Company demanded smoother, clearer film that eliminated *snow and rain.** It equipped its cameras with faster motors and better lenses. Projectors were improved to diminish flickering that strained the eyes and sent audiences into the street blinking and winking. Deliveries were made according to schedule. Prices were standardized. To make up for the expenditures improvements entailed, meager salaries and long work-ing hours prevailed. Actors and directors, for the most part failures on the legitimate stage, dared not complain that they had not re-ceived an increase in five years or more. Stories followed prescribed formulas and were confined to thousand-foot one-reelers. Experimen-tation was discouraged as too costly. Pictures were not made to express any imaginative conception but rather to provide projection machines with a reason for existence. Production expenses were kept at a minimum. The goal: enough releases for a daily change in bookings.

Those who had gone to the Trust for protection found themselves

---

*Fuzzy spots and streaks.

in a ridiculous position. Two-dollar payments did not buy favors. Instead theatres were entangled in the mesh of progress. From the Patents Company came orders to throw out backless benches and install chairs that provided a degree of comfort, and to stop selling candy, popcorn, and soda in the aisles during the showing of a picture. Electric bulbs painted red replaced quivering gas and oil lights over exits. The desirability of cleaning and ventilating theatres was emphasized. Ushers were instructed to "treat patrons like ladies and gentlemen and not like cattle." Pianists were unceremoniously requested to snuff out the everlasting cigarette that smoldered at the piano edge. A suggestion was made to make devotees of school children and newsboys by inviting them to enter free of charge. Metal screens were recommended for safety. The very reforms and renovations exhibitors had hoped to avoid were forced on them with the argument, "It is good business." Elaborate catalogues were published for the benefit of theatre owners. They contained descriptions of new releases, advertising and promotional hints, and illustrated how to modernize and attractively decorate a theatre at small cost. However, nowhere did the Trust interfere with the working conditions of theatre employees. Projectionists, reeking with sweat, ground away in the rear of small stuffy houses for twelve to sixteen hours a day, seven days a week, fifty-two weeks a year at a weekly salary of twelve dollars. Any breaks in condensers, negatives, or slides were charged against their salaries. Teen-agers were employed because they were more readily imposed upon, until the law stepped in and made the employment of anyone under eighteen for this work illegal. Cashiers sat in crude cages along the sidewalk, unprotected from the elements. No one received a holiday except for some extraordinary event, such as a family wedding or funeral. The kindhearted proprietor ran a ball or picnic once a year "to pep up the help," and spoke of his organization as "one big happy family."

Two-dollar pieces rolled in; they rolled in so fast, large baskets were required to transport the deposits. Bank balances ran into seven figures, and as the figures increased the Trust became more exacting. On the slightest provocation subscribers were deprived of a license. One cancellation after another was reported. Within months a reign of terror descended upon distributors and exhibitors alike.

Harry Davis, the Pittsburgh theatre operator and exchangeman was expelled on the grounds he was "retaining first-run film for his own use to the exclusion of his renting patrons." Despite efforts to take advantage of competitive customers, Davis was unable to meet the expenses of his small houses. With the extension of shows from twenty or thirty minutes to an hour and a quarter at the five cent price, he was forced into bankruptcy. Jules Mastbaum, treasurer of Felix Isman, Inc., a realty firm with extensive holdings in Pennsylvania and certain political connections, stepped into the theatre business when he was appointed receiver for the Davis houses. Some said that Mastbaum was appointed because Felix Isman knew how to pull the proper wires. At any rate, several years before, Isman, Davis, and Lubin jointly owned a store show in Philadelphia, and an Isman employee was acceptable to Davis as receiver. Isman also had once been a partner of Archie Sheppard in the Manhattan Theatre, and according to Sheppard, Isman had frozen him out of that situation.

An announcement issued the middle of March, 1909, aroused considerable astonishment and speculation. The franchise of William H. Swanson, who serviced the west and who had many staunch friends in the industry, had been cancelled. At first, like others, Swanson chafed in silence, but his naturally outspoken manner, inherited from the carnival folk with whom he had been raised, forced him to say what he thought of the spying and dictation of the Motion Picture Patents Company. The excuse used by the Patents Company in voting his expulsion was that Swanson had refused to discontinue selling to those who had not paid subscription fees.

Coincident with Swanson's dismissal an advertisement appeared in trade papers:

I MAKE YOU A PROMISE

No matter what happens during the crisis or afterwards, I will take care of you through thick and thin! I will see that my customers get the best of films and the best service on God's green earth and at the very best price that can be made.

THE LAEMMLE FILM SERVICE

Laemmle had asked that the Patents Group be given a chance. No intimation of dissension had leaked out. Week after week the same bewildering copy appeared until April 17, 1909, when Laemmle proclaimed:

I HAVE QUIT THE MOTION PICTURE PATENTS CO.
No More Licenses   No More Heartaches
      Nothing but a straight business proposition.

At an interview Laemmle stated:

"I have been considering it seriously for the past eleven weeks but at the same time I wanted to give the Motion Picture Patents Company a fair chance to see what it could do. They didn't do anything. That's why I went Independent. You see the Motion Picture Patents Company was going to offer protection to exhibitors. It was all right when they assessed the first $10* and I with lots of others thought that the five weeks would give them plenty of time to regulate matters and charge every exhibitor a license fee pro rata according to what a man could afford. You know it is not right that one man that makes $10,000 a year should pay $2 a week and those little fellows in the small towns, who are just making a living, should be compelled to pay $2 a week also which in many cases represents the best part of their profits. The exhibitors throughout the country are losing faith in me. I explained to everybody and told them to pay the $10 and after the five weeks expired the Patents Company would regulate matters. Well, instead of doing that the Patents Company issued another bulletin calling for $6 more. It was not right but I went to work again and told my friends and customers that were hooked up with me that the Patents Company had such a tremendous amount of business on hand they hadn't found time yet. Well, I lost business. Then I got to thinking seriously. I started to figure out matters, and when I just got through explaining to the exhibitors about the second installment of $6 a bulletin reached me from the Patents Company telling the exhibitors to pay $8 for the month of April.

---

*A subscription fee of five weeks' advance was demanded.

"The most ridiculous thing that ever happened came in the form of a statement from the Patents Company that I should act as their collection agency. If they want to collect $2 a week, why don't they go out and collect it themselves. I am in the film renting business and if they want a collecting agency why I can refer them to a lot of concerns through the country that are in that line of business to make a living.

"I was getting letters from all over the country, and people that have done business with me for a couple of years were leaving me, going to the independents. They had waited long enough, they have given me and the Patents Company a fair chance to make good. But the Patents Company remained as silent as a graveyard. They would not answer my letters. They would not answer any letters they received from the exhibitors and film renters and there was the little exhibitor in a small town paying $2 a week like a good boy and I assure you it was like pulling teeth. He paid it with the expectation of receiving the promised protection, which did not materialize, while his competitor a block away was running the same class of film without paying a cent."

This was followed with, "I, Carl Laemmle, the biggest and best film renter in all the world, now ask your patronage."

Kennedy gave the word and *Film Index*, the Trust's paper, titled an article:

THE PASSING OF LAEMMLE

Little Man with the Big Noise
Goes over to the Independents

The article went on to say, "He was despised for his extravagant statements and inferences, tending to cast discredit upon his competitors . . . . in his ready-made clothing store method of advertising.

Cochrane's wit provided Laemmle with a ready comeback:

HAVE YOU A LITTLE WHITE ELEPHANT IN YOUR HOME?

and the Trust was depicted as an elephant hogging a field. With the cartoon of a lamb the Trust was ridiculed for fleecing the public.

Film Index retorted with, "The cheap picture man used junk in the past and will probably continue to use junk in the future. His patronage has always been uncertain." Although the Trust made no direct statement, in a reversal of policy, it made overtures for that very patronage. Insurance companies were prevailed upon to cover Patent Company subscribers previously condemned as too great a risk against fires and accidents. The exhibitor was fed honeyed phrases instead of threats, and he was led to believe he had become a man with rights.

Because of the difficulties under which they were produced and their limited market, Independent pictures in circulation during the early summer of 1909 were of such poor quality they were of practically no benefit to the revolutionists in their fight for life. Newly founded Independents had only two alternatives. They must help existing units to produce more and better pictures, or they must make their own. At this psychological moment several non-infringing cameras appeared on the market. The Columbia Phonograph Company introduced a device invented by Joseph Bianchi, more intricate than any patented by the Trust. John J. Murdock, vice-president of the Western Vaudeville Managers Association and manager of the Olympia Music Hall in Chicago, picked up a camera invented by D. W. McKinney. Financed by John R. Davis, a multi-millionaire, and his friends to the extent of $2,000,000, Murdock formed the International Projection and Producing Company. The Independents relied on foreign film strips, mainly German Agfa or Lumière's sold in the United States by Jules E. Brulatour.

Swanson and Laemmle announced that they would distribute Murdock's product. "Barker Swanson," Film Index called him, and complained of the "Independent movement to coax exhibitors away from a reliable source of film supply." Laemmle was dubbed, "Little Giant of Kenosha." The Little Giant decided to extend his realm. In New York City he opened a factory, the Independent Motion Picture Company (IMP), to supplement the pictures he received from Murdock. Thenceforth a grinning, mischievous, hoofed devil danced through Laemmle ads. Talent was lured with money. On a yearly contract, directors and leads were paid a weekly salary of $125. "The Biograph Girl,"* "The Edison Hero," "The Vitagraph Girl," as unnamed favorites were called, transformed into Imps.

Film Index sharpened its tongue: "Laemmle is cutting up the same didos as he did in the Motion Picture Patents Company camp, great promises and small performances. His advertising is coming to be looked upon as a joke in the trade." Laemmle smiled at the joke. "Every knock's a boost," he said as orders poured into the Imp factory.

Throughout the summer vile names were flung back and forth. "Faker" and "pirate" were favored epithets. The Trust had long since lost its cold aloofness, but *Film Index* kept insisting, "From the beginning of the present arrangement the Patent's Company has not answered its critics."

Actually, Lubin alone among the Patents Group remained insensible to the bickering. The mystery is still unsolved as to why, in the midst of bitter battles, he rented his old studio to a would-be enemy. Whatever the reason, when Mark M. Dintenfass gave up the job of digging slippery salted herrings out of a barrel in a fish store, he found the Lubin plant a safe retreat. Other Patent members never suspected the new *outlaw* films on the market were produced in a loft leased by one of their licensees. But Lubin's actions always were more or less inexplicable. He duped Méliès', a co-subscriber's, pictures and then faced about and placed the facilities of his well-equipped studio at the disposal of an Independent, that a defect in a negative print might be corrected. At this time Lubin also was embarking on a policy of theatre expansion. With George H. Earle, Jr., one of Pennsylvania's best-known capitalists, and Felix Isman, the realtor, he formed a $600,000 theatre syndicate. Here Isman lay the groundwork for corporate practice successfully applied years later by the Stanley Company of America, Warner Brothers, and other large theatre chains. Two corporations were formed. One, privately owned, controlled the real estate. The other, financed by public subscription, operated the theatres. High rentals saved the realty concern from sharing profits with stockholders in the operating company.

---

* In 1909, Mary Pickford left the ingenue parts in David Belasco's plays to become a Biograph Girl.

Another situation arose that threatened to embarrass the Patents Company. Echoes from the bankruptcy hearings of William Friese-Greene drifted across the sea. "Reposing in fancied security owing to the fact that Mr. Greene did not have enough money to come to America and assert his claims as the originator of the moving-picture camera and machine, the creditors of Greene may rudely awaken them (Edison licensees or members of the Patents Company), as he has listed as an asset such items. In his examination by the official receiver, Friese-Greene swore he had sent Mr. Edison a description of one of his patents and that he was the first inventor, adding "They are making a million a year profit and there may be arrangements under which my creditors will be paid in full."

Moving Picture News in an editorial, "The History of Patents," stated, "In 1888 or 1889 Friese-Greene wrote a letter at the request of Mr. Edison enclosing working drawings and designs of a perfected camera which Mr. Edison later patented here. All this came out in evidence in the courts a short time ago. On this evidence, patent No. 12192, which had been granted Thomas A. Edison et al, was declared of no value and the camera brought in evidence, namely the Warwick, using a two-tined fork, was no longer an infringing device on the Edison patents. The issued and reissued patents of Thomas A. Edison were declared null and void owing to prior art."

A Chicagoan offered to prove that "Mr. Edison was instructed how to make the film he now claims to have invented," from film originated by Louis Ducos, a Frenchman who was granted a patent nearly fifty years ago.

These charges weakened the Trust's prestige. Exchange after exchange bolted the ranks. Nevertheless business at the Motion Picture Patents Company was more than satisfactory. Royalties to Edison alone ran over $10,000 a week. But the promise to limit licenses was forgotten. Investments might be wiped out over night, yet show places, without certainty they would or could be served, opened at an amazing rate in suburbs and cities. The conversion of theatre roofs and vacant lots for outdoor showings on warm evenings extended the outlet for films.

Strides in photography made possible the snapping of scenes in natural colors. An exhibit in the United States of the pictures of G. Albert Smith, an associate of Charles Urban of London, stimulated public interest. Urban was wined and dined, toasted as a celebrity, honored as a distinguished visitor, but his hosts refused to experiment with color as long as black and white was acceptable to the public. Urban returned to England without selling his process and several hundred dollars poorer for having accepted an invitation to participate in the industry's favorite sport, poker. The only satisfaction he drew from his trip is that the publicity accorded him increased the number of American movie-goers. In England, Friese-Greene instituted suit against him on the grounds that the Smith process infringed on Friese-Greene patents. Urban lost the case and the color process became public domain. Neither of these men had the business acumen of George Kleine, whose shrewdness saved the leading producers in the United States from a similar fate.

In spite of other harassments, as Murdock crossed the country to organize exchanges or solicit accounts, *Film Index* hounded him with, "Murdock talks quality. It is just talk. The promises of Murdock read like a 'Rube-come-on' story." With word that Murdock was willing to gamble his pictures on a percentage basis, *Film Index* reproved him for cutting into theatre revenues.

Heedless of invectives, scornful of mockery, Murdock, Laemmle, and Swanson abandoned themselves to their ideas. Elastic prices, more for better, less for poorer pictures, aided them. This practice incidentally encouraged bargaining, which still adds zest to the buying and selling of pictures. The pluck and perserverance of Murdock, Laemmle, and Swanson triumphed over threats and denunciations. Newcomers and old-timers alike were encouraged to take chances. Men who had been hesitating invaded the field. Edwin Thanhouser, a long-time trooper, loftily proclaimed that he would improve the movies with a Bianchi camera and his store of dramatic knowledge. Warner Brothers, not quite as sure of themselves, trembling on the brink of financial instability, farmed out productions to equally inauspicious free-lance directors. Harris and Davis reentered the field as producers. Kessel and Bauman, no longer afraid, openly admitted their aims. With Fred J. Balshofer, who had been a Lubin cameraman, they organized Reliance Pictures as their eastern company and Bison Life Motion Pictures as their western outfit. More and more, clear sunny skies through the southwest lured producers. Several operated two stock companies, one in the east and one in the west.

Intruders, pulsating with theories and ambition, procreated like fleas. As Independents multiplied the Trust lost all sense of proportion. It raved and ranted, furiously and bitterly. Without mercy, encroachers paid in kind. H. J. Streyckmans, trade paper editor, rooting for the Independents, recalled the fear of J. A. Berst, Pathé's representative, who testified when questioned why he had become a member of the Patents Company:

> "It seemed to us the Edison Company had some pull
> in the Court of Appeals for having sustained the camera
> patent and we were rather afraid of them."

Streyckmans further reminded his friends that before Kleine visualized a Trust he had:

> ". . . fought like a fiend in an answer which is memorable in the film business, and which it is surprising none of the Independents have followed up and used. He made the startling announcement that the Edison patents were invalid, because the reissues were secured by fraud; that Edison was not the inventor of the camera or idea, and quoted scores of publications describing moving pictures long before the date of the Edison patent.
> "The magic name of the Motion Picture Patent Company, however, had been the panacea for all patent ills, and has brushed away the dark clouds of fraud which Kleine raised on the horizon. Isn't it funny?"

Rubel's cry had carried far, after all.

The Grip Is Tightened

FOR FOURTEEN OR FIFTEEN MONTHS HOSTILITIES PERSISTED. Notwithstanding the strain of combat, Independents showed no sign of weakness. On the contrary, with a fiendish spirit they ingratiated themselves into the hearts of customers of the Motion Picture Patents Company, persuading exchanges to distribute an occasional picture and theatres to run them once or twice a week. The infuriated Patents Group became suspicious of exchanges that appeared to be abiding by the rules. Kennedy, convinced that leniency had encouraged violations, announced that the licensed manufacturers themselves would take over distribution. Thus two objectives would be realized: the Patents Company would be saved from trading with disgruntled middlemen and would get their profits.

To execute this plan, the General Film Company was incorporated in 1910 with a capitalization of $2,000,000. Actually, the incorporators invested only a few thousand dollars. The monstrous figure was publicized to imply invulnerability. Two million dollars or less, 120 licensees were terrified. Kennedy, shielded by the impersonal name General Film, thoroughly investigated each film renter. Small distributors were paid one hundred per cent in notes that matured over a five-year period and were met with profits earned in the normal course of business. Those dealers who also owned large and valuable chains and had liquid finances or political connections were offered partial payments in cash or stock certificates. Wholesalers of no consequence were to get nothing more than the stipulated two-week cancellation notice. All exchanges, no matter how strong, were expected to pay for themselves, except in isolated instances, such as the Pittsburgh Calcium Light Company, which reputedly had been paid over a quarter million dollars in cash and whose president, Richard Rowland, was as other independents bitterly complained, "rewarded" with a high salaried job for services rendered to the Patents Company. More timid Trust members did not like this untempered blow; they argued it was going a bit too far, but Kennedy completely dominated the corporations with which he felt himself to be synonymous. Furthermore, Kennedy saw that his associates were treated more than fairly, Kleine, especially, who had been paid $338,000, only half of which represented the value of film and equipment, the other half representing good will. George Méliès was the only Patent Company member who felt he had been mistreated.

Méliès' aspirations as an artist proved no match for business tactics. His intuitive feeling for beauty, his constructive planning, his well organized sequences carried many over obstacles of ill-conceived designs, disjointed reasoning, uncontrolled temperament and untempered ambition. The man most advanced in production had not kept to the business pace. He refused to listen to the rental plan of his three former assistants, and continued to sell his pictures outright. Exhibitors cared not a whit that his pictures displayed greater imagination and meticulousness than those of other Patent members. The others they might rent; his, they had to buy. This set him at cross purposes with the other Trust concerns, which freely copied his ideas, duped his pictures, and finally expelled him from the Motion Picture Patents Company. When a stock of his prints was stolen he could not stand the financial strain and closed his American branch. Before he died on January 21,1938, at seventy-six years of age, he paced the boulevards of Paris, beseeching indifferent throngs to spend a centime for a newspaper or a square of chocolate. His last days were spent in a charity home. Today the name of George Méliès is little known as a pioneer, whose contributions have been inestimable and indispensable to the industry. A granite statue stands at Ciotat, France, overlooking the Mediterranean, of the brothers Lumière, who had warned Méliès against throwing his money away on a motion-picture camera.

The fate of Méliès was no consolation to the jobbers. They fought to get the best possible deal. But those who protested that the terms were unfair or held out for a better offer soon learned that spying had been so thorough, the most secret transactions were known, confidential records a matter of Kennedy's information. Richard Rowland and other fellow distributors were accused of being Judases. However the Trust received its information, once doubt set in, morale disintegrated, and one by one, exchanges acceded to demands. A few scattered attempts at resistance were made, but by and large jobbers admitted defeat, and Independents lost identity as they were absorbed by General Film. The Trust needed office managers and district leaders so, in instances, even men, who had once resisted but later atoned for the sin, were given consideration. Thus W. W. Hodkinson was made manager of General Film's Salt Lake City branch. A long list of free self-reliant entrepreneurs became employees.

As exchangemen yielded, General Film closed in on theatres. Houses were graded according to seating capacity, appointments, and location, which determined run and rental price. This seemed a fair practice, but favoritism was shown to those in the better graces of the Patents Group or to licensed manufacturers who owned picture houses. Also, once a date was set, a film had to be played as scheduled or paid for without a showing. Changes in bookings were not allowed. Theatre owners, for the most part illiterate and untutored in business ethics, did not know how to combat this colossus and acquiesced to unreasonable demands.

Occasionally men, ejected by the Trust, drifted into production. These units usually were poorly financed and seldom had the capital to carry them through formative periods. Well-financed Independents, such as Swanson, who now produced pictures under the trade name Rex, Laemmle, and several others, banded together to compete with the Motion Picture Patents Company. Their central release agency, the Motion Picture Distributing Sales Company, became a new field for battles when Swanson and Laemmle, supported by their friends, shoved the pictures of other Independent producers into the background. The name-calling that resulted indicated that, given time, Independents might destroy themselves. Kennedy had no doubts — the sovereignty of the Trust was at last definitely established.

Zukor Sees Eye To Eye
With The Trust

WHILE AMERICAN PRODUCERS HAGGLED over commercial supremacy with pictures they advertised as moral, educational, and cleanly amusing, European producers aspired to heighten the artistic treatment of their pictures in an effort to save their companies. Once motion pictures had been extricated from the puerile, toy-like peep-box, film men abroad had little luck. A lower class, resigned to long working hours that deadened desire for recreation and unable to afford the high taxation of theatre seats, and a middle class, suspicious that a new medium of artistic expression might react unfavorably on the moral code laid down for its children, relegated the cinema to carnivals, where they had a place among the freaks, and to scientific institutions, where they were treated as a phenomenon.

The process of extracting films from these widely separated screens was slow and tedious. Tricks of all sorts were tried. Cinematographers opened theatres one flight up where, because rentals were less, admissions could be kept low, and where brown paper, which covered the windows to keep out light, did not seem so uninviting. Some broadcast performances as free, and then, in order to provide for the upkeep of their shows, shamed those who had entered into dropping a coin into a tin can, a tin can so the clatter of gratuities was unmistakable. More elaborate houses had balconies equipped with tables where cordials, wines, crackers, and tea were served. To lend an air of dignity and elegance, ticket takers were dressed in uniforms trimmed with gold braid and brass buttons. All admitted soldiers and sailors in uniform at half price. Even so, cinema theatres remained empty.

In England first and second class arrangements were worked out. A screen, from which oil, applied to make it transparent, dripped on those who sat in front rows, was hung in the center of the room. Plutocrats, on a lark, ventured into these theatres and sat on the fore side of the sheet. Leaner patrons saw the picture in reverse. Compassionate spectators on the right side of the screen read titles aloud so *second classers* might know what was being said. When they stopped, hoarse catcalls demanded, "What's the bloke sayin?" No one minded the bedlam. The poor were accustomed to it; the rich considered these escapades adventures into slums. In isolated spots, such as Birkenhead, England, where townfolk were violently excited by the movies, the cashier was not given a chance to sell his tickets. As soon as the doors were unlocked, the crowd in front of the theatre crashed through in a mad rush for seats. Once inside, a hat passed up the aisles brought more to the thankful proprietor than he could have collected at the entrance. But instances of this sort occurred so infrequently they offered little encouragement.

European producers faced their problem realistically. They set about making pictures with dramatic appeal. Competitions were held to judge the finest productions. The Great Northern Film Company of Denmark enlarged upon the factual film and released adventure pictures. News and topical films, although sometimes faked, were so well produced a theatre in Paris supported a program devoted exclusively to newsreels. Gaumont, who had factories in London, Berlin, and Barcelona, as well as in Paris, continued his chronophone shows (a combination motion picture and talking machine which was synchronized electrically). Sound also was being introduced in the United States. One concern, the Chrono-Kinetograph Company, was capitalized for $6,000,000 to introduce the "speaking-talking" pictures invented by Dr. Isadore Ketsee of Philadelphia, but the life of the company was short. In Russia, where great care was given to pictorial composition, pessimistic, somber dramas were released. The famous Gabriele D' Annunzio directed spectacular historical pageants for Italian Film d'Art. In France producers leaned toward the classics, emulating the dramatic and artistic excellence of the theatre, sparing no expense in the lavishness of settings and costumes. Eclair was an exception. This firm imitated American competitors and produced such pictures as "Alchohol, the Poison of Humanity, in two parts and 41 awe-inspiring scenes." Sarah Bernhardt, prevailed upon to leave posterity a fitting record of her dramatic genius, appeared in a four-reel feature, "Queen Elizabeth."

Immortal Bernhardt! Sarah Bernhardt on a *silver sheet** peddled for sale. Calm, cool, collected Adolph Zukor paid $35,000 for the United States rights.

For over two hours the unprepossessing Adolph with a prospectus under his arm sat in an ante-room of the General Film Company before word came over the switchboard, "Show the gentleman in." He threaded his way across the imposing office. His legs were short, his feet small, his steps resembled those of a hesitant child. His eyes were partially closed and his head tilted to the right. It kept drooping forward slightly and gave him an air of detachment, as if he were engrossed in abstract thought and not wholly conscious of his surroundings.

Fast moving Jeremiah J. Kennedy grew impatient watching the little man who walked so slowly. "I'm sorry, Mr. Zukor, that a luncheon engagement prevents me from giving you much time. Please be concise," he said.

The Trust, secure in its position, had no need to invest in European spectacles. It had its own spectacles, two-reelers, produced from time to time and released as serials, one issue a week. A four-reeler was out of the question. No audience in the world had the brains to concentrate on a picture that ran for more than ten or fifteen minutes. (The cry of the middle Twentieth Century varies slightly. Audiences are described as unable to grasp subtle implications or appreciate artistic treatment. Directors complain they are compelled to make pictures down to the level of public comprehension, which in the United States is set at an average age of twelve years.)

If Zukor were disappointed when he left Kennedy's office, his large hazel eyes in his pale face never betrayed his feelings. His expression remained fixed. Indeed, he did not waste time fretting. Pad and pencil superseded the sewing machine. $35,000! Quite a nut to crack.

---

*film screen

With characteristic lack of imagination the Trust belittled those outside its ranks. Zukor had wholeheartedly desired to play ball with the Patents group. Just because they would not have him was no reason to lose a tidy sum. The Motion Picture Patents Company lost a friend, a friend it cared nothing about.

To succeed with his plan required more capital than Zukor had at his disposal. Timorously, because he knew the antipathy in financial circles toward business ventures tinctured with levity, he approached his bankers, The Irving Trust Company. When the bank professed a willingness to advance a loan, he could hardly believe his ears. The bankers never took time out to explain that they regretted having so long scorned a lucrative source of revenue. Then he had his friends and associates in the theatre chain, Marcus Loew, president, and Joseph M. Schenck, in charge of bookings. Finally, the celebrated Daniel Frohman consented to lend the dignity of the spoken drama to motion pictures by becoming an officer in his corporation. True, Frohman had suffered several failures on Broadway and was hard hit financially, but the illustrious name of Frohman!

Whatever reason Daniel Frohman had for his decision, his brother Charles did not share it. In the opinion of Charles, "People who never came to the theatre at all because they had no sense for drama or comedy, now have a little from watching moving pictures. People who never thought at all now are inclined to think a little by the aid of yellow journalism."

Zukor did not intend to confine himself to foreign pictures. Once he decided to buck the Trust, he would go all the way. A few bad seasons in the theatre made well-known actors receptive to cash-on-the-line propositions. Salaries up to $25,000 a year would be paid for first rate talent. Noted authors would be offered royalties. Nothing was to keep "Famous Plays with Famous Players" from the movies. This, however, was still a secret. The immediate problem was "Queen Elizabeth." Zukor worked on the premise that theatres might shun American-made infringing films but could not afford to withhold from the screen a great drama that featured the world's best-known actress. Progressive members of the Trust saw his point. They fought against conceding to an unknown credit for revolutionizing the industry in the United States, and for the first time brought strong pressure to bear on Kennedy. Grudgingly, Kennedy licensed what might have been a white elephant. Zukor, although he had grown somewhat wary of his benefactors, accepted the gesture.

The Lyceum Theatre, off Broadway, whose halls had mellowed with voices of pampered stars and hopeful lesser lights, opened its doors to plebian entertainment. Here "Queen Elizabeth" made her debut with admissions up to a dollar. Alexander Lichtman, a live-wire salesman, was sent out to test the *feature picture* idea at road show prices and to break into the tradition of complete program buying. Program buying was a system whereby an exhibitor contracted for the right to use a certain number of reels per day, constituting his entire program, at a flat rate per foot of film.

The job was more difficult than Lichtman anticipated. Small town exhibitors, mortally afraid of any new idea, refused to be taken in by the natty, silver-tongued young salesman. Indeed, in many small communities the name, Sarah Bernhardt, was unknown. A weaker man might have been discouraged. Not Lichtman. He pressed on until he understood exactly why he could not sell the picture. When he realized to what extent fear played a part in his failure, he used that very fear as the basis for his arguments. Whenever an exhibitor refused to gamble with "Queen Elizabeth," Lichtman threatened to run the great drama himself in competition to the local show. These tactics made Lichtman's a success story. In cities, in towns, in villages, in hamlets, in communities where the school or fire house took on the role of movie house each Saturday night, "Queen Elizabeth" commanded an admission of not less than 25¢.

Even Pat Powers, toughest of the Independents, lost to motion pictures' super-salesman. But Powers was accustomed to hard knocks and bad breaks. His adolescent years were spent in a forge, where he suffered so many abuses, he finally tossed aside his job and went out to fight the power of capital. As a labor leader he met with little success. A strong arm and a quick temper did not compensate for a lack of mature and disciplined thought. Too much an individualist to return to the oppressive atmosphere from which he had fled, he sought a new means with which to earn a livelihood. His mechanical aptitude led him to take an interest in the various inventions appearing on the late Nineteenth Century scene. He looked upon the talking machine as one of the seven wonders of the world and opened a phonograph shop. From this, like many others, via the Kinetoscope, he drifted into motion pictures. Powers accepted defeat in the Licht-

man battle like a good sport. After all, his only loss was a bookkeeper, the charming Rose Weltz, who crowned the Famous Players'
victory by becoming Mrs. Al Lichtman.

Independents, who observed the results of Lichtman's efforts, attributed his success to an elaborate advertising campaign which
circulated the name of Bernhardt until the great actress became a
country-wide topic of conversation. Each producer decided to create
stars equally popular. A list of characters appeared on the screen.
Lithograph sheets with the name of stars and supporting players
were posted outside theatoriums. Photographs of motion picture
players on postcards sold "12 for 25¢ (assorted) postpaid." Personal appearance tours were arranged. Fictitious accidents were reported merely to publicize a player who might soon be kidnaped
by another company. "The Biograph Girl" disappeared. A few
days later, on April 2, 1910, she was reported mysteriously slain
in St. Louis. Her name, Florence Lawrence, thus was made public.
Laemmle, who had secretly persuaded her to leave Biograph and
become an "Imp", indignantly claimed the story to be a malicious
rumor. His assertion was followed up with publicity on a new
picture, in which she was designated the star. Impersonators, dressed
to represent leading characters in current movies, cavorted about
the streets of large cities. To the delight of New Yorkers, one artful
agent advised the unshrinking violet in his charge to drop a penny
with each step as he walked along 42nd Street. Needless to say, the
actor soon led a great clamoring parade. Executives of one company, seeing the procession from their office windows, attributed it
to the actor's popularity and signed him up under contract at $1,000
a week. The publicity man became an important executive and
frequently was able to "write his own ticket."

The Trust too began to comprehend the potency of publicity. To
the masses it turned with an ill chosen medium, an appeal to ignore
the "films of inferior producers," meaning of course films produced
by Independents. The appeal acted as a boomerang. The cry, "A
trust! A trust!" began to sound.

The paradoxical Lubin came to the Trust's rescue by announcing
that for the first time in history a dirigible would attempt a trans-
oceanic crossing. The voyage, to be made across the Atlantic by
the Vaniman brothers, was to be financed by Lubin. For weeks
preparations went on. Daily the newspapers reported the arrange-

ments, equipment, weather. On trolleys, in the street, at work, men
spoke of the great event. Bets were placed on the outcome of the
adventure. At last the dirigible took off. Before it reached the sea
it crashed. The heroic Vaniman brothers were killed, and Lubin never
did get the "pictorial description of the trip that would have been of
spectacular value to the people of both the old world and the new."
But he did win good will for the Patents Company. The public
agreed, "It takes a big corporation to finance experiments that bring
about progress."

Still, Zukor held the spotlight. Edwin Porter, lured from Edison,
directed "The Prisoner of Zenda," a story of such dramatic quality
it has been produced over and over. The superiority of this production, the first produced on the Famous Players set, and those that
followed at the Zukor studio over other American films was indis-
putable. To save its face, General Film licensed each Famous Players
Company release. The studio became a beehive of activity. Advance
notice of its intentions were eagerly sought, its store of prints, issued
and unissued, an enviable treasure. All this initiated by the man for
whom Kennedy had had no time.

At this time, when Zukor stood in the forefront of the industry,
he received an urgent telephone call late one night which caused him
to rush down to his plant. Fire, dread curse of the film business,
swept through the factory, a factory uninsured. Every dollar Zukor
had earned, every dollar he had been able to borrow, lay in the
flames. The factory was all he had to show for the backaches, the
needle-pricked fingers, the sleepless nights, the years of never-ending
toil. In and out of the crowd he weaved, dazed and stupefied, blind
to intense exertions to save the building, deaf to calls and shouts of
fire fighters, insensible to the shameless, sadistic gratification that
trickled through the mob of onlookers.

Three walls of the building collapsed. The floors caved in. High
on the wall that remained standing, an iron safe was attached. Word
drifted through the crowd that Frank Meyer, a Zukor employee who
had remained to dabble around the factory after all others had left,
had thrown all prints lying loose about the studio into the safe at
the first call of "fire" from the loft below. As the fire raged, the
crowd waited expectantly for the vault to tear away from the ravaged
building. At the time the safe was attached to the wall, Meyer, who
supervised the job, insisted that an extra strip of steel reenforce the

heavy safe. This strip of steel kept the wall from crumbling. When those at the fire became fairly certain that the excitement of seeing a safe tumble through space would not materialize, the crowd began to joke about the condition in which the pictures it contained might be found. Everyone knew film could not withstand the intense heat of fire. Zukor knew it too. Only a miracle saved this man whose vision and daring sent the industry soaring. Wind carried the flames in the opposite direction, so that the intense heat in no way damaged the films.

Fortunatus' Gifts

In 1910, when General Film first tightened its grip on the exchanges, it had 120 licensees. In 1912, only one remained, Greater New York Film Rental, owned by William Fox. An erratic individualist, despised for his impetuous and violent temper as well as for his insolent and insulting manner, when Fox took his stand against the Trust, he was unsupported and unchampioned. Notwithstanding, cajolery, abuse, threats did not budge him. The fate of others did not move him. Never before was he more resolute and self-reliant.

General Film put off this job to the last. The Trust had no illusions about Fox. He was known to be a match for any challenger. In addition, "Big Tim" and "Little Tim" Sullivan, both Tammany Hall Tigers, were counted among his business associates. Winfield Sheehan was on Fox's staff. Sheehan had been employed because he had demonstrated subtle ability in the manner by which he avoided responsibility when bribery scandals, which rocked New York City's Police Department while he was secretary to Police Commissioner Rhinelander Waldo, pointed at him.

Fox proved more unwieldly than General Film had estimated. A weighted roly-poly against brutality, intimidation, and wheedling, he sprang right back into place whenever an unexpected blow threw him off balance. Each time Fox rose, he shrieked protests and complaints. He chose so many crude wily ways of embarrassing his tormentors, passionate hate displaced the cold impersonal calculations of a large corporation bent on deciding the destiny of a smaller company. The annihilation of Fox became an obsession that so possessed General Film, it unconsciously relaxed in its disciplinary measures toward *outlaws.*

Left to carry on without oppressive competition, men, swayed by petty jealousies, illusions of greatness, greed, forgot their common cause. Lost in a jungle of convoluted reasoning, Independents failed to coordinate their forces. For over a year, Harry E. Aitken and John R. Freuler, partners, with a studio in Wisconsin, suffered under the tactics of Laemmle and Swanson, who held the controlling interest in the Motion Picture Distributing Sales Company, and more and more shunted other product into the background. Murdock had already given up his motion picture ghost and returned to vaudeville bookings. When the day came to discuss a renewal contract Aitken-Freuler withdrew their product. With S. S. Hutchinson, another small producer, and Charles J. Hite, president of Thanhouser (in less than a year Edwin Thanhouser, the dreamer, lost his grandiose notions and sold out to Hite), the midwesterners organized Mutual, a company designed to imitate General Film with a national system of exchanges.

Aitken, Freuler, Hutchinson, and Hite, lacking the means for their ambitious undertaking, went in search of a fairy godfather. Crawford Livingston and Otto Kahn, beguiled by the readiness of bankers to break with tradition and advance credits to a speculative business, stepped from lofty Wall Street retreats and waved magic wands of the usual stockbroker's pattern. Thus, before the photodrama was out of swaddling bands, these sorcerers provided it with numerous, doting foster parents.

What remained of the Motion Picture Distributing Sales Company was unable to compete with Mutual. To strengthen their position, Laemmle and Swanson lined up with Kessel and Bauman, Pat Powers, Dintenfass, David Horsley, president of a small company called Nestor Films, and Jules Brulatour. Brulatour, a blank-stock salesman anxious to have an active hand in extending the Independent market, invested enough to win the presidency of the new combine. The company was named Universal Pictures Corporation. History repeated itself. Verbal battles broke up the second meeting of its board of directors. Brulatour was ousted as president. Out walked Kessel and Bauman, declaring that Laemmle and Swanson muffled everyone else's voice in management policies. Kessel and Bauman turned their product over to Mutual for distribution.

Laemmle and Swanson, who felt they should decide when a member might withdraw, sent Pat Powers with nine armed companions to convince Kessel and Bauman they had made a mistake. Not quite clear is with whom they expected to reason, as the trip was made early in the morning, before New York City was fully awake. The offices were locked. In forcing a door to recover prints Universal deemed its lawful property, one clumsy henchman broke a pane of glass and aroused the peacefully sleeping night watchman. Shrill sirens startled drowsy Nineteenth Street. Pat Powers was hustled off to explain the situation to a magistrate. While Powers harried Kessel and Bauman in New York, Swanson staged a raid on their California studio. He found it well fortified; although he put up a good battle, his success was as small as Power's. Kessel and Bauman were free to carry on as they chose.

Before a year was out, C. V. Henkel, Universal's auditor, came forward with charges of corruption. He demanded the appointment of a receiver for Universal Films. The allegation was that, as a result of misappropriating company funds, the firm was insolvent. Specifically Henkel charged $200,000 had been directed to the personal use of the defendants through payrolls padded with salaries for cooks, chauffeurs, valets, etc.; that an attempt had been made to freeze out minority stockholders; that four directors, namely Laemmle, Swanson, Powers, and Horsley, issued promissory notes to the Universal Film Manufacturing Company for their personal holdings in exchanges in Philadelphia, Baltimore, Washington, and New York City, for which the company received no consideration whatever, the profits of the exchanges being divided among the individuals named and not accounted for to Universal. Henkel was said to have received the prize he was after; what it was never was made public. In any event, without explanation Henkel withdrew his charges within two weeks and nothing more was heard of them. But repercussions followed.

The cupidity of his associates and their habit of applying extra pressure when selling pictures of more influential stockholders frightened Dintenfass. He hoped to pull out from under but he wanted to avoid the sanguinary assault that had confronted Kessel and Bauman. First he offered his shares to Powers, then to Laemmle. Neither was interested. In most instances Laemmle and Powers were at cross purposes, but they had the good business sense not to tie up money in Dintenfass's stock as long as they might control its vote by concurring in the treatment of their disadvantageously-placed partner. They told the confused Dintenfass they were about to embark on big things and that, if he would string along for a while, he would be a member of the most powerful organization in the business. Dintenfass was completely disarmed when his name was placed on the New York City ballot in a mayoralty campaign. No member of the firm explained to him they wanted a persuasible Universal executive running the great metropolis. Dintenfass wasn't elected, and it became obvious that he had been only the tool in a canny legerdemain. Panic seized him; his associates were too insidious; he never would be able to cope with their unpredictable stratagems. Too dejected and distrustful to remain at Universal under any circumstances, but incapable of dealing with his partners, Dintenfass appealed to a friend, Lewis Selznick, a diamond salesman, to intercede for him.

One morning Selznick called at Universal on the pretext of selling jewelry. This gave him an opportunity to judge his customers. Breezily he bowed to an empty reception desk. Clerical workers around the room let him pass unnoticed. No one cared that he entered or where he went. Dusty papers and books lay about. The office was cluttered with nonessentials. That friction between executives had demoralized employees was obvious. Selznick found Powers and opened his sample case. Powers was unresponsive so he dropped in on Laemmle. Here was his man! "Mr. Laemmle," he soon was saying, "I can let you have a gem finer than any sparkler on this piece of felt. It's priceless! In your hands it can be as valuable as the magic lamp was to Aladdin. When you hold it you will possess an unrestricted voting power. No longer will you have to ask Mr. Powers or anyone else to play ball; you shall dictate all terms. What I refer to is the stock held by Mark Dintenfass. I can get it for you." Laemmle turned to Cochrane, who was present, and grinned. The time to take over Dintenfass's holdings had come. An Imp was not a Laemmle trade mark without reason.

No objections were raised when Selznick discarded his poorly-paying jewelry line and installed himself as Universal's office manager. Powers did not notice the change. Swanson assumed one of his partners had realized the office needed an overseer. Laemmle considered the job a reward. Besides, to strengthen his position, Laemmle was surrounding himself with assistants who might anticipate eventualities and who had the backbone to stand up under difficulties. Even in his secretary, Laemmle made a careful choice, taking the live-wire Joe Brandenburg, his name shortened to Brandt, from the managership of the *New York Dramatic Mirror's* advertising department. Brandt's job was to see that convincing articles in newspapers and magazines dispelled ill will that had developed when stories of Universal's tactics became public property.

Powers had no objections to the policies or methods of Laemmle as long as he shared equally with his partner, but to stand as a possible victim cast a new light on the situation. When he discovered what had transpired, he allied himself with Swanson and took an option on Horsley's stock. David Horsley was another who had frantically tried to dispose of his minority holdings. Like Dintenfass, he was bounced about until his nerves were strained to a breaking point. Now, with a diabolical contest for leadership, all sorts of bids were made to him. While Powers held an option, Laemmle handed him $97,000 in United States Gold certificates and $75,000 in notes. To prevent any entries of transfers, Swanson, at a Board of Director's meeting, grabbed the company's seal and stock record books and tossed them through a window to a confederate waiting four stories below in the street. Unfortunately for Swanson, the avenue was well policed when the paraphernalia came tumbling down. Books, tools, and men were carted off to jail. Arguments blazed through the courts until Laemmle emerged the undisputed sovereign of Universal, supported by his man Friday, Robert Cochrane, whose resolute, ingenious hand might be detected in every move of the master. Pat Powers was among those ousted.

Conditions were about as stormy at Mutual. Aitken's enthusiasm, his impetuousness, his readiness to take a chance irritated the conservative Freuler. Old friends chaffed each other. And then, without consulting Freuler, Aitken committed Mutual to the sum of $40,000 for an interest in "The Clansman," an emotionally unbalanced novel which the director, David Wark Griffith, who owned the screen rights, conceived as a mammoth production, a twelve-reeler. Freuler, before his motion picture days, had been a small town banker; he did not believe in gambling. The thirty-six year Aitken thrived on speculation. Had not his initiative and daring played an important part in the colonization of central northern United States? Years before Aitken contended, "If films can sell entertainment, they can sell land," and convinced the officers of the Chicago & Northwestern Railroad to finance him on a camera jaunt through remote sections of Wisconsin, Minnesota and the Dakotas. Fertile prairies, forests, wild, rolling landscapes, towering lime formations provided, as Aitken had said, alluring films. With these pictures of teeming abundance, Aitken travelled from city to city. Untold numbers migrated from comfortable homes into the wild country, and Chicago & Northwestern boomed on the stock exchange. When in 1914, Aitken renounced dull, exemplary films for a controversial drama to be treated as a stirring spectacle, he expected some opposition, but he was not prepared to have Freuler bolt the cash box. However, he would not be thwarted. If Freuler wouldn't go along, Aitken would personally guarantee production costs.

Freuler had a weakness. He pushed his own product to the detriment of other Mutual releases. As a result, the majority of Mutual's board favored Aitken, who often spoke for them, but the directors feared that an irremediable schism between Aitken and Freuler might be calamitous for all. Hite stepped up as mediator. He was unable to induce Freuler to relent in his attitude toward "The Clansman," but he did succeed in winning Aitken's promise not to resign from the corporation.

Aitken's $40,000 proved to be only a down payment. Before the picture was half-finished, Griffith informed him that to proceed without more money was impossible. To protect the $40,000, Aitken raised $20,000. A short time later Griffith confessed that the $60,000 was spent and the picture was nowhere near completion. Sixty thousand dollars gone, some of it borrowed, and no prospect of seeing any part of it again. He and Griffith drifted into a lunch wagon in the vicinity of the studio to drown their sorrow in a cup of coffee. On the counter they figured the extent of their bankruptcy. Wynpenny, the proprietor, eavesdropped on the melancholy conversation. His two favorite customers in trouble! Timidly he volunteered the use of $3,000. A Ford dealer at Pasadena, named Hampton; a Los Angeles businessman, and a Mrs. Granger, a widow, came forward with $5,000 each, All this money was not enough. Studio employees, who considered Griffith a genius, chanced their savings until the investment in the picture, which was released under the title, "The Birth Of A Nation," totaled $110,000.

Tension between Freuler and Aitken had abated when Aitken assumed all responsibility for the Griffith production. Aitken, shocked by Griffith's indifference to financial affairs and worried over his investment, had no heart to argue with Freuler over policies at Mutual. Freuler, satisfied that his partner had learned a lesson, magnanimously refrained from mentioning what appeared to be an unfortunate adventure. No one anticipated that "The Birth Of A Nation" would return better than eight hundred per cent on the money invested. No film ever raised such a furor, aroused such conflicting opinions, or had such praise and condemnation heaped upon it.

Everything was again running smoothly at Mutual when fate intervened. Hite was always in a hurry. One evening while driving at great speed in New York City, his high-powered automobile skidded on the slippery pavement of a viaduct, crashed through the rail, and hurtled through space to a level fifty feet below. A brilliant and plucky career was expunged in that accident. Hite's professional life began as a country schoolteacher. From teaching he drifted into newspaper work. In 1906, he became interested in theatricals and booked acts for lyceum circuits. He was a persevering worker and often carried on his job at the expense of his health. In 1908, overstrain brought on a physical collapse. His boyhood friend and physician, Dr. Wilbert Shallenberger of Chicago, was called in to treat him. Instead of collecting the usual fee, Dr. Shallenberger was talked out of a substantial check. Patient had persuaded doctor to finance him in the fascinating movie game. Hite soon serviced the entire west and, by 1911, three years after he had opened his first exchange, owned Thanhouser Pictures. The untimely death of Hite in his thirty-ninth year was catastrophic to both Thanhouser and Mutual. Dr. Shallenberger, an equal partner with Hite, stepped in as Thanhouser's president, but the guiding hand of Hite was lacking. The company went from bad to worse, changed hands several times, and finally was liquidated.

Neither could the raveled threads of Mutual hold together without Hite. Aitken obviously had conceded to Freuler only while he thought the Griffith picture never would reach the theatres. Once Hite was gone, both Freuler and Aitken refused to conciliate. Since to carry on in this manner was not possible, Aitken resigned and formed The Triangle Film Corporation, taking with him the product of Kessel and Bauman. Little was left of Mutual. Freuler's only hope for salvation lay in the fact that Universal was too paralyzed by internal disorders and General Film too involved in its malicious war with Fox to take advantage of his pitiful plight.

The Straw That Breaks
The Camel's Back

INTO THE CALDRON OF DISCORD AND DISCONTENT came twenty-three-year-old Sol Lesser, a West Coast theatre owner, whose partner Lester Kahn, a year older than himself, had just died of scarlet fever. At the studios Lesser listened not only to tirades against the various producers, but to outcries against "radicals, socialists, and anarchists," who demanded increased wages and shorter hours. Unreasonable, impertinent technicians, mechanics, and title clerks refused to be conciliated by the flattery of a credit line on the screen. Rallied by revolutionary speeches they banded together into labor unions. Players too, had grown ungovernable and temperamental. Publicity had gone to their heads. Once they had won public appro-bation they refused to assist at odd jobs around the studios and demanded compensation greater than that paid to legitimate actors. A few featured players insisted on a cut of the profits earned by pic-tures in which they appeared. And each producer ended his com-plaint with, "So, I am compelled to raise my price."

Out of the chaos, Lesser hoped to pull deals that would provide him with adequate features and shorts so he might vie with the growing strength of Tom Talley in California. The more Lesser perceived the situation, the less he liked his job. He trembled in-wardly, but he put on a bold front. He knew that to let anyone suspect he missed the sound judgment of his clear-headed partner, Lester Kahn, would be business suicide. His young bride, who made the trip with him, soon discovered life was not all velvet for the wife of an ambitious man. Lesser's time and energy were burned up in closing satisfactory contracts for the best productions released

102

in the east before they fell into a competitor's hands, or before war-
ring factions awoke to the bargains he had snatched. Although his
wife was spending a lonely honeymoon, this slip of a boy was taking strides that would soon place him in the front ranks as a theatre
operator.

Strangely enough, the farrago, the querulousness, the ferment
acted as a maelstrom sucking a fresh influx into the industry. Mad-
cap Samuel Golfish was caught in the vortex. From the time, when
as an eleven-year-old boy he fled from the poverty of his home
in Poland, his life had been one continuous adventure. Even his
name was a matter of chance. At Castle Garden, immigration authorities were unable to understand his varied jargons and had no time
to translate into words what he tried to convey through pantomime.
To be rid of this gibbering, gesticulating youth they called him
"Goldfish." In those days when he was a poorly-paid hand at a
glove factory, his awkward, confused speech evoked gibes from his
co-workers. These men, who had taunted and mocked him for his
ignorance, must feel a bit chagrined when they read laudatory
comments emanating from Hollywood on the literary bon mots of
this glorified exponent of Mrs. Malaprop. If his press agents are to
be believed, the intricacies of the English language forever remained
beyond his comprehension, and the classic example of his misspeech
is said to be, "You know what I think? I'll tell you in two words:
Um possible!"

No amount of ridicule or hardship discouraged Goldfish. He
was the perennial optimist. Tales of fortune had lured him to the
United States, and he was not to be diverted from his course. He
saw opportunity in every situation. When the glove factory was
called out on strike, he wasn't disturbed. He had the foresight to
perceive that anyone with the sense to avoid the reckless folly of
striving for "um possible" utopias and with the mettle to profit
by the extravagant notions of others, might come out on top. Quite
naturally, the capricious film industry magnetized him. The vari-
ance, the disquietude, the uncertainty were all pabulum for his mind.
To his equally stout-hearted, if more reasonable brother-in-law,
Jesse L. Lasky, Goldfish pointed out that the industry's chaotic
state in the fall of 1913 favored the ready-witted.

Lasky had taken to adventure for reasons somewhat different
from those of his sister's husband. His father was a retail mer-

chant in southern California. To escape the ennui of middle class
life in a small town, he traveled from Hawaii to Alaska serving
as baggage porter, actor, reporter, musician, composer, and producer of vaudeville skits. At times he went for long periods without work. Although privations did not send him scampering home,
it is astonishing that, with the many ordeals that lay behind him,
he would lend his ear to speculation. Yet, as he listened to recitals
of Goldfish's fantastic dreams, he unhesitatingly flung aside the
degree of security he had established as a successful vaudeville
booking agent. A famous Broadway star, Dustin Farnum, was
engaged to be his leading man; Cecil B. DeMille became his director. Adaptations of "The Squaw Man" and other David Belasco
dramas were his first contributions to the screen.

Belasco, dean of the theatre, was already an old hand in the film
business. One day during the summer of 1913, he had stopped
by the Zukor Studio to pay his friend Daniel Frohman a visit and,
incidentally, to watch the direction of a picture. Quite unconsciously
he made suggestions here and there. Next morning, Belasco's mail
contained a five dollar check, salary in full for one day's work as
an assistant director.

Zukor's idea of filming famous plays caught on like wild fire.
It attracted Archibald Selwyn, his brother Edgar, and Augustus
Thomas, noted playwrights. The influx startled James Stuart Blackton. He had become Commodore Blackton, Commodore of the Atlantic Yacht Club, with a palatial yacht spelling his name up and down
the Atlantic coast. He had a home at Oyster Bay, Long Island,
next to that of Theodore Roosevelt, with whom he sometimes went
on fishing trips. For several years, the prestige of a social lion and
sportsman floated precariously about him. He wanted desperately
to bask permanently in its brilliant light. Vitagraph must not be
overshadowed by neophytes if he were to avoid the darkness of
social failure. So, at his factory too, a series of stage successes were
transposed onto the screen. Biograph, to retain its prestige, made
arrangements to film Klaw and Erlanger dramas.

As the famous play conception gained momentum, theatres proud
of staid, dignified, historical backgrounds, were ensnared for pea-
nut and gum-chewing audiences. Classic facades hid behind lurid
posters that shrieked with superlatives describing coming attractions. Advertisements boasted that the interpretations of the si-

lent drama were better than those of the spoken stage. Film salesmen vibrated with regenerated enthusiasm. New high quotas
demanded of them were accepted good-naturedly. In many instances
exhibitors made heated competitive bids for pictures before they were
put into work.

The fortunes of others escaped the attention of the Trust. It was
too deeply immersed in its own troubles to gloat over a competitor's misfortune. Between the necessity of rearranging production plans and its intense desire to destroy Fox, General Film was
not free to take advantage of the rift between Independents or to
put obstacles in the way of parvenus. Months passed and the Trust
remained stalmated in the distressing Fox affair. To be rid of the
whole disagreeable situation they offered Fox $75,000. "My price,
gentlemen," he calmly informed them, "is $750,000."

"That's an out-and-out holdup!"

Fox was indifferent to what they called it. He valued his business at $750,000.

A great corporation lost its dignity and exploded like a steam
valve. In its fury, political contacts, great theatre holdings, strong
financial backing were forgotten. The simple expedient of revoking
Fox's license was adopted. The excuse: Greater New York Film
Rental supplied photodramas to a bawdy house. Fox protested
he had been framed, that films had been placed in the brothel by
General Film itself. Whatever the truth, Fox lost the first round and
bowed to the decision that he might no longer corrupt pictures.

When Fox admitted defeat, talks on a settlement assumed a cordial
tone, and Fox agreed to accept $75,000. Friendly relations reestab-
lished, Fox advised General Film to reinstate his license so that an
active business might be transferred. The Trust accepted the advice,
restored the license, and Fox sued for damages. Nor did he stop
here. His counselor, Samuel Untermeyer, urged the Attorney General,
who already had had several similar complaints, to bring suit to
disband the Motion Picture Patents Company and the General Film
Company on the grounds they violated the Sherman Anti-Trust
Law.

Trust members were visibly distressed. This last step was obviously
more than they could afford. The year was 1914. Beef, steel, mining,
oil, all were being investigated. The Telephone Company had relinquished Western Union to avoid a like suit. Public feelings ran

high against monopolies. Systematic wars against those who restricted trade were the order of the day. Right or wrong, the little
fellow was exalted. General Film dared not chance further damaging
publicity. Before the court brought in its decision, General Film
handed Fox $350,000 to reimburse him for his humiliation and
conveniently forgot that he once had corrupted films.

Aside from the cash award, a great part of which went to his
attorneys, Fox won a shallow victory. The Motion Picture Patents
Company had not kept pace with Independents. With few exceptions,
pictures released by General Films were not worth having. Excluding
the lawyers, the only one to benefit was James J. Darling, the judge
before whom the proceedings were brought. During the trial a sympathetic bond developed between the plaintiff and the jurist, and,
when the case was settled, Fox sent Darling abroad as a foreign
representative.

In Articulo Mortis

THE UNEXPECTED TURN OF EVENTS NONPLUSED JEREMIAH J. KENNEDY. When the facts were no longer refutable, his consolation was that only perfidious machinations had defeated him. Biograph pictures, the very pictures that he released through General Film, began to seep through a new channel, The Kinetograph Company. Biograph competed with herself. In his confusion, Kennedy thus inadvertently admitted how deep his fears were for the future of the Trust.

At General Film the entire force was shaken up. Old employees in the clerical, sales, and executive departments were discharged on short notice. Distrust, suspicion, and consternation led executives to argue among themselves. The Trust had been the logical outgrowth of the business ethics of its age, the natural product of its era. With the passing of years, its decline was inevitable. But Kennedy did not see it this way. He considered the Trust a phoenix-like monument to his genius and was loathe to concede that a social cataclysm had uprooted it. And, Kennedy, the leader, found himself without a friend among Trust members. Vitagraph, Lubin, Selig, and Essanay organized a combine known as VLSE to distribute their pictures. W. W. Hodkinson resigned as a General Film exchange manager and toured the United States to organize Progressive Exchanges so that the pictures of Kalem, now owned by Marion and Long, might be assured an outlet. Reckless and carefree, Marion and Long clashed with the austere Kleine. As the fight was two against one, Kleine "retired" to concentrate exclusively on the importation of foreign spectacles. All former Trust producers copied the very policies and productions of Independents they had scorned.

Selig, when the Trust disintegrated, tied in with William Randolph Hearst, newspaper publisher. The years had proved that the suspicion and fear of the newspapers for motion pictures was senseless. Instead of robbing the papers of revenue, the movies provided them with numerous, consistent advertisers. Malice blossomed into friendship. Hearst recognized the drawing power of a thriller, and when Selig produced the exciting "Adventures of Kathlyn" in serial form, Hearst opened the pages of his yellow journals to the story so that an interest might be stimulated in the picture. Other papers likewise catered to their readers with articles and questions columns devoted to the movies. *The New York Times* assigned its assistant drama critic, Brock Pemberton, who preferred to associate his gifts with the legitimate theatre, to write a column of movie criticism for its Sunday edition. In time, Pemberton became famous as a producer of plays.

Hearst did more than merely cooperate with movie producers. He engaged a staff of cameramen and sent them scurrying for a picture whenever a news item gave any indication of film potentialities. He called his reel International News and released it through Selig. One humourous incident has come out of that old organization. Word flashed on the wires that Vera Cruz was about to be bombarded by the United States. Charlie Mathieu, assignment editor, tossed aside the racing forms invariably under his thumb and made frantic efforts to locate a cameraman. He had fifteen minutes to get a man and equipment on board the train scheduled to meet the "U.S.S. Tacoma," about to leave Newport, Rhode Island for Mexico.

Unaware of the momentous story, Herman Stockhoff, a lanky six-foot-three, strolled into the office. "Don't take off your coat!" cried Mathieu, "you're leaving as a guest of the United States Navy for Vera Cruz."

"For WHERE?"

"For Vera Cruz, Vera Cruz! We're at war with Mexico!"

"But, Charlie," the big fellow demurred, "I'm getting married in two days."

"So you are. Okay, just get this equipment on board. We'll have a man replace you when the ship pulls in at Newport News."

As Stockhoff hopped into a cab he shouted, "Don't forget to call

Linda and tell her I'll be back in time for the wedding."

"Of, course, of course," Mathieu assured him.

The taxi drove off. Mathieu breathed a sigh of relief and dashed back to his racing sheets. Linda was already forgotten. And the United States Government changed its mind about a stop over at Newport News. The gunboat sailed straight for the battle area.

Getting news pictures in 1913 and 1914 had many unexpected thrills and pleasures. Cameramen were hustled about without any consideration for their lives, but they were the acknowledged ambassadors of their corporations and were treated accordingly. Men in public life came to realize that screen appearances had certain advantages. Their doors opened wide to newsreel representatives. Few restrictions were placed on cameramen. They rarely required credentials; cameras were their passports. So well were they received, Ulyate K. Whipple, Universal's ace cameraman, during World War I, tutored the Belgian Crown Prince in the art of *rolling the bones* in a freight car on a railroad siding, while they waited for accommodations to take them to front lines.

Pathé, Universal and Selig-International, the three American newsreels, took pride in and boasted loudly of *scoops* and *beats.* Newsreels were the pets if not the money-makers of producers. Expensive motor cars became a regular part of a cameraman's equipment that he might rush to a story at the amazing rate of from thirty-five to fifty miles an hour.

The belief that movies never would ingratiate themselves into the hearts of people had long since been disproved. Neither false reasoning, misguided ambition, nor selfish restrictions had killed film entertainment. The movies jumped ahead by spurts and starts. And as they did, the organization that had tried its best to hold them in tow reeled and tottered. No one made any serious move to keep it from falling; each member sought to secure his own position. When the Supreme Court, in 1915, finally ruled that the Motion Picture Patents Company, including its subsidiary, General Film, must disband on the grounds it constituted a monopoly, the decision was meaningless. The company existed in name only, shorn of authority and glory. Intrigues, conspiracies, chicanery had been of no avail. The interminable play for power had fomented failure. An inability to adjust itself to changing times predestined ruin. The Trust, through obstinate inflexibility and one-sidedness, had brought about its own destruction. In a dying breath the once-vigorous organization muttered, ". . . . the older institutions have undergone a new life impetus which bodes ill for new and unknown companies and it is not likely new, fly-by-night concerns will appeal to a seasoned exhibitor who has seen a flock of them pass in his time." Then with one mighty heave the junto collapsed.

As the old order passed away, the new order migrated to California. There, clement weather, majestic Sierras, lofty redwoods, Old Spanish missions, boundless deserts, and rugged palisades by the sea presented ideal locations and backgrounds.

Hollywood, in 1914, a small cattle-raising village outside Los Angeles, transformed into a city over night. Rough shacks and sheds stretched out in a long line. Most were flimsy structures, merely of tar paper, chicken wire, and uneven poles supporting a roof composed of linen strips strung on pulleys so the intensity of the sun might be regulated. They looked as if they might collapse at any moment. A few, though sturdier, had long, windowless walls that gave the street a dreary air. None was over one story high. All were studios, leased before completion by a fresh avalanche of cowpunchers, merchants, truck drivers, shipping clerks, and tailors, who had ideas of their own to express in a movie. Several actors, who begrudged the profits made by their producers, set up stock companies of their own in these ramshackle buildings. Cattle-herders and farmers, who turned toward the valley after crossing the Cahuenga Pass and caught a glimpse of this shapeless, nondescript town, were so shocked by the change, they called it Poverty Row or Death's Valley.

Natives soon learned that Hollywood was neither a Poverty Row nor a Death's Valley. The town bustled with activity. Film-shooting in itself became a form of amusement. On each set a grandstand was erected. For fifteen to twenty-five cents anyone was admitted to see pictures shot. And while these crude studios swarmed with people, once buzzing studios in the east took on an air of devastation and decay.

Book Two, Part One

America's Fifth Industry
(1914 to 1918)

War In Europe

NINETEEN-FOURTEEN. WAR IN EUROPE. Charles Jourjon, president of Eclair Films, joined his regiment. F. J. Godsol, American by birth, citizen of France by choice, owner of the largest circuit of picture houses on the continent, and president of Italy's Ambrosio Film Company and Cines Palast at Berlin, was drafted into the French Army. Charles Pathé, who wore the ribbon of the Chevalier of the Legion of Honor for his services to France as a film magnate, bade farewell to his executive staff as one by one the men left for the front. Except as a medium of propaganda, motion pictures had no place in a world hysterical for guns, airplanes, tanks. Down came the curtain on European film spectacles.

One man, Ugo de Seira, official of the Cines Film Company of Rome, hoped to escape the turmoil of war and, at the same time, save for posterity masterpieces of cinematic art. With valuable negatives he left for America. The ship on which he sailed was torpedoed. Thus, Ugo de Seira failed to save the films he so greatly prized.

Repeated shipping losses curtailed eastbound traffic on the North Atlantic to vital necessities. The great European market was lost; business in the United States fell off; factories shut down; workers all over the country were thrown out of jobs. War abroad plunged the United States into a depression. Low admissions saved the industry. Motion pictures were the only form of entertainment the people could afford.

In this fantastic market, William Fox was stranded without product. To add insult to injury, his most immediate competitors, Laemmle and Zukor, had well-organized stock companies. One night Fox

113

complained of his fate to his wife, Eve. She encouraged him to organize a producing unit which he called Box Office Attractions. He also purchased a small company, Balboa Productions.

Thereafter, each evening after dinner the custom in the Fox household was for Mr. Fox to recline in an overstuffed chair, smoking a heavy cigar, while Mrs. Fox related the action of a novel she had read during the day. Each recital, already enriched by Mrs. Fox with suggestions for screen treatment, was repeated by Fox, together with an idea or two of his own, to his director. The director, in turn, supplied a title with *punch* to his interpretation and prepared the tale for the screen. History has no record to show that any author recognized his maltreated plots in these agonizing melodramas and, indeed, Fox thought of them as masterpieces he had created.

When several pictures were ready, Fox, with engraved cards, invited exhibitors of consequence to a premiere of his "Productions Extraordinary." In the West Forty-sixth Street loft building that housed Fox enterprises, Eve Fox decorated two rooms, a Red Room and a Blue Room, to serve as small theatres. William Fox donned evening clothes to receive his guests, but as he greeted them he had misgivings. He wondered if his literary taste were all he had rated it; he wondered if luxurious settings would enhance the saleability of his creations. During the showings he went from the Red Room to the Blue Room listening for comments. The exhibitors were silent. When the lights went up and Fox took his place outside the showrooms to bid his guests good-night, he chewed furiously on his cigar. It almost dropped from his mouth when exhibitors rushed up to congratulate him; to enquire how soon they might book the pictures.

Brief as they were, moments of anxiety were needless. Whether films were good or bad did not matter. What mattered was that United States producers had become aware that so-called artistic foreign productions were no longer a threat and they might now set their own entertainment standards with pictures that rewarded the innocent, punished the guilty, foiled the villain, made gentry of the rich. The rush to see each new release was so great, a film two weeks old was outdated. The unprecedented demand created a stampede into distribution.

Aware that his own black scowl aroused suspicion, Fox depended upon Winfield Sheehan, whom he appointed general manager, to

win friends for the firm. Fox loved this man and gave him his un-
reserved confidence. The bond was so close, Winnie came to be
known as Fox's "Crown Prince."

Late in 1914, the "Crown Prince" set out across the North American continent to open branch offices. Distributors in large cities
dreaded his coming. They accused him of unfair competitive practices; they claimed that wherever he stopped, instead of training a
man, he singled out the most successful local manager and baited
him with a larger salary. Nothing anyone said caused Fox to ask
his "Crown Prince" to alter his tactics. Results were all that counted.
In 1904 Fox stood before a bankrupt arcade, puzzling how to save
it; in 1914 he held the sceptre in an organization nationwide in its
scope.

The success of Fox caused the green eyes of smiling "Uncle Carl"
Laemmle to pop. He recalled his press-agent, lean-faced Joe Brandt
(Joe "Universal" Brandt to the trade press), from a trip, and Joe
issued an announcement that staggered the industry:

"UNIVERSAL PICTURES IS TO HAVE ITS OWN CITY—
UNIVERSAL CITY"

The city, ten miles northwest of Hollywood, had its own railroad
to haul freight and passengers, bungalows for permanent employees,
a sewage system, a lumber yard, a saw mill, a blacksmith shop,
a post office, a hospital, a cafeteria, a corps of automobiles for film
deliveries, and its own private reservoir. Its main thoroughfare was
called Laemmle Boulevard. It boasted an Indian Village and a zoo.
Edison, the electrical wizard (oblivious of Edison the motion picture
magnate) went west to lay the cornerstone for its unequalled electric
light studio. The world had nothing like it. In a series of advertisements designed by Robert Cochrane, the now famous smile was
framed by a horseshoe in which were inscribed the words, "Laemmle
Luck."

Although he was the envy of the industry, a cloud marred the
happiness of "Uncle Carl." Extras in the modern Utopia over which
he was about to rule, unappreciative of all that had been arranged
for their well-being, called a strike in which they demanded an increase in their salaries which were then anywhere from one to three
dollars a day.

Also, "Uncle Carl" was well aware that Universal City, unique
as it was, was not the only strategically located studio in the United

States. With usual French ingenuity, Eclair had built a studio in the wild Arizona country, where petrified forests, rocky tors, lava-capped mountains, and Apache Indians provided interesting backgrounds for "Innocent shows for an innocent public." Just about the time this new studio went into production, France went to war. Before Claude Patin, Eclair's American representative, was able to open distribution centers, the French Consul General at New York ordered him to sail for France. Patin's position was awkward to say the least. His country needed him; his job in America was not finished. Eclair's competitor, Pathé, had sixteen exchanges scattered throughout the United States through which he released pre-war features and serials as well as product obtained on the independent market. In addition, when the last dependable cameraman on Pathé's Gazette dropped his camera for a gun, Pathé himself picked up the camera, with the result that Pathé had the best newsreels of the war. While Patin pondered over his solutionless dilemma, Universal came to the rescue. Patin agreed to let Universal sell Eclair pictures along with its own. In his assistant, Alfred W. Varion, Patin invested a power of attorney and sailed for France.

Other situations developed, other men moved forward. Selznick had held his place at Universal only as long as Laemmle needed his advice in the transfer of stock. Once Laemmle's position was secure, he resented and feared this man who had showed him how to get control. Moreover, Selznick demanded a commission of $39,000 for acting as agent in the sale of Dintenfass's stock. The former diamond salesman's good will was not worth $39,000. For a while Selznick floundered from one company to another. Eventually, another man's ambition provided him with a stepping stone.

In 1914, Emanuel Mandelbaum, owner of a Cleveland chain of theatres, financed by two Wall Street bankers, W. A. Pratt and Van Horn Ely, organized World Film Corporation for the purpose of specializing in the distribution of five-act features produced by unknown independents. Four or five successful months sharpened Mandelbaum's appetite. He wanted to chance production. This led to disagreements with his conservative partners. Here lay Selznick's opportunity. He assured Pratt and Ely they were right, that, with the least risk, the big money was in a string of exchanges, especially if operated by a super-salesman. Mandelbaum resigned. Selznick became general manager of World Film. Of Selznick's super-salesmanship there is no doubt. Coincident with his stepping in as general manager, World Film produced its own pictures.

Zukor surveyed the market. Producers bid frantically, one against the other, for actors and directors. Salaries skyrocketed in a delirious contest for talent. Stars were judged by the salaries they commanded. Actress Mary Pickford, who in 1909 left ingenue parts in David Belasco's stock company to become a "Biograph Girl," with blonde curls her greatest asset, received $100,000 a year, and comedian Charlie Chaplin, his feet insured for $150,000, a salary of $65,000 a year. Fox bragged that no director on his staff received less than $20,000. Lasky engaged a private car to transport his players to the west coast. The Kalen Company sold a penny postcard bearing the likeness of its favorite, Alice Joyce, wearing a $3,000 gown and $1,000,000 worth of jewels. Everything was lavish. The merit of a picture was measured by its cost.

Zukor had no "Crown Prince" to smile for him. Neither had he a Cochrane, the most brilliant advertising man in the business, to coach him, to publicize him. His sole asset was vision, vision that penetrated the kleig lights focused on Fox and Laemmle, vision that carried him beyond the spectacular, beyond the immediate future.

Famous Players Studio was unable to produce more than fifty pictures a year. Jesse Lasky, who owned the rights to many famous stage dramas, had a well trained stock company that included the noted stage star, Dustin Farnum, and was able to produce thirty pictures a year. Zukor wanted these pictures; he wanted them sufficiently to give Lasky equal rights in a joint distribution agreement.

Once this deal was closed, Zukor cemented friendly relations with Hobart Bosworth an independent producer of better-than-average pictures, who agreed to release his output through the same channel as Lasky and Famous Players. This gave Zukor control of a hundred and four feature-releases a year and opened the door to blind block booking — the booking of pictures before they were produced by "date of release, name of play, name of producer, name of star" in blocks of 13, 26, 52, or 104. The contracts were called franchises; some were to run for five years, some for ten, according to the discretion of the seller. Salesmen were trained to use psychology; they were to convince exhibitors that to be able to run this product once or twice a week for 13, 26, or 52 weeks a year over a period of years was a privilege.

Zukor explained his plan to W. W. Hodkinson, who recognized it for what it was — a master stroke. Before 1914 ended, Hodkinson foresook the Progress Exchanges and agreed to distribute the combined product of Famous Players, Jesse L. Lasky, and Bosworth, under the name of Paramount Pictures. Although the producers controlled the voting stock, the distributing company was to remain independent of the producing units.

The presidency of Paramount Pictures, which would distribute the productions of the foremost directors of the day, Edwin Porter, Cecil B. De Mille, and William De Mille, was offered to Hodkinson. To assist him in this tremendous undertaking Zukor hand picked four men: James Steele, whose apprenticeship had been served at Pittsburgh Calcium Light, the first company to bolt to the Trust, became vice-president; Raymond Pawley, Asbury Park banker, with an interest in a New Jersey exchange, was listed as secretary-treasurer. Completing the directorate were Hiram Abrams, Boston jobber, and William L. Sherry, president of the William L. Sherry Feature Film Company of New York.

Whether Zukor favored these men because of their unrelated personalities, which fitted each to a different job, or because of their strategically located and profitable exchanges, which were absorbed by Paramount, is difficult to say.

The full significance of this organization was lost to his competitors. No one considered the reserved low-voiced man with the far-away expression a serious menace who had out-maneuvered them all. Always and everywhere, this little man with a square chin and thin lips, who carried his head slightly tilted, passed unnoticed.

Lasky was different. He was affable. He was curious. His eyes were wide open, smiling. Delicate lips curled up at each end. A dimple in his chin added to his charm. Although gentle of speech, wherever he went he was the life of the party. Whoever met him knew "he was somebody." Zukor knew it too — and saw that Lasky's vibrant personality was not wasted. Zukor, himself, retired into the background to study production methods, costs, all the dry duties of business. Lasky's name was kept before the public.

The industry had not merely made a come back. Its whole structure had changed. Paltry Independents of the year before had become the Majors of 1914.

America's Fifth Industry

I N THIS TEEMING, BLUSTERING RENAISSANCE, Jules Brulatour was
plagued by insecurity. For years he had helped Independents defy
the Trust, and now that their purchasing power was greater than
ever, it seemed he must lose their business. As Lumière's American
agent he had entered into agreements to provide his customers,
the Independents, with a minimum of forty million feet of raw stock
each year. War in Europe made delivery impossible. One day he
realized his contracts did not specify any particular make of film
stock; the collapse of the Trust had released Eastman Kodak's un-
exposed film to the open market. An affinity between Jules Brulatour and the Eastman Kodak Company was a natural. Under
the terms of the Eastman agreement, a verbal one during the entire
lifetime of George Eastman, Brulatour received commission on every
foot of Kodak film purchased by motion picture producers throughout the United States.

Up, up went the commissions. "Lights. Camera. Action," blasted
from a megaphone and burst into many forms.

One producer, shooting at Venice, California, needed a mob scene.
To avoid the cost of a large staff of extras, he sent boys onto the
boardwalk with a batch of newspapers. Nearby in a building he
concealed a cameraman, equipment, and a director. At a given sig-
nal the boys shouted, "Wuxtra! Wuxtra! England 'clares war on the
U. S.!" Everyone in sight rushed to get a newspaper. The camera
ground, citizens scanned each printed page for the startling news,
and pseudo-news peddlers disappeared from sight.

To overcome a customs law, James J. Johnson, manager of

Madison Square Garden and owner of American rights to the Johnson-Willard fight that had taken place at Havana, Cuba, made an ingenious attempt to get the pictures into the United States. He had the film shipped to Canada. At Rouses Point, on the border, he had six assistants set up in a tent a special projector from which he transmitted the pictures onto a printing device in New York State. After all this, the Government ruled that Johnson stand trial. At this dark moment a politician said to Johnson, "For $200,000 I can get the charges crushed."

"Make it $1,000 a state, when and as it is successfully invaded, and it's a deal," Johnson retorted.

"Chicken feed" did not interest the politician. The whole venture was merely an expense to Johnson. By court order the negative was destroyed by fire in a furnace.

Mutual bought itself a war. For $25,000 General Villa of Mexico supplied the action, and Mutual obtained exclusive rights for authentic battle scenes. By this time, Mexican soldiers were movie regulars. Earlier in 1914, Fritz Wagner, a cameraman, by special arrangements with President Huerta, directed Mexican troops on maneuvers and procured exclusive rights for Pathé. Wagner, however, paid dearly for his pictures. The Mexican president, eager to show his enemies the might that protected him, insisted that the cameraman shoot his entire army of twenty thousand men on parade. Cameras in 1914 were not equipped with motors, and Wagner had to crank his by hand. Exciting events did not always make exciting movies. Battle scenes were set up in an electrically equipped bathtub or elsewhere to make them more "realistic" and "authentic," a practice that has continued into the present day. In 1952, for example, Paramount disappointed with shots of the atomic blast near Las Vegas, called upon its special effects department to erect a miniature set, and on it a spectacular blast was produced.

Theatre owners were somewhat slow to move. Each waited to see what his neighbor might do. Feature pictures gave them all a jolt. Longer pictures necessitated larger houses and more comfortable seats. Expensive films called for luxurious surroundings. Thus the scramble and improvement in production forced a scramble and improvement in exhibition.

A $65,000 theatre with ornate plaster reliefs and heavy draperies appeared at Memphis, Tennessee. Richard Rowland and his brother-in-law, James B. Clarke, who with the disintegration of the Trust became large-scale theatre operators, vied with Davis and Harris, each company boasting its theatres were the most beautiful in western Pennsylvania. At Terra Haute, a $100,000 house was erected. A $350,000 structure went up at Long Beach, California. Jacob Fabian, a retail drygoods merchant, installed a Hope-Jones Wurlitzer Organ in a theatre he ran as a hobby at Patterson, New Jersey.

Stanley Mastbaum, and his brother Jules, operators of a chain of theatres in eastern Pennsylvania, built the Stanley Theatre in Philadelphia, in honor of Stanley, who headed the company. Admissions were twenty-five and fifty cents. Emanuel Mandelbaum, ejected partner of World Film, erected a *downtown* house on Cleveland's aristocratic Euclid Avenue. Kleine and Vitagraph built theatres on Times Square, where special feature films acquired prestige with Broadway runs.

Sol Lesser extended his theatre holdings so that it was necessary for him to open an exchange just to book pictures for his own circuit. His competitor, Sid Grauman, the first man to open a theatre in San Francisco after the earthquake and fire, built a motion picture palace and called it The Imperial. Tally also extended and improved his circuit. In Pasadena, a theatre was built and furnished to cater to the whims of local millionaires.

But Mitchell Mark and his brother Moe outdid them all.* The Mark brothers had a reputation for doing the unusual and unexpected. Once, when they were in the hat business in Buffalo, New York, they advertised for a thousand cats. They sought a girl with flaming red hair to ride a white horse down Buffalo's streets à la Lady Godiva. Each spring and each fall they cleaned up shop by throwing whatever was left in stock from the roof of their store to a waiting crowd below. To the children of Buffalo they fed ice cream cones all summer.

Whether in good fortune or bad, the Marks never lost their sense of humor and never refused a favor if they could help it. In a real estate bubble in 1893, they lost most of their fortune. Yet, when a

---

*The writer has the kindliest recollections of Moe Mark. Over a period of months he gave her a penny each day, saying as he did so, "If John D. Rockefeller can give away dimes, I can give away pennies." If the writer returned to her desk and found a penny on the ledge or in the corner, she knew Moe Mark had been in to pay her a visit.

friend asked them to buy his stock of phonographs so he might go to California, Mitchell turned to Moe and said, "I think it will be a good investment." This started them off in the amusement business, ideally suited to their temperaments.

When five-cent arcades were the rage, they opened a penny arcade. And in 1914, when some store theatres still existed whose only form of advertising was to put out a sign, "OPEN," they built in the heart of New York City, a million dollar, 3,500-seat house, The Mark Strand. A marquee extended over the street; a large electric sign blazed across the front. A uniformed doorman, who assisted ladies from carriages or automobiles and announced when seats were available inside, replaced an unkempt loquacious barker. Ushers, trained to march with military precision, escorted patrons to their seats, called all men "gentlemen" and addressed them as "sir." Women up to middle age were called "miss;" those beyond were "madam." All queries about the picture were answered, "The reviews have been excellent. I am sure you will enjoy it." Suffused light and carpeted floors contributed to the elegance within. The management was placed in the hands of Samuel Rothapfel, who had no more to recommend him than the successful operation of a small house at Forest City, Pennsylvania and the confidence of Mitchell and Moe.

Everyone called the Mark brothers fools . . . and rushed to imitate them. On Broadway alone, six first-run houses appeared. Although not every town could support a million dollar-theatre, almost every town had a miniature Strand.

Money! Money! Money! Everything in the industry revolved around money; everything was spoken of in terms of costs, figured in terms of profits. When the Government attempted to levy a $100 tax to help meet the depression of 1914, the industry contested the action. It organized into groups that propagandized against such legislation and spent a fortune in publicity to ask those who remained indifferent to the impending hardship, "Have *you* $100 to throw away?"

At a convention just before the November elections, where those present were sworn to secrecy, a list of names of political friends was circulated, and a speaker cautioned, "Remember we elect all state officers and legislatures this fall who will make and enforce the laws for two years. We should know our friends."

A Pittsburgh circuit knew its friends and used them to dispose of weaker competitors. Any politically-unprotected owner, who refused to sell his theatre to the chain at the price fixed by the chain, was warned that a large pretentious house would be built next to his.

Small theatre owners, themselves, had no mercy for one another. If one store theatre advertised six reels for five or ten cents, a competitior ran eight or nine reels at three to five cents. Exhibitors received from exchanges controlled by men with theatre holdings films that were worn, badly spliced, and *rainy*. Often pictures arrived too late for advertised runs.

A crying need for organization resulted in a meeting at Cleveland, where theatre men protested against film manufacturers and rental interests acquiring theatres for the purpose of exhibiting film in direct competition to exhibitors who were their customers. The meeting ended with a resolution to take positive action to protect the exhibitors of the country from being put out of business by the interests they had patronized and enriched in the past.

Distributors too were unhappy. Producers, they cried, with a get-rich-quick virus in their veins, demanded substantial deposits before producing a story and then delivered inferior films.

But nothing diverted the forward march of motion pictures. Neither a war nor a depression checked them. Self-interest, misrepresentation, greed were unable to stop them. On they went to take their place as America's Fifth Industry, producing in 1914, 68,000 miles of film at a cost of $37,000,000. The total amount invested in the industry was estimated at $500,000,000 with 100,000 people employed. Its *merchandise,* sometimes produced at a cost of $100,-000 for a single release, was shown in 18,000 theatres in the United States alone. Attendance was estimated to be 15,000,000 daily with approximately $1,000,000 a day paid for admissions. And the daily papers at this time devoted more space to movies than to legitimate theatre.

Stock Jobbery

A MERICA'S FIFTH INDUSTRY! So newspapers, magazines, trade papers, the public categorized the field of motion pictures. Leading bankers recognized that the product of the Fifth Industry had become a source of information and requested the suppression of scenes depicting speculation by bank officials. Local 81 of the American Flint Workers Association objected to pictures depicting intoxicated workmen; reformers objected to murder scenes; others too brought pressures to bear. America's Fifth Industry! The words had charm. The bankers reexamined them. This much might be said: those who succumbed tempered their dissipation and insisted on naming a treasurer or comptroller wherever they invested money. The result was a curious admixture — laughless, stiff-collared, stolid citizens, sustained by pigskins engraved in Latin, well-mannered, though often quietly sarcastic and scornful, surrounded by unwitting buffoons, who swore and cursed at the slightest provocation, who chewed on long black cigars and spat across the room, whose collars usually were open with ties askew, and who doffed their coats and kept on their hats in the presence of ladies.

This labyrinth of personalities might have confused an average man, but not the bank representatives, who worked out involved systems to show costs of production and operation, to show where waste occurred, where economies might be employed. The systems were installed; the reckless spending persisted. Men, who had been guided all their lives by impulse and intuition, were not restrained by purchase blanks, cost sheets, stock lists, production controls, release schedules, rental summaries, or balance sheets.

Once bankers ventured through the locks, speculators of all sorts entered the golden waters. The casualness with which corporate setups were investigated made Sime Silverman, "Mr. Broadway," suspicious. In his paper, *Variety*, he ran an editorial headed:

"PUBLIC PROVING EASY PICKINGS FOR MOVIE PROMOTION SCHEMES

Wall Street Bankers Cleaning Up On Cheap Stock 'Shoving' Schemes. One Picture Concern With Desk and Typewriter Gets $45,000 In A Few Weeks. Public Falling Easily For 'Con' Letters."

In editorial after editorial he cautioned against the score of promoters, who in the past had confined their activities to Wall and Broad Streets, and who were displaying an interest in motion pictures. One stock issue underwritten at 1-1/4 was listed on the curb, where it was disposed of in the neighborhood of 4 and over. Between $800,00 and $900,000 worth of the stock was sold with ease, but nobody seemed to know where the proceeds of the stock sale went.

Sime's editorials might never have been written. Film stocks made their initial appearance almost daily on the various exchanges.

Arrow Film a new company headed by Dr. Shallenberger, offered a $350,000 issue. Two million dollars worth of World Film stock was sold. A $4,000,000 issue of Triangle Company was picked up by a public eager to become business associates of Aitken, Bauman, and Kessel, whose directors were John Ince, longtime matinee idol; David Wark Griffith, of "The Birth Of a Nation" fame; Mack Sennett, originator of "The Bathing Beauty Girls."

Anthony J. Drexel stepped from the Blue Book to climb the magic beanstalk that reached into motion pictures. The name and purse of Otto Kahn, a Wall Street power, were linked with a firm that intended to produce a series of pictures featuring opera stars.

W. E. Koch, wealthy manufacturer of surgical instruments, agreed to back W. K. Ziegfeld (brother of Flo Ziegfeld, musical comedy king who glorified the American Girl), president of a school that taught the techniques of photoplay acting. A former English officer, Major Robert H. Reid, had a feature film firm capitalized at

$1,000,000. These were a mere few of the many film stock issues offered.

"Sucker money," Sime Silverman called the cash raised by promoters. He went on to speak of the wild manipulation of a group which seized upon feature films as an easy means of obtaining coin, and had caused Dun & Bradstreet, and other commercial agencies to look into picture conditions. He revealed that profit-showing in several instances came about through bookkeeping-juggling and that new concerns, hard pressed for capital one day, had plenty of money the next; that the ease with which they raised it tended to make them extravagant. "A blow up," Sime wrote, "is looked for."

A "blow up" came.

When Paramount was formed, no place was found for Al Lichtman, who had opened the way for three-and four-day showings when he sold "Queen Elizabeth" as a special release. Backed by William Sievers, St. Louis exhibitor and several other Independents, Lichtman founded Alco Film. His idea was to get theatres in large cities to run features for at least a week. To justify high admissions, each theatre was to be given six month's protection; that is, second-run houses would not get Alco pictures until six months after initial showings.

On November 20, 1914, four months after it was organized, Alco passed into receivership. That day Lichtman resigned; Sievers, Alco's treasurer, went with him. The following day receivership was lifted. With Lichtman's retirement, officers of the company announced that friction between its executives had come to an end and headed advertisements "Watch Alco Grow."

Things began to happen. Lichtman's job was taken over by Harry J. Cohen, who brought to Alco a knowledge of the workings of Davis and Harris, General Film, and Lubin. John D. Dunlop, New York banker, was made a director. Alco became exclusive distributor for All Stars, owned by Augustus Thomas and Archibald and Edgar Selwyn, famous playwrights. Then Richard Rowland, James B. Clarke, James Steele, and others who had advanced sums to Alco, sued to recover their money because Alco had neglected to deliver pictures as promised. William P. Jeffers, appointed trustee in bankruptcy, sued Archie Selwyn for $10,000. He claimed, "Mr. Selwyn agreed to subscribe to $10,200 worth of Alco stock. He paid for two shares at the rate of $100 each. Later he sold his stock for $3,500. A short time later the company went into bankruptcy." Mr. Selwyn, who denied all responsibility for the remaining $10,000 due on the shares never paid the claim. John D. Dunlop, the banker, also stood accused of reneging on commitments to Alco. He had neglected to advance $125,000 to the corporation "pursuant to an agreement under which stock and property of the corporation were turned over to him." Alco settled for forty cents on the dollar. During the trial, J. Robert Rubin, attorney for the creditors, asked Rowland, "Was your position anything but that of an angel?" "Nobody has got me for an angel yet, except this concern," Rowland replied. Later when Metro was formed Mr. Rubin became Mr. Rowland's partner.

Selznick's company, World Film, advertised "Features Made From Well Known Plays By Well Known Players," a slogan not unlike Zukor's "Famous Plays For Famous Players." Confident that the man to whom Famous Players owed a large measure of its success was the man to sell World Film's product, Selznick offered Lichtman, upon his retirement from Alco, the managership of the company's special attraction department. The association did not work out as Selznick had anticipated. Handsome, dark-eyed Lichtman, courteous and pleasant as a salesman, was sharp around the office. His mere presence incited a reign of terror. Selznick had no objection to the fear Lichtman inspired in others, but Lichtman began to lever his assertiveness and irascibility against the great man himself. Once he did this, Lichtman found himself on the less desirable side of World Film's door.

Other gray stories unfolded. *Variety,* which hammered away, had fifty-seven bankruptcies to draw from. J. J. Murdock, like many pioneers, had opened the way for others when he supplied Independents with their first dependable camera. In 1914, his International Projection and Producing Company was unable to get salable pictures to job, and he was forced to rely on the booking of vaudeville skits for a livelihood, only to find his stars competing with themselves. He would book an act at a theatre with admissions ranging from twenty-five cents to two dollars to discover that the star of the skit was appearing next door in a movie, where admissions were ten and twenty-five cents. When he attempted to "fine" those actors who appeared on the silver screen, he merely discouraged them from appearing on the vaudeville stage. The day when an actor considered it shameful to act in a movie had passed.

For a season or two the Warners had enjoyed some success. Sam went to England, where he distributed American-made pictures. The other three, Harry, Abe, and Jack, merged with Pat Powers, and specialized in European pictures made for American consumption. War disrupted their business. Sam returned home and opened the Regent Exchange in New York City. Harry, Abe, and Pat Powers, reorganized under the name United Film Service and combed the market for American films. Jack migrated to San Francisco, where he operated a small exchange.

Kleine, who had conceived the Trust, found himself in a position similar to that of the Warners, except he had an interest in several theatres. When hostilities first broke out he managed to get some Italian pictures to job but within a few months this source of supply was closed.

Firms branded "members of the old Trust" struggled to keep above water. Kalem started life anew in a dilapidated frame mansion in Florida. "Kalem House" the place was proudly called. Essanay built a $50,000 studio at Niles, California. In an effort to compete with heavily financed outfits, Vitagraph erected a fireproof concrete factory in Brooklyn, New York. Edison and Lubin also had modern plants under construction, Edison in New York City, Lubin at Betzwood, a suburb of Philadelphia.

Before construction was completed, fire broke out in both the Edison and Lubin plants. The Edison fire demonstrated the inexplicable impulses characteristic of film folk. Without conscience or mercy, each warred against the other; yet, immediately Jeremiah J. Kennedy, the toughest of them all, heard that Edison's plant was on fire, he placed the entire facilities of Biograph at the disposal of the Edison Company. Lubin suffered a loss estimated at between $500,000 and $1,000,000 from which he never fully recovered.

Meaner stories circulated. Two men were arrested in San Francisco for selling "phony" film stocks. In the east, an *advance* man called on a theatre owner stating he had a prospective buyer for the theatre. An amount too tempting to refuse was offered. The day after the first call, the *buyer* was introduced and requested a thirty-day option. With the option in hand, the pair canvassed the neighborhood and sold stock in the theatre at one dollar a share. Before the thirty days were up the *brokers* disappeared.

Another scheme had police busy. Men with samples of a color print went into fair-sized cities where they confided to a local merchant or banker that they owned a patent on a color process that would revolutionize the industry. Invariably the merchant or banker wanted the studio erected in his city and advanced ten to fifteen thousand dollars for the purpose. That was the last ever seen of the money or the men.

Bubbles burst all around. Firms that failed to attract an angel collapsed; some with angels failed to survive. Even so, except for Sime Silverman, no one labeled film stocks, "sucker investments," and the public continued to pour its cash into America's Fifth Industry.

The $10,000,000 Corporation

IN ISOLATED INSTANCES the Silverman editorials had effect. English firms demanded cash in advance from American distributors for pre-war pictures. The telephone company shut off service without warning as soon as a bill passed its due date. Commercial agencies issued detailed and embarrassing financial reports on film firms.

Nothing of this escaped Adolph Zukor. What disturbed him most was the manner in which *Variety* commented on the investigation by commercial agencies. In Paramount's house organ an editorial appeared which stated:

> "An article from *Variety* treats an investigation being conducted by commerical agencies of stock-jobbing motion picture concerns, and handles the subject in a wholly frank manner to say the least.
>
> "While some thoroughly reputable companies sell stocks the funds are used directly in conducting and establishing the business and the stockholders are reasonably certain of receiving dollar for dollar upon their investment. These may be distinctly classified as stock companies legitimately operating as such and there is seldom the necessity of such stock being offered to the public.
>
> "The manufacturer and distributor operating upon these principles will probably be in a position continuously to supply their customers with a standard grade of pictures to furnish a service that will constantly improve in efficiency and value. The exhibitor feels

confidence in these operators and knows that he, using their service, is building up a reputation and clientele for his theatre upon a class of production and service that he may reasonably expect to receive year after year, a service that will continually increase in efficiency and value. He feels that he is building permanently.

"The motion picture producing or distributing concerns selling stock promiscuously to the public, however, are quite differently operated. Their stock is generally advertised for sale in expensive advertising space, or distributed through brokers underwriting on a basis that is far from being advantageous to the investor, and the public, through these mediums, is assured of the great value of the stock and the really marvelous opportunity to secure holdings of so unusual earning power.

"Little analysis is required to arrive at the simple deduction that concerns taking in funds secured from this sort of selling, a large part of the proceeds of which are dissipated before reaching the business itself, are not conducted in a manner to establish a standing on their own feet so to speak. Their energies are directed more to inflating their stock than to building a film business.

"Exhibitors affiliated with such concerns are building upon sands, which may at any time shift their unstable structure into the sea of misfortune — the shifting fortunes of stock-jobbing.

"The good of the entire industry, as well as the stock purchasers', is best accomplished by the quick detection and speedy elimination of the unwholesome practice of stock-jobbing. Whatever agency or investigation may bring this about is a public benefactor, and to it an industry is indebted for clarifying and cleansing its trade channels."

The ink was hardly dry when Zukor informed the world:

"PARAMOUNT INCREASING CAPITAL TO
$10,000,000"

As promised, Paramount's issue was not offered to the public. It went to exchanges — in return for a controlling interest in the business. That the film world might not misunderstand, Zukor explained:

> "This latest move by Paramount places the organization in a position to give even more efficient service than formerly, and makes it possible for them to offer highly superior facilities to producers.
>
> "The Paramount has under way other plans for the betterment and progress of Paramount releases and Paramount service.
>
> "Paramount was formed not at all for its own selfish ends and for the aggrandizement and profit of its officers. That is an unworthy purpose. The Paramount idea was so big and broad and progressive that it incorporated plans which would mean better times for every exhibitor — better pictures, better theatres, better patronage and better business. The Paramount plan meant better times for theatre patrons in providing them higher class amusement, and the Paramount plan necessitated better and more permanent business for the producers in providing an efficient market for their films."

Notwithstanding Zukor's explanation, wary exchange men invested only as much as was necessary to retain a Paramount picture franchise. This forced Dominick & Dominick and the Hallgarten Company, the underwriters, to buy in a big percentage of of the stock. To protect their money, these investment houses kept a watchful eye on Zukor.

One of the first steps taken by the $10,000,000 corporation was to prove that "only those concerns can win who are conducting their business upon safe, constructive lines governed by systematic, economic business principles," and that it "was not formed for its own selfish ends and for the aggrandizement of its officers." These statements were hardly uttered, when Paramount dictated to newly acquired exchanges exactly what pictures they were to use and withdrew from franchise holders (exhibitors who had obligated themselves to purchase a given number of pictures in a specified period of time under the block-booking system on the strength of the drawing power of top Paramount stars) those stars who proved to be big money makers.

Zukor offered another explanation. "Owing to the enormous salary demanded by its leading lady, Famous Players had found it necessary to first release pictures in which she appeared through big city theatres at a minimum admission price of 25¢ ranging up to 50¢ ." A million-dollar studio was built on the west coast to provide a setting suitable for this star, and Lichtman was reengaged to sell her "specials."

Box Office Attractions lacked the capital to compete with a $10,000,000 giant. Fox approached a coterie of Newark financiers to whom he sold a fifty percent interest in the Fox Film Company for $400,000. Fox's new partners reposed the fullest confidence in him. All voting shares were issued in his name, and a $250,000 insurance policy, with the corporation as beneficiary, was placed on his life.

The sentiments of Fox were as noble as those of Zukor. In a full page advertisement, Fox Film stated:

> "From the theatrical branch of his enterprises alone, Mr. Fox has amassed a fortune far greater than he can ever spend. He has an annual income that is many times larger than he requires. The Fox Film Corporation does not rest on shifting sands of stock-jobbery and notable feats of frenzied finance. Instead it is rooted firmly in the living rock of a sound foundation of financial security. Its directors number such men as Thomas N. McCarter, President of the great Public Service Corporation of the State of New Jersey; Colonel Anthony R. Kuser, Vice-President of the Prudential Life Insurance Company; Uzal H. McCarter, President of the Fidelity Trust Company of Newark, New Jersey. Among the other directors of this corporation are John C. Eisele and Nathaniel King of the banking firm of Eisele & King. These are the men upon whom, with Mr. Fox, the business integrity of the Fox Film Corporation rests. But above and beyond all this is the unique position that Mr. Fox occupies in the producing world. HIS INTEREST AND YOURS ARE IDENTICAL.

"MOREOVER, MR. FOX FEELS THAT HE HAS
A MISSION TO PERFORM FOR THE LESS LUCK-
ILY SITUATED SHOWMAN NO LESS THAN FOR
THE SATISFIED INDIVIDUAL. HIS EFFORTS
WILL GO ON AND ON, DESPITE SORE-HEADED
PRODUCERS, TILL HE MAKES '*STANDING ROOM
ONLY*' BLOSSOM OUT ON THEATRES NOT SO
FORTUNATELY LOCATED BY GIVING THEM
THE BEST PRODUCTIONS AND GREATEST PRO-
GRAMS EVER RELEASED."

A few weeks after the reorganization, Fox entered into a secret
arrangement with one of Col. Kuser's relatives. For $1,000, Fox
became owner of ten shares of Fox Film that this man received
from the Colonel as a gift. These ten shares gave Fox a controlling
interest in the corporation, should he ever need it.

These new corporate set-ups, with *preferred* lists, placed many
distributors and exhibitors in hazardous positions.

Marcus Loew, to assure a beginning and an end for his vaudeville shows, which still depended on movies as a painless way to
empty a house, entered the production field. With Nicholas Schenck,
Joseph M. Schenck and David Bernstein, all executives of Loew's
Inc., he formed a $1,000,000 closed corporation.

Rowland also turned to the production of feature pictures. On
July 4, 1915, he unfurled on The Stem (Times Square in New York
City) an American flag 175 feet in length, the largest national banner in the world to dedicate the inauguration of the Metro Pictures
Corporation, organized that "exchange men can control the output
of their producing units for the benefit of exhibitors." His associates
were his partner and brother-in-law, James B. Clarke; J. Robert Rubin, attorney for the creditors in the Alco-All Star case; George A.
Greenbacker of Portland, Oregon; Joseph W. Engel of New York
City; Otto N. Davis of Minneapolis; James A. Fitzgerald of Detroit;
and Louis B. Mayer of Boston, all exchange owners.

Mayer rose from the sea to take his place as Richard Rowland's
partner. His first recollections were of the wild foamy surf off St.
John, New Brunswick. His father, a Polish immigrant, tried his
hands over a period of years at various odd jobs in the cold, stony,
wind-tossed land. The sea was the only thing that provided him a

livelihood, and that only through the miserable remains of ship-
wrecks that drifted into the Bay of Fundy. As soon as Louis and his
brother were able to support more than their own weight in water,
they were taught to dive for salvage. Throughout the winter they
helped their father dispose of scrap collected in warmer months.
The existence was a desolate one, and to escape it, Louis, when he
reached his majority, fled to the United States, "where all are rich."

At Haverhill, Massachusetts, Louis obtained work in a nickelodeon. He changed his opinion about the financial standing of the
average American. Still he preferred the opportunities at Haverhill
to those at St. John. He lived a Spartan existence and eventually
acquired a burlesque house, which he transformed into a movie
theatre, an amusement place suitable for women and children as well
as men.

The hustle and bustle, the recklessness, the impulsiveness, the
enthusiasm and abandon in the industry, all entranced him, but he
never lost the melancholy that had seeped into his soul as a boy. He
was shy and diffident in the company of people, and although
in ten years he had become a motion picture power in New England, he was perhaps the least known among the partners of the
dapper, engaging Richard Rowland.

Edison, who had looked upon the motion picture as unworthy
of his great genius, watched those he once had scorned pass him
by. In an effort to strengthen his position he merged with Kleine.

The Warners, too, wistfully observed the speed with which others
advanced. They just did not seem to be able to make the grade.
Jack and Sam, now partners, eked out a meager livelihood. The
United Film Service, owned by Harry and Abe Warner and Pat
Powers, passed from bad to worse and finally went the way of
Alco.

To everyone's surprise, Powers reappeared at Universal. Without anyone suspecting, Laemmle least of all, Powers had collected
fifty-one percent of Universal's stock on the open market. Speculation and bets were rife as to how Powers might treat his old foes,
Laemmle and Cochrane. But quick-tempered, ready-fisted, ruddy-
faced Pat Powers had learned his lesson. He knew that, for all his
physical strength, Cochrane, via Laemmle, was better able to cope
with such giants as the Paramount and Fox corporations. In addition, Universal had suits pending against it that required skillful

handling if good public relations were to be maintained. Among the suits was one for $100,000 by Jess Willard, heavyweight champion and idol of fight fans, who alleged he ". . . had worked in a picture under an agreement by which he was to get twenty-five per cent of gross receipts, and that the films were sold by Universal to exchanges owned by them, securing fictitious prices that did not represent a true value of the picture." Administrators of the estate of two victims of a train fire claimed that Universal, contrary to the law, shipped film wrapped in paper instead of in a fire-proof box, and that when the film ignited on the train the fire could not be controlled and caused the fatal injuries. In New England, Universal had to defend violation of fire hazard regulations that applied to the storage and use of films. Although Powers took the position of treasurer away from Cochrane, appointing himself in Cochrane's place, he permitted Cochrane to retain the vice-presidency and made no attempt to displace Laemmle as president.

Millions Float In Space

CARL LAEMMLE MADE SEVERAL TRIPS downtown.* The curious soon learned that the trips were made in an attempt to raise money to buy the holdings of Pat Powers. However, when Powers held out for $1,500,000, Laemmle overcame his desire to buy his partner's share. Such a sum might be used effectively against Universal. Powers and he celebrated their decision to remain together by selling to Universal for $1,000,000 in cash all exchanges privately owned by them, exchanges they had purchased years before with promisory notes of the Universal Company.

The only film product distributed by Universal and not made by it was Eclair's. Through the poor management of Alfred Varion, the company was in financial difficulties. Jules Brulatour sued for $40,000. In court, Brulatour, embarrassed by the description, "pressing creditor," insisted, "I had been most lenient. I allowed the indebtedness to reach $40,000." Why Brulatour, all things considered, had allowed himself to become Eclair's largest creditor, remains something of a mystery. He was a close friend of Universal and a former president of the corporation. He had demanded certified checks before delivery from all other accounts. He had, when he extended a loan to a friend accepted eighty-four shares of stock as collateral and refused to return the securities after they took a substantial upward leap until he was sued.

All in all, Varion had issued notes in the amount of $115,000. Universal offered to settle the debts and incorporate Eclair into its family circle. Like the hero in many of his melodramas, Patin, dis-

---

*New York financial district.

charged by the French Army because of defective vision, returned unannounced just in time to depose Varion for exceeding authority vested in him by the power of attorney, and to save Eclair from Universal.

Actually, Laemmle was relieved. His desires were modest. He wanted only to protect the fortune he already had amassed and was mortally afraid the unrestrained expansion in which he found himself enmeshed might lead to his ruin. Mad he might have been to succumb to the glamour of big business, but he was not mad enough to follow into the super-feature field. His motto was, "It doesn't pay to gamble with your business success." At his insistence, and here Cochrane was unable to overrule him, Universal continued to cater to small theatre owners with complete programs, inexpensively produced. To obtain adequate female talent at low salaries, Universal organized beauty contests. Merger talks with Jeremiah J. Kennedy and Harry Aitken were dropped.

Biograph, having been reduced to producing single reelers, Kennedy returned to engineering. Scarcely anyone noticed he had retired from the field in which he had been the greatest power. When he died in 1932, only a short paragraph in the obituary columns mentioned his passing, and when friends were pressed by a curious reporter for information about him, they refused to reveal whether or not it were true he had died penniless.

Aitken, the man who had dared produce "The Birth of A Nation," with the $4,000,000 bankroll that had poured into Triangle, and no Freuler to frown on the stakes, did not intend to play penny ante. The cost of his productions topped all existing records. He announced his pictures would supplant the spoken drama, whose decadance had made this possible. In large cities he transformed legitimate play houses into "Theatres of Science and Artifice," where "Triangle Plays" were shown at two dollar admissions. On the Great White Way, he leased the Knickerbocker Theatre at a $65,000 yearly rental for his New York runs. And at this time some small towns still had a three-cent show.

The two-dollar admission replaced the $10,000,000 corporation as the favorite topic of conversation. Zukor was hurt. On one of the rare occasions in which he revealed his feelings, he told the public about it, denouncing the two-dollar admission as excessive and unfair. His own policy of running specials had not worked out. All Paramount stars were back in the block. After saying what he thought about two-dollar admissions, Zukor left for his west coast studios. Hardly had he arrived when a telegram from Al Lichtman caused him to pack his bags and return east.

Hodkinson, whom Zukor had placed at the head of Paramount, was all set to release the pictures of the Lasky Company and other Paramount sources of supply without those of Famous Players. All Hodkinson needed were the signatures. All he needed were the signatures that Zukor, the day he returned east, procured under a twenty-five year contractual arrangement for distribution.

Neither Zukor nor Hodkinson discussed the incident. Business at Paramount went on as though nothing unusual had occurred. The date for the annual election of officers arrived. The meeting was well attended. Pawley nominated Hodkinson for president. Someone else nominated Hiram Abrams, the New England representative. When the votes were counted only two had been cast in Hodkinson's favor, his own and Pawley's. Hiram Abrams was elected. Tall, lean, dignified William Wadsworth Hodkinson was stunned. He had not expected to find himself devoid of friends in the organization. For a moment he stood swaying slightly, a tremulous light playing ridiculously on his bald head. Then he gulped, cleared his throat and said, "The votes are against me. I will turn the office over to Mr. Abrams." He did more than that. He and Pawley put on their hats and coats and walked out of Paramount.

Samuel Goldfish, general manager of the Lasky Company, followed them. Whatever the reason, it was cloaked in secrecy. Rumors stated that Hodkinson had carried on his Lasky negotiations with Goldfish. Others said differences between Goldfish and his wife, Lasky's sister, led to the rift.

The resignations of Hodkinson, Pawley and Goldfish by no means ended Zukor's troubles. Goldfish turned to the Selwyns with whom he formed the Goldwyn Company. The combined Goldfish and Selwyn ability presented a serious threat. And Hodkinson owned a strong circuit of theatres throughout the west and, through these theatres, controlled a considerable portion of western bookings. Business at Paramount dropped; its payroll was cut, and Lichtman, who had sent Zukor the warning telegram, was among those let out.

Then there was Selznick—always trying something new. Now he went about saying that World Film would operate on a profit-sharing basis — directors to get a drawing account against twenty per cent of the profits of the pictures they produced. That Selznick adopted this policy because World Film lacked a bankroll with which to pay large salaries unless earned and had no other means of baiting "big name directors" did not pacify Zukor.

Zukor was particularly annoyed because a policy of his own had boomeranged. Long and loudly Zukor had heralded his stars. He had proclaimed their talents until the stars, themselves, were convinced, not only the stars, but George Washington Hill, president of American Tobacco Company. The American Tobacco Company had a $100,000,000 surplus, a $100,000,000 surplus that ought to be invested to earn additional surpluses. Hill sent his advertising agent, Benjamin B. Hampton, out to dangle the $100,000,000 before Paramount, Triangle, Lubin and Vitagraph. Each company opened its books for Hampton's inspection. For months he denied no rumors; he confirmed none. Rumors continued to emanate from his office. Hampton courted this publicity so that little or no attention would be attracted when and if he really did concoct a mixture of tobacco and motion pictures.

In the course of his negotiations, Hampton met Mary Pickford, the star for whom Zukor had built a million-dollar studio on the west coast. She was the most highly publicized star in the business. Hampton succumbed to her golden curls and offered her an option. If he committed the American Tobacco Company, this girl must be its star.

The star read the option and told Zukor that Famous Players would have to pay her $1,000,000 a year to keep her on the payroll. Zukor was in a quandary. If he refused to meet her salary, someone else would reap the benefit of his expensive advertising campaigns; if he paid it, Famous Players would suffer total loss on her pictures. Zukor signed the contract and was doubly embarrassed because he did so at a time stage hands were on strike for a salary of twenty-one dollars a week.

The trend frightened Edwin Porter. Since the inception of Famous Players, he had directed the pictures that led the company into first place. But he was getting old. Younger men than he held the director's spotlight. He did not want to spoil his record. Neither did he want to lose his fortune. For $800,000, he sold his holdings in Famous Players, bought himself a Rolls Royce automobile, and invested his savings "safely" in the Precision Machine Company, manufacturer of the Simplex machine (a projector). Porter had long been interested in the mechanical devices of the industry and had, in fact, been a discoverer of three-dimensional photography.

Hampton's efforts to sign up Zukor's star, unsuccessful though they were, set a new fashion on Wall Street. Now, when a gambler made a *killing,* he invested his money safely in a film star.

In this frenzied market, Selznick struggled to survive. World Film stock dropped. Word went the rounds that the company was on the verge of bankruptcy. "It's a pack of lies," Selznick shouted. Trade papers wanted to know why he spent so much time in conference with Ladenburg, Thallman & Company in the financial district. "To organize a gigantic concern," he explained, "with the assistance of commercial houses — not film brains, mind you. Not because World Film is in financial difficulties, but because I am working out a plan that will revolutionize regular programs." World Film paid a dividend; then the stock, which once sold for between five and six dollars a share sank to one and a fraction.

The *wise* insisted Selznick hoped to merge with VLSE (a combine of Vitagraph, Lubin, Selig, Essanay), with VLSE itself gasping for breath. Vitagraph had been compelled to discharge twenty-seven of its actors. Lubin failed to meet several notes at his bank. Selig's difficulties were political. The United States leaned toward England and France, and Colonel Selig (Colonel, U.S.A.) was accused of pro-German sympathies. Reviews of Essanay's pictures were consistently bad.

No, Selznick insisted, he would not tie in with VLSE, its days were numbered. He had $50,000,000 ambitions. The dream was wonderful — while it lasted. One morning, after all his efforts to introduce a $50,000,000 *angel* to World Film, Selznick awoke to find himself deposed.

With Selznick out, Wall Street raised $1,200,000 for World Film's treasury, and placed William Brady, Adolph Zukor's old friend, at the head of the company at a salary of over $100,000 a year. But he headed a company that had lost its leading lady, Clara Kimball Young. About town she was the constant companion of Mrs. Selznick. At the Selznick residence, she was a frequent guest. James Young gave the situation a diabolical twist. He sued the film executive for alienation of his wife's affections.

Whatever the situation, Clara Kimball Young continued to appear in public with Mrs. Selznick and, if Mr. Selznick was unable to have a $50,000,000 company, he was able to have a $1,000,000 company, a $1,000,000 Clara Kimball Young Company, a company of super-specials that demanded four times the usual rentals. He controlled the company with an actual investment of $1,000 and issued 499,000 shares of the common stock in the actress's name.

And at a time such as this, Aitken admitted defeat by cutting the two-dollar admission in his first run houses.

Adolph Zukor's mask dropped a second time. At a meeting in New York, he rose to his feet, his eyes narrowed into slits, and in a shrill voice cried, "Selznick is a menace! Like a fool he has tossed aside the old contract and program system. The presentation of the Young pictures as a separate proposition and the greatly increased charge to the exhibitor for the product will disrupt the industry." He called on Walter Greene,* Hiram Abram's Boston partner; Stanley Mastbaum of Philadelphia, and Mitchell Mark of New York to support him, in remedial measures, " . . . even if it is necessary to put Selznick out of business."

Trade reporters, eager to decipher Selznick's next move, flocked to him. He was calm, almost jolly. "Why should I discuss Mr. Zukor?" he asked.

"He's trying to put you out of business."

"You take him too seriously. Mr. Zukor has a peeve on. He's sore because I took the jump on him. He intends to do with several of his stars precisely what I am doing with Clara Kimball Young. This talk of my policy being a 'menace to the industry' is ridiculous. The intelligent exhibitor is only too glad to pay four or five times what he now pays for big features if he can eliminate the rest of the trash on the program and double his receipts. And Mr. Zukor knows it is impossible for one firm to put out fifty-two or more good pictures a year."

"As for Greene, Abrams, and Mastbaum," Selznick went on, "they are a pack of jokers. If they don't think it such a good idea, why are they my partners in their respective territories?"

---

*In the spring of 1909, then an independent crusader bucking Trust practices, Walter Greene in advertisements in *Show World,* had said, "Get your film from Walter E. Greene, Boston. Don't pay a license. Wouldn't it make you laugh to think of paying a license on something you have already bought?"

Stanley Mastbaum, who had all the product of the foremost producers tied up by contract, booked for sixty theatres in Philadelphia. Some, he owned. Those he did not own paid him ten per cent to act as their agent. In Philadelphia, it was "book thru Mastbaum" or have a dark house. The Paramount franchise was his mainstay. He played along with Paramount, and Paramount played along with him. What did the few dollars he had invested with Selznick matter? He shelved the Selznick pictures.

Mastbaum had underestimated the producer of the Clara Kimball Young pictures. Selznick opened an exchange in the heart of Mastbaum's territory. Mastbaum was aware that he had a powerful weapon. He was able to supply a theatre with a full year's program; Selznick was unable to produce enough pictures to keep a theatre going for more than a few weeks. A notice, signed by Mastbaum, was circulated. In it, he threatened to pull out of those theatres that ran the Selznick product, any Paramount, Triangle, Metro, or other pictures to which he held distribution rights. Whereupon Selznick instructed his attorneys to prepare papers in an action for triple damages against Mastbaum under the Anti-Trust Act in restraint of trade.

Mastbaum was ignorant of any controversy. "Why," he said, "Selznick is one of my personal friends. I do not know anything about any Selznick pictures. I heard that these pictures were in existence, but up to the present time I have no definite knowledge of such being really the case."

"Very funny! Very funny!" Selznick exclaimed. And he produced a series of letters and telegrams to refresh Mastbaum's memory.

The triple-damage threat had the desired effect. Mastbaum agreed to handle Selznick's pictures and to give him fair distribution.

A new idea in the film business brings about a new cycle. Superfeatures flooded the market. Selznick was right; Zukor produced them faster than anyone else. A million dollars a year no longer satisfied Mary Pickford. To keep his leading lady happy, Zukor made her the star of a producing unit bearing her own name, organized a corporation, Artcraft Pictures, to distribute these specials and, in addition to her salary, gave her fifty per cent interest in the company. This maneuver brought Al Lichtman back onto one of the Zukor payrolls. He was the only man who matched Lewis Selznick as a salesman.

"Black Maria" — first Motion Picture Studio in the U. S., built at W. Orange, N. J. in 1893. Edison's studio tar-papered shack erected at a cost of $637.67.

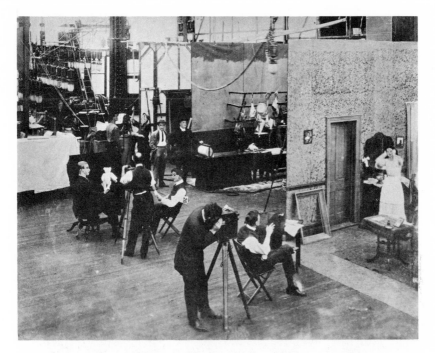

Edison Studio Set 1914 — 1915.

An early Selig Studio showing several different sets.

Early Studio of Adolph Zukor.

1949 *Studio Gates.*

First Hollywood Studio.

The administration building of the Warner Bros. Studio in 1925.

The entrance to the Warner Bros. Studio in 1925.

"One Foot In Heaven," released by Warner Bros. in 1941.

Charlie Chaplin awaiting his entrance in a United Artists picture.

"You Were Never Lovelier," starring Fred Astaire and Rita Hayward; released by Columbia Pictures in 1942.

Shooting "The Desperadoes," released by Columbia Pictures in 1943.

Aerial view of Hollywood Studio.

The Down Payment Plan

IN THE CONTEST FOR LEADERSHIP AND CONTROL, Fox played a lone hand. Like Laemmle, he was not ensnared by the super-special. He continued to make pictures within the means of small theatre operators and catered to subsequent-run houses. Unlike Laemmle, he was not guided by conservatism. He merely had other ideas.

Winfield Sheehan left for South America and Australia, " . . . to liberate theatres." And Prince Winnie did not return until Fox was known as the great emancipator who freed motion picture houses of both continents from the grip of paltry combines unable to give the public its money's worth. Wherever F-O-X decorated a facade, only product bearing the Fox label was shown. Fox demanded that his name be attached to any company with which he was connected. He took pride in the fact that his was the only large company producing every foot of film it released.

He appeared not to be interested in the corporate policies pursued by others or the pictures they produced. Nevertheless, on one occasion at least he released a photodrama just before a competitor who owned the copyrights. He was sued; the resultant publicity increased his profits.

The practice of greeting a competitor with his own story was not confined to William Fox. Four firms produced the "Picture of Dorian Gray" simultaneously. However, "Dorian Gray" was not copyrighted material and Oscar Wilde, resting in his grave, could not protest at the mutilation of his story. All four versions ended happily.

Except for a rare film here or there, critics cried, from top to bottom the industry turned out pictures that were unauthentic, feeble

144

and flat. They ridiculed a soldier for holding his gun in the wrong hand and Rebecca in "Ivanhoe" for wearing French heels and Pickwick for carrying a Gladstone bag. They wanted to know why in the last act of "The Hunchback of Notre Dame" a surgeon performs an operation on Quasimodo and straightens him out so he can marry Esmeralda and how the movies contrived a happy ending for Tess in "Tess of the D'Urbervilles."

"What was originally an industry replete with romantic skylarking adventure," they cried, "has become a prosaic merchandising business."

Variety opened a regular column, DRIVEL OF THE FILM: One item ran:

> "THE CINNAMON TASTERS SECRET. A gorgeous galaxy of scintillating gems. A stupendous eight-reel hydrophobia wonder. A throbbing drama of lavish love and hellish hate. Bristling with adventure. Burning ice house, two knock-outs, a pie-eating contest and an explosion in a sock factory."

Criticism was in vain. The industry saw no reason to overcome its predilection for blatant historical, geographical, and dramatic errors.

The pictures of Fox were often worse than those of his competitors, but education was not his field. He had pictures to sell, and sell them he did — under an ingenious scheme.

First a "missionary" convinced an exhibitor of the outstanding drawing power of Fox product. Then the exhibitor was given to understand the Fox output was practically promised to his competitors. This commonplace psychological trick was used to make a simple theatre owner plead for pictures. When a theatre man was sufficiently anxious, the Fox representative brought out a contract that called for an $800 down payment, "just to convince the home office of your good faith." During the life of the contract the exhibitor was permitted to view four features at a time — one month's supply. The exhibitor might book these pictures in whatever order he preferred, but he was obligated to pay for them in advance. No clause in the agreement provided for rejection of any picture.

Zukor, Aitken, Freuler, Rowland, Goldfish—right down the line

the Fox plan caught fire. Exhibitors complained, "it was an impo-
sition;" they could not afford to deposit large sums at each exchange; that this policy placed them at the mercy of releasing
agents. Once distributors had their money, exhibitors were forced to
accept product, good or bad, or lose their deposits. Even over-
payments were refunded in trade, because home office regulations
prohibited the refunding of cash to an exhibitor.

Many and loud were the exhibitors' complaints. An exchange
might sign up a theatre for a year in advance without mentioning
a super-special in work. When the super-special came out, if the
theatre did not take it, it was offered to a competitor; if the theatre
took the "super, " no cancellation of a picture already under contract was permitted. Often pictures were paid for without a showing.

Frequently after a picture was booked and advertised, an exhibitor
would get a call informing him the film could not be delivered.
Upon investigation he would discover the reason: a variety manager, with a summer policy of movies only, or a saloon keeper,
who showed movies free, had waved an extra five dollar bill before
the booker. A considerate booker might send a substitute. Where a
picture was ordered under the name of a star, he would send the
requested star in an old picture with advertising on a new release.

The demand for down payments continued, still "super-specials"
deluged the market. To give these expensive productions suitable
surroundings, "Deluxe" theatres were erected. On Broadway the
Rialto was built to compete with the Strand, and the Rialto lured
Samuel Rothapfel, the Strand's manager. Detroit opened a duplex theatre with admissions ranging from fifteen to fifty cents.
Shorts were shown in one auditorium while multiple reels were
shown in the other, so that no patron had to walk into the show
in the middle of a photodrama. Wallace, Idaho; Bradentown,
Florida; Eau Claire, Wisconsin; Catawissa, Pennsylvania; all built
theatres with settings worthy of super-specials. John H. Kunsky built
a thirty-one hundred seat house in Detroit, and in Louisville, Ken-
tucky, where an exhibitor once scandalized his neighbors by using
the parlor of his colonial mansion as a show room, a twelve hundred seat house was erected. In Seattle, Washington, a $350,000
theatre had inlaid mosaics of Byzantium design. Even Spokane,
Washington, the city which did not have a movie show until 1908,
came forth with a magnificent picture palace. For all the theatre

expansion, an expansion that far exceeded demand, there were not enough houses to consume the product. To make matters worse, infantile paralysis and influenza closed theatres in many sections of the country.

The irritants that bedeviled America's Fifth Industry increased. In Pennsylvania, a board of censors appointed six hundred police chiefs to act as film spies to report which theatres showed pictures with obscene titles. This practice brought about Sunday closings. In sections where child curfews were in force, theatres were forced to refuse to admit children unaccompanied by an adult, and children began to ask men in the street to take them into the show. When the Society for the Prevention of Cruelty to Animals, which had previously sued Fox for filming a horse taking a six-foot jump in which the rider's leg was broken, took steps to prevent, " . . . any human being from entering a cage, arena, or enclosure with wild animals," the industry answered the attack by circulating pictures of the magnificent zoos in which its animals were housed to prove that it treated wild beasts well, even though humans were permitted to enter cages. Sam Bullock, a Cleveland exhibitor, was arrested for saying, "Censorship was conceived in iniquity and is dying of disgrace." Those who agreed that children must not see shooting or stabbing, even if the violence were to punish the villain, suggested the evil-doer should be drowned instead. In New York, the city fathers ordered those producers still manufacturing within city limits to pack up and move as they constituted a public menace.

The American Newspaper Publishing Association issued a black-list against film companies that advertised nationally through bill boards and posters and slighted the newspapers, until the companies attacked contracted for newspaper space. Young women returning from Hollywood, reported that to obtain employment as motion picture actresses was impossible except at a moral sacrifice and, that conditions on the west coast were so bad, movie-struck girls on a bread line were a common sight. From the film capital also came stories of dream parties and drunken orgies.

Fox was asked to explain why he released to the Locust Theatre at West Philadelphia pictures he had sold to the Belmont Amusement Company, located in the same city. Metro was sued for unethical conduct in negotiating for the services of actors under contract to Vitagraph.

Kessel and Bauman, now associated with Aitken at Triangle, also had to defend a situation. Prints of pictures they had made while distributing through Mutual were no longer usable. When Mutual, who had the American rights to these pictures, asked for replacements, Kessel and Bauman offered various excuses for non-delivery of duplicate prints. Yet these subjects continued to appear in theatres. Investigation revealed that duplicates sold abroad found their way back across the sea onto American screens.

Under an old army game the owner of an exchange bilked three men and a girl. He represented himself as an associate of producers and, for a fee, promised to make the four film stars.

A booker, who wanted to place one of his less successful features in a theatre over a week-end, learned that the theatre manager had ordered a picture from a rival firm. The day before the scheduled showing the booker telephoned his competitor. He pretended to be the theatre manager and asked to have the booking cancelled. When the theatre man came to pick up his feature he was told no print of the subject was available because of the cancellation. Furious, the exhibitor stormed into the office of the first booker, who graciously supplied him with the dullest feature on his shelves.

Into this market Swanson came on a visit. Since the Universal book-tossing episode he operated a chain of theatres in the far west. For old times' sake he dropped into see old friends and old foes. Each had his tale of woe and bitter complaint. Experience had taught Swanson to be discreet. Patiently he listened to each sad story and, recalling his hard-drinking past, he wondered why he had ever taken these people seriously enough to tumble off the water wagon on their account.

Carl Laemmle, J. Stuart Blackton, Jules Brulatour, Pat Powers, Samuel Rothapfel, and others incorporated the Motion Picture Board of Trade of New York City for the purpose of promoting friendlier intercourse among its members; to obtain freedom from unjust and unlawful actions; to diffuse accurate and reliable information as to the standing and character of those engaged in the motion picture business; to reform trade abuses; and to combat adverse legislation. Its affiliate, the Motion Picture Educational League, was organized to play an important part in the coming elections.

The stratagems implied all was not well, and all was not well. Whether anyone admitted it or not, signs indicated that the current business depression was catching up with motion pictures.

Triangle stock, for which optimists had paid over nine dollars a share, dropped to two-fifty. World Film shares, which the year before had sold at five and six dollars, were at one dollar a share. A new series of failures led the *Magazine of Wall Street* to take up Variety's cry and warn small investors against putting funds in movie stocks.

One evening during this period, William Randolph Hearst went to a performance of the Ziegfeld Follies. A blue-eyed blonde in the line caught his attention. Night after night he returned to see her walk, to see her dance, to see her smile. He contrived a meeting. The girl was like a China doll, exquisite, captivating. He did not notice that she stuttered. The fascination was not reciprocated. She secretly laughed at the middle-aged publisher's large sombrero and loose-fitting clothes. She thought his small, closely set, lustreless eyes and his long nose ugly. His elephantine body left her cold. He spoke of his art collections, his trips abroad, his work. The chorus girl was bored. Hearst promised to make her a renowned actress, to provide her with coveted roles. He promised to spread her name throughout the civilized world, to make her motion pictures' queen. A campaign that was to last for over twenty years began. To his wife, Mr. Hearst gave as much publicity as he gave to the actress. Thus his papers carried complete details of prize fights sponsored by his wife to provide milk for underfed babies on one page while glowing descriptions of the histrionic talents and charms of the beauty, Marion Davies, were carried on another. The person who arranged the meeting he repaid with a position on his papers.

Faithful to Hearst's promise, Arthur Brisbane, his editor-in-chief, who once had said, "Motion pictures thrive on the stupidity of the human race," and other equally harsh things, reversed his position and even wrote a scenario to prove himself a fan. Hearst made the girl the most publicized actress in the world. He spent a fortune on sets, employed the best cameramen, and purchased literary masterpieces in a vain effort to make the Ziegfeld beauty a talented performer.

Carl Laemmle was unable to foresee the outcome of Hearst's wild dream. Panic-stricken lest the publisher's extravagance further depress the industry, he counseled the "common show" to return to two and three reelers. "Short films are best," he said; "they are not

so costly and do not present as great a risk." In his over-zealous
desire to purge the industry of speculators and experimentalists and
the intemperate who constantly disrupted production policies and
methods, Laemmle blighted the hopes and dreams of romantic, wild-
eyed young folk by issuing the following statement:

> "The Universal Film Manufacturing Company wishes
> to announce that it has not recommended the school of
> photoplay acting conducted by the Movie Actor's Asso-
> ciation, James Cruze, director.
> "Together with some lurid, highly illustrated printed
> matter, the Movie Actor's Association sends out to
> prospective and actual students a letter of recommen-
> dation from a big wig-maker and from one Dan Meany,
> business manager of Universal Film Manufacturing
> Company. Mr. Meany's letter was issued without the
> authority or knowledge of the Universal and that com-
> pany wishes to state that his letter did not and does not
> now express the attitude of the officials of the Universal
> Film Manufacturing Company toward the Movie Actor's
> Association."

Incidentally, at that time Cruze was negotiating to direct pictures
for Metro, a Laemmle competitor. One of the first films he produced
was "*The Old Homestead*" (1915), which was such a great hit,
it has been reproduced three times since, in 1922, 1935, in 1942.
   Carefully Benjamin B. Hampton followed every move. In the
great tobacco-scented future he conceived for the industry, he dropped
part of the $100,000,000 he had been dangling. For support, Hamp-
ton lined up Frank Harris Hitchcock, Postmaster General in the Cabinet of William Howard Taft and Chairman of the Republican National Convention of 1912; H. H. Vreeland, President of the New York
Metropolitan Street Railways Corporation; Clendenin J. Ryan, son
of Thomas Fortune Ryan. The elder Ryan was a financial wizard
who had made a fortune in Metropolitan Street Railways securities.
At one time he controlled all transportation in New York City. As
a stockbroker, he had helped organize the American Tobacco Company, whose money backed Hampton. In a body these four men
entered the directorate of the Vitagraph Company, and the corpora-

tion which, in the late Nineteenth Century, had been capitalized by its founders at six thousand dollars, was recapitalized in the summer of 1916 at twenty-five million dollars. Accompanying the move was the announcement that a chain of one thousand theatres would be organized where United Cigar coupons would be accepted as theatre tickets. The United Cigar Company operated a chain of retail stores where tobacco was sold.

First National -
The Exhibitor's Revolt

AMERICAN TOBACCO MONEY not only saved Vitagraph, it placed a faltering company alongside those in the front ranks of the motion picture industry. The new investors made it possible for Vitagraph to take over V.L.S.E., and, henceforth, the company was known as Vitagraph — V.L.S.E., or Greater Vitagraph. Under the new directorate, Blackton was superfluous, but no one was able to oust him until he was given a $1,500,000 guarantee, to be met in five equal installments spaced a year apart. The board of politicians, businessmen and financiers better understood Albert E. Smith, who was appointed president in Blackton's place. Thus, years of partnership between life-long friends came to an end. Pop Rock did not witness this strained farewell. He had died the year before, one of the richest men in the industry. Blackton, in his commodore's uniform, moved over to Paramount as an independent producer.

Paramount, itself, was in the throes of reorganization. Super-specials forced Zukor into a defensive position and, in this connection, Hiram Abrams, whom he had made president of Paramount, caused him considerable embarrassment. The Bostonian spoke in favor of low-cost pictures and program bookings while Zukor strove to introduce high priced specials.

At this time Selznick forced Zukor's hand. Clara Kimball Young, after suing Selznick for an increase in her salary of $1,000 a week, completely disregarded her Selznick contract and signed up with Zukor. For a time the two, bitter rivals, let their lawyers run the show, but neither was willing to let legal advice ruin his business. Zukor patched things up between the actress and the producer and agreed to release all Selznick productions as Artcraft specials.

Actually, Zukor was struggling to hold first place. At Greater Vitagraph, Hampton had lined up a galaxy of stars. Goldfish, whose blustering, blundering speech by no means typified his talents, was producing pictures that were among the best of the period. Metro pictures received such excellent reviews the Metro Board of Directors presented Richard Rowland with a sapphire and diamond pin and Joseph Engel with an emerald and diamond pin in appreciation of their brilliant leadership. Aitken now had the backing of Superpictures, Inc., organized by Hodkinson and Pawley and S. A. Lynch, motion picture theatre czar of the south. With $600,000 advanced by Superpictures, Triangle liquidated its debts and Aitken was free to continue his experimental policy. Under the name, Triangle Distributing Company, Lynch, Hodkinson, and Pawley controlled the distribution of these features. John Freuler too, loomed as a Zukor threat. The success of "The Birth Of A Nation," America's first super-special, the production Freuler had spurned, was responsible for this. Freuler's strength lay in his star, Charlie Chaplin, the comedian with insured feet, whom he had lured from Essanay with a yearly guarantee of $670,000.

High-salaried actors, super-salesmanship, business foresight, were not the only weapons with which Zukor's competitors were equipped. They were plentifully supplied with money. American Tobacco stood as a bulwark for Vitagraph. Frederick R. Collins, president of Mc-Clure Publications, was Hodkinson's pillar of strength. A. S. Beymer, of the powerful Keystone National Bank of Pittsburgh, had a say in Metro affairs. A glance into the Board Room of leading motion picture corporations disclosed that the gold coins distributed at meetings* were carried away by a coterie of millionaires, merchant princes, steel magnates, enterprising manufacturers, and influential bankers.

While Zukor, Hampton, Aitken, Freuler, and others vied for prestige, Laemmle held fast to his position of comparative safety. At Universal City, he kept to his course of pictures for small towns and second-run houses and left the million dollar palaces free for those

---

*At one time each member of a Board was given a gold piece each time he attended a meeting. This was courtesy, in lieu of salary, to reimburse a corporation director for any expense he might have incurred in getting to the meeting. Amounts varied. Some corporations gave twenty-dollar pieces; others gave fifty-dollar pieces.

who sought to blaze a trail and win a place in a hall of fame.

Carefully Fox followed the machinations and maneuvers of the super-special foray. He cared little that his name was dwarfed because he felt his competitors had created monsters as deadly as Frankenstein's. A constant supply of new money was needed to appease the insatiable cravings of the hungry corporations. Fresh capital meant a larger Board, a larger Board meant more questions to be answered, and Fox prided himself on the fact that no money invested in his company ever stifled his voice. The Fox corporation was operated, controlled, and directed by one man. Functioning in all three branches of the industry, production, distribution, and exhibition, if skillfully managed, the company could be made to stand as an everlasting tribute to the man whose name it bore. Occasionally he threw a big picture into the ring, but for the greater part other ambitions stirred in his heart.

In 1916, Prince Winnie, who had successfully spread the fame of Fox throughout the South Pacific area, was sent into war-torn, bankrupt Europe. Across the British Isles into France, Switzerland, Germany, Roumania, and Russia, he went. He travelled home by way of Arabia and China. Wherever he stopped he liberated theatres from the grip of "paltry combines" and large electric lights flashed F-O-X.

Except for Pathé, who embarked on his motion picture career with a $500 investment, and who, in 1916, commanded a yearly salary of $100,000 as chief executive of a world-wide distribution agency (when war restricted the output of his cameras in France to photographs of current events, Pathé concentrated almost exclusively on distribution), Fox was the only man in the industry to have his name encircle the globe. This accomplishment deserved a celebration, and Fox, who had a reputation for working twenty-six hours out of every twenty-four and of being surrounded, even on his visits to his barber, by his chief scenario writer, his editor-in-chief, his chief sales executive, his chief attorney, his leading director, the head of his foreign offices, and the general manager of the Fox circuit, decided to risk a two month's leave of absence from his desk. Accompanied by his retinue, he went across the United States to his west coast studios (at the time a campaign was on not to call production centers factories), his first visit to the site, his first vacation in years, his first trip west of Buffalo, New York.

What matter that Fox owed his success to pictures that satisfied the unsophisticated rather than the intelligentsia? Many, more experienced than he, withered under super-special excesses. The death rattles of The Edison Company, Essanay, Kalem, and Selig-Polyscope were heard. For income, Selig now depended on his rights in stories he had purchased. Vitagraph alone among the old-timers had been able to weather the stormy super-specials market. Lubin's notes continued to go to protest, and his bankers, to protect their interests, placed his establishment in charge of Nicholas D. Roosevelt, a descendant of one Nicholas Roosevelt who headed the famous family in the Seventeenth Century. Not until Lubin sold to Vitagraph all rights to his name in the production of pictures was Mr. Roosevelt dislodged from his plant.

Kleine's days too were numbered, but the old warrior would not admit it. Infuriated that Independents had displaced him, he went down to the House of Morgan. The world's most famous financial institution was not ready to engage in film production; too many producers were still in the field. For five years, J. Pierpont Morgan & Company had scattered about the country investigators whose only job was to compile statistics on the motion picture industry. Kleine understood the Morgan mind; he knew those statistics were not gathered merely to satisfy idle curiosity. Perhaps, while they waited, the Lords of Wall Street might like to direct the use of cameras, projectors, lamps, film, and theatre chairs. Control of supplies is a powerful wedge, one often used by financial institutions when entry into a field is under consideration. Morgan & Company nodded its head, and several supply houses, including one owned by Edison, one in which Edwin Porter had an interest, one controlled by William Randolph Hearst, and one owned by Kleine, merged into a $50,000,000 concern.

The penny ante days of motion pictures had passed. Its corporations were now "Titanic," its settings "Spectacular," its productions "Stupendous," and no self-respecting film executive sat in a poker game where the initial stack of chips might be purchased for less than $1,000. The industry had grown to such proportions, David Horsley, now a builder of studios in Hollywood, decided the time had come for the film industry to have representation in Washington, not by delegations but by a congressman of its own.

"Last summer," he said, "I spent nearly all my time entertaining Senators, Representatives, the Vice-President, and other officials who came to California, and almost without exception they suggested that so great an industry as ours should have a representative in Congress. Sombody must make a great sacrifice of time and money and through various means it seems to have devolved upon me to be the goat. I have never been identified with politics, and have no inclination to become so; if I am elected to Congress it will mean a great sacrifice. I would be in Washington looking after the interests of the film business, when I should be in Los Angeles looking after the interests of David Horsley."

Lucky David Horsley. The people of California did not allow him to make this great sacrifice. He also was relieved of negatives he owned to satisfy a $3,000 judgment.

About the only small talk these days centered around the injustice of a government tax on film and who should pay it, the producer or the manufacturer of blank stock; the complaints of extras, who spoke of forming a union because they were weary of turning over forty per cent of meager earnings to agents, who frequently were associated with studios; and the situation in Chicago, where two rival unions resorted to bombs and dynamite in a bitter fight to determine which would save motion picture machine operators from the avaricious clutches of the motion picture executive.

The industry had advanced indeed that labor organizers should vie to control its ranks. Manufacturers, who puffed over the cost of productions, the money worth of their stars, and the spaciousness and magnificence of their studios, shrank from meeting the demands of labor. A simple plan kept low-salaried employees happy. Instead of increasing payrolls, producers increased main title footage with a list of the names of technicians, cameramen, electricians, stage hands, and title clerks, a practice which boomeranged. The flattery eventually brought fame to these workers, and fame brought more lucrative offers.

The extravagance of the manufacturers all but ruined the retailers. Super-specials were of questionable value to subsequent run exhibitors, who usually had to wait six or seven months for the big productions, and received them with scenes missing, whole sections torn and scratched. Run-of-the-mill program pictures lost rather than held customers.

With the possible exception of Stanley Mastbaum, who dictated the terms for distribution in his territory, the plight of those who had first run houses was little better than that of those who had subsequent run houses. Most cities were over-seated and few box offices grossed enough to cover the exorbitant rentals demanded for super-productions. Conditions became so bad throughout the south, theatre owners became careless of their obligations. Some, frantic, resorted to fraud. A few, with a sense of humor, returned films to exchanges with C.O.D.'s attached to cover what they considered their due.

"Will producers never give us a fair deal?" exhibitors asked. "They pay more attention to the destruction of a competitor than to the pictures they produce for us with our money. They were mighty smart to classify us all as dead-beats and get deposits with which to carry on their business. In no other industry does the retailer exist without credit."

Over and over came tales of woe. Outraged exhibitors were at their wits' end. When things seemed the most dismal, Tom Tally asked to see J. D. Williams. He gave Williams, affectionately called Jaydee, a plan. Jaydee immediately wrote a group of men and asked them to meet him in New York. They were: Aaron Jones of the powerful Jones, Linick and Schaefer Circuit of Chicago; Frederick Dahnken of the Turner and Dahnken Circuit in San Francisco; Harry O. Schwalbe of Philadelphia; John H. Kunsky with nine theatres in Detroit; S. L. Rothapfel, the first manager of the New York Strand and of the Rialto on Broadway, and at the time of the meeting, director of Times Square's latest picture palace, the Rivoli; Nathan H. Gordon of Boston; Robert Lieber of Indianapolis; Emanuel Mandelbaum of Cleveland; Tom Saxe of Milwaukee; Earl H. Husley of Dallas; and William Sievers of St. Louis.

Of all who attended the meeting, Sievers had the most modest circuit, but at home in the Mound City, he was a popular man. His genial smile and kindly manner made many friends, and whenever he dropped into St. Louis' Palm Restaurant, Spyros Skouras, an ambitious, ever-watchful bus boy, made it a point to clear his table.

The men met at the Hotel Astor on April 23, 1917, to discuss the Tally plan. Sometimes arguments were so stormy, Lieber, who presided, could not tell whether they had come together as friends or foes. For five days they wrangled in a smoke-filled room. At last they emerged, tired, bedraggled, thick-voiced, to tell the world they had formed First National Exhibitors Circuit, an organization prepared to demand reasonable, dependable service for $20,-000,000 worth of theatres.

The United States
Enters The War

JAYDEE WILLIAMS, WHO WAS APPOINTED MANAGER of the new company, immediately grasped that, to producers, First National appeared simply as one more buying agency. He persuaded his associates to finance the production of pictures. Each agreed to contribute a percentage according to the number of seats in his circuit, and each, according to his investment, was to receive a percentage of profits made from the distribution of such pictures. First National combed the market for talent and found itself struck with star-madness. Its first contract, which carried a yearly guarantee of $1,360,-000, gave First National sole distribution rights to all pictures made by the star Mutual had baited with $670,000. This star was Charles Spencer Chaplin, one who had been a controversial figure all his life. To escape the poverty he suffered in England, he came to the United States and, during this period, when the English Government called upon him to take his place in the British Army, he refused. On the other hand, when the United States Treasury Department billed him for income tax, he refused to pay it on the grounds he was an English citizen. Whatever his personal problems he was reputed to be the greatest artist on the screen, and the contract created a wave of terror. Zukor for Paramount, Lichtman for Artcraft, hastened to inform the industry that henceforth Paramount-Artcraft pictures might be purchased on the open market, no strings attached. Fox sent out word that in the fall he would cancel all existing contracts; that exhibitors might start the new season with a clean slate. Goldwyn and Triangle agreed to abolish the deposit system.

Advertisements became humane documents. The sudden generosity of producers touched the heart of the industry. Exchanges agreed to extend five days' credit to theatres in good standing. Harry Crandall, Washington, D. C. theatre owner, inaugurated motion pictures' first profit-sharing plan, which provided that each employee, no matter what his job, receive one week's extra pay each Christmas and in addition a week's vacation annually. In Philadelphia, Stanley Mastbaum, to placate disgruntled exhibitors, offered a greater variety of subjects to choose from. This step meant opening Philadelphia to additional producers, and the Paramount product, which he had favored in the past, suffered as a result.

Zukor resented this and openly accused Mastbaum of running a local monopoly. In other communities, where exhibitors cooperated in a buying pool, all contributed to the expense of operating such a pool and all had a voice in its policies. In Philadelphia, Mastbaum charged those exhibitors he serviced ten per cent of the price of each feature and spoke for all. Mastbaum ignored the tenor of Zukor's charge and, on November 26, 1917, circulated his "waste bomb," an eight-hundred word telegram to fifteen producers in which he asked them to unify the industry and prevent waste "through an amalgamation of the entire industry into one gigantic concern." Fox, who in advertisements referred to himself as "the world's greatest showman," lost no time in declaring, "I am William Fox, and I always will be." Others proclaimed such a step would be in the nature of a trust. Each was jealous of his independence and his name. Yet the chaos that kept producers in a constant state of jitters made many wonder why they were.

Vitagraph, before which Benjamin Hampton once dangled $100,000,000 of American Tobacco money, the company into which he eventually brought $1,000,000 of that money, received a like amount from Henry Ford, when the concern failed to meet a $200,000 payment due on still another $1,000,000 obligation. Henry Ford had not parted with his million dollars because of any love for motion pictures. The automobile manufacturer was, in fact, puritanical and objected to them, but he had indiscreetly declared that munition manufacturers, eager to bring the United States into the war, had financed the Vitagraph production, "The Battle Cry of Peace." In Hampton's language that spelled libel, and he spelled well. However, The Finance and Trading Company, affiliated with the Guaranty Trust Company of New York, holders of the unpaid notes, were unimpressed with Hampton's money-raising aptitudes, and Hampton was out.

A trade paper announcement that Mayer had signed up an actress to be starred in a vehicle which he would produce as an independent precipitated his withdrawal from the Metro Company.

At Triangle, Stephen A. Lynch blamed W. W. Hodkinson for a lack of profit; Hodkinson blamed the product. Lynch, with more ready cash, bought up the shares owned by Hodkinson and his satellite, Raymond Pawley, and became president of Triangle Distributing Corporation. Hardly had he taken over when he offered his holdings at cost price. The only person to appreciate the bargain were the directors of S. A. Lynch Enterprises, of which he also was president. Lynch Enterprises relieved Lynch of his Triangle holdings, and Stephen A. Lynch with Sol Lesser, now known as motion pictures' Little Napoleon, and Louis B. Mayer, organized a state's right distributing company. Like everyone else, Lynch knew little about the undersized Mayer except that everything Mayer touched turned into gold. This tie-up exemplified the complicated set-ups which existed in the industry.

In thirty years, in good times or bad, the industry had not once run a smooth course. To further complicate conditions, the United States entered the war against Germany. Would the industry suffer as it had in Europe? Would a people involved in a war go to the movies? As a form of insurance the producers turned their studios into battle grounds. The fashion of sex-flavored titles, such as "Where Are My Children?," "The Neglected Wife," "The Easiest Way," "The Uneven Road," pictures advertised "for adults only," gave way to the fashion of war-flavored titles, such as "The Honor System," "The Fall Of A Nation," to which children as well as adults were admitted. The Mayor of Boston sued a newspaper for libel when he was represented as owning an interest in "Where Are My Children?". A picture without a war background was taboo.

In Congress tax discussions intensified. Manufacturers of raw stock said the producers should meet any tax that might be levied. Producers thought any tax should be met by the public at the box office. Theatre owners cried a war tax on admissions would be the death blow to their theatres. Some argued against paying any tax, insisting that it was proposed by a House leader who at the eleventh hour wanted to "jam through a joker" that would penalize every good salary in the country except his own.

Adolph Zukor pointed out to the United States Congress that motion pictures were a valuable aid to the government in the prosecution of its war plans; that thousands of small theatre owners throughout the country operated without a profit, and that a tax such as the government proposed would force them to close their doors. "The result of this in turn," he concluded, "will reflect directly on the government because it will entail a loss of income and surplus profit tax from the great producing and distributing organizations whose profits will thus decline."

John Freuler insisted, "The motion picture is simply a form of publication, a form of thought transmission using pictures instead of printed words," and as such, "an important means in the education of a free people which made it unfair to subject them to an amusement tax."

Pat Powers laid his case before Woodrow Wilson, President of the United States. "Mr. President," he said, "if this tax goes through it will break me. It will put me out of business."

C. C. Pettijohn, counsel for Exhibitors Affiliated Association, advised exhibitors, ". . .not to pay the burden."

A whispering campaign reached the ears of these men which made them realize their protests might be interpreted as unpatriotic. Objections to the tax ceased abruptly. At a meeting in New York City a resolution was unanimously passed in which a motion picture admission tax was described as fair and just, and it was decided that a wide publicity campaign should be inaugurated to tell the public what the tax stood for. A public eager to "do its bit" responded graciously. Without a murmur movie goers paid the ten per cent levied at the box office.

In controversies over taxes, promises made under duress and complaints of bad business had been forgotten. However, when Zukor announced he would spend $1,000,000 on a national advertising campaign to teach the public how to know which were the best photoplays before they saw them, men remembered that Paramount-Artcraft pictures were to be had on the open market, no strings attached.

"There are no strings," Mr. Zukor insisted.

"No strings, indeed," exhibitors replied. "A salesman calls on us, displays his collection of stars and pictures; we make a selection, and without flicking an eyelash he quotes prices steep enough to knock us off our feet. We protest and are told to take the entire block for a little more. This is followed by a suggestion that, if we don't, our competitor might be a little more reasonable. In this way, lemons are included in the deals on which there are 'no strings attached.' "

Complaints soon died down. An unanticipated rush at the box office opened a frenzied market. People, suffering from the emotional conflicts of war, flocked to the movies, eager to see anything that depicted the supposed conditions their brothers, sons, and lovers faced on distant fronts. Exhibitors in need of product gladly forgot promises to cancel contracts, release deposits, and dispense with block bookings. They accepted product under any terms. The demand for motion pictures was unprecedented.

The Administrative Bureau

THE BOOM LASTED A FEW MONTHS and then subsided. The United States settled down to the tedious job of providing for a war. White collar workers entered factories to turn out bullets, airplanes, tanks. Women became taxi drivers, street-car operators, machine operators, to relieve men for duty in the armed forces. City girls became farmerettes. Everybody toiled extra hours to make up for the nationwide shortage of labor. War workers were too tired to seek entertainment. Smallpox and drought ravaged the south. The Fuel Commission ordered theatres that required heating to close one day in each week. Everything seemed bent on the destruction of the motion picture industry.

Contracts contained no cancellation clauses, and producers would not assume the burden of circumstances that prevented exhibitors from running all pictures bought. "An agreement is an agreement," theatres were informed. An agreement is an agreement! Theatres wondered. A road man's job rarely lasted longer than a year in any given territory so that when a salesman made his rounds, the exhibitor could not accuse him of getting business on false promises; a new man had no need to explain why promised lobby displays, extra paper, and other items never arrived or why a big advertising campaign had not materialized.

In the slump of 1918 the unbelievable took place. Exhibitors did not plead; they did not complain; they did not argue; they did not hold stormy meetings. They merely exercised care when buying. Results were disastrous. Some studios ceased all production for a full week. Others closed for an indefinite period. Triangle discharged

164

over one hundred employees at its Culver City plant. Fifteen hundred of Universal's twenty-nine hundred employees received pink slips.

Universal's Board of Directors consolidated executive positions, and Carl Laemmle became director general as well as president with Joe "Universal" Brandt to assist him as general manager. Hardly twelve years had passed since that day in Chicago when Carl Laemmle set out to find a five and dime store site. His twenty-five hundred dollars had swelled into millions. His small neighborhood theatres had grown into a world renowned corporation. But Laemmle was not happy. Caution, timidity, frugality had not been enough. The unhealthy state of his corporation worried him. He had begun to enjoy the glamour and prestige attending his position; the mere protection of his fortune no longer was his only aim. Naturally, Laemmle's promotion necessitated a statement. A press conference was arranged. But, what had happened to smiling Uncle Carl?

"Every business concern," he said, "has a deadly fear of being considered anything but the richest company in its line of business. All of us are guilty of letting the public, including the exhibitor, think that we have the fattest bankroll imaginable and that nothing short of an earthquake can shake our foundation. It is time to stop bluffing. We have been asked why we discontinued our one, two, and three reel program pictures. An audit of our books shows that in a recent six-month period we lost $3.08 on every positive print, not on every negative, but on every positive. And in that period we shipped 24,810 such reels. This has been going on for eighteen months, but every time we hinted we might discontinue the short stuff we received pleading letters urging us to stand by the little exhibitor who needed the short stuff. So we stuck and took our loss (Had Laemmle forgotten how, a short time before, he had pleaded for the short reel?) thinking that we could turn the loss into a profit by getting the exhibitors to pay a little more. But instead of paying more, they paid less and less, hammering the prices down and down until we finally had to quit releasing short stuff altogether. We now have on our shelves 371,000 feet of perfectly good negative. These are comedies and dramas. They cost us close to a million dollars, but we cannot release them because we lose money on every positive reel made from them. I seriously and solemnly venture the prediction that all of us, the producers, the distributors, the exhibitors, will become ripe for the receiver unless all of us get more money from the only source it is possible to get it from, the public. The industry must have an operation. Raising all admission prices is the operation that will either kill or cure it."

Confessions became the order of the day. Hodkinson, who with Pawley was now selling pictures under a states' right arrangement, conceded that it was time to "live and let live." Brady announced that he would cut expenses at World Film by relinquishing one of the jobs he held. Unless the salaries of stars were cut, Goldfish announced, the industry "would go to the dogs."

Selznick, who had never forgiven Laemmle for refusing to pay him a commission on the purchase of the Dintenfass stock, read the confessions and released a statement to the trade press. "Not long ago we were told that motion pictures were in their infancy. Now we are told they are on their deathbed. To the sick, all are sick. Carl Laemmle confesses that Universal has close to a million dollars tied up in shorts; he wails that the picture business faces disaster; that everyone will be ripe for the receiver. The only salvation he can see is for someone to pay him more for his dead stock than he ever asked for it. Mr. Laemmle doesn't seem to figure that brains are of much use in this business. He says that even after they found they could not sell his kind of pictures at a profit they went on and made a million dollars worth more. Mr. Laemmle's cure for the condition he himself created is higher admission prices. But Mr. Laemmle, the exhibitor, does not take much stock in Mr. Laemmle, the producer. At the Broadway Theatre he reduced prices from $1.00 to 15¢. The industry is not in its infancy. Neither is it on its death-bed. It is afflicted with minor ailments; one of the worst of these is the presence in its midst of men who blame general conditions for their own stupidity."

Turning on Goldfish, Selznick wanted to know, "Why does Samuel Goldfish say that the stars should get less when he offers some of the juiciest contracts in the business?"

A feud between Zukor and Rowland was carried on in trade press advertisements, in which they clearly indicated that each was determined to break the other. Concession after concession was made to first-run theatre owners. When Rowland told them to " . . . write your own tickets for product," Zukor was satisfied. Rowland was where Zukor wanted him. Abruptly dropping the fight, Zukor began to buy in theatres in principal cities to assure first-run showings for his product.

Before they too became vulnerable to a Zukor attack, Pathé, Triangle, Goldwyn, World Film, and First National decided to amalgamate. Each agreed to play a limited role, one to produce features, another serials, etc. The theatres controlled by First National and the production and distribution facilities of all would place such a group far out in front. For weeks Williams, Aitken, Goldfish, each company head, carefully studied the papers drawn for the merger. Back and forth they sent the contracts, suggesting changes, soliciting provisions, questioning the smallest details. Not one could bear to put his name to an agreement which granted another privileges he was denied.

The threatened merger forced Zukor to reexamine Paramount's position. Fox and Pathé both had well-established connections abroad. The time had come for him to have them also. With Leon Gaumont all but bankrupt as a result of the war, Zukor made a deal whereby Gaumont agreed to distribute Paramount-Artcraft pictures on the continent.

Zukor realized that even though Pathé, Aitken, Goldfish, Brady, and Williams had failed to make the compromises required for a successful merger, they were able motion-picture men and, as such, stood as a threat to Paramount. Nor did he belittle the First National setup. Many of its $20,000,000 worth of theatres already were closed to his product. At Burbank, California, First National had under construction a studio that soon would meet if not surpass his own in production. And this at a time when other exhibitors refused to renew their contracts because they resented a sales practice which "suggested" it might be expedient to contract for some of Paramount's minor stellar luminaries in order to obtain brighter stars. Zukor turned penitent. He placed Hiram Abrams, who said his code was the golden rule, at the head of a new department, the Administrative Bureau. This bureau was created ". . . for the purpose of establishing closer cooperation within the industry, especially between the producer and the exhibitor." Whatever this meant, theatre owners were satisfied. Across the country they were heard to say, "Zukor got nowhere with his tricks. He has learned his lesson." Gladly and freely they signed contracts that " . . . practically brought them into partnership with Paramount."

Zukor's uncanny foresight had not failed him. Once again, before anyone realized it, he had delivered a master stroke. The Administrative Bureau issued a Paramount "White Paper," a contract that stipulated the exhibitor was to use a given number of Paramount pictures each year over a period of years at a designated minimum price. What matter that Paramount owned only a limited number of theatres! Its new franchise arrangement provided an assured outlet.

Ruefully Sigmund Lubin observed Zukor's triumph. For years he had struggled to keep abreast of the times, but he had not been able to overcome the streak of ill fortune that pursued him since his Betzwood plant went up in flames. One by one, his theatres passed from his hands into those of the Mastbaums. Now, Wolff Brothers, famous banking house headed by Pennsylvania State Senator Clarence Wolff, wanted the rebuilt studio. Like many others, they were eager to have an active say in America's Fifth Industry. For several years they had had their eyes on the place, but had waited patiently until it might be had at a price. During a period of prosperity, Lubin had not been able to recoup his fortune. In 1918, with the industry passing through its worst days since the young cameraman Edwin Porter rescued pictures in motion from the suffocating scorn of Thomas Edison, Lubin's position was hopeless. Across Betzwood's 250 acres he walked for the last time, his head bowed, his step heavy. Gone was the breezy, witty Lubin; all that remained was a sad broken old man, who went back into the optical business and died of a nervous disorder in 1923.

Watch With Twelve Faces

IN FRANCE AND ENGLAND IN 1918, the trend turned upward. Civilians reconciled to war, craved diversion. Service men, especially American doughboys on leave, sought inexpensive entertainment. But, in the United States, the principal market, business showed no improvement.

S. A. Lynch, facing a slump in the south, tied in with five other substantial users, all with states' right status, and organized the Anti-Bid Association. Its plan was simple and ingenious. When a new feature, particularly one expensively produced was shown to them, five expressed dislike and rejected it. The sixth would say, "I don't know, maybe it will go, maybe it won't. Make a worthwhile proposition, and I'll gamble with it." Thus every sixth picture automatically went to a member at his price. Besides Lynch, at least two of the other members were affiliated with producing companies, First National and Universal. The left hand had no need to know what went on in the right hand.

Other groups had other schemes. Over-zealous, self-protective measures stifled production and further depressed the industry.

Aitken's dream turned into a nightmare. The magnificent masterpieces he had envisaged came through as disjointed incoherent spectacles, unsalable at the box office. Adolph Zukor meanwhile opened his exchanges to Hearst and other Independent producers, and three of Aitken's ranking directors, David Wark Griffith, John Ince, and Mack Sennett, took advantage of this opportunity to remove their hats from a peg at Triangle, where their status was that of mere employees, to a rack on the Famous Players-Lasky lot,

169

where they might operate as bosses. H. O. Davis, Triangle's production manager, claimed that the company was not progressive, it had not kept abreast of the times and hampered his creative ability. And Aitken, who had broken with Freuler because his old partner was too conservative, released Davis from his contract because the production man's ideas were too radical. Reduced to part-time operation, Aitken advertised, "Pictures to Order," and explained, "The great studios of Triangle have ample capacity for more than fifty companies so that, in addition to Triangle Programme and special productions constantly in work, we are in a position to undertake the making of motion pictures of the highest quality to individual order."

For a time old banking friends in Milwaukee and Chicago kept John R. Freuler going, but the one-time conservative went through money faster than they could or cared to supply it. On May 8, 1918, the Central Trust Company of Illinois attached Mutual's funds, and the company that had become famous as the producer of comedies with the English pantomimist Charlie Chaplin went out of existence. Pathé without explanation farmed out its stars. Claude Patin, who had rescued Eclair from Universal, was not able to nurse the company back to health. He remained in the United States long enough to settle Eclair's accounts and then returned to France. Neither could the veteran George K. Spoor carry on. Bitterly he complained about "... .film companies that hogged the market with mammoth productions," closed his shop, and invested in a processing machine capable of carrying ten million feet of film a week. Sometime later he backed P. John Berggren, a Swedish physicist, who invented a camera which provided depth or three-dimensional pictures.

Run! Run! Run! Running here, running there, running for this, running from that. Such had been the lot of Adam Kessel. As a boy he ran errands. As a young man he dodged behind posts, scurried among crowds, hid under grandstands, ran into all sorts of corners to escape plain-clothesmen who robbed horse racing of its flavor. Later, as a producer, he ran from one big outfit to another, Universal, Mutual, Triangle. Often, weary of the struggle, he would say, "I wish I could get away from all this. I'd like to live in the country." No one believed him; his life was too interesting, too exciting. Then, one day, flush after a season of good bookings, he bought a chicken farm along the shore of Lake Champlain, at Douglass, New York, on which to spend his holidays. Now, with the odds against motion pictures, he found it more profitable and enjoyable to take care of his barnyard than to sit in a swivel chair with his heels on a desk in a stuffy office reading scripts, studying reports, planning pictures, scanning reviews, and he dropped out of sight in movie circles.

The Triangle "Pictures to Order" idea appealed to Robert "Hustler" Cochrane. He publicized Carl Laemmle as a generous broadminded benefactor, willing to turn up the lights at Universal City that small producers might use the facilities there to cut down their overhead expenses.

Samuel Goldfish alone appeared optimistic. For the first time in the history of motion pictures, he made a payment of interest on all money up as advance deposits. Producers resented the precedent he set; exhibitors were so delighted the thought never occurred to them that the step was merely a blind to keep them from asking for the return of their deposits.

These were dreary days for all. Performers who had earned from $15,000 to $20,000 in 1917, had no money with which to meet income tax payments. Offices of the Department of Internal Revenue became confessional booths, where penitents admitted that, to create imposing roles in daily life or to surround themselves with luxuries which made the parts they played on the screen enchanting, they had failed to provide for the slump.

At World Film, which was embarrassed by rumors of graft in connection with a war tax on films, the bank balance dropped so low, Will Brady was informed the company could not afford to pay him $100,000 a year as director-general. At a substantial cut in salary he preferred foot lights to Kleig lights. Julius Steeger replaced him. The position of Steeger was complex and obscure. In S and S he was a partner of Joseph M. Schenck, a power in various amusement fields. Joe Schenck and his brother Nicholas owned Palisades Amusement Park, a summer playground on the Jersey cliffs facing New York City. The brothers, stockholders in the Loew Theatre Corporation, booked acts and arranged special day and date picture showings for Loew, United Booking Offices, Fox Variety Theatres, and the B. S. Moss Circuit of vaudeville houses. Once before, with Marcus Loew, Joe Schenck had engaged in production.

S and S was an outgrowth of that old company. All S and S pictures were released through Select Pictures, a new firm which Selznick founded when he discovered he was a mere stepchild in the Zukor outfit. Joseph Schenck's bride was Norma Talmadge, whom he had elevated from the rank of extra at Vitagraph to stardom at S and S. When Steeger, close associate of Joe Schenck, stepped into World Film, word went around that his object was to open an outlet for S and S other than Select Pictures. In this way Joe Schenck's favorite would not have to compete with Lewis Selznick's favorite.

While others complicated their lives, Adolph Zukor simplified his. When the first tint of red appeared in the black, he explored his personnel. As a result, Zukor became aware that William Sherry considered alcohol a necessary attribute to happiness. Such a man, Zukor felt, might not be able to stand up under stress, and Sherry parted from the company "by mutual consent." Hiram Abrams took over Sherry's duties; then let it be known that he and his assistant, Ben Schulburg, hankered to express their ideas in production. "Let them," Zukor said, "as Independents!" Al Lichtman and Sidney Kent in Paramount's sales department were given their jobs. "As Independents" meant no affiliation with Paramount-Artcraft, for Zukor was disposing of his interests in associate production units. Even Commodore James Stuart Blackton was out.

Selznick's status, however, remained something of a mystery. Under the trade name Select he offered pictures on the open market. In this company Zukor retained a fifty percent interest, although he had sold his highly-prized Loew stock to help finance Paramount-Artcraft when credit tightened at the banks. That the great sacrifice of Loew stock might not be in vain, Famous Players-Lasky took over full ownership of Paramount-Artcraft, the releasing concerns which had been operating independently, and the names Paramount and Artcraft ceased to exist legally except as trade marks. Walter Greene, who had been president of Artcraft, was transferred to Famous Players-Lasky sales department.

Besides the executive shake-up, personnel in every department was weeded out; salaries were cut as well. This tendency on the part of businessmen to reduce their staffs as a first step in economy sent labor up in arms. The cry "Business is bad!" brought the retort, "We did not benefit when it was good, and executives continue to fish at Palm Beach, golf at Pinehurst, take cures at French Lick

Springs, and live like monarchs." When workers attempted to organize, 250 representatives of film manufacturers, film supply houses, and theatres, signed a document which requested the courts to enjoin union officials from interfering in the motion picture business and impeding freedom.

A melancholy market favored Stanley Mastbaum. In these precarious times theatre men in and around Philadelphia dared not shift for themselves. Stanley Mastbaum decided to test his strength. Backed by George H. Earle, Lubin's old partner, he opened sumptuous offices in New York City. He beckoned and theatre men streamed into his office, where he described in detail the idea in back of his "waste bomb," the telegram in which he had exploded the idea about organizing a film booking system to save waste. He boasted that within three months no picture house would get a picture except through him and those who did not book through him would close their doors. Was this a first step in a plan to amalgamate the entire industry into one gigantic concern? A sphinx-like silence greeted all enquiries. With awe and trepidation, the entire industry waited for him to indicate how far he proposed to go. Manufacturers wondered how soon he would be their partner or their foe.

Twelve producers contributed $358.33 each, purchased a $4,300 watch, and presented it as a token of admiration and esteem to the man who might soon dictate to them all. On the dial, instead of numbers were twelve tiny portraits, the faces of the heads of the twelve concerns that had donated toward its cost. Stanley Mastbaum thanked them and without dropping a hint went about his business. He worked ceaselessly, night and day. His wife could not prevail upon him to spend an evening with her. Not even an attack of tonsilitis kept him from his desk.

To the world Stanley Mastbaum might have been an important man, 38 years of age, but to his mother he was merely, "my boy." Fannie Mastbaum heard he ran a fever and demanded to see him, so early one afternoon he took a train for Philadelphia. One glance at her son, and the mother ordered him to bed. She was too late. During that night, March 7, 1918, Stanley Mastbaum died of septic poisoning. Thus, the most meteoric rise in the industry came to an end before the twelve men on the watch learned whether their gift had served them.

When in 1909, Jules Mastbaum, then an employee of Felix Isman, acted as receiver for the Davis motion picture houses, he noticed the swift progress of the industry. Often he had thought he might like to go into the business, but profitable real estate ventures presented themselves and did not leave him time for other enterprises. In 1911, with Maurice Fleisher as a partner, he came into possession of several motion picture theatres, which he asked his younger brother Stanley, an Oriental rug salesman at Gimbel Brothers, to manage. Before long Stanley dictated the policies of the theatre and realty business, booked all pictures in and around the Quaker City, and gave the company its name, Stanley. At the time of his New York invasion, in partnership with his brother Jules, Fleisher, Felix Isman, Abe Sablotsky, and John McGuirk, he owned 78 theatres and booked for a total of 167 in Eastern Pennsylvania.

Actually the industry did not know whether to sigh with relief or mourn the loss of a savior. But it respected its dead. Five thousand persons attended his funeral, among whom were producers and distributors, business associates, competitors, friends, employees. Among the long list of notables who acted as honorary pall bearers were: Senator Clarence Wolff, Adolph Zukor, William Fox, Carl Laemmle, Felix Isman, Samuel Goldfish, Joseph M. Schenck, Hiram Abrams, Walter E. Greene, Louis Selznick, Richard Rowland, George H. Earle, Marcus D. Loew, Abe Sablotsky, John McGuirk. Before his casket was closed a cast was taken that his face might live in bronze for future generations. With funds raised by subscription a small building was erected at the Eaglesville Sanitarium for consumptives to stand as an everlasting tribute to the memory of Stanley V. Mastbaum.

On March 20, 1918, barely three weeks after the death of Stanley Mastbaum, Mitchell Mark died of a cerebral hemorrhage. Days went by, the Strand Theatre Corporation, with theatres in New York City, Buffalo, and Rochester, made no attempt to elect a new president. Stories circulated that with the death of Mitchell the company would fall to pieces. Nevertheless, business at the office proceeded in the usual methodical and harmonious manner that had characterized the management of Mitchell Mark. Weeks after the death of his brother, Moe Mark, without fuss, became president of the Strand Theatre Corporation. The Motion Picture Industry did not understand the sentiment of Moe for his fifty-four-year-old brother. At Moe's insistence the president's chair had remained vacant for a while. He knew no better way to respect the memory of Mitchell, who, once, to help a friend, bought some worthless talking-machines and, with that sorry stock, in a musty, ill-lighted store, twelve feet by fifty, entered the amusement field in which he amassed a fortune of $2,500,000.

Epidemics

FROM WASHINGTON CAME WORD that men in the industry were
in disgrace. Felix Malitz, who before the war had specialized in
foreign films, was sentenced to five years in prison and fined $5,000
for smuggling rubber into Germany.

Under indictment was Frank J. Godsol, charged with participating
in the dissemination of enemy propaganda. Six reels of life behind
German lines stood as evidence against him. A group of New York
motion picture men contended the pictures had been purchased in
Scandinavia before the United States entered the war, while the
country was still neutral, and showed how Godsol had changed the
titles in an attempt to bring the pictures within war regulations in
an effort to avoid losing his investment. The Attorney General's
office remained unconvinced and while it was preparing its case
to prove that, in spite of the substitution of titles, the pictures were
pro-German, the French Ambassador, M. Jusserand, accused Godsol
of bribing his way out of the French Army into a position on the
French Buying Commission. The Ambassador further contended
that Godsol used this position to obtain over $6,000,000 in com-
missions on purchases from the Pierce Arrow Motor Car Company.
Godsol, under the name Elie Heliopoulos was a salesman for Pierce
Arrow and sold Frank J. Godsol, secretary and interpreter to the
French Purchasing Commission in the United States, trucks and
tanks for war use. In addition to the graft charge, Heliopoulos was
accused of bribing various French officers and officials who aided
him.

Godsol's name changed frequently, but the name Heliopoulos lived on to reappear more than ten years after Godsol's death in 1935. In 1872 in Cleveland, Ohio, Godsol started life the son of Russian immigrant parents with the name Joseph Frank Goldsoll. When he left for France at the turn of the century he called himself Frank Joseph Goldsoll. During the war because, he said, Goldsoll was too Germanic, he became Frank Joseph Godsoll, later Godsol.

The French Ambassador demanded that Godsol be extradited to France. While the merits of Godsol's plea that he could never get a fair trial in France were being studied, Godsol married one of his mistresses, the French actress Constance Elsie de Vere. As his wife, she was unable to testify against him, and M. Jusserand lost his key witness. Godsol's attorneys, John Barry Stanchfield of New York and Senator Joseph W. Bailey of Texas, in a series of press releases designed to make a great philanthropist of their client, told of his heavy contributions to French and American war charities and loans. They merely neglected to mention that of the $3,000,000 subscribed for Liberty Bonds, $2,000,000 were reconverted into cash within twenty days through a resale of the bonds at the rate of $100,000 a day. They won public sympathy for him and succeeded in getting delay after delay so that Godsol was not tried until all war hysteria had passed. After the war he was exonerated of all charges, and his Pierce Arrow commissions were declared legitimate. However, he never returned to France, and, when he finally retired from the motion picture business, he went to Switzerland, where he died in 1935.

The story connected with the name, Eliopoulos, follows: An article in the July 19, 1943 issue of *Life Magazine* related that one Elie Eliopoulos* and his brother George were under indictment for smuggling narcotics into the United States. In 1927, Elie and George, with another brother Anthanasius, while looking for a new venture for their already substantial capital, entered the illegal narcotic field with headquarters in Paris, where the House of Eliopoulos functioned as the central bank and clearing house for the biggest share of the world's illicit trade in opium, morphine, and heroin, ever organized up to that time into one system. They prospered until 1930, when a tightening of the French laws forced them to move to Turkey. The pressure of the law was now attracting a new class of men into the

---

*Heliopoulos is the same name. The Greeks sometimes use, sometimes drop H.

trade, men practiced in other fields of crime, including hijacking and blackmail. The Eliopoulos brothers adapted themselves to the new conventions of their business. One New York broker, who failed to complete a transaction was, via trans-Atlantic arrangements, given a beating in a speakeasy. Another United States broker paid for one thousand pounds of morphine. When he went to load his shipment at a European port, he was offered another thousand pounds at the same price he had paid for the first shipment. He opened his cases and discovered them to be filled with sawdust. His outburst sent him to jail. Soon it became the custom of all sides to betray one of each four purchases to authorities. The brothers betrayed a large prepaid shipment to the United Customs agents, and, as a result of this betrayal, a customer went to jail. After several profitable years the restrictions imposed by the League of Nations were becoming too annoying and forced the brothers to retire.

In the autumn of 1941, Elie and George came to the United States, secure in the belief they were protected by the statute of limitations. However, men they had betrayed had not forgotten them, and in New York they were arrested.

When the Life article appeared, the writer was engaged in research for this history. Becoming quite excited, she sent a letter to the Department of Justice asking if this Elie Elioupolos might have any connection with the French Purchasing Commission back in World War I. An agent of the Treasury Department came to investigate her notes to see if they contained any useful information, and gave the writer the following facts: The father of the narcotic pedler Elie Eliopoulos was a Greek banker also named Elie. He, or perhaps his son, went to Paris during World War I and received authority from the French Purchasing Commission to buy war equipment, food stuffs, and supplies. At one time Elie Eliopoulos went to Russia to buy for the French. He undoubtedly knew or was associated with Godsol. After the war, the Eliopoulos family concentrated in fields where big money was made faster than in banking.

Apparently the Eliopoulos family always had some contact with people in the motion picture field, for, upon arrival in this country, an executive very high in motion picture circles vouched for the credit of Elie Eliopoulos at a hotel on West Fifty-seventh Street in New York. A lawyer for the motion picture executive became the Eliopoulos lawyer, and after the arrest of Elie and George, the brother of the New

York executive, also prominent in motion pictures, had Mrs. Elie Eliopoulos as his house guest on the West Coast. The Eliopoulos brothers were tried and found guilty. The statute of limitations saved them from jail sentences; they were merely deported as undesirable aliens.

As if the gods had a hand in the dark recesses into which motion pictures were sinking, an epidemic of Spanish Influenza swept across the country in 1918. Added to the list of war dead were those unable to escape the pestilence. "Epidemic Casualties" became a regular feature in newspapers and periodicals. Among those who succumbed were Harold Edel, twenty-nine year old successor to Rothapfel at the New York Strand; J. T. Turner, partner of Fred Dahnken since the days they had both prospected in the Klondike; Forty-three-year-old Recha Laemmle, wife of Universal's president; Mrs. Abe Warner; R. W. Lynch, brother and partner of Stephen, himself on the danger list. Frightened by the *calendar* of the dead, the masses avoided public gatherings and crowds. In congested areas health authorities ordered theatres closed. Exhibitors were forced to pay full damages for films destroyed when a delivery truck burned, and manufacturers not only refused responsibility for seeing that an exhibitor received his show on time, but charged him for any losses sustained in transit. However, to force exhibitors, whose doors were boarded up, to accept deliveries was impossible, so studios ceased all production for a five-week period.

Never was time more opportune, *The London Times* and other English papers wrote, to free the British from the yoke of American movies. Their campaign to divert the $1,000,000 or more spent annually in the United States to build up the film industry in Britain was so intense, England placed an embargo on all American-made pictures. Canada soon followed England's lead. France too barred American productions, except those of a factual character. Producers here lodged a formal protest at Washington against these actions. There, the representatives of the people, quick to argue, slow to move, did little about the situation, and the producers themselves were too engrossed in problems at home to work out retaliatory tactics.

Vitagraph charged Louis B. Mayer, abetted by J. Robert Rubin, Metro lawyer, had stolen Vitagraph's most publicized actress, Anita Stewart, and asked $250,000 damages. Mayer and Vitagraph came to terms out of court; then Mayer actually did not quite know what to do with the actress. He was bombarded with war stories "made to

order for her." Mayer did not want a war story; he was not convinced the war would last much longer. Mayer's partner, the sartorial
king, Richard Rowland, famous for his green gabardine suits, his
purple socks and shirts, sapphires and diamonds, became furious
when he heard that Mayer had signed up the actress as an individual and not on behalf of the Metro Company. The Board of
Directors supported Rowland, and Mayer, along with Rubin, withdrew from Metro.

Stephen Lynch, mystery man of the industry, recovered from his
illness to face serious problems. In addition to the loss of three top
directors at Triangle, thieves had stolen a large supply of its prints.
Some were located in an opium den in Seattle in a box labeled
"hardware" and consigned to a town in Java. Many never were
traced. The five-week shutdown made even the production of pictures
to order impossible. At Triangle, Lynch's investment was at stake;
in another situation his reputation was at stake. Alcott and Kraus,
partners in several copyrighted pieces, in an affidavit stated that
Lynch with William Oldknow, a stockholder in S. A. Lynch Enterprises, and Frank G. Hall of Weehawken, New Jersey, had organized
a concern, the United States Exhibitors Booking Corporation, capitalized at $1,000,000, ". . . for the purpose of misleading and de-
frauding owners of moving pictures and plays by enticing and persuading them by means of the high-sounding name of the corporation and the supposedly large capital to sell photoplays on credit."
Alcott and Kraus further charged that when they had requested
a financial statement, the outraged Hall took them into the stock
room to show them they were dealing with the owners of two valuable negatives. That brought the asked-for credit. Only upon demanding payment, when payment was past due, did Alcott and
Kraus learn that the company was insolvent; that the pictures shown
to them were not the property of the firm, but the personal property
of Stephen A. Lynch and that the trio had formed similar dummy
corporations in various sections of the country.

In 1918 motion picture cases clogged court calendars. Mark
Dintenfass sued to collect $5,000 on a note given to him by Carl
Laemmle on June 10, 1913. Walter W. Irwin, about to resign as
Vitagraph's general manager to accept a vice-presidency at Famous
Players-Lasky, filed a $3,000 claim against Edison, Kleine and all
former members of General Film, contending that he, as a lawyer,

had advised the Trust to settle with Fox out of court.

The epidemic of legal actions involved Harry and Abe Warner, who were sued for payment on pictures they had bought in partnership with Pat Powers, and they, in turn, sued to hold Powers responsible. Contrary to the tide, the Warners were passing through a period of affluence. A picturization of Ambassador Gerard's "My Four Years In Germany," which Sam, Harry, Abe, and Jack owned in partnership with Mark Dintenfass, was about the only hit of the season.

A lively controversy also was going on in Chicago, where local politicians charged that the Deputy Superintendent of Police and Movie Censor for Illinois, Major L. C. Funkhouser, had pro-German sympathies. Forty other charges were cited against him, the most serious of which was conduct unbecoming an officer, neglect of duty, inefficiency and inattention to duty. As evidence against him, they produced scenes he had ordered cut from various motion pictures. Funkhouser contended that he had been framed, the victim of the city's crooked political machine, which in this case was financed by an irate film clique anxious to get him out of office at any price because he often cut vulgar and obscene shots from their photoplays. He pointed to his past record; he showed how he had cleared up the bad name that had clouded the City of Chicago; he produced editorials from the *Chicago Tribune* and other local papers to prove his integrity. For five weeks the court listened to charges and counter-charges before it retired to study the mass of testimony. In a few moments it returned. This was all the time needed to weigh the material that had taken more than a month to present, and find Major Funkhouser guilty and deprive him of his rank and position.

A stampede in which six children lost their lives revealed that politics in New York City was hardly less corrupt than politics in Chicago. The tragedy occurred when smoke, the result of a faulty furnace flue, seeped up through the floor from the basement of the New Catherine Theatre on New York's lower East Side. About two weeks after the fatal event, Mrs. Ellen A. O'Grady resigned as Fifth Deputy Police Commissioner. Known for years of devoted and conscientious service, her resignation brought a storm of protest. Under constant pressure from the newspapers, Mrs. O'Grady broke down.

"My position," she said, "is hopeless. It is impossible for me to enforce protective regulations. Commissioner Enright has taken authority out of my hands and placed it in the hands of the president of the New York League of Exhibitors, an association that serves the Motion Picture trusts."

"Why don't you go over Enright's head to Mayor Hylan?"

"Who him?" shouted Mrs. O'Grady, and there ended the interview.

William Fox too was in the courts, his identity hidden under the alias Louis Jacobs. His attorneys, Rogers and Rogers, on his behalf, asked the court to prohibit the Superintendent of Buildings from approving plans submitted by Aubrey M. Kennedy for the Symphony Theatre on the grounds that they contained a number of violations that constituted peril to life and limb. Kennedy wanted to erect the Symphony Theatre at the corner of 95th Street and Broadway in New York City, one block south of the street on which two Fox houses stood side by side. Fox at the time was having difficulty competing with himself let alone meeting the competition of an outsider. The jurist in this case, unlike Judge Darling, ruled against Fox and was left to spend the rest of his days on a bench deciding the fate of other men instead of becoming a special Fox foreign representative.

A contest at Washington, D. C. had Robert Cochrane and George Creel, Chairman of the Committee on Public Information, as opponents. This was one contest in which Cochrane did not assign any part to Laemmle. With the decline of the Selig organization, International News moved in with Pathé, and the reel's name was changed to Hearst-Pathé. But neither was happy; each begrudged the credit the other received. For some time Hearst, that he might have an established outfit if he broke away from Pathé, tried to gain control of Universal News. Universal resisted all offers. Now, Creel refused to permit Universal Film to release a picture entitled *The Yanks Are Coming,* and Cochrane said this was Hearst's revenge. He contended that by maneuvering Carl Byoir (later famous as the public relations man who raised funds in the United States for Chiang Kai Shek) and other former Hearst employees onto the Committee, Hearst was able to exert undue influence on Creel. Under Cochrane's unmerciful attack, Creel crumbled and, to save the Government's face, Secretary of War Newton D. Baker came to his rescue.

Also on the court calendars of 1918 was the settlement of the estate of Samuel Long. The estate, willed to his widow, totaled

$583,911. Half of this was in cash, half in stocks and bonds. Although Sam Long was president of Kalem when he died on July 18, 1915, he owned not one share of Kalem stock; the motion picture stocks he owned, totaling between $40,000 and $50,000 were in Paramount and other companies. Long's associates apparently respected his judgment; at the time of his death, Kalem in which the total original investment was $5,000, had assets of $5,590,737, of which $4,905,000 represented shares in other corporations. Great distances and diverse ambitions separated Long's old partners. Frank Marion, although he retained an interest in the Kalem Company and had been its president since the death of Long, left the company's management to William Wright, an engineer, who believed that features which ran over four reels failed to justify expense of production. So completely was Wright identified with Kalem, he was nicknamed William Kalem Wright. Inasmuch as he had no reputation as a motion picture producer to uphold, he boasted that Kalem's bid for fame rested on its ability to process a million feet of film a week for others. Marion, onetime newspaper reporter, as a dollar-a-year Public Information Commissioner, represented the United States in Spain and France. Most of his time was spent in Europe spreading propaganda. One one occasion he returned to the United States to become acquainted with his six-month old son, born to his wife while he was on government business.

Kleine's story was less gratifying than that of his old partner, Marion. By the time the merger of the supply houses of Kleine, Edison, etc., was finally consumated, Kleine was out. Unable to induce the Morgan people or anyone else to restore him to a position commensurate with his ability as a producer, he turned reformer. Supported by George K. Spoor, he prodded the United States Attorney General, and suit was brought against the Stanley Company and the Saenger Amusement Company of New Orleans on the grounds these two combination theatre-distributing corporations constituted a trust. Time, indeed, had shifted the scenes, recast the actors.

The indictment charged that the Saenger Brothers, like Jules Mastbaum and his associates, had tampered with competitors' employees; compelled theatres to sign up with their buying groups at preposterous terms under threat to put them out of business; threatened hesitant participators in the plan with slander; and if a man resisted all this, by divers means caused contracts for exhibition of film entered into by conspirators to be broken or cancelled, coerced those manufacturers with which they did not have reciprocal contracts into letting them have a picture already booked for a first run by a dissenter, ran it a few days prior to the advertised showing, and otherwise intimidated competitors.

Kleine did not stop even after Mastbaum admitted, "We may have been bad boys once, but we are not now." Like Canute, the king who chose to test his authority on the tide, only to have the sea swirl about his feet, Kleine appealed to the Priorities Committee of the War Industries Board to "use the knife" on the industry to stop production, eliminate salesmen, cut positive prints by twenty-five per cent, and control distribution "for the good of the nation and possibly also for the good of the industry." This advice he accompanied with startling views on censorship, in which he suggested that not only motion pictures, still pictures, and posters, but electric signs as well should be censored by a board of three to five broadminded persons. "After careful observation over a period of years," he summed up, "I have come to the firm conviction that electric light signs when used over a theatre act as an irresistible magnet to the morbid and curious who might otherwise pass."

The industry had just succeeded in convincing political Washington to classify motion pictures, because of their propaganda potentialities and because of their value as a form of relaxation for the people, as an essential. The fear which Kleine provoked made him a pariah in film circles, already harassed and weary.

The phrase "for the good of the nation" was indeed cynical; years later Kleine's name was linked to those of Nazi sympathizers. However, a deep affection for the industry must have existed somewhere in his heart, for he donated to the New York Public Library his large and valuable collection of trade publications, many of which served the writer in her research for this history.

Armistice

WITH SUCH GRAVITY DID ADOLPH ZUKOR regard the crisis, he permitted the impossible to transpire. When his star, Mary Pickford, the girl he had fashioned into America's Sweetheart, advised him of her new terms, he failed to renew the option on her contract. The highest paid actress in the world was out of a job. Zukor had built and rearranged his organization around her; he provided her with publicity that brought her love, respect, esteem. The step required an apology; he granted one of his rare press conferences. "What can I do!" he said. "I am besieged by theatre owners who cry that they lost money on her pictures. Their losses are so great I am forced to give them rebates. How can I cut my prices and at the same time increase my expenses? Miss Pickford's demands are too unreasonable. My position is much the same as Siegel-Cooper's. When B. Altman & Company moved from their location opposite Siegel-Cooper, the latter took a lease on the vacated premises to block competition. They succeeded. Altman got the competitors and became the center of a lively shopping district. It wasn't long before Siegel-Cooper was out of business. Well, I'm looking ahead, not backwards. Any step that tends to deprive the exhibitor of his legitimate profit is a step in the wrong direction."

The Siegel-Cooper gag fooled no one. A fortune had been spent publicizing Mary Pickford. If her contract were allowed to lapse, reasons, good reasons, must exist. Famous Players-Lasky stock dropped from 85 to 22-1/2 a share. This drop forced Zukor to launch a new line of attack with which he hoped to divert attention

185

from Famous Players-Lasky. "Which are you," he asked, "exhibitor or producer? It is a psychological law that the mind cannot do two separate things equally well at the same time. Not only does the producer-exhibitor build a barrier about his own business, limit his own field, establish his own competition, but he creates one of the gravest perils that has ever confronted the motion picture industry." This was a direct slap at First National, which from the start Zukor considered a dangerous rival. First National's answer was to sign up at $250,000 a picture, the girl Zukor had made America's Sweetheart.

To Fox the Zukor-First National feud served as a warning. In Asia, Europe, Australia, South America, practically all over the world, except in the United States, Fox operated theatres on a large scale. In his own country, his theatre holdings were confined to twenty-six "ten-twent'-thirts" in New York City and its environs, where three or four acts of vaudeville, sandwiched between inexpensively produced "Productions Extraordinary" or "Photoplays Supreme" stood the brunt of audience catcalls. Zukor might be content to meet First National with arguments; not so Fox. Without further waste of time he informed Winnie Sheehan, to whom he confided all business plans, and Mrs. Fox, whom he consulted on artistic problems, that he was about to invade each and every town that supported a First National theatre. His first step was to take a long lease on a newly-built St. Louis theatre, the Victoria.

Although in the industry Fox was disliked for playing the lone wolf, he had soft spots. Deep in his somber, dismal soul reposed a recollection of the kindness and tenderness of those who nursed him in a charity ward when he was ill as a boy. Despite the pressures on his time, demanded by the bitter struggle for survival in which he was engaged, Fox attended elaborate banquets as the guest of honor while Felix Warburg and others high in financial circles paid tribute to him for his "unselfish philanthropy and tireless effort on behalf of the poor." Winnie Sheehan, on behalf of William Fox, gave away thirty gold watches to that many persons who acted as committee heads in a successful Red Cross Drive. One exhibitor friend told this story. "I called at the office to see Bill. At the reception desk I asked where I could find Mr. Fox. 'At the Red Cross.' And Mr. Sheehan, is he in? 'No, he's at the Red Cross.' Where will I find the bookkeeper? 'At the Red Cross.'

Where are all your stenographers and clerks? 'At the Red Cross.'
Well, suppose I wanted to pay a bill, where would I pay it? 'At
the Red Cross.' "

Fox's endowments were so generous, America's best known
editor, Arthur Brisbane, wrote of the motion picture man's great
altruism. At the Riverside Theatre in New York City, auctioning
of trophies of famous battles to war bond purchasers was a regular
part of each performance. One evening a Liberty Loan worker disposed of several articles with greater success than usual. Inadvertently, as he was about to walk off stage, he put his hand in his
pocket. Out came a bullet which he had overlooked. The auctioneer stopped, turned back to the audience and said, "This was shot
by a Hun at Chateau Thierry. What am I offered for it?"

When the figure reached $1,000 a man at the back of the theatre
sent an usher to ask the auctioneer what he would accept to retire
and allow the show to proceed. The bond salesman consulted the
audience. After much shouting $50,000 was agreed upon. "Sold!"
the man called from the audience. The salesman started backstage
when another voice shouted $51,000!" The loan worker settled back
to start his work all over when a young sailor rose and called,
"That $50,000 was a sporting proposition. The man who made
it should be given the bullet." The war worker thought for a
moment and decided the sailor was right. Half way through the
next turn four naval officers went down the aisle and arrested the
sailor for making seditious remarks. The entire house rose to see
what was going on. The team on the stage signalled the orchestra
to play and walked off. All the way up the aisle the confused boy
was booed and taunted. He pointed to his uniform and produced
several Liberty Bonds to disprove the charge. The man who bid
the $50,000 tried to intercede for the sailor, but was brushed aside.
The man was William Fox.

When Fox opened the Victoria in St. Louis, a man of whom he
had never heard looked upon him as a competitor. A back street
theatre operator, Spyros Skouras, wondered how the new show place
might affect his business, already tottering under the epidemic and
neighborhood competition. Everything Spyros Skouras had was
tied up in his theatres. These theatres represented more than money;
they represented a place in life. The first $300 that he and his older
brother Charlie had been able to save went into a small run-down

house. Spyros had kept his job at the Palm Restaurant and Charlie continued to work as a waiter to raise additional money to renovate the place. They scrubbed and cleaned and worked until they accomplished the impossible, making their theatre an inviting resort. As soon as they were able to devote full time to the theatre business they opened a second house. Just before Fox took title to the Victoria, they had purchased their third small theatre.

In addition to business worries Spyros and Charlie had another complication — their younger brother George. On the boat from Greece, he gambled away the train fare that was to take him from New York to St. Louis. In St. Louis, Spyros simply was unable to make him understand that a man or woman with a questionable reputation might be interesting but encumbered the progress of a respectable businessman. Charlie, more worldly than Spyros, often came to George's rescue, but like Spyros, he kept a watchful eye on his youngest brother. To keep George from mischief the older brothers set him to the most laborious tasks around the theatres.

The man the Skourases emulated, William Sievers, was in trouble. Although the local First National franchise holder, his theatres were so deeply in the red he found it necessary to supplement his income and became manager of the Victoria for Fox.

In spite of its $250,000 a picture star, the plight of First National was critical. The war and the epidemic cut its income. Inflamed by anxiety, fractional strife became apparent in the ranks of franchise holders. Each blamed the other for bad business. At the same time each wanted to buy in stock while it was low. The west lined up against the east. Dahnken, supported by Tally and others of the west, procured up to sixty per cent of the stock on the New York Exchange. The other forty per cent was held by Max Spiegel, son-in-law of the deceased Mitchell Mark; Walter Hayes, a Strand Theatre Corporation stockholder; Moe Mark; J. D. Williams. The sixty per cent gave Dahnken the control to shape policies in the production units. The easterners offered Dahnken $150,000 for his holdings. When he refused, feelings became so bitter, Spiegel, Hayes, Mark, and Williams, were glad not to be eased out altogether.

Bad as the plight of the manufacturers and jobbers, that of theatre owners was worse. Few had public backing or personal resources to carry them over a long stretch of profitless business. The majority were small operators struggling to eke out a livelihood.

In Cleveland, the Exhibitors Affiliated Association, composed of theatre owners, met to discuss ways and means to improve their position. Charles C. Pettijohn, member of the Shriners, Elks, and Knights of Pythias, and the association's counselor, presided. Although he had a homespun, awkward appearance, his speech inspired confidence, and he was the idol of small theatre owners. He had cried against their bearing a tax burden, he fought their battles for them, and insisted on their rights. At the meeting when he rose to address the members, he shifted his bulky weight from one foot to the other. For a moment he remained mute, thinking. The members knew he was about to say something momentous. In a strong clear voice he told his listeners the time had come to insist on open bookings, fair prices, and an elimination of extravagance and waste. "If the industry is to survive," he warned, "manufacturers must moderate their tactics."

Col. Jacob Ruppert, beer king, baseball magnate (noted for his black suits with large satin lapels) also had ideas on how to save the movies. With Mr. Pettijohn he agreed that the waste, especially overhead expenses, was too great. To overcome these excesses he organized a corporation, the Film Clearing House, which settled in the Kleine office and proposed to store, inspect, and deliver film for manufacturers, large or small, at reasonable cost.

World War I had brought about changes and innovations. Men found themselves in strange occupations. Manufacturers turned from peacetime wants to wartime needs. Industries, especially those engaged in providing guns and ammunition, developed with Arabian Nights speed. To fill contracts for war explosives the du Ponts of Delaware enlarged their plant many times. For several years the du Ponts purchased from the Eastman Kodak Company film *junk* which they used in the manufacture of munitions. Through a newly discovered chemical, the process was reversed, gunpowder refuse might be turned into film. Whether business was good or bad, as long as a motion picture industry existed, it represented an outlet to the du Ponts. With peace they would bring the Eastman monopoly of film blank stock to an end.

Then one day in November of 1918, epidemics, embargoes, fraud, extravagance, scarcely mattered. Rumors spread of an armistice. Before confirmation, the world went wild. Drunk with joy, men and women, without closing their desks, their drawers, their doors, rushed from their offices. Factory hands laid down their work. Housewives forgot the dinners on their stoves. In large cities and small the populace crowded into the streets. Traffic was unable to move. Whistles shrieked. Sirens blew. Church bells tolled. Strangers kissed each other, laughed and cried together. Ticker tapes, telephone books, important letters, ledger sheets were shredded and tossed about like confetti. The armistice rumor was false, but by the time a tense tired world recovered from its delirium it awoke to find itself at peace. The movie industry? It too awoke, to find itself with a stock of unmovable war pictures on its shelves.

Book Two, Part Two

Wall Street Invasion

(1918 to 1929)

The Million Dollar Blackjack

TRAPPED BY THE EPIDEMIC, the war, and now by peace itself, producers, distributors, exhibitors were in a quandary. From east to west and back again Abrams and Schulberg unsuccessfully sought a connection. Neither was Ben Hampton able to find a place. Blackton, who when speaking of life in California, once said, "I never will make another foot of film in the east," returned to Brooklyn, where he owned a glass-enclosed studio. His estate at Oyster Bay on Long Island, where in former years he had boated with his neighbor Teddy Roosevelt, was gone. Every dollar he could raise went into two pictures which he turned out in a hurry. Extremely patriotic, Blackton persisted with nationalistic themes. No market existed for these films, but his old friend, Albert Smith, took one off his hands, although at the time to keep Vitagraph alive Smith had turned the company into a serial producer. Blackton was relieved of the other by Col. Ruppert, who saw in it an opportunity to prove the value of his Film Clearing House. Neither picture reached the public, and Blackton was saved from despair only when word came that his son, twice wounded in the war, was homeward bound.

At Triangle conditions appeared so hopeless, Aitken suspended production indefinitely, leased his Culver City studio to Goldwyn, and left for Europe in an effort to make contacts abroad. Universal, Mutual, and First National gave employees vacations without pay. For a while Hodkinson and Pawley tried to exist as state's right distributors. They finally released pictures they had under contract through Pathé.

In an effort to survive several producers turned to picture-counterfeiting. They rearranged scenes of negatives three or four years old, rewrote lines, and released the results as current attractions. Some exhibitors, instead of advertising a picture known to be dull under its own title, substituted a title similar to a hit. Fox met the emergency by providing Sheehan with an assistant, James E. MacBride, political writer, former President of New York's Municipal Civil Service Commission, and manager of Judge John F. Hylan's successful campaign in a New York City mayoralty race.

For a few the depressed state provided opportunities. Louis B. Mayer, with idle cash, an idle star and, since his break with Metro, theatres without first-class product, played good Samaritan. He rescued Nathan H. Gordon, who had the First National Franchise for New England, by purchasing a half interest in his concern. This gesture automatically made Mayer a First National partner. The distribution advantages that went with this connection encouraged him to put his star, Anita Stewart, to work. Joseph Schenck bestowed an agreeable surprise upon his wife. Second rate distributors would no longer trade her talents. He disposed of his interest in World Film and worked out a deal whereby she too was to become a First National star. Jacob Fabian, whose retail dry goods business had prospered during the war, had money to invest. Although his Paterson theatre had suffered along with all others, his confidence in motion pictures' future remained unshaken. He not only extended his theatre holdings in New Jersey, but gambled on a First National franchise for part of the state.

The time had come for the du Ponts to market their film raw stock. Pat Powers, who desired to protect himself with additional sources of income when Universal found it necessary to declare a holiday, took courage from the du Pont action and opened a film blank stock manufacturing plant at Rochester, New York. The idea was to entice Eastman Kodak's trained employees with a small increase in salary. George Eastman's answer was to bind his employees with a one-way contract. The contract gave him the right to discharge the workers at will, but did not permit them to resign without a release.

George Eastman had had a hard, tough climb, too hard, too tough, to sweeten success. From his middle teens until he was twenty-three, he stood behind iron bars in a small, dimly-lighted cage counting the deposits of Rochester merchants. Neither his social standing nor his family connections entitled him to rapid promotion at the bank. Because of this, in 1877, when the United States Government announced the purchase of a naval base at Santo Domingo, he decided to try his luck as a merchant in that wild, virgin territory. Cautious, he thought to wait until he saw what was required before investing in any stock. With thrift, a credit to his frugal Yankee ancestors, he planned his wardrobe. Included were only the barest necessities, with one exception — a camera and photographic supplies.

A few days before he was scheduled to sail, Eastman went through his trunk and discovered that the silver nitrate, packed with his camera, had spilled and ruined his clothes. An evil omen. Superstition had killed his enthusiasm, and he returned to his job at the bank. Instead of losing interest in photography because the caustic ate away his wardrobe, he plunged headlong into an intensive study of the subject. He joined camera clubs and carried on a correspondence with amateur and professional photographers. By 1879 his correspondence was nationwide. Whenever possible he recommended a dry plate of his own make. Each night he rushed home from work to fill orders or to stimulate sales. After another two years he resigned from the bank a second time, and with his savings of $3,000, he opened a shop for the purpose of manufacturing dry plates.

Eastman had one interest — photography and how to apply it to increase his fortune. His business became an obsession. With flexible film on paper he made snapshot excursions commonplace. Whether or not he invented an item made no difference; the camera and its accoutrements he regarded as his special domain. In 1887, Hannibal Goodwin, an Episcopal preacher in Newark, New Jersey, detected that the transparency and flexibility of celluloid made an excellent base for film. Eastman patented the discovery. Until 1914, when the courts decided otherwise, the Eastman Kodak Company claimed full credit for this invention. The preacher did not live to receive the award. He had been accidentally killed in 1900. But his widow and associates collected $5,000,000.

By any and all means Eastman shut out competition, and, at the same time, sympathetic attachments. Prosperity did not buy friends. He left middle age a kinless, lonely man. When he entertained, his guests were business associates who considered his invitation a command. Among his prized possessions were twelve gold plates. Every

Sunday he invited eleven acquaintances to eat from these luxurious dishes. One man misread his invitation and came a week too early. Eastman sent him away without dinner. He apologized for this rudeness by explaining an odd plate on the table spoiled the golden setting. The little bank in which he had once served as a teller became a great institution, guardian of one of the world's great fortunes, Eastman's. With the same ardor that he devoted to business he applied himself to philanthropy. He endowed various universities with sums totaling almost $60,000,000. He established museums and hospitals, but he never relaxed in his commercial policies, and, when he committed suicide in 1921, he was one of the world's wealthiest men.

At the age of sixty-five, when he was faced with the du Pont and Powers competition, a million-dollar laboratory which housed apparatus and machinery not to be found elsewhere sprang up almost over night at Fort Lee, New Jersey. Huge rollers were installed to carry film from the roof to the basement through dark rooms, hypo rooms, printing rooms, drying rooms, inspection and shipping rooms, in one continuous operation. The plant was able to apply mechanically coloring, temperature, humidity, and all processes operated by hand in other laboratories. Sen Jacq was its name, and though the facilities of the laboratory were well publicized, the name of its owner remained a secret during construction.

When the building was completed, Jules Brulatour invited the heads of all laboratories servicing the motion picture industry to examine the Sen Jacq fittings. After a tour of inspection the guests were seated at a sumptuous banquet, and the mystery of Sen Jacq was solved. George Eastman was introduced as the guest of honor. He addressed those assembled. "Gentlemen," he said, "it is not my intention to go in the processing end of the business unless I am forced to do so. As long as you resist the temptation to develop second-rate film, not a wheel will be permitted to turn here. But, if you do not properly protect the interests of my patrons, and this laboratory becomes the only one where prints may be made on Eastman stock, I shall be compelled to set it in operation."

Relatives Aplenty

THE SEN JACQ LABORATORY was simply one more thorn to prick the spirits of disconsolate men. Many studios were closed, none operated full time. Across the country dust distorted the alluring smiles of movie queens high on billboards; rips and tears defaced the features of virile hard-riding cowboys. Although to post them hardly seemed worth the effort, "For Sale" signs replaced colorful movie posters. Common show owners, who once despaired of holding theatre properties now despaired of selling them.

Then, without warning, the incredible happened. As soon as a "For Sale" sign appeared so did a buyer. Small theatre operators, unfamiliar with the intricacies of finance, did not comprehend what was taking place. How could they comprehend that men with fortunes made in war stocks wanted to turn gold into real estate, any kind of real estate? How could they comprehend that the recently enacted Prohibition Law made any movie house attractive to a former saloon-keeper, whose one desire was to get into a business that did not require specific training? Because they did not comprehend these things, they became suspicious of the motives of would-be purchasers. Perhaps their properties were worth more than they realized! Prices went up. The new prices were met. "For Sale" signs came down. Even so, buyers appeared, often with offers beyond good judgment.

The Livingtons and the Kahns invested in theatres. The House of Morgan plunged, and one of its partners, Henry P. Davison became a member of the Loew Board. Loew stock appeared on the Curb Exchange, and the name of the company spread throughout the east and south. The time had come when entertainment, especially theatre, stocks might be offered to the public on a large scale. In this era, with its growing tendency to look upon the movie theatre as a legitimate business and not merely as a decadent art form, a corporation was formed by Eugene du Pont of gunpowder fame; Messmore Kendall, a lawyer identified with copper interests; George H. Doran, book publisher; Major Edward Bowes, a capitalist; Frank H. Hitchcock, his Vitagraph experience behind him. Because they were unable to find a picture house to meet their requirements, they built one — the Capital, 5,500 seat theatre on the southwest corner of Fiftieth Street and Broadway in New York. Paintings and sculpture decorated the corridors; a great marble staircase led to upper floors. Throughout the house were comfortable mohair chairs. Admissions ran up to $1.65. Major Bowes confessed to being an outstanding showman and so he was appointed manager in charge of programs. All bookings were made with the socially elite in mind. As a special attraction, Aimee Semple McPherson, evangelist, was given a contract which guaranteed her $5,000 a week and a split of any intake over $50,000.

The elite failed the theatre. To save their investment, the illustrious list of stockholders called in Samuel Rothapfel, known to the public as "Roxy." The son of immigrant parents, he became a small-town showman and later successfully launched the New York Strand, Rialto, and Rivoli. He was the only executive at the theatre without a blue book listing. Upon taking over the management, he reduced admissions to $1.10 tops and introduced a new high in motion picture theatre entertainment by setting off each feature picture with an elaborate ballet, familiarly known as "Roxy and His Gang." The feelings of Major Bowes were saved by electing him vice-president at an increased salary of $25,000 a year.

Big theatres were the rage, and 1919 became known as the million-dollar theatre era. E. H. Hulsey, owner of twelve Texas show places, built the largest house in the state at San Antonio. To bring an air of culture into their St. Paul and Minneapolis theatres, Finkelstein and Rubin removed all advertising from their screens. Jacob Fabian built an elegant motion-picture palace in Newark, New Jersey. Harry Crandall provided suitable settings for senators and diplomats in Washington, D. C., and Sid Grauman, in an effort to outdo all, erected Grauman's Oriental in Los Angeles. The program of big theatres increased the impetus to buy. Everywhere and anywhere, at figures ridiculously high, men sought a means to turn cash into a *grind* show.* Theatre owners reasoned, "If my house is worth so much to an inexperienced operator, it is worth more to me." This fantastic line of reasoning set the wheels of the motion-picture industry turning with renewed energy. Exhibitors reorganized their shows, cleaned their houses, redecorated their facades. They signed up for new product, contracted for billboard space, and committed themselves to increased lineage in newspapers and magazines.

Activity in the theatres inspired extravagant moods. Producers in rosy speeches spoke of their aims; they promised fewer, bigger, better pictures; they promised that henceforth not the star, but the story would be "the thing."

Thus a bit of wishful thinking, especially on the part of untrained men who hoped to lure patrons from a brass rail to a plush seat, restored life to the motion picture industry.

The scholarly Ben Hampton was so impressed by what he heard, he formed a new corporation which he called Great Authors, Inc. Harry Aitken returned from abroad and, to the relief of Stephen Lynch (reputed to be the most active speculator in the market, both on the long and short sides, in motion picture issues) bought out the holdings of the S. A. Lynch Enterprises in Triangle. Aitken reorganized Triangle in a small studio. With the profits of "My Four Years In Germany" the Warners established themselves as producers, and Abe went west to purchase land suitable for a studio site.

Their partner in the Gerard venture refused to go along with them. He had other ideas. Like David Horsley, Mark Dintenfass wanted to serve the people. The desire to devote himself to the utilitarian life of a politician had remained with him since the days his partners at Universal had convinced him he was destined to become a public servant. Again, like Horsley, Dintenfass was not called upon to make the supreme sacrifice; the people relegated the responsibility to his opponent in a New Jersey gubernatorial race.

Increased production raised the hopes of William Sherry. He saw an opportunity to reestablish himself as an independent distrib-

---

*A name derived from the turning of the machines.

utor on a nationwide scale. Unlike Zukor, he believed salesmanship required "good sportsmanship," and the film man's hangout, the Hotel Astor Lobby, buzzed with delightful stories of Sherry's fishing excursions, his motor trips, his picnics, his gay night club parties.

Frank Godsol, having been declared innocent, became a partner of Coleman du Pont, who spent $4,000,000 of his war-time gunpowder profits on a highway which he presented as a gift to the State of Delaware. Godsol and duPont provided the Goldwyn Company with funds with which to meet obligations on which only interest had been paid, and to purchase Triangle's large old glass-enclosed studio at Culver City. A tie-up with Lee Shubert and A. H. Woods, theatrical producers, safeguarded the company against a story shortage.

A smiling, shiny-headed, undersize man, with an Horatio Alger history, had maneuvered the Goldwyn deal. Years before, when a Castle Garden inspector who was unable to understand him, stamped his card Goldfish, he accepted the designation good-naturedly. A name did not seem of any particular importance in the life of a man. Maybe this was the American way. If changing his name was one step toward the success for which he had come to the United States, what difference did it make! In the course of years he had become president of a great corporation; his business associates were high in society. They spoke of family traditions and backgrounds. He thought about his name. It did not connect him with his ancestors; it did not describe or identify him. He had accepted it lightly. Why shouldn't he discard it lightly, discard it to take a name that symbolized ability, power, wealth, prestige; a name he had made famous; the name of his company, Goldwyn. The thought became parent to the deed, and little Sammy Goldfish became Samuel Goldwyn, The Great Goldwyn. Things are apt to go this way in the motion picture industry; instead of a man giving his name to a company, a company gives its name to a man.

Fox too had come a long way. The Prince of Wales, later King Edward of England, on a visit to the United States was his guest at the Academy of Music, a F-O-X combination vaudeville and motion picture palace located east of Union Square in New York City. That Fox might have a setting befitting his position, he erected on West Fifty-Sixth Street in Manhattan's Hell Kitchen a four-story structure the width of a city block. It contained innumerable stages, the sizes of which were regulated by accordion walls operated on pullies strung in ceiling tracks, a developing plant, printing plant, warehouse, carpenter shop, gymnasium, restaurant, and administrative offices. Fox's office was an immense hall, panelled in chestnut wood stained to imitate oak. Colored glass windows, which gave the room a cathedral-like air, shut out from view the slum dwellings of the street on which it was located. Visitors approached across a long carpeted floor to his desk in front of the windows, and he sat much like an emperor receiving his subjects. But he had not been able to eradicate the spectre of poverty that had hovered over his youth. As strong as his desire to build an imposing structure was his instinct to economize, and second-hand bricks, a Fox trade mark, went into the rear of the building.

In the revival, Selznick set up his son Myron as a producer and solved the Zukor-Selznick mystery. When Selznick complained that his product did not get fair distribution at Paramount, Zukor agreed to release Selznick from his contract, provided Zukor was permitted to retain fifty per cent interest in the Selznick company, and further that Selznick would not produce or release pictures under his own name. Selznick accepted; Select Pictures resulted. The arrangement nettled the spirited Selznick and, in 1919, when his son Myron, not bound by a Zukor contract, came of age, a huge electric sign on the Great White Way flashed "Myron Selznick Productions." In vain, Zukor accused Selznick of breach of contract. The contract was with the father; the advertised productions were the son's. In an attempt to shame Selznick, Zukor claimed the breach was a moral if not a legal one, and let fall in the film center, "Selznick gives too much advice to his son and too little attention to the time clock."

"If that's the way Zukor feels," Selznick reiterated, "I'll buy out Select, time clock and all."

The argument provoked smiles even in movie circles where humorous situations are often regarded as serious. Who in films did not provide for a relative? Hadn't that very practice led Zukor into an arcade? And hadn't Zukor made room for his son Eugene at Famous Players-Lasky? Sidney Kent, Famous Players' sales chief, placed two brothers in lucrative positions on his payroll, as did Winnie Sheehan at Fox. Blackton's son had acted as his father's assistant. Albert Smith placed five of his six brothers in important

Vitagraph posts. The twenty-one-year-old Loew twins, David and Arthur, held executive positions in their father's corporation. Even small theatres were family affairs. Papa ran the projector; mama took cash.

Zukor accepted Selznick's offer. He anticipated what would happen to his investment at Select with the Myron Selznick Productions in competition, especially since Charles C. Pettijohn had a long time contract to act as legal advisor and assistant to the Myron Selznick president, and Sam E. Morris was to organize independent theatres to provide constant access to screens.

Sam Morris, at the time, comparatively unknown in the industry, had been born in Oil City, Pennsylvania. That decaying town offered little to his parents so they moved to Cleveland. There, after a meager education, Sam went to work in his father's tailor shop. Ambitious, his father's shop did not offer much in the way of opportunity. He flitted around for a while and then drifted into the film business. When he had saved a few hundred dollars he opened a nickelodeon of his own. Lewis J. Selznick first became acquainted with Sam's cold persistence, his ability to wear down an opponent, when he tried to sell Sam film. Later, when Sam agreed to take over the Cleveland territory for World Film, Selznick had a chance to observe at closer range Sam's inability to see any but his own point of view, a trait which served him well when he had a hard bargain to drive. When Selznick broke with World Film he knew that he would again one day engage the talents of Sam E. Morris.

Charles C. Pettijohn, on the other hand, had the ability to present a convincing argument with his eyes open to both sides of a question. In fact, when he represented the independent theatre owners he fought their battles so well he was the idol of the men. Now, he not only advised Selznick how to handle exhibitors, he organized the American Fiscal Corporation for the purpose of selling stock in Pennsylvania. His plan established him as a super-salesman as well as a brilliant lawyer. The son of an Allentown jeweler was engaged for small part in a picture. For weeks before the picture reached Allentown, it was advertised as a film with local talent. When the local talent finally arrived, stock salesmen were planted in the theatre lobby. Once the stock-selling campaign was over the jeweler's son was told he was better fitted for his father's business.

Zukor, with the cash he received from Selznick, organized another small producing outfit, Realart. The purpose of this company was twofold. It would produce pictures of about the quality of Myron Selznick's to harass his erstwhile partner. At the same time it assured Zukor a place in the industry if the authority he wielded at Famous Players-Lasky rebounded against him.

Stanley Mastbaum's Dream Takes Form

ALTHOUGH PRODUCERS, in an impetuous moment, had promised fewer, better, bigger pictures, their energies went toward speeding up their plants to turn out films as fast as possible. Advertising and publicity stressed the story, not the star. Lest the star era had really passed, Charlie Chaplin, to protect himself, asked for a few minor changes in his contract about to come up for renewal. First National did not see things his way. One Friday afternoon in 1919 the comedian posted notice to the effect that his set was closing down; he was going abroad for an indefinite period for a much-needed rest. Newspapers throughout the country commented on the state of his health. A flood of fan mail revealed that thousands of movie goers were fearful that the pathetic little tramp who caricatured their stifled emotions might never again appear on the screen. Perhaps Charlie Chaplin expected the world to find a comic twist in any of his actions, for the following Tuesday he was seen devouring a hearty luncheon at the Hotel Alexander in Los Angeles in the company of Mary Pickford, David Wark Griffith, and Douglas Fairbanks, the current Paramount heart throb. A few days later the foursome announced that, under the trade name, United Artists, they would produce the finest pictures the world had ever seen, and that theatres might have these pictures on a percentage basis. Oscar Price, former Assistant Director General of Railroads, was to head the corporation. William Gibbs McAdoo, transportation expert and son-in-law of President Woodrow Wilson, was to leave his $12,000-a-year post as Secretary of the United States Treasury to act as their general counsel at $50,000 a year. Hiram

Abrams was to be general manager of distribution with his "Gold Dust Twin" Benjamin Percival Schulberg to assist him.

For publication, Adolph Zukor, at the time acknowledged to have the most fertile mind in the industry, said, "I congratulate the members of the United Artists Distributing Association." Secretly he invited Mary Pickford to spend a few days at his country residence outside the society colony at Tuxedo Park, New York. His estate, was an ideal place to talk to a friend. It was laid out in the English manner, with a day and a night house, a dining-room with a huge window through which might be seen an unobstructed view of the countryside, a private theatre, formal gardens, two natural swimming pools, an artificially built pool, tennis courts, and an eighteen-hole golf course that rambled over five hundred acres of velvety hills. Zukor told Mary that he was worried about her; he wanted her to take a vacation before she wore herself out; he wanted her to have a vacation at his expense. He was willing to let her have $1,000 a week for five years if she would retire from the screen for that length of time. Mary was not ungrateful, but she enjoyed playing America's Sweetheart; because she enjoyed it she did not find the role too strenuous.

The stubborness of the demure actress sent Zukor into conference with his partner Jesse Lasky, Famous Player's production chief. One course was open to them; they must find another whose unsophisticated charm would captivate the world as Mary's had. A blue-eyed girl with long golden curls. Mary Miles Minter, was given a 3-1/2-year contract which carried a guaranty of $1,300,000 and the stipulation that her innocence must never be questioned. That their star might have the finest vehicles money might buy, they purchased the rights to all plays owned by the Charles Frohman Estate. The great Charles Frohman, who had compared motion pictures to yellow journalism, had perished in 1915 when the Lusitania was sunk by a German submarine. Salesmen were put on a bonus plan and provided with the United Artists' sales talk whereby exhibitors were to have pictures on a percentage basis. An Advisory Board, composed of representative exhibitors throughout the country, who were invited to express opinions regarding the director, the star, the story before a picture went into work, was established. The directors, stars, and stories were presented in such a way, the exhibitors did not dissent and, therefore, were not in a position to complain when the finished pictures appeared.

The spurt of activity that had started with Prohibition spread with the return of doughboys and the entrance of European immigrants into the United States. Many an oldtimer, who had himself achieved the seemingly impossible, stood aghast at the sudden transformation of 1919, and shied from the accelerated competition in which any and every feature picture was stupendous, magnificent, spectacular, unsurpassed, or colossal. Adolph Linick and Peter Schaefer of the Jones, Linick, Schaefer Circuit in Chicago, sold out to Aaron J. Jones, who stayed on as a First National franchise holder to fight the rising strength of Balaban and Katz, who played the Famous Players product.

Abie Balaban and Sammy Katz had come a long way in a short time. Twelve or thirteen years before, for a dollar or two a night, they were rivals, competing with each other as back-street musicians and singers. Now, as partners, they were building a $2,500,000 house in the Loop.

Exhibitors soon became aware that only those who strengthened their positions ensured them. John H. Kunsky consolidated theatres in and around Detroit. Emanuel Mandelbaum built several houses in the Cleveland district. The Saengers, although under investigation, extended their holdings in Louisiana and Mississippi. Sol Lesser joined forces with the Gore Brothers and formed the West Coast Theatres Corporation.

Jules Mastbaum was at Mount Clemens, Michigan, trying to rid his body of racking rheumatic pains, when he became aware of the tremendous change taking place in theatre control, a change in which he had no part. His pains suddenly became imaginary; his company, not he, needed treatment. As soon as he could pack his bags he left for home. At last Stanley's dream would come true, and come true it must if the Stanley Circuit were to survive. With the backing of John McGuirk and Abe Sablotsky, former partners in a saloon, and the Wolff Brothers, bankers, he recapitalized The Stanley Company at $15,000,000, renamed it The Stanley Company of America and bought, built, and leased theatres in Pennsylvania and New Jersey until the Stanley circuit became the largest in the country with no close rival.

Vitality had indeed come back into the industry. Now, no self-respecting film executive sat down to his old-time favorite pastime, the game of poker, where a pot contained less than $15,000 to $20,000.

The Bolsheviki

FOLLOWING THE WAR, A NEW MENACE, the Bolsheviki, cast its shad-ow. The first to comprehend its evils were Wall Street angels. When Franklin K. Lane, Secretary of the Interior, implored the coun-try to resist a Red invasion, their fears were intensified. The capitu-lation of Russia had not satisfied the Bolsheviki; they wanted the world, and the motion picture served as a weapon to help them get it. The time had come to stop thinking of motion pictures as a mere time-killer, a delightful dissipation, and to recognize "the fore-most entertainer and educator of the world's millions of people" for what it might be: a useful medium for propaganda purposes.

Talk spread that the Republican and Democratic Parties wanted to buy into the newsreels to carry their platforms to a greater number of people, that churches intended to run their own motion picture shows, and that Henry Ford, automobile manufacturer and former Vitagraph partner, who issued a weekly educational short (which many exhibitors refused to run because of its hate content) was ready to invest $120,000,000 in a production company. He wanted a series of feature films through which to carry out a pro-gram of religious bigotry via which he hoped to become President of the United States. But Wall Street, cautioned by Standard Oil bankers and others, had no room for the caprice of an individual or the ambitions of politicians who might not necessarily serve its ends. The motion pictures must concentrate on preserving a system; it must maintain a *status quo*.

As a first step, Famous Players-Lasky's capital was increased by $20,000,000, and the stock was placed on the big board. Kuhn,

Loeb, & Company underwrote the issue, and Dominick and Dominick and the Hallgarten Company, who had taken a licking on an earlier Paramount stock issue, shared the deal.

At the Goldwyn Company the Coleman du Pont ante swelled; a million dollar Goldwyn issue appeared on the curb. Eugene du Pont, Coleman's cousin, poured money into a company known as Associated Exhibitors, formed in association with Pathé exchanges for the purpose of catering to the needs of the Capitol Theatre (in which Eugene had an interest) and other deluxe houses. As is usual, fresh money brought about reorganization. Charles Pathé, elevated to the position of Officer of the Legion of Honor by the French Republic, was just an old-timer in motion pictures. No place existed for him in the new setup, and the name of Paul Brunet, his assistant, replaced his as president of Pathé, Inc.

The Loew people erected booths in their theatres where an issue was sold so that Loew's patrons might become his partners. Although Loew's stock could be had on the Curb Exchange at 17 a share, the underwriters offered the theatre booth issue at 20 cash, 21 on the installment plan.

A Canadian syndicate, made up of a race track owner named Lumsden; the owner of a string of horses, Charles Rohrback; and a pool room operator named Buckley, bought into the Myron Selznick Company with $3,000,000 in cash. These backers demanded the company's entire stock of negatives as security. The Utica Investment Company, its Board of Directors a mystery, floated $2,000,000 worth of ten-year, eight per cent collateral sinking fund bonds. With the new money, Selznick was able to purchase a fifty per cent interest in thirty exchanges.

Friends of Oscar Price, a group with Guaranty Trust Company backing, induced him to leave United Artists' Big-4 in the hands of Hiram Abrams and form Associated Producers' Big-6, composed of six successful directors.

On one point bankers, brokers, producers, exhibitors agreed. Bolshevism must not poison the American people. It was to be combated before it had a chance to cause unrest. The result was a series of anti-Bolshevik pictures that depicted starvation, unsanitary living conditions, lack of comfort, and restrictions on free movement in the Soviet Union. More imaginative directors produced stories subtle in tone. They turned out films in which they showed that

business success brought connubial bliss, in which the happy, contented, quiet home life of America's Four Hundred, the good people,
was emphasized, and in which philanthropy accompanied the ac-
cumulation of gold. Most of those who attended the common or
grind show were simple folk. Without suspecting their entertainment
was designed to limit their political outlook, they developed a taste
for luxury. So, without intending to, the motion picture not only
directed men's minds in economics and politics, but dressed their
wives and decorated their homes.

The Bolshevik threat under control, Wall Street turned to the
problem of protecting its investments. Those who had helped Loew
extend his chain of theatres now wanted assurance that the theatres
would have sufficient product. True, Joseph Schenck, a former Loew
partner and brother of one of the vice-presidents of Loew's Incorporated, would give the company first choice of pictures starring his
wife, whose contract called for $8,000 a week, or her sister Con-
stance, whose salary was $6,000 a week, but he would be unable
to   produce enough to keep the houses adequately supplied. Bankers
and brokers, unwilling to trust to luck, wanted a say in mass production and provided Loew with $9,000,000 with which to buy
that say, and for $9,000,000 Richard Rowland agreed that the Metro
Company might become a Loew subsidiary.

At Goldwyn the situation was reversed. Coleman du Pont was
unwilling to speculate on the debut of his pictures. He worked out
a deal whereby Cousin Eugene invested another slice of his war
profits in the Goldwyn Company that that company might buy an
interest in the Capitol and other first-run houses. Thus Coleman was
assured of a first run in key cities and Eugene was provided with
additional product for theatres under his control.

The ego of William Randolph Hearst was pained. Although the
pictures starring his Ziegfeld beauty had unrestricted space in his
papers and, although Famous Players distributed them, they sold
at a loss. Hoping that with talent he might develop profits, he organized Cosmopolitan Productions. However, only masculine names
were to be classified as stars. Except for the blue-eyed blonde, all
actresses were to be billed as leading ladies.

Word of his intentions reached his mother, Phoebe Hearst. Shortly
before her death she visited his duplex apartment on Riverside Drive
in New York. While he remained with friends in the living room, she

examined his curios and his paintings, his statues and his suits of armour. She ran her hands over his leather draperies and stepped with care on his Oriental rugs. As she wandered through the rooms she compared this apartment with his marble ranch house on his estate at San Simeon, California, an estate so large it had its own private railroad. There he had intended to reconstruct an Irish Castle, and had brought one, stone by stone across the sea for the purpose. Meanwhile the old stones lay scattered about the ground. Everything he touched was expensive and intemperate. On the balcony that overlooked the sitting room in the apartment she noticed a projector from which William flashed films onto the wall below. "William," she called down, indifferent to his friends, indifferent to his high standing in society, indifferent to his age, "William, these extravagances will ruin you. You will die broke." The sentiments of Phoebe Hearst impressed none in the room. All looked upon her as an old woman who did not understand that big money was required to make big money.

And big money, big enough to embrace another continent, was the order of the day. The time had come to bring Europe back into line. Throughout the years the English had ignored the pleas of Friese-Greene, but they could not ignore the strides made in the United States. A scarcity of British-made pictures forced them to lift the boycott on American product, an action that provoked the cry, "Britain for the British." One association passed a resolution that asked the British government to protect the film industry in the United Kingdom against American invasion. Among Members of the House of Lords one group floated a $25,000,000 issue with which to open a studio in England. For something between $5,000,000 and $7,000,000 Charles Pathé relinquished his English holdings, a fifty-two per cent interest in Pathé Ltd., to Lord Beaverbrook, the English-Canadian newspaper magnate. Thereafter Pathé confined his investments to France, where a company in which he was principal stockholder enjoyed a monopoly in the raw stock field. France continued her embargo on American-made films. In Italy new production units were set in motion. Germany and Sweden released pictures that threatened America's prestige.

Richard Rowland, most of his downy blond hair gone, but otherwise still youthful in appearance, called on European motion picture owners. His argument, that American producers must meet the foreign distributor half way as long as exchange rates were unequal, impressed those he called on, and he worked out reciprocal agreements in almost every country on the continent.

Fox sent Winnie Sheehan abroad to save mankind from falling under the influence of a "heavily capitalized Teuton company that aimed at Prussianizing the whole world through screen control." By dazzling actors and directors with contracts drawn up in the American manner (with tremendous salaries), Winnie broke up an intrigue of German bankers and munition makers with eyes on the movies.

Bennie Schulberg left his friend Hymie Abrams to protect his interest at United Artists, which was still in a formative state and did not require the services of two top executives, and followed Sheehan across the sea. No one was in doubt about the reasons for his trip. The only question was which actors and directors he would line up to add to United Artists' Big-4.

Goldwyn and others quickly perceived advantage in bringing European talent to the United States. In a matter of months, European production, young, yet full of promise, would be completely demoralized and disintegrated.

Again it remained for little Adolph Zukor to comprehend the full magnitude of the situation abroad. Lord Beaverbrook, one of England's wealthiest men, had invested millions in the Pathé Company; he had bought up theatres throughout the British Isles. Lord Beaverbrook was a smart man, as smart as Rowland, Fox, and Goldwyn. In addition, British resentment of America's dominance in motion pictures had reached an all-time high. Of what use to keep buying up foreign talent? Of what use to make reciprocal sales agreements as long as antipathy for the American trade mark existed? First Zukor went into Canada, where resentment against products made in the United States was not so strong. There, with Canadian personnel, he formed Famous Players-Lasky Films, Ltd., to sell Famous Players' pictures in Canada. Then he left for England. There, in partnership with Major Davis, a British capitalist interested in using films to promulgate the League of Nations, he built a studio for the purpose of producing with British casts, and made arrangements for subsidiaries in France, Belgium, Scandinavia, Poland, Spain, and Czechoslovakia.

The deal consummated, without fanfare to indicate that he was the John D. Rockefeller of the world's most publicized industry, he left for home. In his pocket reposed a $400,000 pearl necklace for a dark-eyed, dark-haired woman, who, years before, on a government land-grant farm in Dakota had traded beads with Indians.

Warner Brothers' first theatre The Cascade *opened in New Castle, Pennsylvania early in* 1903. *Seated* 99 *persons; chairs were rented from an undertaker. Movie patrons stood when a funeral was held.*

Ushers dressed as cowboys were featured by Manager James Barnett of the Florida Theatre, Miami, during engagement of "Montana".

Paramount Building, Times Square, New York City

Queue awaiting admittance into 43rd Street entrance of Paramount Theatre, New York City

The striking auditorium of the Radio City Music Hall, Rockefeller Center, New York, the world's largest theatre, with 60 foot high proscenium arch, and stage a full city block in width. Shown in the picture is part of a capacity audience of 6,200 persons watching the celebrated Rockettes, world-famous precision dancers, in one of their routines. In the pit can be seen the Radio City Music Hall Symphony Orchestra.

Wall Street vs. Poverty Row

A DOLPH'S HOMEWARD TRIP WAS FAR DIFFERENT from his first westward journey in 1888, when doubled up in pain he tossed in a steerage berth for seventeen days. This time he had de luxe quarters on the luxury liner Mauretania. As the ship steamed passed the Statue of Liberty, Adolph Zukor leaned against the rail peering at the billion-dollar skyline, vastly different from that day when he stood transfixed before buildings six and twelve stories high, with a burning desire to become a part of all they represented. Well, he had become a part! In his vaults lay a deed to one of the most valuable plots of ground in the world, the plot on which the Putnam Building stood on Broadway between Forty-third and Forty-fourth Streets. When and as he gave the order, the Putnam Building would come down to make way for a thirty-story skyscraper, a combination theatre and office structure to be known as the Paramount Building. But little Adolph Zukor was not happy.

From the start the repressions of Wall Street clashed with the temperament of Poverty Row. Men who had been trained when to smile and when to frown, when to sit and when to stand, found difficulty in fraternizing with men who did not understand the niceties of a modulated voice, whose English was laughable, who acted on impulse rather than reason. Especially difficult did men who supplied money find executive salaries of over $100,000 a year justifiable. No bank official dared vote himself or his associates salaries that so disregarded public opinion. Where their incomes were as great or greater, sources such as bonuses and dividends were discreetly ascribed.

Most victims of this scorn, with characteristic nonchalance, threw it off with shrugs of their shoulders. Maybe they were illogical! Maybe they were ignorant! Maybe they had no manners! So what? Highfalutin bankers provided them with the where-with-all just the same! Besides, they were quickly catching on to the ways of their new associates. Delmonicos became their favorite eating place. Stock tickers became a conventional part of their office equipment. Motion picture men were well represented in the board rooms of the best brokers. Mack Sennett, independent producer of slap stick comedies released by Famous Players, cleaned up as much as $1,300,000 on his security transactions alone. Joe Schenck showed his contempt for small stakes by sitting in on a stud poker game where $300,000 changed hands.

The willingness of motion picture men to play at high finance was not enough. When Wall Street went over the bills it wanted to know why retail prices were paid for whiskbrooms, mops, and other para- phenalia bought in quantity; why unionization was permitted so that projectionists were able to demand anywhere from $32 to $65 a week. It was distressed when it discovered that for every actor who appeared on the screen thirteen people were at work around the studio. It was suspicious of an industry that paid its labor (even though that labor was called talent) the salaries paid on Poverty Row, which frequently ran to more than five hundred or a thousand dollars a week. A display of creative imagination was looked upon with contempt and misgiving. If a picture or theme brought a profit, why experiment with new ideas?

Kuhn, Loeb & Company appointed H. D. H. Connick of their firm chairman of Famous Players-Lasky Finance Committee, so that he might report on the conduct of the film company. Victor Smith, brother of Albert, at the request of friends on " The Street " gave up his Vitagraph post and went to California to demonstrate to the Famous Players West Coast personnel how monied interests liked things done. Efficiency experts were installed on the various sets and seventeen persons were employed where thirteen previously did the job in back of each working actor. With the entry of Connick and Smith came the exits of Daniel Frohman, Walter Greene, Zukor's brother-in-law Albert A. Kaufman, and Walter Irwin. Except for Zukor, who remained silent at the departure of old friends, and Lasky, who kept as far as possible from the administrative ends of the business, about the only old-time executives left at Famous Players were Sidney Kent and Al Lichtman.

Sidney Kent struck a receptive chord in Wall Street. He was the type of self-made man they understood and admired. At the age of fourteen he stoked boilers, before he was twenty he roamed the desolate Wyoming country with five other men in an effort to establish camps and posts in that wild territory, he built pipelines and railroads, and when he tired of the lack of financial reward in adventure, he returned to civilization to become a salesman. Men of finance liked his unimpassioned approach to any situation, his cold self-assurance, his deliberateness. But in-again-out-again Al Lichtman was having the fight of his life. That he had risen from usher to actor and from actor to film salesman and from film salesman to film executive impressed no one. What was unusual about his climb? In fact, it was exceedingly annoying, because Lichtman never forgot it. His habit of telling jokes that dated back to the days when the Avon Comedy Four sold newspapers on street corners proved to be the last straw, and he was out.

Old lower-salaried employees who had stood by the company in dark hours also disappeared from the payroll. Still Zukor made no comment. "Where does Zukor stand in all this?" reverberated throughout the industry. Zukor realized all eyes were on him. If he dissented, organizational changes would take place just the same, and his weakened prestige would be obvious. If he said nothing, any changes might seem to be made without his consent. As a capping gesture, word spread that Kuhn, Loeb had insisted that Connick be placed on the Famous Players payroll. An aggrieved Zukor finally spoke. He said Kuhn, Loeb had not made such a request; he, himself, had engaged Connick because he was so impressed by the man's ability when he met him at the bankers' office. Who had chosen the other four Kuhn, Loeb representatives on Famous Players' Board never was revealed.

At Metro, W. J. Hiss, an efficiency expert, former director general of the Red Cross, saw that funds poured into that company's treasury were dispatched with care.

A fierce, open conflict raged at Goldwyn. Sammy, with his malapropisms, his indifference to petty details, his notions that authors should be trained to write only for the screen and were more important than actors, and that he, himself, was a creative artist, tried the patience of his associates. They regarded as an affectation his pocketless suits fitted to show the lines of his small figure. This man, who was an industry thorn as well as the butt of its teasing, had been foolhardy enough to import the first futuristic picture ever made, "The Cabinet of Dr. Caligari," a U-F-A release. In 1919, the U-F-A, the German film trust, was in financial difficulties and used the modernistic background because with it weird effects could be created and production costs kept down. If "The Cabinet of Dr. Caligari" chagrined Goldwyn's financial backers, it amused his competitors. Critics called it "an insult to human intelligence." Theatre-owners, who had booked it without a screening, sued Goldwyn for "malicious and wanton damage to their reputations." Historians of the films now list it as one of the greatest pictures ever produced. In a two-week period Goldwyn stock was hammered down from 17 to 9. The movement of the stock ticker, which carried other amusement stocks with it, was interpreted to be a "downright fight for control on the part of financial interests." A shakeup was apparent. The names of Frank Hitchcock (known to be a protector of big money interests and now a regular on motion picture executive boards) and William Braden, a copper magnate, appeared on the Goldwyn directorate. Chase National Bank also was linked to the company.

When Samuel Goldwyn was accused of extravagance, he knew his position was in jeopardy. That his pictures usually earned high praise from the critics and set a standard for quality seldom equaled, was of no consequence. When Felix Feist, Goldwyn's sales manager, refused a flattering offer from Loew, Goldwyn understood where he stood; only one reason might account for Felix Feist's refusal, a more flattering offer from the Goldwyn backers. Samuel Goldwyn, the uneducated Polish boy who had led his company into an enviable position tendered his resignation as president of the corporation whose name he had adopted as his own. The move was not an easy one, and he did not make it without strings attached. He demanded that his $2,000 weekly salary continue until the expiration of his contract, and that he be permitted to retain his stock holdings in the corporation. His offer was accepted by monied interests alarmed at the rate the Goldwyn bank balances shrank; they wanted someone with a sense of responsibility, someone who had an understanding of the value of money, someone who spoke their language to act for them.

The presidency of Goldwyn Pictures Corporation was offered to

Messmore Kendall, boulevardier, member of the alimony-paying circle as well as the Sons of the American Revolution, who lived in a house that had been Washington's headquarters at Dobb's Ferry, who was personal counsel to the du Ponts, member of the Advisory Board of the Chemical National Bank, director of the Andes Mining Company, the Quebec Mining Company, and the Capitol Bus Terminal. His background and his legal training were enhanced by his short experience at the Capitol Theatre and at Associated Producers. When, in September of 1920, the presidency of the Goldwyn Company was offered to him, he informed the Board that he would accept it only on condition that they would provide him with additional capital so that the company would not suffer because of forced economy.

Nothing To Fear

POVERTY ROW HAD SAVED THE WORLD from the clutches of Bolshevism only to find itself conquered by its ally. Wall Street reasoned in simple terms. It had, because of threats of a hostile ideology, plunged headlong into motion pictures, which counted stories, talent, ideas as assets. Hardly proper collateral for monies advanced! Tangible assets, real property, since they might not entirely supplant the incorporeals, had at least to supplement them. If production units in which big money was invested would buy up theatres, Wall Street would have a degree of protection as well as an assured market place for the intangibles it controlled.

First National had a theatre tie-up. So did the Goldwyn Company, through the cousins Eugene and Coleman du Pont. Nowhere were bankers as deeply entrenched as they were at Famous Players-Lasky. And hardly a year before Adolph Zukor had asked, "Which are you exhibitor or producer?" He had gone on to say, "The producer-exhibitor builds a barrier about his own business, limits his own field, establishes his own competition, and besides creates one of the gravest perils that has ever confronted the motion picture industry." Only those who had accepted financing were aware of the pressures.

Without comment from Adolph Zukor, Famous Players-Lasky bought into the S. A. Lynch Enterprises and two concerns owned by Alfred S. Black of Boston, the Exhibitors Film Booking Office and the New England Theatres, Inc. To Stephen Lynch and Alfred Black, Adolph Zukor explained the new aims of Famous Players-Lasky, placed these two men in charge of their respective territories and informed them they were to carry out their jobs in their own ways, that

218

he placed no restrictions on the methods to be used. In New York, Famous Players became allied to the B. S. Moss Vaudeville Circuit. Through the purchase of Stanley Company of America stock, the name of Adolph Zukor appeared as a member of its Board of Directors. Harry O. Schwalbe, secretary-treasurer of First National, owner of that company's franchise for Eastern Pennsylvania, was affiliated with Jules Mastbaum in a booking office which was a subsidiary of the Stanley Company. Thus Zukor was growing not merely into a formidable foe, but was in a position to learn First National secrets.

Uneasiness increased among First National executives when word drifted in from the mid-west that Famous Players was aiding local independents to break the Fox monopoly in Denver. The Denver independents, who had accepted Zukor as a savior, were unaware that Famous Players' theatre holdings at this time dwarfed those of Fox. In addition to its other alliances, Famous Players drew up a working agreement with A. H. Blank, proprietor of twenty theatres throughout Iowa and Nebraska.

Common knowledge had Wall Street divided into two factions, the Morgan group on one side; the du Ponts on the other. Each was willing to pour money into the contest until one or the other was broken. Every day brought fresh news. Famous Players, which always topped the list, came into control of theatres in Cincinnati, Indianapolis, St. Louis. The full extent of its holdings remained unknown and a tenseness developed waiting for additional news to break.

Adolph Zukor announced the betrothal of his daughter Mildred to Arthur Loew, one of the Marcus Loew twins, and all agreed, "This is it. A Loew-Famous Players merger puts this combined group out in front." All were mistaken. Adolph Zukor was jealous of his position. So was Marcus Loew. Neither intended to relinquish his place to a friend, a banker, or anyone else. Because of family ties one concession was made — to operate as friendly enemies through cooperative agreements. In many houses Famous Players-Lasky had the picture franchise and Marcus Loew the vaudeville franchise.

Stories drifted up from the south. At the head of an army of twelve men, variously called the wrecking crew or dynamite gang, Stephen Lynch marched through Georgia, Louisiana, Mississippi, and Arkansas. Small exhibitors sold out at the Lynch price or went out of business. Newspaper editorials throughout the south blasted the cold-blooded tactics. News items related how person after person was put out of business. On marched Lynch. The Saenger Circuit, a large Louisiana concern, ran full-page advertisements to bolster the spirits of smaller exhibitors. "The methods they are using," E. V. Richards, Jr., Saenger's general manager wrote, "are as near Bolshevism as anything I know of. They hope to gain a hold for each tentacle of their octopus by threats and brute financial force, and the independent exhibitor who has worked years to get his theatres in paying class and has striven night and day to make motion picture fans of his town's population is a mere pawn in the operation of this huge octopus and classed by it as worthy of no consideration." Richards pleaded with exhibitors not to be frightened by Lynch and his gang, to refuse to succumb to threats, and when Lynch entered New Orleans, the Saenger Circuit conceded to his demands. By this action the Saenger theatres were relieved of responsibility in a government action for trust practices pending against the circuit and passed the responsibility on to Famous Players.

That much of the ugly publicity was intentional became apparent after a while. The name Lynch was used to frighten men into giving up their holdings. Almost daily, terrified small-town exhibitors arrived in Dallas, film center of the southwest. Their stories were much alike. Lynch or a member of his crew had told them they would accept the proposition laid down or face ruin.

Stories also drifted in from the mid-west. A Famous Players-Lasky salesman working out of the St. Louis Exchange called on B. Uran, a Mattoon, Illinois, exhibitor and informed him that he would have to pay $400 to $550 for the quality product he formerly had at $75. Uran, whose house could not stand these prices, discontinued Famous Players showings. An advertisement in the local papers read:

> Mattoon can't see Paramount Pictures . . . It is about
> the only town in the state where you can't see Paramount
> Pictures . . . You can see Paramount Pictures in New
> York, Chicago, Charleston, and Arcola . . . Why not
> Mattoon? Is your theatre manager at fault?

Exhibitors across the country asked Zukor for an explanation. He denied knowledge of the situation and referred all inquiries to Sidney Kent, head of the sales department. Kent laughed the situation off with, "Gerard Akers, our St. Louis exchange manager is a high-pressure salesman."

Other high-pressure Famous Players exchange men placed adver-
tisements of the Mattoon type in Natchitoches, Louisiana; Lebanon,
New Hampshire; and other small cities. The exhibitors went back to
Zukor and demanded to know what the shock system concealed.
Zukor assured them, "You have nothing to fear."

"If I have nothing to fear," Mrs. Pauline K. Dodge, a Vermonter
asked, "how are my children to be fed?" Her story: Alfred S. Black
paid her husband a visit. He wanted to purchase three theatres
owned by Dodge. Dodge set a price which Black refused to meet;
instead he threatened to return and put Dodge out of business. A
few months later Dodge died. When Mrs. Dodge attempted to renew
the lease on one of her theatres, she discovered Black was her landlord. He offered her $700 for the equipment in all three houses.

J. E. Beane of Hillsboro, New Hampshire, had a call from Fred
Eames, a Black employee. Eames offered Beane $1,500 for his
theatre. When Beane held out for $5,000, Eames threatened to build
a theatre in Hillsboro and charge five-cents admission until such time
as Beane sold out; then admission on the new house would be raised
to thirty cents. Admission into the Beane house was twenty-five cents.

If Famous Players continued to absorb small theatres, Universal,
which catered to this type of exhibitor, would have no market for its
pictures. Pat Powers was alarmed. In addition, he had always
remained something of a misfit in the company where Laemmle and
Cochrane worked together like two peas in a pod. He was greatly
relieved when his partners consented to buy out his holdings.

Meanwhile Lynch and his crews made their way across the south
into Dallas. Coincident with their arrival in that city, a Dallas banker
received a wire from the Federal Reserve Bank of New York placing
$1,000,000 to the credit of Southern Enterprises of Texas, a Lynch
company. A few days later, E. H. Hulsey, First National Franchise
holder and owner of a chain of theatres throughout Texas and
Oklahoma, called on his banker, the same banker who had received
the Federal Reserve wire, and asked for a loan. Hulsey's account was
in excellent standing; nevertheless, the loan was refused.

Hulsey, to protect himself against a Lynch attack, had allied himself with exhibitors in Texas and Oklahoma; he had fortified himself
with an abundance of product — Goldwyn, Metro, Select, Fox, United
Artists, Universal, and Independent, in addition to First National. In
a series of advertisements in the Dallas, Houston, San Antonio, and

Oklahoma City newspapers, he assured the public he would not let the proposed plans of a large company intimidate him, that he would fight to a finish.

Abruptly his promises to fight to a finish disappeared from the papers. Furthermore, he ceased to talk against the tactics of Lynch. First National franchise holders refused to believe that Hulsey had secretly turned his franchise over to an enemy, but Paramount pictures began to appear in the Hulsey houses.

Jaydee Williams stepped into the Texas situation and dropped $180,000 of his personal fortune in an effort to carry on the contest, but he was unable to match the unlimited resources backing his opponent.

While the Lynch-Hulsey rumors were still hot, word came through that for $1,000,000 Jake Wells let Lynch have his Atlanta, Savannah, Augusta, and Knoxville houses.

Tom Tally found himself speculating which of his patrons came to see his shows, which to evaluate his properties. At First National board meetings he wondered who present was a Zukor representative. The long-legged cowboy, who had given up the freedom of the plains for life in a stuffy arcade, decided he was too old a contestant and for $1,000,000 sold his theatres and his Southern California First National Franchise to Sol Lesser, a younger man.

William Sievers too, had had enough. Mild, easy going, the schemes and plots were too much for him. To the three Skouras Brothers (who in partnership with E. H. Birent and Leo Rossieur, Jr., raised $350,000) went his theatre properties and his local First National Exchange. This deal, although it had an ill effect on the morale of First National franchise holders, placed Famous Players at a disadvantage in St. Louis, for it gave the Skourases a virtual first-run monopoly in that city.

The Skourases, unlike Sievers, were relentless, determined and aggressive. They worked seven days and seven nights a week. Their staffs worked just as long. Each theatre had to pay. And each theatre was adjusted to its section. In a red light district, the Lyric Theatre conformed to the conventions of its neighborhood. That downtown houses might rival those in any city, Spyros Skouras, the head of the company, went to Chicago and New York to study at first hand *high class* theatre management.

If Wall Street via Adolph Zukor, via Sidney Kent, via Stephen Lynch, etc., intended to wage a war of nerves, J. D. Williams in-

tended not to let them. Jaydee bolstered First National's position by
signing up for the pictures of Oscar Price's Associated Producers
for distribution. Many franchise holders still were loyal. Harry
Crandall, who had been approached innumerable times, resisted all
pressure. So did Harry Schwalbe, in spite of his Mastbaum connection. Gordon and Fabian and others were not intimidated. Supported by Robert Lieber, First National president, and Schwalbe,
Jaydee prevailed upon all franchise holders known to be staunch
to reorganize under the name Associated First National Pictures
Incorporated and Associated First National Theatres Incorporated.
The plan provided:

> That the country be divided into twenty-three territories,
> and that the franchise holder in each territory dispose of
> sub-franchises to independent exhibitors;
> That each territory be assigned an established cost for
> every negative price paid by Associated First National;
> That each sub-franchise subscribed for by an individual
> exhibitor will immediately and automatically establish the
> rental value (the percentage of the valuation of each pic-
> ture in the respective territory) the individual exhibitor
> will pay for each production released by Associated First
> National;
> That ownership of a franchise will guarantee an exhib-
> itor the sole and exclusive right to Associated First Na-
> tional attractions in his established locality (in larger
> cities to be determined by zones. In smaller towns it will
> carry with it as a protective measure the exclusive privi-
> lege to exhibit First National attractions in the munici-
> pality);
> That exclusive exhibition rights will make it impossi-
> ble for the exchange serving the territory to book any
> other theatre in any zone or theatre locality where an
> independent exhibitor previously obtained a franchise
> for Associated First National pictures;
> That the exhibitor holding franchises will pay rentals
> for attractions equivalent to their franchise percentage of
> interest in the main franchise in the respective territory
> (In brief — if a theatre holding an Associated First Na-
> tional franchise is rated in that franchise as 5% of the

associated theatre strength, the rentals of that theatre will be fixed on all productions released as 5% of the valuation of each picture in the territory as a whole);

That franchise costs are secured to exhibitors in stock in the exchange against which, as permanent security, is the exchange's territorial franchise and equity in all contracts which the national organization has with stars and producers, releases made and the physical assets of film on hand;

That no dividend over 10% would be declared, and that all profits would be employed toward buying pictures for the free use of sub-franchise holders;

That ownership of a franchise will protect exhibitors against price opposition and the menaces of a fast growing form of competition wherein theatres controlled and financed by producer-distributor interests bid up rentals at personal loss to prevent independent exhibitors from obtaining meritorious screen material;

And that no sale or transfer of franchise is valid without the consent of all other franchise holders throughout the country.

Upon presentation, capital stock in the amount of $10,400,000 was over-subscribed. Those exhibitors lucky enough to obtain a franchise agreed with the advertisements that had introduced them that they had achieved "independence at last."

Hardly had the ink dried on Associated First National territorial contracts when an automobile escorted by a brass band playing full blast left Grand Central Station in New York. The car and the band travelled at a snail's pace, west on Forty-second Street to Broadway, north on Broadway to Universal's office at Forty-eighth Street. Along the line of march, office windows became alive with faces. People in the street stretched and strained their necks in an effort to see President Harding. Who else could be in the car? Who else? Carl Laemmle. Smiling Uncle Carl was out in the cold. Like Selznick, the Warners, Blackton, Smith, Hampton, and others who did not have protective theatre connections, Uncle Carl had been frozen out by Famous Players on one side and First National on the other, but he did not intend to freeze unseen.

Court Actions

IN ALL ITS HAPHAZARD UNCERTAIN HISTORY, the industry was never in a more bewildered state. Small theatre owners, although they feared extinction, failed to throw support to independent producers. Instead they organized to fight for the advertised product of larger companies who scorned them. As a result, Ben Hampton, who had proved himself the small exhibitor's friend, was forced to retire. He had fought for them at conventions, he had provided them with the best independent product on the market. That he might continue producing for small houses, he once had forced a Los Angeles banker into giving him a loan by throwing on the banker's desk a package of bonds and saying, "You sold me this bunch of Los Angeles City bonds; you guaranteed them, and if you don't take them as collateral I will go to the people with my story."

Sidney R. Kent (oblivious to the fact that others might recall the days when Zukor, his boss, had an interest in a penny arcade or the years he himself had spent as a pipe layer in uninhabited country) informed the trade that "Paramount Pictures are to be strictly a class product. Unless an exhibitor has a modern house, Famous Players-Lasky does not care to rent him its pictures." To introduce this "class product," the tactics of dance halls, cafes, and sellers of questionable stock issues were used. Four girls, selected for beauty, shape, and eloquence, were entered into a competition to see which one could obtain the most play dates.

Famous Players put small exhibitors in their place by refusing point-blank to serve them. Fox employed a different strategy. By removing original titles, "The She Tiger," "Sink or Swim," etc.

and substituting titles entirely different, "The Love Thief," "The Yankee Way," etc., he sold as new issues pictures the theatres had shown before.

Conditions in the studios were even more chaotic than in the field. Monied interests demanded a reduction in salaries to stars. Production heads staged talent raids by offering performers well publicized by a competitive firm three to ten times their current earnings. Some stars were given $50,000 merely for signing a contract. Often the new agreement carried the clause, "If you can get out of your present contract sooner, we will be glad to have you start your new contract then." This practice encouraged bursts of temperament and bad acting for which a star either was given an increase to go on with his picture in good spirits or he was released to accept the new offer. On the other hand, studios maintained a "salary check list" which prevented a salary increase to freelance performers during layoff periods. These unknowns, eager to prove their histrionic ability, were employed by the day only to discover a day meant anywhere from eight to eighteen hours. They were hired for one picture and, while waiting for a change of scene, asked to do bits in another.

James Stuart Blackton, unable to cope with the plots and counterplots, left for England, where he hoped his knowledge of United States production methods and operation might aid the competitors of Lord Beaverbrook, Adolph's Zukor's British partner.

At Famous Players, Zukor, who until this time had avoided a clash with the bankers, was in a bitter one with their representative H. D. H. Connick. Under Connick's supervision, Famous Players' personnel suffered constant changes and rearrangement. Connick now announced new policies and spoke of Famous Players' aims. As his voice grew louder, Zukor's voice became lower. Their conflict was paraphrased in a song, "Oh, say can you see by Connick's red glare that so far he has failed, and Zukor's still there."

At Metro, Marcus Loew announced that Richard Rowland, president and Joseph Engel, treasurer, had resigned. Loew offered only one explanation for the retirement of these old-timers: he, Loew, was first and last a theatre man, he had not entered production to conquer new worlds, but as a matter of self-preservation, and he would gladly swap Metro for the Zukor theatres. However, late in 1920, Marcus Loew stopped the theatre building that had been rampant for about a year in his organization.

Aaron Jones had seen enough. A man's business wasn't his own any more! He decided to retire while he might still dispose of his holdings without dictation. One by one, the Jones, Linick, and Schaeffer Theatres, once the largest circuit in the mid-west, were leased to other theatre operators or for other purposes. Balaban & Katz, now Chicago's big fry, took over most of them and inherited the Associated First National franchise.

Rumblings among Associated First National franchise holders indicated that sub-franchise holders were not receiving the protection they had anticipated. Jacob Fabian, speaking for the executive board, issued the statement, "We intended to value 'Mighty Lak A Rose" at $300,000 and only put a valuation of $500,000 on it so YOUR company would not sustain a loss on other pictures." When the exhibitors were billed, the rate was at a $600,000 valuation. The Fabian statement left them somewhat confused because almost every picture came through at increased valuations. Where were the promised free pictures? That something brewed was obvious. At a meeting, the Associated First National board of directors appointed Richard Rowland general sales manager to assist Williams. The connections of Rowland were somewhat enigmatic. In partnership with his brother-in-law, James Clarke, he owned the First National franchise for Western Pennsylvania, although he was known to disagree with the policies set by Clarke in Pittsburgh, where they operated a dozen theatres. Through James Steele, also a stockholder in the Rowland and Clarke Theatres, he had representation on Famous Players-Lasky's board of directors for, while Steele no longer held an executive post in the company, he still retained sufficient stock to remain a director. For a decade Rowland had been a business ally of Godsol, and, while with Metro, he had tried to bring about an amalgamation of that company with Goldwyn Pictures. From the industry's earliest days, things had a way of changing when Rowland was around. He had been the first to capitulate to the Edison-Kennedy-Kleine trust, and his company was one of the few well paid when the Trust took over. Jaydee accepted Rowland as his assistant with his usual grace but hinted how he felt in a speech at a Chicago dinner, where he said that an unwritten law in film circles in New York decreed that unless a man had control of the stock of a corporation he could not hold a high executive post in that organ-

ization for more than three years. He concluded his speech by point-
ing out that both he and Schwalbe had overstayed their time.

In a court action, Triangle stockholders charged that Harry
Aitken had depleted the company's funds. They claimed that "stock
which had been underwritten at 10¢ a share had been sold at $8
a share, that Harry Aitken had wasted and diverted from the treasury
at least a million dollars and had transferred without consideration
to the Western Import Company, which he controlled, Triangle
assets worth $400,000." On the witness stand, Aitken's vocabulary
was limited to, "I do not remember." Inasmuch as other stockholders remembered, Aitken settled out of court for $1,375,000. In
an effort to give the impression that Triangle had assets and inspire
a market for the stock, Aitken sued Stephen Lynch for an accounting.
The strategy failed and Triangle was forced into involuntary bankruptcy. His memory and his business were not his only losses. About
town his wife was the constant companion of H. D. H. Connick.
However, she also suffered a loss. One evening while she and
Connick danced at a road house jewelry worth many thousands of
dollars was stolen from her.

Two court actions involved Pat Powers. A suit for commissions
was instituted by stockbrokers who had handled the sale of shares
in his Rochester plant. A public desirous of easy money was convinced that the Powers' raw stock securities would fall heir to the
phenomenal rise that had attended Eastman Kodak. When Powers
saw the clamor for his shares, he withdrew sales rights from the
brokers and filled the orders himself. In the second case, a judgment
of $51,400.58 was awarded in favor of the U. S. Printing and Litho-
graphing Company against Powers and the Warners for credit
granted by the plaintiff during a period of the Powers-Warner
partnership. This judgment broke the Warners, who moved their
offices three times in one year and closed the West Coast plant that
Abe had opened so hopefully with the profits from Ambassador
Gerard's picture.

Hiram Abrams too was hailed into court. Like Aitken, he suffered
loss of memory. The full story of United Artists was told, and the
public learned that the idea that led to the luncheon at the Hotel
Alexander of the Big-4, Charlie Chaplin, Mary Pickford, David
Wark Griffith, and Douglas Fairbanks, had been born in the brain
of Bennie Schulberg. Awed by Abrams' executive ability, Bennie

was satisfied, when the dream became a reality, to let Abrams run things, provided he received his share of the profits. Arrangements were verbal, and when Bennie returned from his European trip, he found it necessary to bring his "partner" into court to refresh his memory.

George Eastman almost exposed the industry to a serious investigation, but as soon as the Government charged Eastman with running a monopoly, he disposed of his holdings in Sen Jacq. He said he had entered the developing field only as an object lesson to make independent laboratory operators (by Brulatour called "jelly fish") understand their responsibilities.

Will Hays
Needed The Money

To ADD TO THE PANDEMONIUM, Massachusetts, Connecticut, New York, Pennsylvania, West Virginia, Ohio, and other states threatened rigid censorship. Such clouds brought together the producers who glorified the bathing beauty, picturized the suicide attempt of a jilted actress, made a star of a murderess and, according to William Allen White, "made a nasty sex thing out of my book." Controls of this character might not only rob pictures of entertainment value but might dangerously increase political patronage. In Pennsylvania the state allotment rose from $2,700 a year in 1911 to $76,640 in 1920. At the suggestion of Adolph Zukor, William A. Brady was engaged to educate the people of the United States on censorship evils and to combat the efforts of politicians to bring it about. With pompous speeches that revealed little, Brady toured the country. Wherever he went he gave in to at least one point raised by local politicians. In one town he agreed that children under sixteen should not be admitted to a motion picture theatre. Always his concessions proved costly to exhibitors and of little consequence to producers. Infuriated independent theatre owners claimed he not only played politics, but that he played it as Adolph Zukor's stooge, pleading Zukor's cause, and they engaged their own spokesman, New York State Senator, James J. Walker.

Walker, who was given a retainer of $1,000 a month, not only pleaded for the bathing beauty and other risque scenes, but exposed what he called "trustifications" and urged cooperation between the various branches of the industry. He accused a fellow senator of accepting a $100,000 bribe from major motion picture interests and, in turn, was accused of accepting his retainer from independents while serving as Senator and even during a period of two and a half months when he was ill and performed no service. Name-calling, instead of bring about cooperation, increased bitterness.

Tragedies and scandals added to the unsettled state of affairs. In Washington, D.C., ninety-five persons were killed when the roof of Harry Crandall's Knickerbocker Theatre caved in after a snowstorm. The nation was shocked to read of the deaths of Wallace Reid, the screen's greatest idol, and Olive Thomas, talented and beautiful wife of Jack Pickford, Mary's brother. Both had been poisoned by narcotics. That narcotics played an important part in the social structure of Hollywood soon became apparent. William Desmond Taylor, a director, was found murdered. Although his murderer was never brought to trial, evidence was strong that extortion and drugs figured in the crime. The names of many women were linked with that of Taylor, among them the comedienne Mable Normand and the blue-eyed Mary Miles Minter, who was arrested four times in one day for driving irregularities, even though her $1,300,000 contract with Zukor and Lasky carried a clause that her innocence must never be questioned.

One scandal followed another. Harry Cohn, producer of a movie comic strip was named corespondent in the divorce action of John Howard Cromwell against his young wife. Valiantly Cohn tried to save the position of Mrs. Cromwell. On the witness stand he said he could not have written a letter brought in as evidence because he did not know how to spell "rhinitis," and he did not know the meaning of the word. Before the final curtain, Rose Barker Cromwell became Rose Barker Cohn.

The names of a director and a star, both male, were linked. Contributing to juvenile delinquency was a frequent charge against directors and booking agents. Hollywood became known as the modern city of iniquity. So many lurid stories, some true, some untrue, were spread, producers warned all, players, directors, craftsmen, to mend their ways, only to be told to keep their own linen clean.

Max Spiegel, son-in-law of the deceased Mitchell Mark, was found guilty of raising $400,000 by forging stock certificates. His family apologized for the incident by committing him to an insane asylum and his mother-in-law, Mrs. Mitchell Mark, made partial restitution to those who had been swindled.

In 1917, four years before, a stag dinner was given to honor "Fatty" Arbuckle, a leading screen comic, at Boston's Copley Plaza Hotel. About midnight, when everyone began to yawn, a young Boston attorney suggested that the party move on to a cozy little place at East Woburn. About twenty of the men, among them Adolph Zukor, Jesse Lasky, and Hiram Abrams, went. At Mishawum Manor, the resort, ten or twelve young women greeted them. When the party broke up at four in the morning, a bill of $1,050 was paid. The men left, satisfied all obligations had been met and that everyone present had had a good time. About six or eight weeks after the dinner, Daniel H. Coakley, a young Boston attorney, informed the motion picture executives that, with the assistance of his friend, Nathan Tufts, District Attorney of Middlesex County, Massachusetts, and $100,000, he would be able to settle without notoriety breach of promise suits arising out of the Mishawum revels. At this time, Zukor was negotiating with Wall Street. Rather than scare off bankers, he settled.

Who or why the matter was dug up in 1921 remains a mystery. Whether politicians were out to get Tufts, who was removed from office as a result of the publicity, or whether someone in New England had a grudge against Famous Players-Lasky, Zukor in particular, has never been definitely determined publicly. Whatever the reason, the story broke unfortunately for "Fatty" Arbuckle. At the time, another scandal in which he was involved was front-page news on every paper in the United States. He was on trial in San Francisco in connection with the death of Virginia Rappe while he was having sexual intercourse with her. Although acquitted of rape and murder, the scandal ruined the comedian.

Lack of discretion and harmony existed everywhere. Wall Street regretted it had become involved with businessmen who considered themselves artistic and who were, therefore, impossible to control. Exhibitors cried, "Trustifications." Graft to members of various fire departments was exposed. Unions were demanding increased pay and shorter hours for craft and unskilled workers. Mechanics and technicians called periodic strikes. Theatre musicians stated they had been discharged when they asked for one day off each week. Salary kickbacks were revealed. Reformers demanded censorship. A district attorney threatened to prosecute when one press agent arranged the fake suicide of an actress and had the police drag a lake for two days and another arranged the fake kidnaping of an acrtess. A third agent

sued for reimbursement of $8,000 he spent to please the Creel Com-
mittee in getting Italians to kneel down and pray to President Wilson
as they did to saints.

Standard Oil, Harriman, and Astor money had gone into pictures.
With the stock break caused by the Arbuckle-Rappe scandal, The
Street as a whole wished it might find a way out without loss of face.
Money tightened. Interest ran up to sixty per cent with twenty-five
and thirty per cent the average. All motion picture issues dropped.
Famous Players fell from 90 to 40. Goldwyn broke to 4, and the du
Ponts, who were unwilling to stave off the trend as long as Sam
Goldwyn retained his stock, allowed him to gain control. Loew's hit
10. This was one situation producers were not able to laugh off.
Again they met; then announced that motion pictures would emulate
baseball with a self-appointed arbiter.

Through the grapevine, word leaked out that a member of the
cabinet of Warren Gamaliel Harding had been asked to take the
job. The Democrats proclaimed the whole set-up was nothing but a
deal between the administration and the industry. Reformers, however,
considered the rumored name a victory, as the man was known to be
a church-goer. Democrats kept protesting. Private citizens urged an
investigation be made into the practices of motion picture lobbyists.
And, all the while, small theatre men worried. The arbiter was to
receive $100,000 a year plus a $15,000 expense account. From whom
would the money come? The only explanation they received was "A
good man comes high."

The "good man" turned out to be Will H. Hays, who was giving
up the $12,000 a-year job as Postmaster General, with which he had
been rewarded for carrying the Harding campaign to a successful
conclusion. His $100,000 contract stipulated that he might step down
anytime he wished, but no one had the power to relieve him before
the contract expired.

On the evening of March 16, 1922, Will Hays was introduced
to his new associates at a banquet at the Hotel Astor. Present were
1,500 persons, among them the Secretary of Labor, J. J. Davis;
John F. Hylan, Mayor of the City of New York; Arthur Brisbane,
Hearst editor; Channing Pollock, reformer. Mr. Hays rose to speak.
His nose was long and thin, his upper lip protruded, his ears stood
away from his head. The audience did not stir. All listened attentively
to hear what this man had to say, for on his words hung the fate

of a great industry. His speech was long. Here is part of it:

"I received the offer out of the sky from gentlemen I do not know personally, for whom I have never done anything, and to whom I have as yet never promised anything except my best efforts to cooperate in making pictures more worthy of such a huge industry and such sincerely right-minded men as appear to dominate it.

"I have no political affiliations of any kind in this work, and no one has asked me to have. There is nothing I know of that pictures want of the national administration.

"I hope to help develop the highest moral and constructive efficiency in films, but will be neither a censor nor a reformer, as the words are properly understood.

"I have no leaning toward eradicating sex from pictures. It would eradicate interest from pictures, and when pictures have no interest they can do nothing because no one will see them.

"I am against improper censorship of pictures as much as I am against improper censorship of the press or pulpit.

"I admit that I am floundering around at present, and do not know exactly what I shall propose beyond the primary principles underlying all such proposals.

"I have been asked about such things as uniform release prices, franchises being held up to keep out competition, etc., about all of which I know absolutely nothing— but I hope to find out, and when I do, my advice along these lines will be guided by the same ideals as my views on other phases of the business— square dealing and the good of the majority always come first.

"I believe that the leading producers can dictate a tone of production which will force less responsible and less organized producers to follow clean, worthy standards.

"I know nothing about the technical end of pictures, either manufacturing, exhibiting, or distributing. I hope to learn, however, and right now I am going to school like a child to master this great industry of art, science, and commerce.

"I accepted my post for three reasons — first, because it offered a chance to engage in a public service; second, because it offered a chance to retire from politics; third, because I needed the money."

Will Hays Tackles His Job

WILL HAYS' STATEMENT THAT ONE OF THE REASONS he had agreed to become "High Arbiter" was because it offered him a chance to retire from politics must have tickled the funny bone of William Gibbs McAdoo, who, to escape film madness, had gone back into politics.

Although the Federal Government among other things inquired into mergers, and national censorship threatened, Mr. Hays knew of nothing that pictures want of the national administration. Inasmuch as he had so much to learn, adjustment to the life of a schoolchild kept Mr. Hays busy. As assistants Mr. Hays appointed Courtland Smith, brother-in-law of Arthur Brisbane, and Charles C. Pettijohn, a native of his home state, Indiana. For their advisory ability they were to receive $25,000 yearly. Another of his staff was Thomas Patten, former Postmaster of New York City. Later, Carl E. Milliken, former Governor of the State of Maine, was made secretary of the organization. Independents, ever fearful of producer-distributor moves, were frightened by the mere name of the new Hays' organization, Motion Picture Producers & Distributors of America, Inc.

Assisted by Charles Pettijohn, who had fought against block booking when he represented independent theatre owners, Hays drafted a standard block booking sales contract form. Exhibitors did not trust it, but they agreed to try it out. Whenever it came time to sign up for product they found themselves between the devil and the deep blue sea. They had just come through a season in which Famous Players-Lasky had let them have pictures on a percentage basis. The contract carried a minimum guarantee that

235

covered each picture's normal flat rental, allowed Famous Players to fix admission scales, and gave the distributor, but not the exhibitor, the right to change playing dates.

The Chicago territory had a problem of its own which Hays was expected to solve. Balaban & Katz, now a powerful organization controlled by the five Balaban and two Katz brothers, demanded a sixty-day protection clause. Men who had applauded the Hays appointment were not making life easy for him. Sam Spring, First National general counsel, in a "pep talk," advised salesmen to "make the exhibitor squeal, holler, yell. Make him call the police and the fire department, but get better prices. The good salesman is one who can sell poor pictures; anyone can sell good pictures." And Jaydee, the former exhibitor, proclaimed, "I will make exhibitors the janitors of their own theatres."

Coupled with its other woes, the industry again was in a depressed state. Hard times, an aftermath of the war, made itself felt at the box office. Only fourteen cameramen turned their cranks in Hollywood. Retrenchment was obvious everywhere. Winnie Sheehan, now the balance of power between Fox and his Prudential Life Insurance friends, before he started on a trip to the branches, made a list of those to be erased from the payrolls of each Fox office after he left it and while he was enroute to another city. In this manner he was not available for comment. The Universal staff was cut to the bone. Joe "Universal" Brandt became plain Joe Brandt, an independent producer. Famous Players-Lasky, Loew, and Goldwyn drastically reduced their personnel. Several studios shut down completely. Extras went back to the bread lines or drifted into other occupations. Salaries of actors and directors were slashed from 25% to 75%. Panic seized everyone not under contract. Directors, few of whom in this star era had contracts, were the hardest hit, a number going from $2,000 to $500 a week.

Speeches became the order of the day; loyalty, the keynote. Employees in all departments were reminded of the loyalty they owed their corporations. Anyone who did not evidence loyalty by accepting a cut in salary had a blackball against his name, a ball that might bounce at any time, perhaps at the expiration of a contract. The high salaries of actors and actresses were given as the main reason for the industry's lack of profit. However, many office and studio officials had incomes, which included bonuses and stock rights that ran up to $1,000,000 a year.

The "High Arbiter" was not expected to concern himself with salaries while stories that degraded the industry persisted. Frank Tilley, an English editor, wrote that in Hollywood he found, "an unholy alliance of favoritism, incompetence, and graft at the studios, which prevent a showing of box office profits." Hearst, the newspaper man, ignored Hearst, the producer, and ran a campaign in his publications against narcotics, still easily obtainable in the film capital. The head of a fake school of picture-acting was charged with impairing a minor's morals. One producer paid the husband of a star to keep the star's scandals a secret. The parties and life of Hollywood personalities continued to provide sensational material for spicy magazines.

Hays left for the West Coast. There he told players and producers alike that he wanted "the city to be a model industrial center." He set restrictions on costumes, said who might and who might not wear sweaters, and asked all to respect the national Prohibition Act. Satisfied he had done a clean-up job, Hays returned east, only to have another bomb burst. The chauffeur of Mabel Normand, one of the actresses exonerated in the Taylor murder, shot and seriously wounded C. S. Dines, Denver oil man, vacationing on the West Coast. H. A. Kelly, alias Horace A. Greer, the chauffeur, said that when he walked into the Dines' apartment, he found "Miss Normand was in no condition to stay longer," and asked her to leave with him. Dines, clad in underclothes and socks, tried to prevent her, and the only way Kelly was able to get her out was to shoot Dines. Although others were present, including another actress, Edna Purviance, no one except Kelly remembered exactly what had taken place. To use Kelly's expression, "They were all hopped up."

Rumors of a rift between Zukor and Lasky spread. Zukor had Lasky "on the carpet" for the manner in which their Vine Street lot was always out in front in the big scandals.

Distraught, Hays announced he would ban pictures of performers involved in scandals. The Normand and Purviance pictures, however, were not banned. He arranged special showings for children; he asked producers to cease making pictures that might be offensive to the American public; he lined up women's organizations, rotary clubs, and civic groups in his drive to lessen public animosity.

Nevertheless, fear of censorship increased. The industry mobilized to forestall restrictive legislation, and the intensity applied to this task led Dr. Crofts, chairman of the Federal Interstate Motion Picture Commission, which had the backing of the Rockefeller Foundation, to charge that legislators had been intimidated.

In the drive against censorship, H. D. H. Connick went up to Albany to see Governor Miller. "Our business," he said in a prepared statement, "is purely manufacturing, distribution, and exhibition," and then contradicting a statement by Zukor that Famous Players-Lasky "has only a few theatres, surprisingly few," he went on to say, "We are, I presume the biggest theatre owners in the world. We have over four hundred theatres in this country and Canada, and we have $65,000,000 invested between our holding companies and our subsidiaries. We have 140 subsidiaries, and they would add up to about $65,000,000. These theatres are not little bits of cellars, nor are they downstairs. We have theatre holdings costing two-and-a-half-million, and we have one project on Broadway which will probably cost us $8,000,000. It will be a thirty-story building. We are building and building all the time. We have just completed $8,000,000 worth of theatres in Canada in the last few months. This is not a sentiment with us. This is a business. We are going to get shot if we don't pay dividends. You know what they do with a corporation in Wall Street that don't pay dividends? They take him out and stand him against the wall, and that is the end of him."

That little speech, while it did not save the industry from censorship in New York State, did cost Connick his $50,000-a-year job as chairman of the Famous Players-Lasky Finance Committee.

Within a short time, just by standing pat, Zukor had conquered two foes, Connick and Selznick. Selznick's company was in such bad straits, Sam Morris preferred to cast his lot with the struggling Warner brothers. Charles C. Pettijohn now spoke for Mr. Hays and, through Mr. Hays, for large successful producers. In his most persuasive oratory, Mr. Pettijohn told independent exhibitors that he gave up speaking for them because they were unable to pay him enough.

Reestablished as the "Little Chief," Zukor saw no need for Realart and the extra distribution expense it entailed. A wire was dispatched to exchange managers giving them twenty-four hours in which to discharge their staffs, turn over all prints and accounts to Famous

Players-Lasky, and close their offices. Sidney Kent, who had stood staunchly by, was made the "Little Chief's" spokesman. He picked up where Lynch and Black had left off, and his sledge-hammer tactics frightened exhibitors and producers alike. One picture did not reach second-run houses until a year after its initial showing. When he was asked if exhibitors would be compelled to show all pictures under the percentage arrangement, he retorted, "It's coming as sure as hell. There is no way out. Imagine the pin-headed attitude of men who don't believe it!" What at first appeared to be a friendly gesture also proved to hold sinister implications. In the Rocky Mountain section, Famous Players offered product at reduced rates. Subsequent developments revealed that Kent had sent a letter to the branch manager at Denver, where Vitagraph still had a foothold, in which he said, "I want you to kick out every Vitagraph account you can find, irrespective of the terms you have to make just so you cancel the contract and get them out of the way."

Albert Smith had brought his old friend, James Stuart Blackton, who had had little luck in England where the market was on the verge of cracking up, back into Vitagraph. In a triple-action suit under the Sherman Anti-Trust Law, they listed damages to the extent of $2,000,000, based on the claim that the defendants conspired to control a large number of first-run theatres for the purpose of restraining trade and suppressing competition.

Hays found that to create an impression of stability was increasingly difficult. As if the $6,000,000 claim of Smith and Blackton were not enough, his job was further complicated by the many changes and constant moving about of big names. Lichtman went from place to place before he ended up as assistant to Hiram Abrams. Schulberg floated around until Zukor reengaged him. Richard Rowland became First National's general manager, and William's prophecy came true; he and Schwalbe were ousted. Joseph Schenck shifted distribution on his pictures from First National to United Artists, where he took on the title of president. Louis B. Mayer, who had devoted all his time to production, went from First National back to Metro. Sol Lesser, through his West Coast Theatres, took over the Turner and Dahnken houses and, with them, the First National franchise for northern California. Pat Powers, who had retired to open a golf course which catered to a restricted clientele, found the golfers too dull, the life lacking in excitement, and bought into two English concerns operating in the United States, Robertson-Cole and Film Booking Offices. Hearst transferred his feature picture productions and the accompanying newspaper space from the Lasky lot to the Goldwyn lot.

The du Ponts, in a coup, regained control of the Goldwyn Picture Corporation. They appointed Godsol president in Goldwyn's place. Godsol, who had bought an interest in the Tecla Pearl Corporation and had placed his wife in charge of its management, arrived at his office at seven each morning and worked until midnight, and then made a round of speakeasies and gambling houses before retiring for three or four hours' sleep. When he arrived at his office in the morning he jammed dollar cigars into the mouths of assistants still suffering from morning mouth. He demanded that these assistants display even greater attachment to their jobs than he did to his, despite the fact that his was made easier by a retinue of valets, maids, secretaries, masseurs, barbers and bookies, who even accompanied him on cross-country trips. He boasted that he would produce better pictures than Samuel Goldwyn at less cost. On the other hand, in contrast to Goldwyn, who was always short of money because he had no pockets in which to carry it, Godsol's pockets bulged with the money he carried.

Goldwyn turned independent and through First National released the Samuel Goldwyn pictures. The Goldwyn Company, which had spent $30,000,000 on productions and $24,000,000 on publicizing the Goldwyn name, sued to restrain Sammy from using "Goldwyn" on his pictures. The judge who presided in the case, unwilling to deprive a man of a name to which he had contributed so much, ordered him to state in any advertising, "Not connected with Goldwyn Pictures Corporation."

Selznick, to placate creditors, turned over Select and Selznick Pictures to his two sons, making Myron president and David vice-president of both corporations. Extravagance had caught up with Lewis; young blood at the helm did not save his corporations. His productions had been among the most garish, the most costly; his advertising the most spectacular. In his heyday, a Selznick electric sign blazed on every corner of the Great White Way. Before his sons were out of their teens he paid them handsome salaries. He never questioned a usurer's rate of interest. Suddenly, he had no need to; his companies were bankrupt. The usual list of pitiful stories followed. One woman lost $26,000, her entire fortune. She had bought Selznick stock that had been offered by the American Fiscal Company, when Charles C. Pettijohn was the lawyer. An old woman, who earned $17 a week, lost her savings of $500 and $250, which she had borrowed when she was told her $500 would go if she did not put up the additional amount. The Selznick family did not seem to be in want. One son, David, was betrothed to the daughter of Louis B. Mayer of the Metro Company. Lewis still resided in his $18,000-a-year Park Avenue apartment and travelled around in a Rolls Royce. And he was just as nonchalant as when his stock issue was offered for sale, at which time he had informed exhibitors, "Henceforth it is up to you whether this stock will be worth a million or nothing. If we work with and for each other, we will split a fortune. If we split hairs, I lose a lot of time, a little money, and both of us lose a big bite on opportunity."

Poor Will Hays! Things moved so fast for the $100,000 a year schoolboy. To make matters worse, reformers who had once hailed him for his standing as a churchgoer, now said he was a mere blind for the industry.

The Producers Strike

T HE LYNCH, BLACK, CONNICK, VITAGRAPH PUBLICITY was not
to the taste of Adolph Zukor. To close a deal was one thing;
to have details of the deal spread abroad was another. When a
group of theatre owners complained to him, Zukor promised that
wrongs would be righted. He kept his promise by demanding the
resignation of Lynch and Black and placing their circuits under
the direct supervision of Famous Players' home office. To be rid
of the triple action suit, Zukor agreed to play a year's output of the
Vitagraph studios in first-run houses in key cities.

But Zukor had acted too late. So many reports had circulated,
the Federal Trade Commission opened an inquiry to determine
whether or not the character of the business conducted by Famous
Players-Lasky constituted a monopoly. The company was charged
with:

(a) Threatening to build or lease or to operate theatres in competition with exhibitors who refused to sell or lease their houses;

(b) Threatening to cut off or interfere with the film service of
such exhibitors who refused to sell or lease their theatres;

(c) Secretly offering higher rentals, effective upon expiration of
leases held by exhibitors who refused to sell or lease such
theatres;

(d) Temporarily reducing the price of admission charged by
theatre owners and controlled by the respondents below that
charged by exhibitors who refused to sell or lease their theatres;

(e) And of attempting to coerce and intimidate motion picture

242

theatre owners or exhibitors by divers means and methods including block booking.

Former employees and associates were among those called to the stand. Al Lichtman testified that from the start Zukor sought to merge the functions of producer, exhibitor, and distributor, and that survival was almost impossible for the small producer. "He is like a man in a strange city who wants to gamble," Lichtman (who always related a story to illustrate a point) said, "and is told there is only one gambling house in the place and it is crooked. Just the same he takes a chance and wins $1,000. But on the way out he is confronted, and all but $100 is taken from him."

Alfred S. Black admitted he paid less rental to Famous Players-Lasky than to other companies.

William Wadsworth Hodkinson said independent producers could not approach the United States market via Broadway showings, a practice which had become important because of prestige value, as New York's first-run theatres were under the domination of the principal companies, Famous Players-Lasky, First National, Goldwyn, and Metro.

Hiram Abrams revealed why Hodkinson had received only two votes, his own and Pawley's, at the 1916 meeting. Zukor, immediately upon receipt of the wire in which Lichtman informed him of Hodkinson's plan to sign up all Paramount producers except Famous Players-Lasky, dropped everything at the West Coast studios and returned East. Upon his arrival in New York, Zukor went into conference with Lichtman, Abrams, and Greene at his Riverside Drive apartment. There, Abrams agreed to line up Steele and Sherry for the vote against Hodkinson.

From William Sherry came a version of his experience. In his merger with Paramount, the agreement provided that he would retain the franchise for the New York Exchange, the most profitable in the chain, receive a block of stock, a weekly salary of $1,000, and two percent of the New York profits. Sherry received the stock and the salary, but Zukor delayed signing the contract. In the meantime Zukor asked Sherry to distribute an independent picture he had backed, "Joan The Woman." When Sherry told Zukor he did not like the picture, Zukor promised to make good any loss. Under these conditions Sherry agreed to take the picture for $125,000, $100,000 in cash and $25,000 in a note. To raise the $100,000

Sherry placed his block of Paramount stock, worth several hundred thousands dollars as collateral. In the meantime. Paramount stock dropped and the banker, to cover the loan, sold Sherry out. The transaction made him so nervous, Zukor advised him to take a vacation. When he returned, Zukor took over the operation of the New York Exchange, transferred Sherry to the purchasing department, and cut his salary from $1,000 a week plus a percentage of profits to $250 a week. A short time later Sherry resigned. Sherry tried to reestablish himself as a states' right exhibitor, but he was unable to meet the competition of the big companies. He asked Zukor to make good his promise. Instead Zukor advanced $15,000 as a loan and cancelled the $25,000 note. Thereupon Sherry signed an agreement in which he waived all other claims. Unable to meet the $15,000, Sherry gave up all attempts to make a comeback and went to Florida to live.

Independents complained that Famous Players-Lasky would not look at their pictures and told of their difficulties in getting their product into even smaller Famous Players-Lasky houses.

The Dodges, the Beanes, and others told how they lost their theatres.

Connick too, poured out his heart. He spoke of Zukor's ambition, his sense of superiority.

"What do you mean," he was asked, "by superiority?"

"Superiority is domination," Connick answered.

"Then you would say, wouldn't you, that Caruso dominated the opera field?"

"God Almighty had a lot to do with Caruso, but He had nothing to do with Famous Players," Connick answered vehemently.

Others testified that Zukor planned to make his control worldwide; that he even tried to invade India.

Col. Alvin Owsley, National Commander of the American Legion, testified that during the war he had made a study of the American soldier in Europe. He found that in four million men, one out of every five could not read the English language. In his efforts to determine the easiest way to teach these men, he found the motion picture the best medium. Upon his return to the United States he wanted to continue his efforts to reduce illiteracy, but found it impossible to lease theatres for this purpose.

During the investigation the fact was established that rental prices had increased 400% in a short period of time.

Zukor followed his usual policy and made no comment. Two important witnesses, agents for the Federal Trade Commission which conducted the inquiry, were scheduled to appear against him. With word that Holland Hudson, one of the investigators, due to overwork was threatened with lung trouble and was not able to testify because he had gone to Saranac Lake, Zukor made no comment. Neither did Zukor have anything to say when the other investigator, William E. Clark, advised the Commission that he could not run around and testify because his physician said he had heart trouble and was to confine himself to desk work.

Pete S. Harrison, publisher of *Harrison's Reports*, a four-page paper in which he fought for better pictures and more equitable deals for independents, asked, "Has someone paid hush money to stop the Famous Players-Lasky investigation?" Pictures not of a Broadway first-run quality were frequently released in other parts of the country weeks and even months before they were shown in New York City to avoid the Pete Harrison criticisms.

Huston Thompson, Chairman of the Federal Trade Commission, averred that pressure had been brought to bear upon him, and the name of George B. Christian, President Harding's secretary, was mentioned in connection with the disposition of the case.

Variety stated that stories circulated in the trade to the effect that "Will Hays might have something to do with the squaring." Will Hays who had said he knew nothing that "pictures want of the National Administration," and who knew nothing about the industry, but "would go to school like a child to learn," had no time to answer his critics. The one thing he had learned was that his job required him to win good will for his members, and he kept his public utterances to statements pointed toward that end. Producers did little to simplify life for him.

Talk along Film Row soon switched from the Famous Players' case to picture-buying. A year's protection for Deluxe houses which presented "road shows" at high admissions became common practice. Fox advised his customers that he would willingly permit them to reject two pictures, "The Net" and "Does It Pay", if they so desired. Sidney S. Cohen, owner of five neighborhood theatres in New York, suspicious of Fox's generosity, pleaded with exhibitors to watch their step. "The Fox pictures," he said, "must be good, and Fox undoubtedly hopes to get higher rentals for them. He's a business man — not a philanthropist."

Sidney Kent followed Fox with the announcement that Famous Players pictures were to be had on the open market, that they might be seen before buying. Optimists, who refused to allow cynics to influence them, argued that Famous Players needed good will. Soon Kent's actual intention became obvious. If Famous Players-Lasky presented its pictures as pre-release showings in large centers and accompanied these showings with spectacular exploitation campaigns, the company would be able to get increased prices for its product by basing prices on the receipts stimulated by these drives. Or, with its pictures free from contractual obligations, Famous Players, by calling its own theatres "demonstration laboratories," might give all pictures "pre-release" showings across the country. In this manner it controlled all first-runs under the excuse that this was a means of presenting new product to customers, thereby giving theatres something for which they long had fought, the right to see before buying.

The situation reversed itself, exactly as it had when Kent previously had announced that Famous Players intended to release pictures under a percentage arrangement because "percentage is not good for the lazy." To check the receipts of exhibitors playing percentage pictures, the Hays office organized the Federal Checking Bureau. In their reversal of attitude, exhibitors fought for block booking; they agreed to accept a dozen, two dozen "lemons" if only they might get one good picture. They hardly said, "Boo," when "World Struggle For Oil," a propaganda picture produced by the Sinclair Oil Company of Tea Pot Dome fame, was offered to them. Outside pressure alone saved them from the film.

The standard contract form was so loosely worded, litigation was constant. All exhibitors asked that it be modified. Charles C. Pettijohn, who had helped Will Hays draft the form, informed the theatre owners, "The producers are going to use the uniform contract regardless of what exhibitors think of it. Many contracts have been printed. We can't make up new ones every few days."

After this speech, Pettijohn set out on a country-wide tour and, under the auspices of The Motion Picture Producers and Distributors of America, Inc., popularly known as the Hay's office, he established arbitration boards or Film Boards of Trade. Exhibitors commented that arbitration is not supposed to be compulsory; to force anyone to surrender his constitutional rights of trial by jury is against the law. Nevertheless, for opening the arbitration offices, Pettijohn's salary was increased to $34,000 a year under contract. The salary of Hays, his boss, who was given a ten-year contract, breakable by him but not by the producers, was reputed to be $150,000. The appropriation for the organization was increased to $1,000,000 a year.

Independent exhibitors, when told that any who criticized productions would be disciplined, threatened to strike; instead they organized into large buying combines. When they did, the producers went on strike; one and all refused to sell any group composed of small theatre owners.

Merger   Madness

THE ECONOMIES THE DU PONT GROUP hoped to see with the ousting of Samuel Goldwyn failed to materialize. Under Godsol, production costs rose until the sales department could not possibly set prices high enough to cover them, and the du Ponts point blank refused to put additional monies into the tottering firm.

That Marcus Loew desired to occupy Zukor's throne was a thinly veiled secret. Never was time more opportune. The children, Arthur and Mildred, were not getting along. Talk of their separation took some of the family pressure off Loew. With the government at his heels, Zukor dared not make any move to extend his holdings. Loew bought the stock of Frank Godsol and William Braden and merged the Goldwyn Company with Metro. "Elimination of waste," was the announced purpose of the amalgamation. The Cosmopolitan Productions of William Randolph Hearst were included in the deal. Hearst, who announced that the public had been played down to long enough, was an asset although his pictures, also produced for a mental age of twelve, never were a box office success. He had considerable political influence in California and in New York. He was, in fact, about to place his hat in New York City's mayoralty race. A Hearst tie-up meant good notices in his newspapers, which at the time ran articles against monopolies. Most important, when he purchased a story for any of his publications, film rights were included in the publication price. This practice, which the Authors League of America called unfair, gave him something of a monopoly of the film story market. Authors had little to say about their stories once they signed away movie rights. Hope Hampton, actress-wife of Jules Brulatour, sued Fannie Hurst, short story writer, claiming $150,000 damages in a libel action, when Miss Hurst criticized the screen play of her story, "Star Dust."

Mayer too had a good spot in the amalgamation. In fact the combine was named Metro-Goldwyn-Mayer, with Mayer vice-president in charge of production. The little fellow had come to be looked upon as an important factor in production. He had in work a $6,000,000 picture, "Ben Hur." The cost alone caused Mayer and the production to be regarded with awe. Never had anyone dared invest that much in one film. To give it a realistic flavor, it was to be photographed in Italy, but there, authorities created so many obstacles, the filming of this story, first a Kalem* film hit eighteen years before in 1908, and reproduced innumerable times by M-G-M under a variety of titles, among them "Quo Vadis," was eventually completed on one of Hollywood's super-colossal sets. Because Mayer's favorite expression was, "Let there be action!" the picture contained a chariot race more thrilling than any cowboy and Indian chase ever shown in a horse opera. The race Mayer thought was the high spot of the picture. It epitomized his social ambitions. As he became more prosperous, Louis B. Mayer made a point of being seen riding a horse at certain hours. He studied diction and manners. He followed the advice of his attorney and friend, J. Robert Rubin. He entertained lavishly and had his home decorated by highly-paid motion picture set designers. Late in life he changed his religion. But on his face remained an expression as forbidding as the dark stormy surf that had molded his character.

The merger called for a speech. Godsol made it. "Joint distribution," he said, "will put an end to dictation of prices by exhibitors. If a sufficient number of pictures are in the hands of one distributing agency, exhibitors who persist in their strangling methods will soon find themselves facing a shortage of pictures and they will be willing to deal on a fair basis." One aspect of his "fair basis:" If the pictures of one large company (A) were given a break in the non-competing theatres of another large company (B), the circuit of A would reciprocate by placing the pictures of B in its non-competing houses, giving a year's protection; that is, a year would pass before smaller

---

*"Ben Hur" was one of the stories Kleine and his associates used without permission of the author. When sued for copyright infringement, Kleine accused the estate of Lew Wallace of ingratitude for the publicity the author received.

theatres might obtain the films.

As expected, Loew set his heart on a newsreel; Zukor had one, Paramount News. Inasmuch as International was still bound by contract to Universal, Hearst organized Hearst Metrotone News for Loew.

From the floor at a convention of the Theatre Owners Chamber of Commerce the methods of Loew, who considered himself something of a genius, were scathingly assaulted, and he was called a menace. Less emotional members pleaded for him, and he was permitted to resign to save him from the humiliation of expulsion. Thus ended his membership in an organization before which he had once declared that he was first and last a theatre man, that he was not looking for new worlds to conquer, that he would gladly exchange his production unit for Zukor's theatres.

If Zukor's hands were tied, First National's were not. To meet the new industrial colossus, Metro-Goldwyn-Mayer, First National accepted financial aid from an old friend, Dr. A. H. Giannini, president of the Bank of Italy and the Commercial Trust Company. Hayden, Stone, & Company, through one of its partners, Richard B. Hoyt, also came to the company's rescue.

Outside monopolistic competition was not the only threat that faced First National. A similar condition existed within its ranks. Many of its founders had sold their holdings to competitors. Richard Rowland, who had replaced Jaydee Williams, never succeeded in stimulating a sense of pride among new members toward the organization. They had bought into the company because it was a good business investment. They had not fought for its growth and had no sentimental attachments to it. First National's directorate was an example of the intricacy of the motion picture set-up. Nathan H. Gordon, in bad health, sold his thirty-eight New England theatres including his First National franchise to Famous Players-Lasky. The Skourases worked out a booking arrangement, whereby they divided downtown St. Louis with Famous Players and were in partnership with Famous Players in several houses in Indiana. The Saenger and Blank chains, both subsidiaries of Famous Players, held First National franchises. And Sam Katz made no attempt to hide the fact that he was out after the scalps of several of his First National partners.

Sam was only thirty-two. He was still punching hard, trying to tear himself away from any connections with the Chicago ghetto in which he had spent his childhood. He never cared how arrogant he was, whom he hurt, or what anyone thought of him. Assisted by Abe Balaban, who organized the shows, and Barney Balaban, the brains behind their real estate deals, he had stifled competition in Chicago. Now he wanted to do the same thing in Minneapolis and Detroit. However, Finkelstein and Rubin in Minneapolis and Kunsky in Detroit were not novices. They had played some tricks themselves; they had resisted others before Katz. Because of their battles, First National meetings invariably were a tug of war.

Rather than let Sam Katz violate First National's unwritten law, the Board of Directors worked out a compromise whereby Balaban & Katz were permitted to enter into partnership with Kunsky and Finkelstein & Rubin. To forestall further trouble along these lines, a great booking combine was formed. Those included were Balaban & Katz, the Stanley Company of America, Kunsky, the Skourases, Finkelstein & Rubin, the Saenger Circuit, the West Coast chain, and Abe Blank.

Joseph Schenck reviewed the conditions his company faced. Metro-Goldwyn-Mayer had the Loew chain. First National had its franchise holders. Famous Players-Lasky, as Connick had told Governor Miller, had one of the largest circuits in the world. United Artists, nicknamed the "Old Folks' Home," was without screen control. Schenck was a director of the East River Bank of New York and the Bank of Italy, institutions which carried motion picture accounts. Besides access to competitors' accounts, his banking connections gave him an opportunity to analyze business trends. Loew Theatres, where his brother was first vice-president, played along with him, but how long he would be able to count on this outfit with Metro-Goldwyn-Mayer in the picture was a question. If United Artists was to survive it must become a Loew unit.

Douglas Fairbanks, the swashbuckling, broad-jumping matinee idol, was receptive to the proposition; Mary Pickford lukewarm. When Schenck spoke to Charlie Chaplin, the comedian grew thoughtful. He recalled the statement of Sam Katz, "Schenck must come to us with his hat in his hand, and I will not play Chaplin." He recalled his uncertain days as pantomimist on the vaudeville stage, and the $60 weekly salary he sometimes received. He recalled how well nickelodeon proprietors accepted his first pictures. "There are higher aims," he said, "than economy. Honor and independence for example. I do not want to be associated with a trust that will use my pictures as a club to force men into line. Block booking is just a means to foist film junk on the exhibitor. I owe my rise to small theatre owners. I will not keep my pictures from them."

Chaplin insisted that the big chains could not afford to reject good independent product, and he had enough confidence in his talent to sell it on the open market. No power of Wall Street could move this little man who always found a way to help the underdog. His arguments won over Mary Pickford and Douglas Fairbanks.

Universal, lacking the creative ability of a Chaplin, made a desperate attempt to obtain theatre affiliates. The company was too late. All important chains were tied up with producing units that cast Universal into a shadow. The only new accounts Universal succeeded in getting were second-rate vaudeville circuits. Laemmle and Cochrane were practically forced to carry on their policy of complete programs for subsequent run houses. But at times Laemmle must have laughed at his more glorified competitors. He was five times as rich as Marcus Loew; two and a half times as rich as Adolph Zukor.

Loew's Inc. with M-G-M, Famous Players with its many theatres, First National with its franchise holders, completely overshadowed the Fox organization. For the first time in his life, William Fox, with assets of $24,509,470, issued a financial statement. He had to to get the support of Halsey, Stuart & Company, which placed the stock of the Fox Corporation on the Curb Exchange. With coins jingling in his pockets Bill Fox went shopping. His first purchase was an $8,000,000 interest in Lesser's West Coast Theatres. This brought Fox into partnership with First National, as Lesser was a First National franchise holder. Working eastward Fox made theatre deals in St. Louis, Chicago, and Baltimore. In New York he organized two corporations, Fox Interstate Theatres, Inc., and Fox Metropolitan Theatres, Inc. The purpose of these two corporations, which opened sumptuous offices in the Ambassador Hotel, was to acquire a large chain in the east. As a start, options were placed on over a hundred theatres.

Federal Trade Commission or no Federal Trade Commission, Adolph Zukor had seen enough. Like Fox, Sam Katz was reaching out to control a nationwide chain. And Zukor felt Katz might as well control the chain as a Zukor partner. A casual inspection revealed the Balaban & Katz stock had been watered for the deal. The contract included a yearly salary of $150,000 for Sam Katz, who was to take over theatre management. Katz would not go into a new field without his line up—his brother and the five Balabans. Two of the Balabans, Abe, who was to remain in charge of the Chicago territory, and Barney, who was to be brought into New York as a real estate expert, were to get almost as much as Katz.

The defense of trust charges were so costly, Wall Street had informed the industry that money would be available for improvements but not for law suits. To get The Street to consent to a combine of this magnitude, John Hertz, founder of the Yellow Taxi Cab, who had invested heavily in Balaban & Katz, worked out a plan whereby a separate company called Publix would take over all theatres under the joint control of Famous Players-Lasky and Balaban & Katz. Hertz presented this plan to bankers who had financed his taxicab deals and, with their blessings, Publix Theatres came into existence.

Zukor soon discovered that the government was simpler to handle than Sammy Katz. People spoke of the "mad scenes from Balaban & Katz." Of candidates for first place none came close to Sammy. His mental gymnastics were impossible to follow; his actions impossible to anticipate. Although he had not hesitated to water stock for the sale to Famous Players, when the deal was closed he sent a $100,000 check to a Chicago orphanage.

As soon as news of the deal leaked out, Famous Players stock jumped to a new high. All previous successes were dwarfed when compared to the newly formed Publix Company—the *Katzenzukor Outfit*. This giant octopus spread its tentacle and across the country first and second run independent houses vanished. Those theatres that continued to get Famous Players pictures at all received them anywhere from twenty-eight days to one year after first run, because Katz demanded this protection.

On Times Square, on the plot that ran from Forty-third to Forty-fourth Street, appeared the most splendorous theatre the world had ever seen—the Paramount. Its motif was French Renaissance, and no French Renaissance design was omitted. It was built with a lobby to accommodate hundreds of standees when the theatre overflowed. Set in the wall of its Hall of Nations were stones collected wherever Famous Players-Lasky had a foreign office. A thirty-one story office building adjoined the theatre. Kuhn, Loeb & Company, the Hallgarten Company, Marshall Field, and Glore, Ward & Company, offered a $10,000,000 mortgage bond issue on the edifice. So imposing was the theatre, page after page of congratulatory messages appeared in *Variety,* one from Hiram Abrams, who had just died. His instructions to insert the message was one of his last acts, and Al Lichtman, his successor as general manager of United Artists, saw that it appeared. The Famous Players-Lasky Company, itself, was so enamoured by the magnificence of the structure, the name of the company was changed to Paramount, Famous Players-Lasky.

Despite the Hertz plan, the Federal Trade Commission charged an attempted monopoly of film theatres. Experience had taught Zukor that time took the sting out of many things, especially government actions. Paramount had plenty of time, and the brains of Wall Street and Poverty Row in addition.

The dream of Stanley Mastbaum tore at the heart of his brother, Jules. If Zukor were able to get away with a corporation of this magnitude, why shouldn't he? First National franchise holders, frightened by the speed with which Paramount spread, agreed with him. Several circuits, among them, the Jacob Fabian, the Harry Crandall, the Mark Strand, the Rowland & Clarke, the Davis Chain of Pittsburgh, became subsidiaries of the Stanley Company of America. Through New York, New Jersey, and Pennsylvania, Mastbaum swept like a cyclone. In Atlantic City he formed a $10,000,000 realty corporation, and no other company was to open a theatre there.

The business genius of Jules was demonstrated in several ways. A large stockholder in the Sentry Safety Control Company, he set the policies of that company. The Sentry Safety Control was a fire device, and the Fire Marshall of Philadelphia ruled that no theatre within the city limits would be given a license to operate unless equipped with this instrument. It rented at a minimum charge of $250 per annum; it cost $22 to manufacture. Similar inventions were on the market, but this is the only one that had the Fire Marshall's approval.

As a power in the industry, Mastbaum moved his executive offices to the Bond Building in New York City. The elegant simplicity with which these offices were furnished reflected the refinement of his taste. Blue carpet covered the floors from wall to wall. The desks were walnut, some hand-carved, the chairs, leather. Monk's cloth draperies framed the windows. In charge of the New York office was James McKeon, close friend of Jimmy Walker, the New York

State Senator, who on a retainer fee fought for independent theatre owners. McKeon and Walker shared a suite for entertainment purposes at the Hotel Biltmore. Later, while Mayor of the City of New York, Walker resigned rather than face impeachment proceedings for accepting graft.

As a next step, Jules merged First National and Stanley. He also met with William Fox and talked of a gargantuan organization composed of Fox, the West Coast Theatres, Stanley, and First National. But like his brother Stanley, Jules did not live to fulfill his dreams. In December of 1926, in his fifty-sixth year, he died unexpectedly of an acute attack of appendicitis. Monuments to Stanley were a building for consumptives and the Stanley Company of America. A monument to Jules who left an estate valued at $12,245,-136, is the Rodin Museum in Philadelphia, erected by his widow to house his collection of two hundred pieces of the sculptor's work.

With the death of Jules, John McGuirk stepped into the presidency of the Stanley Company. This step practically placed two men in the chair, for "everywhere that Johnny went, his friend Abe was sure to go." John McGuirk and Abe Sablotsky were inseparable. They had been friends and partners as long as they could remember. Their crude speech and raucous laughter intermingled. They almost looked alike. They were heavy set, with potbellies. Derby hats were part of their attire in and out of doors. The derbies were so well known, they inspired jokes on the Philadelphia vaudeville stage, especially in the McGuirk and Sablotsky houses. One comedian told this story:

Abe Sablotsky was walking down the street with a friend the other day. When he came to a Catholic Church he tipped the derby on his head.

"Why did you tip your hat, Abe?" the friend asked.

"We just passed a Catholic Church."

"But, you're not a Catholic, Abe."

"No," Abe answered, "I'm not. But McGuirk is. And this is his hat."

M-G-M
To Be Our Best Friend

WHEN M-G-M STEPPED OUT IN FRONT, *Looie* B. Mayer, as production chief, visualized himself as a sovereign. His belief was so obvious, Mike Levee, First National's West Coast studio head, saluted him with a salaam whenever they met, and Looie accepted the greeting in all seriousness. Then, as top Katzenzukor boy, Zukor became the industry's top man. Whatever the dreams of anyone else, whatever the deals, Zukor emerged the czar.

Mayer thought about the situation when he took his morning rides. He thought about it in his office. He thought about it on the sets. He thought about it until it became an obsession. Mayer hated Zukor. He hated him ever since the days, when as a small, unknown Boston theatre owner, he had suffered under the blows of Famous Players' hammer. One day, late in the spring of 1926, Looie turned his work at the studio over to assistants with strict orders that they were to put action into motion pictures and started on a lecture tour. The sole purpose of the trip, scheduled across the country, was to enlighten the public, to tell the masses of people what he knew about Zukor, to tell them that he, not Zukor, held the most important place in the industry.

Before he was gone very long, the Julian Oil scandal broke. He was exposed as one who had lent the petroleum company money at usurer's rates and had sold its stock to guests in his home when he knew the company was in financial difficulties. Even so, he continued to say what he thought about Zukor.

A bust of Adolph was placed in the Paramount Theatre lobby, and the words of Looie became more biting. The more vehemently he

256

spoke, the weaker his pictures came through, but his assistants continued to follow his instructions, and plenty of action raced through his films. So things went until the 2nd of June. On that day, *Variety* reprinted a letter that Eugene V. Brewster had written to the editors of his various publications:

"This is to notify you of a very important business arrangement I have just made.

"I, President, Editor-In-Chief, and sole stockholder of Brewster Publications, have entered into a business arrangement with Metro-Goldwyn-Mayer studios, the details of which are too lengthy to explain here, but the part that concerns you follows:

"From now on, for a period of one year at least, Metro-Goldwyn-Mayer are to be our best friends among the producers, and we are to be their best friends. We are to favor them in every way possible in the way of covers, galley pictures, interviews, etc., etc., and when it comes to expressing views on their stars and criticizing their pictures we are to be as favorable as possible. In other words, if they have a picture or a star, which you do not think as good as they do, or as important, we are to say nothing that will injure that star or that picture. If we cannot say anything favorable, we won't say anything at all — at any rate we will leave out the bad things. Wherever you can serve their interests in any of our pages, please remember you are serving your own.

"I have said this to you before. I do not believe in tying the hands of my editors and critics; but nevertheless, here is a case where we must make an exception. The Metro-Goldwyn-Mayer studio is only one of a dozen of producers, and you must remember that M-G-M are our friends, and in a way part of our organization. Of course, you must do this in such a way that it will not reflect discredit upon our magazines, and it must not be obvious publicity. They understand just as well as we do that there must be a limit, because otherwise the value of our magazine would be impaired. We want to be fair with everybody, but we certainly cannot knife our friends, and I consider Metro-Goldwyn-Mayer as such, and we must certainly treat our friends far better than we treat our enemies.

"Sometime ago I wired you to be friendly with First National and Colleen Moore, because they had done several favors for us. I believe that these obligations have been fully paid, and I am inclined to release you from any obligation under it. However, Colleen Moore is a friend of mine, and I shall always speak kindly of her, but you are under no obligation to treat her differently than you would if I hadn't wired you aforesaid.

"I know you will cooperate in this matter."

Looie cut short his tour. He rushed back to the West Coast and fired Corliss Palmer, though he had promised his friend, Eugene V. Brewster, to make a star of her. A reason given for her discharge was that she was named as corespondent by Mrs. Eugene V. Brewster in her divorce suit. This, of course, drove Brewster to write his editors another letter about Metro-Goldwyn-Mayer.

And through all the excitement, Adolph Zukor remained silent.

Warner Bros. and Vitaphone by arrangement with Western Electric and Bell Laboratories presented the world premiere of DON JUAN with a Vitaphone score and program of Vitaphone all-talking shorts on August 6th, 1926, in New York City.

Premiere, Roosevelt Theatre, Chicago.

Tokyo, Japan

Premiere, City Theatre, Amsterdam, Holland.

At the "Menteng" Theatre — Djakarta, Indonesia.

Sound Makes Its Debut

WITH IRRITATING REGULARITY, inventors came forward with such technical improvements as films for larger screens, color photography, three-dimensional pictures. George K. Spoor kept trying to make a comeback with the invention of P. John Berggren. Fox, to protect himself, formed a company called Grandeur Films and purchased patent rights to a wide screen. His partner in this enterprise was Harley Lyman Clarke, at forty-six, the youngest utility magnate in the country and owner of several theatre supply companies.

A number of sound instruments were offered to producers. C. Francis Jenkins experimented with color pictures and sound on film. He also worked on a television device that made him famous as the father of television. Again to protect himself, Fox bought into two sound patents, Tri-Ergon (patented in Germany on March 3, 1919) and Case (a sound on film system developed by two young inventors, Theodore W. Case and Earl I. Sponable). No other producer thought this protection necessary. The Tri-Ergon patent was seven years old; what reason to suppose the situation would change in another seven years! Too great an expense was involved; new sound proof studios, actors who could speak well, cameras that did not squeak, royalties to those who controlled sound patents. Besides, the public was content with a black and white silent screen. Other things held the spotlight, such as Sid Grauman's new Chinese, a preview or premiere, theatre.

In the pavement outside the theatre, Sid had film favorites' footprints, nose prints, palm prints. Seats at a premiere cost anywhere from five to eleven dollars each and went only to celebrities. A carpet was laid along the sidewalk that the privileged few might enter like royalty. Huge arc lamps played on them and a microphone carried their greetings and anticipations over the radio. Crowds lined the street and blocked traffic to get a glimpse of Ronald Colman, Janet Gaynor, John Gilbert, Harold Lloyd, or Lillian Gish as they entered. Traffic was blocked for streets. Although these premieres served as great publicity vehicles, few inside the theatre had eyes for the screen. Everyone was too busy checking how others were received, what they wore, what they said. Nevertheless for a producer to open his big pictures at Grauman's Chinese had become a must, as a singer appearing at the Metropolitan Opera House.

At St. Louis, a city that still was a consistent hotbed of abuses, bicycling, kickbacks on film rentals, etc., the Skourases opened the Ambassador, a theatre that was the talk of the Mississippi Valley. Built at a cost of $5,500,000, it occupied the equivalent of six floors of office space. Society leaders, politicians, newspaper and film men from distant places came to the opening. The formally dressed Skourases, proud and happy, remained in the lobby to greet their guests. George noticed a rather stout woman with several children tugging at her skirts at the rim of the crowd. She kept staring at him as if she wished to speak to him. After everyone left the lobby he lingered a moment at the door. The woman approached. "You don't remember me," she said.

He remained silent.

"We were good friends once, in the old neighborhood," she ventured timidly. "You shanghaied me, you and doc. You put me in a hospital to get a dope cure. I'm married now. These are my children. I owe it all to you, and I want to thank you. Every time you bought or built a theatre I came down to see it. I'm glad you are a success. You deserve it. God bless you."

George, in a desire to say something to hide his embarrassment, commented on how stout she had become. The woman never heard him. She had disappeared into the crowd. As he left the lobby, George Skouras compared his old friends and his new. He mingled in society now, with people who discussed drama, golf, horses. He wondered if any of them considered the Ambassador an achievement.

While so many reaped fortunes, the four Warners still struggled to survive. In their desperation they approached Joe Brandt, who in association with Harry Cohn and his brother Jack, had formed an independent company, Columbia Pictures. Columbia had produced some fairly good movies, and as Charlie Chaplin had said, theatres could not reject good pictures. They did not need the Warner tie-up and turned it down.

Without substantial backing the Warners could not survive. Harry made a trip downtown and aroused the interest of one of the few financial houses that had not earned commissions on a movie issue, Goldman, Sachs & Company. Every dollar the Warners received went into expansion. They built a $1,500,000 theatre in Hollywood and the Warner Theatre on Broadway. For $2,000,000 they purchased the old Vitagraph Company. Albert Smith and James Stuart Blackton, the only two original Patent Company members who had survived as producers, were anxious to get what they could out of their company before the agreement with Famous Players-Lasky expired. The Warners, on the other hand, wanted to use the balance of the contract as a wedge to bring them into contact with the Zukor outfit.

Since that day Sam Warner had pawned his watch to purchase a travelling show of motion pictures, he felt as if he were on one continuous merry-go-round, with a creditor on the horse in back of him. Even now, despite the Goldman, Sachs support, he and his brothers verged on bankruptcy. He was desperate, and as a desperate man he lunged for the brass ring, and caught it. The prize was sound pictures.

While Sam went to California to organize a studio, Harry took over in the East. He completed negotiations that Sam had begun with Western Electric Company, a subsidiary of American Telephone & Telegraph, which owned sound patents. The agreement provided a royalty for the Warners on every Western Electric sound instrument sold if the Warners would introduce sound pictures.

In California, Sam caught a cold that confined him to bed. Meanwhile Harry, Abe, and Jack produced films which synchronized music in the old Vitagraph Studio which they called Vitaphone Pictures. Sam's cold developed into a sinus infection. Harry, Abe, and Jack pushed on. Late in October of 1927, "The Jazz Singer," starring Al Jolson, musical comedy star, opened at the Warner Theatre on Broadway. A brilliant audience attended to see this new form of entertainment, a form of entertainment Leon Gaumont had tried for years to present to the public. None of the Warners was present to greet their guests or see how "The Jazz Singer," which treated the theme "the show must go on," was received. They were in California at the funeral of their brother Sam.

Few professional critics said anything pleasant about the performance. Columnists ridiculed the squeaks and scratches. Producers considered the story treatment a retrogression. The seventy-nine year old Alva Edison, who once was interested in movies merely to supplement his talking machine, issued a statement for the press in which he said, "Americans don't like talking movies. They prefer the restful quiet of silent film shows." Even so, Harry Warner and his brothers returned East famous, famous enough to demand five-year contracts from exhibitors on percentage basis. The public had enjoyed itself.

"Where
The Hell Am I Heading?"

MOTION PICTURE STOCKS had become notorious as speculations. Professional trading was obvious. Bears pooled one way; bulls pooled another. Fraudulent issues appeared. Executives were known to gamble in their own corporate issues. Stocks changed hands frequently. Men directed the affairs of a corporation during periods in which they owned not one share of the company's stock. The shares of Famous Players turned over five times in one year. Nevertheless, Goldman, Sachs sold Warner securities as fast as they were able to have them printed. Zukor offered the Warners $10,000,000 for their company. Fox offered them $12,000,000. The Warners held out for $40,000,000. Forty million dollars, Zukor decided, was too much to pay for a novelty. Fox did not have to pay that much; he had his own patents.

J. J. Murdock, who years before had been eased out of the picture game and who now was manager of the Keith-Albee Vaudeville Circuit, quickly perceived that *talkers* would cut deep into vaudeville. With little loss of time, Murdock merged with the film interests of Joseph P. Kennedy, a Boston promoter, and with the Radio Corporation of America (R-C-A). Kennedy, backed by John J. Raskob and Mike Meehan of Wall Street, had bought the American interests of Pathe'and an English firm, Film Booking Offices, popularly called F.B.O. David Sarnoff, president of R-C-A, became chairman of the board of the combined corporation, known as Radio-Keith-Orpheum (R-K-O). Kennedy was appointed president and general manager. Offices were opened in the Bond Building, which once housed the great Jules Mastbaum. Elevator operators were instructed that when Kennedy, a man with three favorite words, "retrench-ment," "culture," "economy," entered a car it was to run express to his floor. No passengers other than those who accompanied Kennedy were to be taken up in the public elevator. "Retrenchment" was accompanied by discharging many workers. To accomplish "culture," Kennedy, a Harvard man, informed the trade that per-sonnel replacements would be made only with college graduates. Some people were confused because in previous utterances, Kennedy had praised the calibre of the industry's men. "Economy" was to be accomplished, he informed the trade, by putting not more than $75,000 into any R-K-O picture.

"What kind of pictures are we going to get for $75,000?" the harassed exhibitors wanted to know.

Kennedy answered with an advertisement in which he said, "A Titan is born."

The industry went from one extreme to another, and whichever way it went the exhibitor worried.

Estimates indicated that $3,000,000 had already been spent on sound experiments and that $24,000,000 had gone into the recon-struction to make studios soundproof and to improve cameras so that they need not be wrapped in blankets to stifle noise.

The exhibitors repeated a familiar question: "Who will pay for all this?"

They soon found out. Rentals increased ten times. Where a silent version sold for $40, the sound version sold for $400.

Finally the exhibitors asked, "How far can producers go?"

Sam Morris, now Warner's sales manager, was the first to answer. He simply could not resist depriving independents of a hit, even though he had to change a picture's title to remove it from the block. The picture, renamed "Old San Francisco," was sold on a road show basis. First and second runs were practically closed. In a twelve-month period, three thousand independents either shut or sold their houses. How much further would the business narrow? In desperation, one man placed this advertisement in *Variety* and other trade papers:

Where The HELL Am I Heading?
The bull slinging season is on. This year I'm wearing ear muffs.
I've been pumped full of hot air season after season.

Now I MUST talk—and talk straight out—up, and down, and AT. I either get hell or the sheriff gets me.

I'm just a two-theatre exhibitor, an independent. I was in this game when a two-reeler was a feature. At one time I made a profit. In the last two years I've made a mere living. I'm spending some of this money now on these ads to shout MY battle cry, and to broadcast, "Watch your step," to others.

What is sapping the life blood of my two theatres?

What the hell is anyone doing to fight the menaces that are stabbing at the heart of my business? What's keeping people away from my houses?

Is it Radio that keeps 'em glued to their Morris chairs every night? If it is what is anyone doing about the Radio menace?

How can I fight over-seating and over-building?

What about this "Presentation Craze?" Am I in the picture business or am I running a side show?

Why must I be taxed the fat overhead salaries for fatheads, when I book their "Economy Wave" pictures?

Why must I take a dozen "duds" to get one possible box office HIT? Why must I pay for a nightmare of colors to tell me how great pictures may be—maybe, and most of the stuff hasn't been put through the sausage grinder yet?

Where the HELL am I heading?

How can I meet these threats

I WANT TO KNOW

I guess there must be others like me who want to know—who must know, or blow up.

If things don't get better, I'm going to take up bricklaying where a brick's a brick, and no gold paint's on it.

If anyone's got the answer, for Heaven's sake, shoot —write me personally. I'm desperate. For good reasons I can't sign my name. But you can reach me by addressing

JUST AN EXHIBITOR
Box 400, Variety

Cease And Desist

THE R-K-O AMALGAMATION STARTED A NEW CYCLE. Zukor looked longingly at First National. He had lined up so many of its franchise holders only one short step would put him in control of the company. He dared not take it. The government had ordered him to "cease and desist" block bookings. While the government's eye did not keep him from gathering in small circuits, to go after First National might tease the government into extending its order. More tantalizing, an even greater prize than First National was available. Marcus Loew had died. His heirs lacked the urge that had made him a famous man. Arthur, especially, found love and trips around the world more exciting.

The estate of Marcus Loew owned 400,000 shares of Loew's Inc. Loew's Inc. controlled the well-equipped Metro-Goldwyn-Mayer studios. Loew's stock, valued for tax purposes at $42 a share, sold on the exchange for about $75 a share. The Loew family, through their representative Nicholas Schenck, who succeeded Marcus Loew as president, asked $50,000,000 cash for the 400,000 share block, which represented a third interest in the company. Forty million dollars was to go to the Loews, $10,000,000 to Schenck. A block which gives control frequently sells at a higher price than on the open market.

The Warners, who now had a respected reputation on Wall Street, spoke of approaching the Loews. While they consulted their bankers, Halsey, Stuart & Company, the bankers of William Fox, agreed the stock was a good buy. They advanced him $10,000,000 for a year, which they raised via a sale of short term notes to their customers. They also sold a $16,000,000 stock issue in Fox Theatre Corporation. The balance of $24,000,000 came from three different sources: Bankers Security Company of Philadelphia; The Chatham & Phoenix Bank, which advanced $3,000,000; the American Telephone & Telegraph Company, which advanced $15,000,000 at twelve per cent interest per annum through one of its affiliates, Electrical Research Products (Erpi). With A. C. Blumenthal, a real estate broker and friend of Mayor James J. Walker, Fox formed the Foxthal Company for the purpose of handling the transaction.

Everybody connected with the deal was happy. Fox because, with the acquisition of the Loew shares, he outstripped Adolph Zukor and became the most powerful figure in motion pictures; Halsey, Stuart because Fox let them have $1,000,000 for "financial advice" in addition to regular commissions. The commissions were shared with others who had participated in the sale of Fox securities; the "financial advice" money was not. The Telephone Company was happy because the Fox action kept the Warners, who also were interested, from getting the 400,000 shares. At the time, Western Electric, a Telephone subsidiary, was in the midst of an involved conflict with the Warners.

When the Warners entered into a sound deal with Western Electric, the Telephone Company claimed ownership of almost two thousand basic sound patents. Now, Radio Corporation of America made a similar claim. Case and Tri-Ergon had patents owned by Fox. Lee DeForest, American pioneer in wireless telegraphy had fifty-odd patents covering various talking picture devices. Several others, including Louis Gerard Pacent, had been granted talkie patents. Of all the devices, the Western Electric was the most expensive and was constructed to carry only Western Electric recordings. In addition Western Electric was slow in filling orders. The Warners, anxious to have their houses wired, signed up with Pacent, whose apparatus sold for about one tenth the price of Western Electric equipment, and who was in a position to make immediate installations. Western Electric would not tolerate what it considered an infringement and brought suit against the Warners. The Warners, on their part, claimed Western Electric had promised them a commission on all talkie apparatus sold and were suing for such commissions.

To further please the Telephone Company, Fox agreed to use

Western Electric sound equipment exclusively and to shelve his Case and Tri-Ergon devices. At the time, Fox, who owned only United States rights, suggested to A T & T that they, in partnership with him, buy the German rights to Tri-Ergon. A T & T advised him the Tri-Ergon instrument was worthless; they were not interested in it. They also requested Fox not to tie up money in the foreign patents. For his cooperation, the Telephone Company accorded Fox an added privilege, exclusive license to make a sound newsreel. This privilege was a bit hard on the Hearst-M-G-M newsreel, which had to pay Fox a royalty for the switch over from a silent to a sound reel, and on the exhibitors, who were forced to rent the Fox Movietone News for a period of not less than five years under contract.

A few days after Fox bought the 400,000 share block of stock, Halsey Stuart and the Telephone Company instructed him to purchase enough additional shares to place absolute control of Loew's in his own hands. They also sanctioned his purchase of a controlling interest in British Gaumont which, like its American competitors, produced, distributed, exhibited. Under the Fox purchase, the English circuit was to be equipped with Western Electric sound instruments. To cover these two deals, Halsey, Stuart and the Telephone Company helped Fox raise another $20,000,000.

To protect himself before he entered into the Loew deal, William Fox, accompanied by Saul E. Rogers, his general counsel, called on United States Attorney General Mitchell; his assistant John Lord O'Brian; Colonel William J. Donovan of the Department of Justice; a Mr. Thompson, Donovan's assistant; and other government officials. At first they thought Fox would not encounter difficulty if he acquired the stock; then they thought he might. As Fox pondered over his uncertain position he received a call from Col. Claudius C. Huston, treasurer of the Republican National Committee and close associate of Herbert Hoover, President of the United States. Col. Huston asked Fox why he did not contact Louis B. Mayer, "He's a nice fellow." A hint to the wise is sufficient; Fox talked to Mayer. The purchase price of the block of Loew securities was increased by $2,000,000; the $2,000,000 to be divided as far as Fox knew among Mayer, his associate in production, Irving Thalberg, and J. Robert Rubin, M-G-M attorney. Col. Huston called again; this time to tell Fox that everything was clear in Washington. That settled, Fox made a deal with First National franchise holders whereby they let the balance of power in the West Coast Circuit swing to Fox in return for which Fox said nothing when The Stanley Company absorbed First National.

The Stanley-First National merger was financed through Richard B. Hoyt of Hayden, Stone & Company, and Clifford B. Hawley of E. B. Smith, a large Philadelphia banking house. Spyros Skouras, a First National franchise holder, came east to attend the closing at Philadelphia. On the train from New York to Philadelphia he met Mr. Hoyt, whom he had seen at First National Board of Directors' meetings. Skouras's English was bad, his words blurred. Hoyt did not always understand exactly what was said, but he got the general idea. The man had a Hoyt philosophy, a Hoyt business outlook, the aspiration to leadership of a Hoyt, the astuteness of a Hoyt. In theatre partnerships, when a film salesman called, a common practice when bartering was to shout and yell, walk up and down, even argue bitterly among partners as to what was an equitable deal; another was for one partner to assent to any price quoted only to be stopped from entering an agreement by the *no man* until the price was *right*. Spyros Skouras had a more subtle routine. Either he, Charlie, or George would start the film buying negotiations. Without making the slightest concession, after a while, the one with the salesman would be replaced by another of the brothers, who after a while was replaced by the third. The one replaced went off for a rest or massage and came back later to take his place arguing with the worn-down salesman. A firm friendship developed between the corseted banker and the mid-western theatre owner.

When the Stanley-First National deal was consummated, Irving Rossheim, lawyer and bank representative, was appointed president to succeed John McGuirk, who willingly stepped down into the inactive position of Chairman of the Board. Why McGuirk relinquished his place without resentment, Rossheim soon understood. The dizzy swirl was too much for the seasoned motion picture man. Friction to the extent it existed in the ranks of both companies was without precedent. Pressure had forced the resignations of Robert Lieber and Richard Rowland. Although the stockholders had ratified the appointment of Rossheim, almost every member of the Board coveted his chair. When Rossheim insisted that a dividend be passed, he heard one long grumble; McGuirk had given twenty cents extra.

Rossheim was unable to make the Board understand that payment of a dividend would leave a dangerous hole in the reserves of the company that had to meet the Fox-Loew-West Coast group as a competitor.

The Cathedral Of
Motion Pictures

ALTHOUGH FOX HAD CLOSED HIS EYES to the Stanley-First National merger, he had not closed his eyes to the fact that Zukor had the most publicized theatre in the world. Like Marcus Loew, William Fox considered himself a genius, and as a genius he had to excel in all things.

Herbert Lubin, a cousin of the one-time producer, Sigmund Lubin, had under construction a six thousand seat house, the largest theatre ever designed, a "Cathedral of Motion Pictures." It was named Roxy to honor the great showman, Samuel Rothapfel, who agreed to move "His Gang" and their colossal stage entertainments over from the Capitol. This step meant that Edward Bowes would no longer be Vice-president in-charge-of-nothing. In fact he not only took over the Capitol presentations, the production of which he learned under Rothapfel's tutelage, but he organized "Major Bowes Amateur Hour" on the radio. All amateurs introduced on his program signed a contract which gave Major Bowes a cut of all their future professional earnings.

The Roxy ran into more money than its builders contemplated; it ran into more money than S. W. Straus & Company, underwriters of its bond issues, could raise. Fox, with better Wall Street connections than Lubin, came to the rescue, and the Roxy became a Fox house. Sometimes Fox wondered whether he had a cathedral or a white elephant. The theatre was just far enough from the entertainment center to miss the crowds. During the 1950's, theatre builders, aware of traffic and parking problems, were not interested in a Main Street site, but Fox did not have the parking problem to help him in the

271

late twenties. The ironic part of the Roxy story is that Fox took over the theatre mainly to dwarf Zukor's achievement, and all the while Zukor wondered where Paramount headed. Zukor wondered how soon the theatre he had built with such pride would have a potato night and an opportunity night. Katz, as head of Publix, introduced all the homey policies that had made Balaban & Katz successful theatre operators in Chicago. Publicity at the Paramount smacked of corn. A ten dollar book of theatre seats sold for nine dollars.

The Roxy was not Fox's only source of irritation. Independent theatre owners in and around New York, who had been invited into the sumptuous offices in the Ambassador Hotel to receive options on their houses, complained that by not picking up the options on time, Fox had interfered with their buying programs. The options provided that all contracts between the theatres and producers or distributors had to be sanctioned by Fox, and if product were needed between the date of the option and the date of expiration, permission had to be obtained from Fox. In addition any talking devices installed had to be instruments in which Fox was interested. During the life of the options exhibitors sat tight. When option dates came due, Fox instead of picking them up, renewed them. Theatre owners threatened to sue because, they said, Fox was stalling, only to discover that the sole assets of Fox Interstate Theatres, Inc. and Fox Metropolitan Theatres, Inc. were the stock certificates, the corporation seal, and the furnishings of the hotel suite. When Fox finally picked up the options he paid much less than the amounts agreed upon in the original contracts because the theatre values had greatly depreciated.

While Fox concentrated on involved financial problems, his Crown Prince Winnie went west to supervise production and refit the studios for sound. Wherever Winnie worked, he spread a wave of fear. Whose name would appear on the lay-off list "to take effect after his departure and while he was enroute?" Just before he left the west coast, he gave such a list to Eugene Castle, then in charge of the newsreel crew there. One of the names listed was that of Sanford E. Greenwald (in 1944, a Lieutenant Colonel in the United States Army Air Corps), a man Sheehan had never met but a name he objected to. Castle scratched his head in a quandary. No cameraman Greenwald's equal was available; how could he be replaced? Castle simply put another name on the payroll, and everytime Sheehan visited California, Castle sent Greenwald on a trip.

The personnel situation had reached such a state throughout the industry, writers, directors, even stars, threatened to unionize. But where they banded together, they were inexperienced as labor traders and won few concessions. The Hays office stepped into these quarrels and arbitrated them so well the salary of Pettijohn, nicknamed Fixer, went up to $50,000 a year. Hay's salary went up to $200,000.

Many were the accomplishments of the Hays office. In a speech at Dallas, Pettijohn revealed that because "distributors were tired of being dictated to by exhibitors," he was inaugurating a fight for relief from theatre-chain oppression. So great was his success, producers asked Hays to tackle their problems abroad. With great fanfare Hays and a retinue left for Europe. The English stood tight on a reciprocal arrangement. The French insisted he state his promises in writing. When Hays left for home, he had agreed to continue the quota policy and had assured his newly made friends, friends who had threatened one member of his staff with deportation, that American exhibitors would show European pictures regardless of merit or pay a fine.

Spyros Skouras
Takes New York

W HATEVER MOTION PICTURES' PROBLEMS, the investing public did
not lose confidence. An industry must be profitable to pay such
salaries: $130,000 a year, plus a bonus of $757,000 to Adolph
Zukor; $104,000 plus a bonus of $606,000 to Sidney Kent. In
1929, David Bernstein, mere treasurer of Loew's, received a $164,000
bonus on a salary of $104,000. Forty-odd bankers sat on the
Boards of leading corporations. Moreover, according to the New
York Times, the industry had moved up, had stepped up to become
the fourth largest industry in the United States, surpassed only by
agriculture, steel, and transportation. All issues rose. Paramount
preferred climbed to 131. Warners, which went on the market at
10, touched 37.

The prestige of the motion picture magnate had become so great,
Louis B. Mayer was a frequent week-end guest of Herbert Hoover
at the White House. This friendship dated back to 1928, when
Mayer attended the Republican Convention as a delegate and promised to deliver the industry to Herbert Hoover, the Republican Party's
candidate for the Presidency of the United States. True to Mayer's
promise, Hearst-Metrotone News, the M-G-M newsreel, devoted an
overwhelming amount of space to Mr. Hoover.

Several film executives now felt that to take an active part in
politics was a social duty. Like the Hearst-Metrotone Newsreel,
the Fox reel supported Herbert Hoover. The political philosophy
of motion picture producers made life somewhat easier for Will
Hays. According to *Variety*, an insistent report indicated that the
Republicans looked to the former Postmaster General to deliver the

274

screen throughout the country to the party.

Two years before the Presidential election, Senator James J. Walker ran in a New York mayoralty race. On that occasion local theatre owners subscribed better than $150,000 toward the cost of his campaign. Pettijohn once received $30,000 for getting subtle Republican propaganda into newsreels, and from the Democrats he received a fee for preparing a reel in a New York Gubernatorial campaign. At one period, Hearst, a power behind the throne in California politics, hoped to be Mayor of New York City. Scandal defeated him, but in his newsreel his views were so boldly flaunted, the reel was hissed out of many theatres, and Hearst, his name so discredited, eventually had to change the name from Hearst Metrotone News to News of the Day. News of the Day was chosen because it implied the theatre's views were merely the news of the day.

While competitors sought benefits through political connections, Harry Warner sought to capitalize on the advantages he had gained through sound. As soon as Fox and Zukor stopped bidding for his company he started on a quest for theatres. Internal conflicts made The Stanley Company vulnerable. Harry called this to the attention of Waddill Catchings, the Goldman, Sachs' man on his Board of Directors. The result: both The Stanley Company of America and First National Pictures became Warner subsidiaries late in the summer of 1929. The deal was financed by Goldman, Sachs in association with Hayden, Stone & Company. This merger stands perhaps as the most sensational single event in the history of motion pictures. In less than a year the Warners had reversed their circumstances from a deficit of $1,234,412 to a spectacular first place in the industry through sound.

In this deal the friendship of Richard Hoyt for Spyros Skouras bore fruit. Sypros Skouras was asked to manage the theatres. A dream come true, a dream that Spyros often had cast from his mind as too fantastic. The Ambassador, he had felt, would exist as his supreme achievement. Much as he might have desired to manage a great chain he never really believed the opportunity would be his.

When Spyros Skouras arrived to officially take up his post in New York, the staff of the Stanley Company watched him walk across the blue carpet of the reception room into the firm's largest private office. A retinue of *yes men* followed him. What would happen now? Who would remain with the company? Who go? Mechanically, Mr. Skouras nodded to executives on hand to greet him. Inside the great office he walked to one of the windows, where he remained a moment. His silky straight black hair brushed against the edge of the monk's cloth drapery. His small childish nose was pressed against the window pane. His eyes dropped to the street. The neon and electric lights of Boardway burned brighter than the fire of Prometheus. He raised his eyes and let them wander toward the river. The gray and purple mist over the Jersey shore held his gaze. It was like the light over the olive covered hills in Greece, where as a boy he tended sheep. In those far-off days he used to dream of being an important man, an educated man, a priest. How was he able to comprehend that he might become the head of the foremost theatre circuit in the world. And the achievement was so simple! Yesterday he was unknown. Today he ruled over a $100,000,000 empire, so much better suited to his temperament.

The moment for dreams was over. A comment by one of the men brought Spyros Skouras back into the room. He passed a pleasantry and smiled; he smiled as if he were about to ask a favor. The smile faded and in his eyes flashed a light as sharp as the blade of a sword. In a tone of voice that did not bear contradiction, he said the company, that part of it that was to be retained, was to prepare to move from its blue carpeted halls to the Warner Building on West Forty-Fourth Street, which had cement floors and factory-like windows that swung on a chain. The cornerstone of the building had been laid by Jean A. LeRoy, a poor machinist.

LeRoy had been chosen to lay the cornerstone in an impressive ceremony because he was one of the industry's romantic figures. He had invented a motion picture projector that was perfected in 1894, but had considered the invention so non-essential he never bothered to patent or market it. "Washing the Baby," a picture he produced as an Edison release was buried in the cornerstone.

Few noticed the transition from beauty to efficiency. Everything moved so fast; everyone was so busy. Under the direction of Spyros, assisted by George and Charlie, small circuits in Connecticut, Massachusetts, New Jersey, Pennsylvania, and Ohio, were bought up with alarming speed. Over all this, Spyros Skouras was master. He was so completely the master, callers sat for hours, for days, in his anteroom, hoping he might eventually keep his appointments.

When he came into an office, clerks dug their heads deep into their work. Everyone stopped talking. Many wished they might stop breathing. Spyros Skouras had to account to no one, except to Harry Warner.

R-K-O and Paramount had no intention of letting the Warners get the jump on them. The scramble for theatres became wilder than ever. And the public loved it. Paramount reached 146-3/4 and divided two for one. Warners skyrocketed to 139.

Warner employees became such excited speculators, Harry Warner sent a round-robin through the offices, which each employee was requested to sign. The round-robin was an assurance that the signer would not gamble on the stock market. The logic of this might be difficult to follow. Setay, a firm controlled by Harry Warner, which dealt exclusively in securities, had a complete list of Warner employees and counted 150 of them as customers. Goldman, Sachs also had a profitable outlet among Warner employees. Late in the summer of 1929, the Wall Street firm sold two issues at a special price to Warner employees who promised not to dispose of these securities before the date they were scheduled to appear on various stock markets. The idea, of course, was to keep the price up until November, when the stocks were to be offered to the general public. Warner employees were so grateful for being allowed in on the ground floor they held the stocks as promised. Several executives who had bought large blocks were not so naive; they sold out as soon as they were able to realize a point or two. In the October, 1929 crash these issues became worthless.

While the public clamored for stock issues, producers clamored for theatres. The more theatres they bought, the more sound installations they demanded. The more sound installations, the greater the confusion, despite the fact that manuals of procedure were issued and an expert on sound made the rounds of a circuit as well as experts in buying, advertising, public relations, seating, standing, ventilation, lighting, music scheduling, auditing, projection, insurance, cleaning, usher training, and manager training.

The width of Western Electric's sound film differed from R-C-A's. David Sarnoff offered R-C-A equipment for any picture, but Charles Bunn, Western Electric general sales chief, announced, "I do not know the meaning of interchangeability." His salesmen passed upon the sound instrument in a theatre before permitting a film exchange that handled pictures made under a Western Electric license to rent film to that theatre.

Interchangeability or not, the Warners wanted music for sound pictures. With $8,500,000 supplied by bankers who had received it from a public eager to transform cash into Warner stock, Warner Bros. purchased Harms, Inc., a music publishing house. This deal served several purposes. It provided the young sons of Sam Morris (now a Warner vice-president) and Harry Warner with lucrative executive posts. It placed several composers at the disposal of Warner talkies. The use of music copyrights was a wedge that might be used to force exhibitors to book Warner pictures.

The scramble for theatres, the agitation over sound, did not keep Spyros Skouras from installing reforms in the circuit under his management. One morning he called an executive meeting. That day, Si Fabian, who had taken his father's place on the Stanley Board, and who held an executive post in the theatre company, had an appointment to take his mother to luncheon. When Mrs. Fabian arrived the meeting was in full swing. Si came out to excuse himself, told his mother what was going on, and asked her to have luncheon with his secretary.

The two women went into the Lincoln Hotel grill. Neither ate. Tears rolled down Mrs. Fabian's cheeks. "How can they do it!" she cried. "How can they take bread out of their mouths!" She referred to what her son had told her about decisions already made at the meeting: Char women at the theatres were to be reduced from $11 and $12 a week to $10 a week. Theatre managers were to work twelve hours a day, seven days each week, for $40.

Mrs. Fabian had worked with her husband, had nursed the business, had watched it grow. It was like a child to her. Neither she nor her husband ever gambled in their corporate issues. They did not pay the highest salaries in the business, neither did they pay the lowest. She felt her child had been wronged.

A short time later, because of personal differences with Harry Warner and Spyros Skouras, Si Fabian resigned. His secretary became secretary to George Skouras. One of the first things she did was to ask George why Spyros had reduced the salaries of scrub women.

"To economize," he answered.

"But, if he wanted to economize," the secretary pressed, "why didn't he cut men making $2,000 a week to $1,500, or men making $1,000 to $750? Many such are on the payroll. That would be a real saving. Those men might not have quite as much to lose at the race track, but they would not have to change their mode of living."

"Oh," George laughed, "you're a Bolshevik. Those men can fight for themselves."

Thus Spyros Skouras took New York. Why not? After all, Richard B. Hoyt gave him the key to the city.

Book Three, Part One

America's Fourth Industry

(1929 to 1934)

The Stock Market Collapse

WELL PAVED BOULEVARDS EXTENDED FOR MILES where for generations muddy paths had been the only roads. Building after building covered what had been pasture land fifteen years before. Palatial studios replaced tottering shacks. Millionaires Lane supplanted Poverty Row. The world's most glamorous city emerged on the site of an unknown sleepy village. In Hollywood were reflected the expansion, the magnitude of the motion picture industry.

Its suburbs were studded with estates. A forty-room *bungalow* was built by the sea for Marion Davies. At Pickfair, Mary Pickford and Douglas Fairbanks, now married, received in imperial style. Every star, every first rate director, every top executive boasted a large house, an English garden, a tennis court, a stable of horses and, most important of all, a swimming pool. Their homes were protected from vulgar public gaze by high picket fences. The men and women of Hollywood were publicized as the best dressed persons in the world. The parties of Hollywood were reported as important social events. The guests of Hollywood were feted as royalty, Hollywood style. The doings of Hollywood personalities became looked-for gossip; the private life of Hollywood, newspaper items. For the first time in the history of the Fourth Estate, a money value was placed on news. Columnists became high-salaried writers to report on the length of Adolph Menjou's mustache, the eccentricities of Greta Garbo, the latest date of John Barrymore. More and more Hollywood personalities were *glorified*; more and more film executives emerged as people of importance . . .

. . .a Zukor — feted guest of Ricse, Hungary, acclaimed its greatest benefactor, recipient of a medal of honor from his native land . . .

. . .a Mayer — week-end guest of the President of the United States at the White House. . .

. . .a Kennedy, Joseph P., Esquire — associate of, spokesman for financial giants.

Less and less consolidations, amalgamations were mentioned. Yet, on they went, daily creating new highs in stocks which were devoured by a public greedy for all sorts of securities. The list of Wall Street names on film boards of directors increased until they equalled the number of showmen. Powerful names also cut deep into the Electrics — Rockefeller with control, Morgan with a minority interest in Radio Corporation of America; Morgan in control, Rockefeller with a minority interest in Western Electric.

Schooled by Wall Street, Fox, under an arrangement similar to Paramount's whereby he paid off in stock, absorbed additional theatres in the east, the mid-west, and the far west. The Warners extended their holdings in New England, Pennsylvania, and Ohio. R-K-O sewed up independents. Experience had taught Zukor that the government cannot afford the legal talent of a powerful corporation. He bought theatres in Indiana, Illinois, and Missouri.

A new race was on. Nothing impeded the furious pace — neither the cries of independents, the exposés of the socially minded, nor anti-trust suits. Office clerks in distributing centers, without foresight to see that a greater number of accounts provided greater opportunities, imitated their superiors in treating small theatre owners with contempt. Salesmen, with a misguided sense of loyalty, bullied customers into selling theatres to large chains. District managers, in the confidence of home office officials, regarded their own double dealings as a proof of cleverness. Company heads, so important, their offices had two doors, a front door and a back door from which they might emerge unseen, never doubted the brilliance of their deals. They bowed only to the superior intelligence of financial wizards, and soon they, in company with their clerks, salesmen, and district managers, were out both doors.

Jaydee Williams' name disappeared from motion picture annals. Joseph Godsol was living in Switzerland. The Selznicks pledged jewels that Lloyds of London once insured for $192,000 to cover a $420 loan. Richard Rowland went from one company to another in secondary roles. Irving Rossheim returned to Wall Street as a full time legal consultant.

Talent groups on the West Coast, technicians, stage hands, actors, sensed disaster for all and voiced protests through strikes. Three hundred musicians in St. Louis joined them; they asked that a minimum number of musicians be employed in drop-pit houses.

Will Hays, arbiter, started west to crush the uprisings. Those who paid the subscriptions that kept Hays in office weighed his abilities and decided not to waste them. At Chicago he was prevailed upon to return east, convinced that a recital of his achievements would better serve his sponsors. So, Hays returned to New York, called a meeting, and for two hours read a report which described how successful he had been in warding off censorship. Modest, he failed to relate the success of a spy system he had developed to check on independent theatre owners.

Cannon Chase, with a keen sense of things obscene and pornographic, cried Hays merely laid a smoke screen for indecent pictures. *The Christian Science Monitor*, also incensed, said that Hays carried on propaganda under cover. *The Churchman* stated, "The publicity director and secretary of the Federated Council of Churches were paid by the Hays organization." Nevertheless, the Hays report was hailed a masterpiece by film executives.

The strike in the west was settled without concessions. So was the St. Louis strike. However, the St. Louis strikers had the satisfaction of a tribute. Spyros Skouras, who negotiated the settlement, said, "Without music movies never would have made the grade. Music aroused emotions where directors failed. Music has enriched almost every film presentation."

The strikes settled, the cries against Hays quieted, executives concentrated on the all important job of reshaping corporations. Rumors indicated that Paramount and Warners would join forces, Paramount and R-K-O, Warners and R-K-O; that all major companies would form one gigantic corporation. Pictures were the incidental means of keeping a corporation in operation, not only for corporate heads, but for many of the picture-going public. Stocks! Stocks! Stocks! Stocks of any kind were wanted. . .until October 29, 1929. On that day all issues on the New York Stock Exchange fell 20 to 40 points a share.

At ten minutes to three that afternoon, a group of film men milled about the Hotel Astor lobby, outside their favorite haunt, the board room of a Stock Exchange firm. Quotation calls, ninety minutes late might be heard. But the men in the lobby were too stunned, too bewildered to care what was reported. They had already been wiped out.

Millionaires became paupers. Edwin Porter, the first man to introduce a story film in the United States, lost his Rolls Royce and his fortune. Back to work he went as a mechanic in a mechanical appliance shop. Spyros Skouras studied the suicide clause in his life insurance policies. The losses of the Skourases were placed between $3,000,000 and $4,000,000, much of which had been borrowed from banks. Mack Sennett, originator of "The Bathing Beauty," dropped his fortune, estimated between $5,000,000 and $8,000,000. James Stuart Blackton filed a pauper's oath. Eugene Brewster, who shortly after writing to his editors in 1926 divorced his second wife to make Corliss Palmer (who in turn divorced him) his third wife, listed his assets at $500 and his liabilities at $7,396. "Bad investments," he said, "are responsible for the loss of my fortune." "And your wives?" a reporter asked. After a moment's thought, Brewster answered glumly, "We geniuses have no business getting married."

Gloom spread over Hollywood. All eyes in filmland's capital turned eastward. Who would gather up the strings that controlled the puppet city?

Not Joseph P. Kennedy; he and his partners had cleared profits in the mergers. While remaining R-K-O's financial adviser, he was stepping up to the less strenuous job of chairman of the board.

Not Adolph Zukor; he concentrated on his theatres. To meet conditions, he employed Max Schlosberg, formerly with Gimble Brothers, and J. S. Middleton, formerly with Kresge, to transform Publix lobbies into chain stores with vending machines and booths to handle the sale of music records, candy, peanuts, popcorn, and soda pop.

Not Nicholas M. Schenck, Arthur M. Loew, or David Bernstein. They were busy defending a suit by minority stockholders who claimed they had been injured by the sale of stock to Fox.

Not the Warners, who ignored a government ruling and discontinued First National as a separate entity. They were engaged in readjusting their organization.

Not William Fox. Recovering from injuries sustained in an automobile accident in which his chauffeur had been killed, he held bedside conferences with Prince Winnie to discuss the millions Fox owed on notes as well as production and operation costs. Like Metro and Universal, Fox Film arranged for a four-week lay-off period.

Will Hays met the emergency by issuing a new code of morals which provided that motion pictures shall not ridicule the law, natural or human; that the use of liquor shall be restricted in scenes depicting American life; that the sanctity of the institution of marriage shall be upheld; that scenes of passion shall not be introduced; that sex perversion or any reference to it would be forbidden on the screen; that the subject of white slavery would not be tolerated; that dances which emphasized indecent movements would be regarded as obscene; that profanity shall not be used; and ministers of religion must not be treated as comic characters or villains.

Neal O'Hara, Evening World movie critic read the code and wrote, "Will H. Hays has sent the movies out to the dry cleaners and they are coming back sweet and pure." It was the only comedy relief in the whole situation.

The Fox Voting Shares

DURING THE FIRST DAYS OF THE WALL STREET CRASH, the market value of Fox's holdings in Loew stock fell to $30,000,000. This represented an immediate loss of over $50,000,000. Whatever happened to the country or the film industry, Fox felt his position was secure. He had a tie-up with American Telephone & Telegraph. He had his two friends, John Edward Otterson, graduate of Annapolis, a retired Navy Lieutenant, and, in 1929, president of Electrical Research Products, Inc. (sales contact organization for the Telephone Company's subsidiary, Western Electric), and Harold (Harry to intimates) Leonard Stuart of Halsey, Stuart & Company, with whom Fox played golf.

Fox had another valuable ally, Harley Lyman Clarke. Clarke was a close friend of Albert H. Wiggin, chairman of Chase National Bank, and an acquaintance of Harold Stuart. In Utilities Power and Light Corporation, of which he was president, Clarke was a partner of Samuel Insull. He was owner of International Projector Company and National Theatre Supply Company (which had one hundred per cent representation of bankers on its board) from whom Fox purchased equipment. In the Grandeur Company, Fox and Clarke were fifty-fifty partners. Time and again, Clarke told Fox that he had several million dollars in cash; Fox had only to say the word anytime he wanted money.

The crash had eaten up Fox's cash reserves; he said the word. In reply he received a curt, "No." The answer shocked Fox, but he knew people well enough to know they can be this way. He approached his friend and financial adviser, Harry Stuart. Fox's indebtedness at Halsey, Stuart already had been reduced to $12,000,000. Although his credit was not questioned, Fox offered personal holdings as collateral. Harry was sorry, said, he, himself, was in financial difficulties and was unable to raise money.

Neither was John E. able to induce the Telephone Company (where part of the Fox block of Loew stock was pledged against the $15,000,000) to increase the Fox loan. Fox approached Chase National Bank and Kuhn, Loeb & Company. They too were, "Sorry!" He went to Dillon, Read & Company. He called on the National City Bank, with whom he traded all over the world, and on Field, Glore & Company. Not a bank, not a broker had money to advance him.

The Fox companies were liquid; they made money. Fox offered to put up as collateral properties worth twice the amount of money he wanted on loan. He offered to put up property he owned personally. No one had the cash he needed. Wall Street had closed its doors to him. To emphasize how securely they were bolted, the Paris branch of the Guaranty Trust Company asked him to withdraw his account from that bank.

In England, Reginald McKenna, former First Lord of the Admiralty, later Chancellor of the King's Exchequer, and, in 1929, chairman of one of Britain's great banks — Midland — which had collaborated with Chase National in working out the Gaumont British deal, attached his funds. The attachment was followed by a suit for $6,000,000 still due on notes given to Gaumont British. In stating the amount due, the attorney had failed to take into consideration the money attached. Thus Fox was given an opportunity to file an answer. The breathing spell was of little use. Hardly had he caught his breath when his friends Otterson and Stuart maintained that, by taking on Gaumont British, Fox had placed money due Halsey, Stuart and the Telephone Company in jeopardy.

Had these friends forgotten? They had been consulted before he made the purchase. They had agreed to it. Cablegrams, telegrams, telephone calls had been exchanged on the subject.

Fox analyzed his position. In 1925, when stock in Fox Film was first offered to the public, the company was recapitalized for a million shares of stock, 900,000 A shares, 100,000 B shares which carried the voting control. All the B shares were owned by William Fox. If Fox were unable to meet his obligations, his companies naturally would fall into bankruptcy, and the voting shares would be wiped out automatically. Harry Stuart and John E. Otterson could not possibly be in a conspiracy to ruin him!

Fox decided to sell some of his assets and offered his West Coast holdings to the Warners, who agreed to take them over for $55,000,000. With $55,000,000, Fox would pay off pressing obligations — $15,000,000 to the Telephone Company, $12,000,000 to Halsey, Stuart & Company, $3,000,000 to Chatham & Phoenix Bank, the balance due Gaumont British — and have a comfortable surplus besides.

News of this deal brought Otterson back as a friend. He came up to ask a favor. He came up to ask Fox not to sell his West Coast Theatres to the Warners, the Telephone Company's worst enemy. No reason existed, Otterson informed Fox, to sell to the Warners. Zukor wanted to buy the West Coast circuit. "If you agree to sell Zukor an interest," Otterson said, "the Telephone Company will prove its friendship for you. It will buy the whole thing for $55,000,000 and sell Zukor half of it. The Telephone Company will own the other half, and it will give you three years to regain it."

Fox broke off negotiations with the Warners only to learn that the Telephone Company merely wanted to thwart the return of the $15,-000,000. The Telephone Company explained: Once Fox returned the $15,000,000, they were afraid he might install Tri-Ergon equipment in his theatres and fail to renew his Western Electric license. The West Coast Theatres in Warner hands certainly would have meant the loss of that circuit's business.

In the weeks that followed, Fox hardly ate or slept. He developed a nervous stomach. Lines cut deep into his face. He dared not talk on the telephone; a test had proved that someone listened to everything he said. He did not know where to turn for help. But he was not a man to be easily downed. If he were unable to raise money in usual channels, he would raise it in unusual channels. To the theatre owners of the United States, William Fox addressed a plea. He asked help in the raising of $35,000,000 to save his business from the clutches of Wall Street. His courage caused men across the country to speak of him with respect. Exhibitors lauded his determination, his defiance. They hailed his refusal to admit he was trapped. They were proud one of their ranks had the spirit to defy the powers of high finance. They also had long memories. They recalled his film substitutions, his high prices, his theatre acquisition tactics, and they were afraid to help him. In the end, William Fox might devour them.

However, the appeal to theatre owners brought Otterson and Stuart on another visit. Stuart, as usual, wore a carnation in his lapel. Both apologized. "The crash has upset everyone." They suggested that Fox form a trusteeship for the purpose of reorganizing and re-financing Fox companies, the trusteeship to be composed of Stuart, Otterson, and Fox, and to provide that two out of three had the right to decide any question. Fox rejected the proposition; where-upon Otterson, as spokesman for the Telephone Company, and Halsey of Halsey, Stuart, Fox creditors of notes not yet due, de-manded a proxy of Fox's voting shares. "You are insolvent," Otter-son said, "and the Telephone Company and Halsey, Stuart are going to take your companies over."

The public airing of his financial difficulties broke the morale of his organization; his salesmen lost heart to solicit business where they formerly had dictated terms. Frantic, on the verge of physical collapse, Fox called on Charles Evans Hughes, lawyer, former Gov-ernor of New York State, former Justice of the United States Supreme Court, former Secretary of State of the United States. He detailed to Mr. Hughes how he had arrived at his high position. He related his troubles. Charles Evans Hughes shook the hand of William Fox and promised to help him.

The next day the Government announced it had started action against William Fox, Fox Theatres, and Fox Film, requiring them to divest themselves of Loew stock. At the time Charles Evans Hughes, Jr. was Solicitor General of the United States Government.

Fox wondered if the action were coincidental. He, after all, had once offered $2,000,000 to influence the Department of Justice to con-sent to the Fox-Loew merger; he had told the full story of his life to Charles Evans Hughes, Sr. On his promise, Hughes had shaken the hand of Fox. Fox believed that hand shake.

One Friday, late in 1929, word reached Fox that a bear raid would attack Loew stock on the following Monday. A further devaluation of Loew shares would make the collateral on the Telephone Company note due in April of 1930 insufficient. Fox would be ruined.

Three times during this period, Will Hayes called to see Fox. Each time he spoke of a man who was willing to buy the Fox voting shares. On the third visit, Fox forced Hays to admit the man was

Harley Clarke. That Friday afternoon, Fox advised Hays, in view of his difficulties, he would let the Fox voting shares go for one third of $100,000,000, the price at which Fox valued them. Clarke telephoned from Chicago to say the price was fair; that he would close the deal on Monday.

"Monday will be too late," Fox informed him. "I must have an advance of $6,500,000 before ten o'clock on Monday morning to stop a raid on Loew shares. Clarke promised to see that Fox had that amount before nine thirty on Monday morning.

Fox, who no longer trusted Clarke, appealed to the New York representative of Eastman Kodak Company. For years, Fox had purchased enormous quantities of supplies from Eastman Kodak. The New York representative left for his home office that night and, on Monday morning at 9:45 a telephone call came through from Rochester. Eastman Kodak had placed $6,300,000 to the credit of William Fox at the Bankers Trust Company in New York City.

Fox put a staff to work. In five minutes, thirteen telephone calls were made. Thirteen brokers had orders to deliver Loew securities to the Bankers Trust Company. Without apology or explanation, Clarke walked into Fox's office at ten thirty. The raid, of course, had not taken place. Clarke came prepared to pay over $33,000,000 for the Fox voting shares. With them he wanted the Fox block of Loew securities at a price and the Case and Tri-Ergon patents for nothing. The extra demands forced Fox to reject the whole deal. He was right back where he had started.

As Fox's attorney, Charles Evans Hughes advised Fox to accept the trusteeship proposed by Otterson and Stuart. When the agreement was presented for his signature, Mr. Hughes asked, "Shall I continue as your attorney or do you wish my firm to become attorneys for the voting trusteeship?"

Fox wanted Mr. Hughes as the attorney protecting his voting shares, especially since Hughes and one of his associates, Richard Everett Dwight, had drawn up the trustee agreement, and asked the famed lawyer to act for the trusteeship. Mr. Hughes had failed to explain that, if he were to act as attorney for the trusteeship, legal ethics placed the Hughes firm in a neutral position, one in which it was not supposed to act for either Fox or Fox's opponents. From that day on, Mr. Fox never again saw Mr. Hughes in reference to the trusteeship. Mr. Hughes went back into the Supreme Court, and

Richard Everett Dwight became the attorney for the trusteeship. Fox was somewhat amused when Dwight took over. He recalled an incident years before when, as an attorney on the General Film Company staff, Dwight handed him the check that covered the $350,000 settlement.

A mysterious premature release to the New York Times, revealed a plan to wipe out the Fox voting shares through an exchange of stock. This exchange would have reduced the value of the Fox holdings to about $2,700,000, over $30,000,000 less than he might have obtained from Harley Clarke.

The plan might have been carried out, if at a meeting the evening the release had been given to the Times (the day before the item appeared in the newspaper) Dwight had not lost his temper, a loss of temper which prompted him to abrogate the Trust agreement. One fiery word at the meeting led to another. Fox asked why the agreement failed to incorporate a clause that provided for the resignation of Otterson as a trustee as soon as the $15,000,000 was repaid. Dwight answered that "his client" (meaning Otterson) expected to remain a trustee, that he never intended to resign, that if Fox insisted on any such thing, the trust agreement was off. Fox insisted.

Whoever had given the item to the New York Times tried to kill it, but the Times had already gone to press. The next morning, when he saw the article, Fox, for the first time, fully comprehended where he stood. Wherever he stood, he needed cash. The Rockefellers had offered him $1,450,000 for a plot of ground on West Forty-Ninth Street. They contemplated a large development to be known as Rockefeller Center. Perhaps they still were interested? They were, at $800,000. This barely covered the mortgage; no use to sell.

Meanwhile a Boston lawyer named Berenson charged that Fox mismanaged the companies, that he had incurred financial obligations he was unable to meet, that he was about to pay himself and other stockholders dividends which the companies could not afford, and asked that a receiver be appointed.

The course of events in the Fox situation alarmed the President, Herbert Hoover. Never in United States history had a corporation of this size gone into receivership. The bankruptcy of Fox Film and its subsidiaries would be a national catastrophe. It might cause a panic.

Col. Claudius C. Huston, President Hoover's personal representative, came up to New York. He spoke to Fox. A few days later he had Christmas dinner at the home of his friend, Albert C. Wiggin. He spoke to Wiggin. Wiggin informed Col. Huston he resented White House interference in the business conduct of Chase National Bank and suggested that Huston go home and mind his own business.

Instead, Huston went to Henry Ford. Ford once had fought banking interests, and Huston thought the automobile manufacturer might have some sympathy for Fox, but Fox once, during Mr. Ford's anti-Semite campaign, had forced the Detroiter's hand by threatening to show in the Fox newsreel every accident in which a Ford car was involved. Herbert Hoover was so desirous of saving Fox Film from bankruptcy, he wished to talk to Mr. Ford about the situation. The Colonel asked if Mr. Ford would telephone the President of the United States. Mr. Ford did not make the telephone call, but he volunteered to help Mr. Fox; he would introduce the film man to Walter S. Gifford, president of American Telephone & Telegraph Company. Mr. Fox and Mr. Gifford were acquainted already.

Fox refused to believe he had no way out of his dilemma. His defiance became a nationwide topic of conversation. His troubles were aired in the public press. Fox's next step became a matter of speculation.

That next step led to another banker, Dr. A. H. Giannini, head of Bancamerica, formerly Bank of Italy, a California bank that long had supported motion picture ventures. Bancamerica, in collaboration with Lehman Brothers and Dillon, Read & Company, presented a plan for Fox refinancing.

The plan acted like an explosion.

Halsey, Stuart released a forty-five page open letter denouncing William Fox and made a bid for the Fox concerns. Radio Corporation of America also made a bid. One cry sounded over and over — a corporation as large as Fox Film has no right to be controlled by 100,000 shares of voting stock owned by one man.

Fox was worn out by worry; he lost over thirty pounds; he kept going on nervous energy. His wife was ill, in need of an operation. Her name, like his, had been slandered. Fox felt that things could not be worse when he received a round-robin letter. The first signature was that of Winfield Sheehan, who, in 1912 when under questioning because of scandals in the office of Rhinelander Waldo, had been given a job at one hundred dollars a week by William Fox. In 1929, Sheehan's salary in the Fox Organization was $130,000 a year plus extras. Others to sign the letter were: Saul E. Rogers, general counsel, who had worked with Fox on the Loew deal; A. C. Blumenthal of the Foxthal Company; Courtland Smith, formerly of the Hays office and since 1926 in charge of Movietone News; John Zanft, a director; and James R. Grainger, sales manager at Fox Film. The letter asked Fox to concede to the Halsey, Stuart group.

Despite this and all that was said against Fox, the stockholders at the annual meeting held on March 5, 1930, voted 914,405 in favor of the Bancamerica plan; 33,085 against it.

Immediately Sheehan asked the court for an injunction against the Bancamerica financing plan. Fox, he contended, was obsessed by the idea that Halsey, Stuart and the Telephone Company were involved in a conspiracy to ruin him. He also claimed that he, Sheehan, had more intimate knowledge of general business details, production details, and distribution details than any other official, executive, or employee of the company. As for Fox's statements, they were merely a smoke screen to cover selfish motives.

The New York Evening Telegram published Sheehan's picture. Under it was one word — Ingrate.

The drama was over. Halsey, Stuart and Telephone Company notes fell due, and Bancamerica withdrew.

A few minutes past midnight on a Monday morning in April of 1930, William Fox let Harley Lyman Clarke, friend and equal of Otterson and Stuart, have his voting shares for $18,000,000. For an additional $500,000 a year, under a five-year contract, whereby Fox was to act as chairman of the Advisory Committee, Fox agreed not to accept a post with any other film concern or to compete in any way whatsoever against the Fox corporations. To the last he refused to relinquish his rights in the sound patents. However, he did agree to let Fox Film use free of royalty instruments built according to Tri-Ergon principles.

Thus the voting shares, which had caused such a furor because they represented only ten per cent of Fox Film stock, and because they were held by one man, William Fox, passed over to one man, Harley Lyman Clarke, who, with three voting shares valued at nine dollars, controlled the $500,000,000 Utilities Power & Light Company.

A. C. Blumenthal was relieved of a $3,000,000 indebtedness to

Foxthal. He was given a $500,000 bonus in addition. Sheehan received a five-year contract that called for $250,000 the first year and went up $50,000 a year, plus $250,000 for signing the contract. Smith, Zanft, Rogers, and Grainger were all taken care of under the transfer.

All commissions, expenses incurred by all factions, and lawyers' fees, including $520,000 to Hughes, Scherman & Dwight and $250,000 to Mr. Berenson of Boston who started an action that alarmed the President of the United States, were paid from the treasuries of the Fox companies.

Almost twenty-six years before William Fox stood outside an arcade pondering how to save it. That arcade he had built into an organization that encircled the globe. Now, once again he stood outside, this time speculating where he might have avoided a false step.

The victor, Harley Lyman Clarke, accompanied by Winfield Sheehan, Saul Rogers, John Zanft, Courtland Smith, and James Grainger, celebrated with a march of triumph that ended at the Fox Film Cathedral — the Roxy Theatre.

The Patience Of
Adolph Zukor

Fox WAS A DEFEATED FOE — but no one would ever know whether
Adolph Zukor preferred Fox or his successor as an adversary.
This ability to stand as if on sidelines and watch a conflict between
ambitious rivals without indicating in which direction his sympathies
lay was a strong point in Adolph's genius.

In the Fox incident, Zukor regained motion pictures' throne. What,
if at the time internal dissension existed at Paramount? The fracas
was between Sam Katz and the Balabans on one side, Jesse Lasky
and Sidney Kent on the other.

What of it that Sam Katz demanded unreasonable protection for
the theatre department and tied up pictures with double-feature bil-
lings in towns in which Sidney Kent struggled to rewin the confidence of independents?

What of it if Sam Katz tied up more Paramount pictures than he
needed to keep practically all product from small exhibitors at a time
Sidney Kent was crying, "Save the small exhibitors," and assuring
them they might have features even though they did not contract
for shorts?

What of it that Barney Balaban closed real estate deals without
taking anyone else in the organization into his confidence?

What of it that A. J. Balaban felt a yearly salary of $75,000
entitled him to executive expression and moved into production?
What of it that Lasky chafed at this move and came east to raise
a fuss? What of it if this fuss culminated in the purchase of the
balance of A. J.'s. contract?

What of it that soon after Lasky's name disappeared from film
titles?

What of it that the name of Zukor also disappeared?

What of it that Katz took over where A. J. met with little success — in production?

What of it that the names of John Hertz, Yellow Taxicab king; William Wrigley, Jr., chewing gum king; and Albert D. Lasher, Chairman of the Shipping Board during World War I, all men who backed Katz enterprises in Chicago, replaced the name of Zukor relatives on Paramount's Board of Directors?

What of it that Hertz questioned Kent about Paramount film rentals? What of it that the questions angered Kent because he felt Hertz had no right to pry into production or distribution? What of it that the mental gymnastics between Hertz and Kent culminated in Kent's resignation? What of it that this resignation was of such a character Kent's contract was not impaired, and Paramount was able to purchase it intact for a little over $200,000.

What of it that Zukor's long time partner, Jesse Lasky, announced, "I am not resigning; I am merely taking a three month's leave of absence?" What of it that those three months became forever?

What of all this to a patient man?

Although Adolph Zukor had assured the President of the United States, "There is nothing to fear; as far as I know the country is prosperous, almost 5,000 employees, earning between thirty-five and fifty dollars a week, were dropped from Paramount payrolls. Others had salaries cut from five to twenty-five per cent. Dividends were slashed almost in half. Executives, whose salaries ranged from $50,000 to $350,000 a year, were called upon to make the sacrifice of accepting their bonuses wholly or partly in stock.

Such a step required an explanation. "There has been," Zukor said, "a drop in industrial securities. Motion Pictures are not depression proof."

His utterances, his policies, his talents were not unappreciated abroad. Count I. Szechenyi called at Zukor's New City estate and decorated him with the Hungarian Cross in recognition of his artistic treatment of motion pictures, and the Government of France conferred on him the Chevalier of the Legion of Honor in recognition of his part in the promotion of cordial relations in the motion picture field between France and the United States.

However, in the United States, the holder of a mere three hundred shares sued on a transfer of stock. The suit led to a rumor, denied, that Paramount-Publix needed new financing. Denials were awkward when the stock, which once sold at 137 a share, touched 7. But then, Paramount was not the only stock that fell; all across the board prices dropped at an alarming rate. Among other film issues, Warners went from 134 to 3; Fox Film from 106 to 2; R-K-O from 50 to 1.

Denials became more awkward when additional cuts in Paramount-Publix salaries were announced.

Denials became impossible when Paramount-Publix sold its half interest in Columbia Broadcasting Company for $5,200,000 and, in addition, made arrangements to defer payments on certain obligations.

When Paramount-Publix went theatre shopping it had in its pockets a small amount of cash and a large roll of common stock certificates. Paramount-Publix guaranteed to redeem these certificates provided they were held for eighteen months, at anywhere from $85 to $120 a share. And now Paramount-Publix stock sold on the market around $7.

The stock arrangement was a merger custom in and out of film business, but thoughts of losses on the difference between $85 and $7 dumbfounded the taxicab king, the chewing gum king, and the former chairman of the Shipping Board. In bringing them into Paramount, Katz had made a mistake. As long as they had only his words to go by, they never questioned the business genius of Sam Katz. When, at close range, they saw theatre losses pile up; when they saw how he took theatre control out of the hands of experienced managers and attempted to run each house from a desk in his New York office; when they saw production costs mount after Sammy had assured them that once Lasky was out costs would go down; when they saw the hostility his personality provoked, they decided they, not he, were better fitted to decide policy at Paramount-Publix.

The famous statement, supposedly made by Zukor, "The Republicans gave us the depression, but God gave us Sam Katz," gave way to "The Lord giveth and the Lord taketh away." John Daniel Hertz replaced Sam Katz.

Still, Adolph Zukor was patient.

He was patient although his troubles were manifold. Sam Katz, claiming he had been wrongfully discharged, sued for $265,298, the balance due on his contract. In Chicago, where Paramount through its Balaban & Katz holdings was the largest operator, an ugly strike was called. The union had become bold enough to dictate how many projectionists each theatre should engage. Rather than take dictation from a union, 107 theatres switched off their lights. When the lights were switched on again, strike breakers from the east stood in the projection booths. Late one night, after show hours, three theatres were bombed. Chicago police issued an order, "Shoot to kill." To this strikers responded with explosions of stench bombs at almost every performance. In one theatre two persons were hurt. For two months the strikers carried on their war; then agreed that all theatres seating up to four hundred persons might engage one operator, all others two. A blanket cut of twenty per cent in salary was accepted.

While settlement was a relief, the strike had not been the most serious of Zukor's problems. Stockholders in a suit charged collusion and conspiracy between the directors of Paramount-Publix and the directors of Balaban & Katz. The bill claimed that a plan had been devised to unlawfully saddle an obligation to rebuy 30,000 shares of Paramount-Publix stock onto the Balaban & Katz organization. These 30,000 shares were held by a group of Great Lake Theatre owners who had sold their houses under the eighty-five dollars a share guarantee. The court was asked to appoint a receiver for the Balaban & Katz chain pending litigation.

Worse, A.C. Blumenthal of Foxthal fame, holder of twenty-five $1,000 debenture bonds, claimed that the rights of bondholders were prejudiced by a loan of $13,875,000, against which Paramount had pledged valuable assets consisting of twenty-three feature pictures. The money had been borrowed to repay loans to the Bankers Trust Company, the National City Bank, the Commercial National Bank, the Empire Trust Company, and the Central Hanover Bank & Trust Company.

Was the patience of Adolph Zukor enough?

Albert Warner   Sam Warner

Jack Warner   Harry Warner

Barney Balaban　　　　　　*Marcus Loew*

Adolph Zukor　　　　　　*Louis B. Mayer*

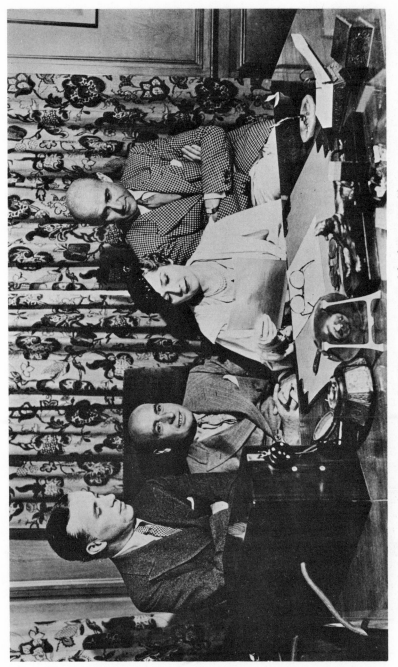

Charles Chaplin, Al Lichtman, Mary Pickford, Sam Goldwyn

*Will H. Hays who delivered a talk via Vitaphone on the program of
DON JUAN August 6th, 1926.*

The Miracle Men
And The Titan

THE WARNERS LOOKED ABOUT and dubbed themselves "Miracle Men." And "Miracle Men" they were. They had more theatres than any other circuit equipped with sound; they produced the best talkers; they had clever sales tactics. A Warner salesman would call on an exhibitor whose house was wired for sound and sell him a block of pictures. The next day another salesman would call and produce a list of the same pictures. When the exhibitor explained he had purchased those very pictures the day before, the second man would say, "The man who was here yesterday sold you the pictures. I am from Vitaphone to sell you the scores." The score rentals were higher than those for the pictures. Those exhibitors who complained were asked the trite question, "What do you think this is a charitable organization?"

Other reasons also caused the Warners to consider themselves "Miracle Men." John J. Raskob owned 300,000 shares of Warner stock. Raskob was close to the du Ponts of Wilmington, who in turn were close to the Morgans of Wall Street. Raskob's holdings again illustrate the interlocking of film issues. In 1929, Raskob, in a syndicate with Walter P. Chrysler, automobile maker; Mike Meehan; and others, identified on the books of M. J. Meehan & Company simply as account No. 433, shared profits amounting to almost $2,000,000 from a pool in Fox securities. At the time the pool spent $24,000 on newspaper men in a publicity campaign designed to put Fox Theatre stocks before the public. Raskob also was a backer of Joseph P. Kennedy, president of R-K-O.

A new flotation to meet Warner commitments was underwritten

by Goldman, Sachs in association with Hayden, Stone. The name of Spyros Skouras, friend of Richard Hoyt of Hayden, Stone, was mentioned as a possible Warner vice-president. The Warners never had considered Spyros, Charlie, or George for a directorial berth. The Raskob faction let it be known they had full confidence in the managerial ability of the Warner brothers and were quite satisfied with a Warner dictatorship. When interviewed, Harry Warner proclaimed indignantly, "There is no foundation for any report of disagreement or friction between the Warners and the Skourases."

With "Nothing to say," the mysterious, silent Skourases, as they were called, resigned, and under a salary and percentage of profit basis moved over to the Publix chain. While the Skourases were not dubbed "Miracle Men," they were able and, within a few weeks after stepping into their new jobs, negotiated a deal which provided that a New Jersey exhibitor surrender a half interest in two of his houses for twenty-one years to Paramount in exchange for a Paramount franchise. Although they had "nothing to say," little doubt existed on film row about the way they felt about the change. At this time, in January of 1931, Paramount was fighting receivership and the Warner outfit was the strongest in the industry.

However, Harry Warner had justification for his indignant remark that friction did not exist between the two sets of brothers. The Skouras resignation had no bearing on the Skouras position in the mid-west where the Skourases remained partners with the Warners and with Paramount-Publix.

Although personal animosity existed between Harry Warner and John Edward Otterson, Warner Bros. arbitrated its difference with Western Electric. The film company received $2,500,000 in cash, $1,300,000 in negotiable promisory notes, and surrendered all rights to participate in future royalties.

Other incidents came to light to further reveal the Warners as "Miracle Men." In a six months' period, between January and June of 1930, the Warners made millions trading in their own stocks. Hardly a year later, the balance sheet of the Warner Corporation showed a loss of almost $8,000,000. One stockholder, Harry Kaplan of University City, Missouri, brought suit in which he claimed the Warners paid excessive salaries to certain stars and to kin of directors. The company, his charge said, "paid out many millions of dollars in transactions in which Harry Warner, Albert

Warner, Jack L. Warner, Waddill Catchings, Sam E. Morris, etc.,
or some of them, had personal interests adverse to the corporation.
As an example they purchased with funds of the corporation at
excessive prices the businesses of various music publishers to create
a job for a young man who had just left college and was the son
of the vice-president. Profits that amounted to $18,000,000 have
wholly disappeared, and the company has operated at a loss ever
since."

Others joined Kaplan. Executive salaries went under fire. A gift
in 1928 of fifty thousand shares to Goldman, Sachs was questioned,
as was a gift of ninety thousand shares to Renraw (Warner spelled
backwards), Inc. This issue later split two for one and sold as
high as a hundred dollars a share. The suits were a nuisance; not
more than that. The decision stated that the Warners had operated
within the law.

However, the "Miracle Men" had not completely escaped the
pattern of the times. Warner dividends went undeclared. Stars and
feature players were asked to take cuts from fifteen to forty-five per
cent. No one, no matter how well worded his contract, could afford
to refuse. Home office publicity made or broke a star. While their
own talent was taking cuts, the Warners were negotiating with Cosmopolitan Productions. In return for publicity in Hearst publications,
they offered William Randolph's lone female star an advance of
ten thousand dollars a week against profits. In an effort to keep
their bankers happy, the "Miracle Men" asked their employees to
patronize banks that had extended loans to the company.

Like the "Miracle Men," "The Titan," sobriquet chosen by Joseph
P. Kennedy for R-K-O, had powerful connections. Most of its directors were directors of R-C-A; many were interested in General Electric
Corporation and in Westinghouse Electric & Manufacturing Company. Hiram Brown, successful shoe manufacturer, was president.
Although Kennedy had resigned and was back on Wall Street, he
remained a "Titan" friend.

Radio Corporation, affiliate of "The Titan," manufactured the
most practical sound apparatus on the market and made so many
concessions to small theatre owners, the powerful Western Electric
Company, to meet the competition, conceded to interchangeability.
While the pictures of "The Titan" were by no means masterpieces,
neither were they prohibitive in price, and Mr. Brown split the

product into zones to protect small theatre owners.

The greatest claim to the designation "Titan" was R-K-O's association with the Rockefellers, who were ready to acknowledge an
interest in motion pictures. The princes of Standard Oil broke ground
in the two square blocks extending from Forty-ninth Street to Fifty-
first Street, between Fifth and Sixth Avenues, for a development to
be known as Rockefeller Center. Rockefeller Center was to contain
two theatres, one, The Music Hall, to be devoted to motion pictures, supported by elaborate stage presentations. That the Music
Hall might have the very best in stage shows, Samuel Rothapfel
(Roxy), was engaged. A lease on the Music Hall was given to
"The Titan," with whom the Rockerfellers were associated through
their financial interest in R-C-A.

Dishes Sell Pictures

"The slump is over," Joe Schenck declared during the summer of 1930. "The entertainment world is entering on a new period of prosperity." And at United Artists, he ordered salaries cut ten per cent. In some companies wages sank so low, charwomen, doormen, and porters spoke of unionizing.

R-K-O and Loew's cut admissions in half. Fox Theatres admitted two persons on one ticket. In some sections, Warners slashed admissions from 40¢ to 15¢; Paramount reduced matinees to 10¢. Yet, these companies refused to sell Southern independent theatre operators who charged less than 15¢ admission.

Theatre after theatre went dark. Paramount found that to close a house on which it paid a yearly rental of $184,000 was cheaper than operating it. Miniature golf courses sprang up across the country to further rob motion picture theatres of revenue. Competition became more intense. An M-G-M telegram to its out-of-town salesmen requested telephone books of the rural communities they served. Letters went to people listed in these directories telling them in which nearby town M-G-M pictures might be seen.

The Hays office was asked to economize, requested to take old carpet and furniture when it moved from quarters on Fifth Avenue to quarters on West Forty-Fourth Street, and further told, "After a cleaning and polishing everything will look as good as new." Mr. Hays, in turn, suggested that producers economize by saving leader on film instead of junking it.

Wall Street, distrustful of Hollywood visionaires, sent sleuths into the studios to check on costs.

Independents received something of a shock when the United States Government indicated that it too suffered from the depression. To enforce the "cease and desist" order the records of the case had to be printed. The cost would be $25,000. And the richest country in the world, after spending hundreds of thousands of dollars on the prosecution, could not afford the cost of the printing job. Such a hullabaloo followed this announcement, one-twentieth of the records were printed. Arguments against blind block booking in the section selected were so weak, the "cease and desist" order was reversed.

Harrison's Reports revealed that producer-distributors paid certain critics weekly bribes and that one company placed a well-known critic on its regular payroll. More and more concealed advertising appeared in feature pictures. Such items as Boston Garters; B.V.D's.; Hart, Schaffner & Marx Clothes; Listerine; Lysol; Murad Cigarettes, The Magazine Of Wall Street were prominently displayed in movies. The bolder they were displayed, the stronger Pete Harrison in his four-page sheet denounced sponsored concealed advertising. Harrison's crusade was picked up by newspapers all over the United States, including the New York Herald-Tribune, New York Times, New York World-Telegram, Colorado Post, Cleveland Plain Dealer, Brownsville (Texas) Telegraph, Mankato (Minn.) Free Press, Oil City (Pa.) Derrick, Toms River (N.J.) Morning Sun, Bartlesville (Okla.) Examiner, Manhattan (Kansas) Chronicle Mercury.

Late in May of 1931, although Paramount was not the only company cited, Paramount lawyers asked the Postal Authorities to cancel Harrison's second class mailing privileges, and gave Peter Harrison twenty-four hours in which to abandon his campaign against sponsored advertising, "or suffer the consequences." Pete Harrison had an answer, "Paramount," he said, "is unappreciative of the free space its pictures are getting," and intensified his campaign against hidden advertising. The government did not take away Harrison's second class mailing privileges and the Paramount lawyers never indicated when the twenty-four hours were up.

Many things vexed the big outfits. Ohio guardians of public morals, the Censors, cut bits from productions; then ran a collection of these clips at private showings for $1.50 a head. The double-feature was a conspicuous sore spot, and producer-owned chains fought this practice bitterly. They lost, not only because they, themselves, ran two features a night in former *class* houses, but because of public demands. A boy, who was able to take a girl to a show that ran almost three hours, did not have to worry about additional entertainment expenses after the show. The large chains objected to premium nights in small houses.

"Are you trying to keep our family trade away?" exhibitors cried, "Dishes sell pictures."

But not even dishes did a good enough job. Bad times had hit the industry. With bad times came law suits. Stockholders sued for accountings. They especially wanted large executive salaries and bonuses explained. Ralph Hendershot, writer of a New York column entitled Wall Street, illustrating with instances in the motion picture industry, warned against the "bonus racket." Pathé stockholders sued to recover money allegedly spent wrongly before the studio and other assets were sold to R-K-O. Loew stockholders claimed that officers of that corporation had made an illegal profit when they sold the Loew block to William Fox.

This suit revealed many things, and upon his return to New York after a round-the-world trip, Arthur Loew discovered that while he had been away, several executives had voted themselves the right to purchase stock under a *special arrangement* in lieu of bonuses. Irving Thalberg, director, was to get 100,000 shares; Louis B. Mayer, producer; J. Robert Rubin, attorney; David Bernstein, treasurer; were to get 50,000 shares each. Arthur Loew threatened to resign. However, fellow executives talked to him, and Arthur remained with the company.

Anti-trust suits once again crowded the court calendars. Harry Kaplan, the Missouri theatre operator who had pressed the suit against the Warners, formed a stockholders protective committee and instituted action to force the Skourases to take up at a satisfactory price stock held by stockholders in Skouras Enterprises, stock guaranteed by the brothers. Kaplan, an old partner of the Skourases, figured that something between fifteen and twenty dollars a share was a fair price. As a result of this action, Skouras Enterprises went into receivership; the brothers were relieved of their guarantee. The Skouras attorneys received one of the largest fees ever paid in this type of action.

Depressions have a way of arousing a sense of social consciousness in public officials. In a government action against the major companies, Judge Thatcher of Pittsburgh ruled the Arbitration Clause in standard contracts illegal. The decision, however, left the independents cold, especially when Will Hays declared, "The decision is an aid to the industry. Distributors and exhibitors will clarify their relations. A new system of voluntary arbitration is now being evolved." A new zoning set-up also was being evolved.

While others struggled to get their bearings, Carl Laemmle carried on as usual. He held no place of glory. He was just plain Uncle Carl. But neither bankers nor a depression had had much effect on Uncle Carl's balance sheet. He had not overreached himself in buying theatres; he had not acquired a *Cathedral*; he had not invaded the million dollar production field.

Except for a rare picture, such as "All Quiet On The Western Front," which was awarded every competitive prize for the best picture in 1930, he contented himself with complete programs for neighborhood houses. At no time during the depression was it necessary for him to change his mode of living. His annual endowments remained the same, and he never forgot his native town of Laupheim in Germany on his list of contributions, a charity to which his whole organization made donations.

In February of 1931, he was presented with a handsome bound volume of letters written by exhibitors to mark his silver jubilee in the business. But nothing touched the veteran film man as much as the homely mark of affection shown by his employees at the time his grandchild was born. From that day on "Uncle Carl" became "Grandaddy Carl."

To The Victors

THE REINS SNATCHED FROM WILLIAM Fox, Harley Lyman Clarke moved his office to New York, where he installed a $10,000 desk, a duplicate of one he used in Chicago. The desk was equipped with a secret device. When he pushed a button part of the top raised and exposed a complete set of loose leaf ledgers. These books were kept up to date and covered all Clarke enterprises. Collecting clocks was another Clarke hobby. An assortment of all kinds and sizes decorated the walls of his office.

Without explanation, the office door of Saul E. Rogers was padlocked. Winfield Sheehan, who "had more intimate knowledge" of the corporation than "any executive or employee of the company," the man who received a bonus of $250,000 simply for signing his revised contract, was given a two-year leave of absence with pay to nurse his liver. Courtland Smith moved over to Pathé News. John Zanft went into free-lance production.

On the directorate also, name changes occurred. John E. Otterson, Murray E. Dodge of Chase Securities (subsidiary of the bank), W. S. Ingold of Pynchon & Company (market place for General Theatres and other Clarke securities), Charles W. Stuart, brother of Harry, replaced former Fox satellites.

Mr. Ingold, like Mr. Clarke, owned one share of stock. The Fox stock had been purchased in the name of General Theatres Equipment. In fact the purchase was made to provide General Theatres with substance. This company had outstanding an issue of 1,800,000 shares and practically no assets. Upon becoming owner of the Fox shares, General Theatres deposited the certificates at Chase National to secure a General Theatres bond issue of $30,000,000.

Clarke got together $15,000,000 of Fox Film cash and called a meeting of theatre managers. Throughout his half-hour address he forced air through his nose or cleared his throat. In spite of this habit, which some of the men attributed to nervousness, the sales force agreed that Mr. Clarke was a gentleman. He was a university graduate. He was president of Fox Film. One old-timer, who said the way Clarke spoke, made him nervous, lamented, "I miss the boss. He certainly could crack the whip. Remember his three hour sermons. How he'd bully us! And the way he razzed the Indies! I'll never forget how he'd boost his product. The biggest kick I got out of selling the melons was to go him one better."

Mr. Clarke had more important things on his mind than the selling of pictures; the purchasing of equipment, as an example. His instructions were to the point. Each and every house was to be redecorated; all purchases were to be made through National Theatre Supply, a subsidiary of General Theatres Equipment. One man declared that he had renovated his theatre six months before, that everything was in fine shape. "We don't want everything in fine shape as under Fox," he was told, "we want everything in superfine shape as under Clarke." This man who had laid a new carpet six months before ordered another for his theatre at cost plus fifteen per cent to National Theatre Supply. A California manager replaced a new marquee.

Harold Franklin, in charge of the West Coast chain (Wesco), came east to explain to Clarke that these unnecessary expenditures caused Wesco to show a loss. Franklin's contract called for a percentage of profit, and he did not intend to permit useless replacements unless these replacements were not taken into consideration at the time of accounting. The balance of Franklin's contract was purchased for half a million dollars.

By and large the loyalty of theatre managers was beyond the expectation of Clarke. Their buying spree remains unmatched in the history of show business. On every transaction, National Theatre Supply received a minimum of fifteen per cent for handling. And all the while a story was circulated in which Mrs. Fox was accused of being extravagant. In a warehouse was some $200,000 or $300,000 worth of props she had purchased years before after she had discovered that the studio rented items such as these for ten per cent of their value per week. A not uncommon practice was to hold such a prop for five weeks (pay fifty percent of its value for rental), return it, and then re-rent the same prop at a later date. From time to time, some of the pieces she had purchased were used as theatre decorations; some were rented to other studios when not in use on the Fox set. When confronted with the stories, Mrs. Fox maintained that she considered the work a hobby and had never received remuneration for it.

John W. Pope, famous as the boy wizard of Wall Street, wired his clients not to buy Fox stock and to dispose of any they had. Chase National Bank, which through Chase National Securities, had just underwritten a new issue, complained to the New York Stock Exchange, and Pope "went on the carpet." He was exonerated because he showed that the financial condition of Fox Film as of December, 1929, as reported by Clarke during 1930, varied as much as $6,000,000 in three different statements. Nevertheless, Pope told friends, "I'll have to watch my step. Chase will be after me for this." Pope died a few months later, on November 21, 1931, but Chase National took many years to dispose of the Fox issue that Pope had warned against. A secret remained locked in the $10,000 desk: whether any of its books agreed with any of the financial statements made public.

Many things harassed Clarke. A Wall Street paper refused to print a statement by him that a picture entitled "Big Trail" would gross $4,000,000. The paper had the audacity to say it doubted Clarke.

In California, where United Artists claimed that Fox Film exercised monopolistic control, the court decreed that Fox Film had no right to exclude independent theatre owners from contracting for film just because Wesco had a theatre in opposition, or to prevent independent exhibitors from showing two features on one bill, to stop them from giving away premiums, or to grant a theatre owned by Fox West Coast (Wesco) unreasonable protection.

William Fox kept insisting he was able to show Clarke how to make a profit, a right he had as chairman of the Advisory Committee. He reminded Clarke that Fox Film might use Tri-Ergon patents free, and that to sign a fifteen years contract for the use of Western Electric equipment was a waste of money. On top of this, Fox sued Western Electric for infringement of his Tri-Ergon patents.

Another thorn was A. C. Blumenthal, who asked for additional commissions in connection with the Loew-Fox deal, of which he claimed to be the master mind. The stock, pledged as security on $20,000,000 worth of notes held by Chase Securities, Western Electric, the Graybar Corp., Hayden, Stone & Co., Dillion, Read & Company, Chemical Bank & Trust Co., Manufacturers Trust Company, Old Colony Corporation, Bancamerica-Blair, and The Atlas Corporation, had depreciated to $6,609,000. The government had ordered a Fox-Loew divorce, and the note holders were claiming the shares because the $20,000,000 had gone in default.

The Gaumont holdings too had been lost, and Fox Film was involved in litigation in an attempt to recover the £4,000,000 invested in that deal.

A financial report which showed operating expenses of 1930 exceeded those of 1929 by $12,000,000 provoked Harry Stuart to inform Chase National that Harley Lyman Clarke must resign or Halsey, Stuart would not participate in raising money to renew Fox notes amounting to $55,000,000. Harley Lyman Clarke did not resign. Halsey, Stuart withdrew from the situation, and its clients lost approximately $35,000,000 in Fox securities.

The wild purchasing spree of Fox Theatres had not protected General Theatres Equipment. Its stock fell from 66 to 1/8. The company was in bankruptcy. Pynchon & Company; Hammons & Company of Boston; West & Company of Philadelphia, organized as a banking insitution a year after the signing of the Declaration of Independence, all deeply involved in financing General Theatres Equipment and other Clarke concerns also in receivership, failed. Chase Securities alone was left to see Clarke through. Albert Wiggin took Charles W. Stuart's place on Fox Film's Board of Directors.

In the autumn of 1931, Albert Wiggin, who had tied up one third of the capital of one of the world's largest banks in Fox enterprises, retired as president of Chase National Bank on a pension of $100,000 a year. He was replaced by Winthrop W. Aldrich, son-in-law of John D. Rockefeller and a director of the Telephone Company. Mr. Aldrich also replaced Mr. Wiggin on the Fox Board. General Cornelius Vanderbilt joined Mr. Aldrich as a Fox director. The day his appointment was announced Fox Film stock dropped ten points.

Again talk began to spread that Harley Lyman Clarke would resign. To this he declared, "I like the show business and will stick as Fox president. What is experience?" Despite his statement, the new directorate displaced Mr. Clarke as president, but apparently agreed with him on the question, "What is experience?" E. R. Tinker, president of Chase Securities Corporation, and a vice-president of Chase National Bank, became president of Fox Film. C. E. Richardson, another Chase official, was elected vice-president and treasurer of the film concern.

William Fox called to pay his respects and tell Mr. Tinker that he would gladly assist in any way possible. Mr. Tinker thanked Mr. Fox and said, "Why the job was wished on me, I do not know. I didn't seek it. I practically told them I didn't understand it; but they said they all had confidence in me and could agree on me in common as the man to run these companies." He did not explain who the "they" were, and he never consulted Fox.

Mr. Tinker's first move was to dispossess Fox Theatres from the Fox Building on West Fifty-sixth Street. He wanted no trace of this extravagant concern around. Fox Theatres had paid out more than $1,500,000 in legal fees alone! The legal fees, by the way, had been rendered to General Theatres Equipment and its subsidiaries. He informed several high-salaried executives that their contracts had not been ratified by Fox's board of directors. He sent out a letter in which he said any contract signed by a vice-president of Fox Film was subject to repudiation by the directorate. This raised such a storm of protest, a "pardon" letter followed, and Mr. Tinker moved upstairs with the title chairman of the board.

The presidency of Fox Film went to Sidney Kent, who had just sold his Paramount contract for $200,000. True to movie tradition, Kent moved in escorted by an entourage of *yes men*, including his brother Percy, his brother-in-law Robert Kane, and Jesse Lasky. Winnie Sheehan miraculously cured of his liver ailment, returned for active duty. An agreement provided that he was to have Kent's confidence in financial matters.

Not even Sidney Kent was able to save the Fox companies. In May of 1932, Fox Metropolitan Playhouses went into receivership. A short time later, Charles Skouras became receiver of Wesco, which went into voluntary bankruptcy. Other Fox subsidiaries quickly followed. In June, Judge Martin J. Manton, who later served a jail sentence for accepting bribes, appointed a receiver for Fox Film. In another decision, Judge Manton authorized Fox Theatres to accept $22,500 in settlement of its suit for $1,577,500 against American Telephone & Telegraph Co.

William H. Neblett, Los Angeles law partner of Senator McAdoo, filed in the U. S. Court of Appeals at San Francisco, charges of fraud in the bankruptcy of Fox West Coast Theatres. He named federal Judges William P. James and Harry A. Hollzer of Los Angeles and former U. S. Attorney Samuel W. McNabb. Judge James, he said, failed to disqualify himself in the bankruptcy proceedings at the time of the adjudication, although his son-in-law, Albert W. Leeds, was secretary, treasurer, and a director of the Fox concern. Judge Hollzer, he alleged, brought about the appointment of Mr. McNabb as bankruptcy referee before he resigned as U. S. Attorney. He accused Mr. McNabb of permitting the fictitious sale of Fox assets to the Wesco Company for a fictitious bid of $15,433,000.

In New York, Fox Film went into receivership, and it became impossible for A. C. Blumenthal to enter judgment for a balance of $350,000 plus interest due him on a note given to him for his part in the Loew-Fox deal. A. C. cried that receivership had been obtained solely to obstruct payment to him, and he entered into another of his many court squabbles. Nathan Burkan, A. C's. attorney, declared, "The proceedings hereto and herein are collusive, sham, fictitious, and in bad faith, and of ulterior motive."

Stench Bombs

Lay offs across the country reduced staffs in all departments. Over two hundred workers were let out at Warner's. Paramount shut down its Long Island studio. At Metro feature players were cut 35%. Star after star reported himself a bankrupt. In the film capital, the whole social structure was upset. Hollywood Blue Book wives, not sure who was broke and who was not, were in a quandary whom to invite to parties. Talented musicians peddled apples, the only profession open to them.

Rumblings of bad business became so intense, booth men in Chicago in June of 1931 donated a week's work without pay to exhibitors in that city. In spite of this good-will gesture, labor relations were anything but good. Law suits that revealed the amount of executive salaries and bonuses increased resentment.

Stories emanated from Hollywood that by working actors excessively long hours they were railroaded through pictures; that producers continued to maintain salary check lists which were used to block the raising of a player's salary during free-lance or lay-off periods; that often an actor was laid off without pay for a long spell during the shooting of a picture; that the only place salary vouchers might be cashed were at employment agencies where placement fees were deducted; that producers were financially interested in these employment agencies. One story Louis B. Mayer denied: that he had told his staff writers any attempt on their part to organize would jeopardize their jobs.

A story that could not be denied came out of Chicago. In that city, where non-unionized house managers received $35 for a sixty-six hour

315

week and unionized janitors received $40 a week, where booth men had worked a week without wages, between five thousand and ten thousand persons lost their jobs when one hundred theatres closed their doors rather than concede to a union demand for two projectionists in all booths.

The projectionist strike spread eastward. A movie patron never knew when a stench bomb might explode at his feet. Tear and mustard fumes were used. In a Brooklyn theatre, seven persons were injured when phosphorous, hurled from a balcony, burst into flames. A calliope placed in front of a Manhattan theatre was played so loudly the audience inside was unable to hear the talking picture on the screen. A parade under a movie marquee of two or three men bearing union banners was a common sight.

A Bronx exhibitor charged Sam Kaplan, head of local 306, with conspiracy. The theatre owner complained that men planted by the union stamped their feet, constantly changed their seats, engaged in loud and profane conversations, and otherwise annoyed patrons during performances.

The charges prompted police to raid Local 306 and seize its books. Three members of his local turned against him, and Sam Kaplan was placed on trial. Kaplan, they said, was cruel, merciless, and unscrupulous; he ruled by force; he coerced, intimidated, and used physical violence upon members who opposed his wishes; he expelled those who did not agree with him, and then had them attacked by strong armed men. They further charged that Kaplan had used Union funds for trucks and sound equipment to help one of the political parties in New York State during the 1930 campaign; that $300,000 deposited by apprentice operators was being dissipated, and that Kaplan accepted a salary of $21,800 a year for the presidency which formerly had been an honorary post that paid $250 a year.

Former Supreme Court Justice Charles S. Kelby, counsel for Kaplan, called the three who had testified against Kaplan traitors in the pay of exhibitors and pointed out that under the Kaplan regime the number of jobs available to members had been doubled, and that salaries had been raised.

The court was unimpressed. Kaplan was questioned about twenty-two sticks of dynamite found in the projection room of Loew's Paradise. Kaplan insisted he could shed no light on the situation, and no one was able to prove that he had anything to do with the placing of the dynamite in the theatre; nevertheless his trial which had been a civil action became a criminal action. Max Steuer, one of the foremost lawyers of his generation, was engaged to defend him.

Kaplan was accused of using union members as *cannon fodder*. He and his two companions, described in court as bodyguards, were searched. Guns were found on them. All had permits because their lives had been threatened.

Not even the great Steuer was able to overcome the effect created by the firearms. Kaplan was denounced as a "real menace" to organized labor and to unionism. Finally, he was ousted as head of the union and, with five aides, sentenced to serve six months in jail. Kaplan asked why he was given such a light sentence if the Court really believed him guilty of the horrible things of which he had been accused unless it simply wanted to keep him inactive for six months.

Whatever theatre owners suffered at the hands of unions was mild when compared to what they suffered at the hands of organized gangsters. A resourceful Brooklyn exhibitor solved his problem by inviting a neighborhood *mob*, which systematically dropped stench bombs in his house during performances, to become members of his theatre organization. After that competitors got the bombs. The net result: no competitive house within twenty blocks.

Financial Readjustment

H IRAM BROWN FOUND THE FILM INDUSTRY simply did not conform to commercial standards. He had remained faithful to Mr. Kennedy's promise: retrenchment. He had cut weekly operating expenses from $1,400,000 to $950,000. He went as far as to offer pictures at less than old Pathé prices. Still they did not sell. Mr. Brown did admit that, although productions in general were not of a high character, those put out by the "Titan" were bad by comparison. However, shoes, even mismates, always might be sold at bargain prices. The hot summer of 1931, the financial crisis in Germany, Britain going off the gold standard, all might have been responsible, Mr. Brown said, for R-K-O's ill luck.

When a company cannot sell its product, it has money troubles; when it has money troubles it is vulnerable to manipulation. To an experienced observer one thing was obvious in mid-October of 1931: R-K-O issues were in the clutches of astute bears. By November 5th short commitments were almost 149,000 shares. This daily average continued until November 12th, when the stock declined sharply. The price of the stock fell from $50 a share in April to 75¢ a share. With two exceptions, this drop, which amounted to fifteen thousand per cent, was greater in this space of time than any on record since the establishment of the first stock market at Amsterdam in 1630. The two exceptions were issues of concerns in receivership, Insull Utility Investment Company and the Kreuger & Toll Company. At one time, R-K-O's stock had sold for $90 a share.

On November 10th, while short sales were at their height, a letter went to shareholders in which they were informed that each four shares of Class A stock was to be exchanged for one share of common stock,

318

and that the shareholder had the privilege of purchasing a $5 debenture to replace each confiscated share. As an alternative to this devaluation of seventy-five per cent, receivership was threatened. Depression-poverty stockholders, many of whom no longer had five dollars for each share with which to save seventy-five percent of their holdings, were stupified and before they came to their senses were besieged by a battery of proxy hunters. Across the country, district managers, salesmen, clerks, every R-K-O employee had orders to forget pictures and concentrate on proxies. No one was too important to sit at a telephone and tell a shareholder where to place his signature. Executives went on a house-to-house canvas saying, "Sign here please." The directorate was determined to assure a majority vote on its refinancing plan.

The stampede was so frenzied, the Seventy-second Congress heard about it, and Clarence C. Dill, Senator from Washington, demanded an investigation into all motion picture financing.

This was too much for Mr. Brown. Early in 1932, he turned the presidency of R-K-O over to Merlin Hall Aylesworth. Mr. Aylesworth had an imposing record. In 1914, he was chairman of the Colorado Public Utilities Commission. Three years later he became Public Relations Counsel for Utah Power & Light Company. He helped organize the National Electric Light Association, and, at the time he accepted the presidency of R-K-O, he was president of National Broadcasting Company, a post he continued to hold.

A senatorial investigation leads to questions, and no one in connection with R-K-O did the Senate Banking & Currency Committee, which acted on Mr. Dill's demand, desire to question more than Mike (Michael J.) Meehan. Meehan's name was linked to a huge bull pool on R-K-O stock in 1930 as well as the bear pool of 1931. During both these years his associate, Joseph P. Kennedy, was R-K-O's financial adviser. On the advice of three doctors, Mike Meehan travelled abroad.

The committee contented itself with the testimony of Ernest W. Stirn, an economist connected with the Graduate Department of the University of Chicago, who had invested in R-K-O stock. Accompanied by William J. Morgan, former Attorney General of Wisconsin, who volunteered to act as counsel without pay to guide Mr. Stirn through his presentation, Mr. Stirn explained details of the most drastic stock squeeze in history. He claimed that R-K-O violated the laws of

Maryland, its home state, which forbade the reduction of the stock of a solvent company. He stated that Radio Corporation of America, already a heavy shareholder, had obtained an option to purchase all unsubscribed conversion stock and debentures, and that minority shareholders had been forced to surrender or abandon their holdings because of a decline in price and the five-dollar assessment. Others did not subscribe for the debentures because the company report indicated "manifest insolvency." Thus R-C-A, through its options, obtained $67,000,000 worth of R-K-O assets for $11,500,000, which was practically the price of the $5 debentures.

He gave a table of short selling and showed how it started with 13,800 shares of stock and crept up to 149,000 shares. He traced the rise and fall of the price of the stock; he testified that when dealt in over the counter, "the rigging of this stock upwards was as outstanding as the short selling I have just outlined."

A. J. Cookman, another stockholder, followed Mr. Stirn and told The Senate Committe that, "R-K-O gave me close to a respectable price." Under examination he admitted the company did this to settle his suit based on an illegal conversion of R-K-O securities. "At one time," he said, "I thought it was the duty of the Stock Exchange to look into the stock conversion, not to leave it to a one horse lawyer. I sent them letters and telegrams telling them so, but I never received any satisfaction." He related how he also took the matter up with directors of R-K-O because as far as he was concerned, "the whole thing looked too close to Radio Corporation of America." Only, however, when he brought suit in which he charged a violation of the Maryland law was he given a settlement.

The most conspicuous achievement of the investigation was the fulfillment of the threat; R-K-O went into receivership.

Over two and one half years of depression had Congress embarassed, even though Wall Street continued to insist no depression existed, the country was merely going through a "financial readjustment." The R-K-O inquiry forced other investigations. Along with bankers, financiers, industrialists, and others, who claimed that activities and mentalities such as theirs had brought about America's greatness, Harry Warner was asked to appear before the Senate Banking & Currency Committee. He was about fifty at the time, but he did not look more than forty. Under a barrage of photo-flash lights he smiled. He posed for each and every news photographer.

His bearing and appearance were decidely those of a well-established executive. All marks of the shoemaker, the trade of his youth, were gone. He obviously was nervous as he agreed to testify under oath, but he answered all questions in a soft, even voice.

"The three Warner brothers," he was asked, "realized a profit of $9,521,454.50 by buying and selling their own stock?"

Harry denied this. He and his brothers had made only $7,394,459.

Yes, he and two of his brothers had sold their stock at 54 and bought it back again at 23. He explained — they did not know the earnings of the company were falling off when they sold their holdings; certain financial columnists inflated the value of Warner stock at the time. These same columnists deceived the brothers a second time. They gave unfavorable reports on the stock as the brothers bought it back. He did not see anything peculiar about the fact that on January 1, 1930, although he and his brothers owned only slightly more than ten per cent of the stock, they held three of the eleven memberships on the board of directors. Another thing the brothers did not know is that dividends to stockholders were to be passed; the $3,365,000 lent to the company by the Warners received interest as usual. This loan was covered by guaranteed debenture bonds.

"Why did you," Harry Warner was asked, "trade in Warner securities under various names?"

"We found when we traded in the names of Harry or Albert Warner it influenced others."

The examination over, Harry Warner left for home satisfied and calm.

An investigation into the transactions of Fox Film followed that of Warner Brothers. In the course of the inquiry, Miss Grace Roberts, daughter of a railroad president, took the stand. She revealed that Hayden, Stone & Company sent her a pamphlet which described Fox Film's Silver Jubilee issue and that, after Mayor James J. Walker participated in a Fox Silver Jubilee celebration, Richard Hoyt personally recommended the issue to her as a "house stock." Later she discovered that she had purchased the holdings of a member of the firm and that all firm members had "dumped" the stock. When she complained to the New York Stock Exchange, she was informed that to discipline a firm such as Hayden, Stone for misconduct was not within its province.

Harley L. Clarke too, had his day before the Senate. He traced the formation of General Theatres Equipment Company and told how the corporation had a write-up of more than $26,000,000 in one item. The transaction was simple one. General Theatres took over a company called International Projector Corporation, which had one million shares of common stock valued at something over $2,200,000. On the books of General Theatres Equipment valuation was given as $28,488,000.

"How did you justify this $26,000,000 mark up?" Mr. Clarke was asked.

"On prospective earnings."

The committee desired more detailed information. Murray A. Dodge, vice-president of Chase Securities and a financial advisor to Harley Lyman Clarke and Albert H. Wiggin, was called to testify. Mr. Dodge informed Ferdinand Pecora, the committee's counsel, that because the projector made by International was too new he refused the invitation to participate in financing the company. However, under his advice, Mr. Wiggin had his family's company, The Shermar Corporation, take a part of the financing. The bankers who participated in the pool earned commissions that amounted to $4,-000,000 on this one issue. Shermar lost $2,000,000.

Before he finished, Mr. Dodge explained how General Theatres Equipment gained control of Fox Film and how Harold L. Stuart had been eased out of the picture. "In April of 1930," he said, "various groups were making effort through court action in New York to oust Mr. Fox as the dominant figure in the affairs of Fox Film. While court hearings were being held Harley Lyman Clarke conceived the idea of gaining control of Fox Film through having General Theatres Equipment purchase the stock control. Mr. Wiggin and others concurred in the plan."

"Is that when this conversation was held?" Mr. Dodge was shown the transcript of a telephone conversation between Mr. Clarke and Mr. Stuart, excerpts of which follow:

Stuart: "I have been put out on the end of a spring board and told to jump off."

Clarke: "What do you mean?"

Stuart: "Well, for one thing Blumenthal knew what was going on and I did not."

Clarke: "Well, if he got any information he didn't get it from me.

> If you want to play ball with me, you tell me what you
> have on me, and if you have anything on me, I will come
> clean with you. I have a reputation as well as you have."

Stuart: "I don't think you ought to talk to me like that. I feel as
though I have been pushed out of the picture."

"It was," Mr. Dodge admitted.

"Bankers frequently quarrel among themselves over a choice
bit of financing business?" Mr. Pecora asked.

Dryly Dodge answered, "Bankers are human like everybody
else."

How very human was proven in a couple of notes Mr. Dodge had
written to Mr. Wiggin. Harry Stuart, with John Otterson as his ally,
suspicious though he was, continued to play along with the Chase
National group until early in 1931 when he issued his ultimatum
and refused to help refinance the $55,000,000 Fox loans. Mr. Pecora
surprised Mr. Dodge by asking him to identify the notes which were
confidential inter-office memoranda.

They read:

> "We are doing everything to prevent a fight as the Lord knows
> this financing is difficult enough without being torpedoed by
> Harry Stuart. He is evidently bent on getting control of the
> management of the company through John Otterson and will
> use the same methods that the two of them used against Fox
> to obtain their ends. It would be a very profitable and advan-
> tageous thing for Stuart and Otterson now that they know
> they will not have our backing in throwing Clarke out of Fox,
> to make this financing himself and so obtain control of the Loew
> stock and the company for $55,000,000.

(The second memo obviously was written after the withdrawal
of Halsey, Stuart.)

> "With Halsey, Stuart out it is possible for me to discuss the
> whole financing with Kuhn, Loeb & Company again, a thing
> I am loath to do unless necessary, as the split up of the gravy
> would hurt my feelings."

To what extent, the Banking & Currency Committee wished to
know, were bank loans used for stock speculation. Presidents of more
than forty banks were subpoenaed to Washington. Also called was
Richard Whitney, scion of one of the country's first families and
president of the New York Stock Exchange, who a few years later

went to jail as an embezzler. Mr. Whitney told the committee that 25,000,000 people lost money that amounted to over $50,000,-000,000 in stock dealings, only a small portion of which was represented by motion picture issues.

All went under the label, "Financial Readjustment."

The Paramount Failure

Close on the heels of A. C. Blumenthal's claim that the rights of Paramount stockholders were prejudiced by the $13,875,000 loan, stockholders brought suit in which they asked that Chase National Bank be removed as the trustee of a $15,000,000 bond issue on the ground that the bank was guilty of "breeches of duty; wilful, selfish, and reckless misconduct; gross negligence and bad faith, and has therefore demonstrated itself unfit and disqualified longer to continue as trustee." Cited as an example was the sale of a half interest in Columbia Broadcasting System for a sum that did not represent its true value. Also cited was the pledge of twenty-three feature pictures at a time when the trustee had known for some months that the operation of Paramount-Publix "has been carried on under recurring, severe and oppressive losses of at least $1,000,000 a month."

Charges of this nature invariably culminate in a resignation. John Daniel Hertz, who held the losing card, became a partner in Lehman Brothers, bankers and brokers. The move did not save Paramount-Publix. In January of 1933, Federal Judge William Bondy appointed Charles Dewey Hilles of the Republican National Committee and Adolph Zukor receivers in equity of Paramount-Publix.

Samuel Zirn, attorney for bondholders, protested that the trustees represented banking interests and demanded the appointment of a third trustee. The court concurred. C. E. Richardson, who represented Chase National Bank as vice-president and treasurer of Fox Film, resigned his Fox posts, to accept a place beside Zukor and Hilles.

Shortly after, with the consent of the receivers, Paramount-Publix, a corporation with 501 subsidiaries, declared itself bankrupt.

325

In the course of the bankruptcy hearings, Ralph A. Kohn, former Paramount-Publix treasurer, explained how the money was raised against which the twenty-three features, valued at over $10,000,000, were placed as collateral. In February of 1932, National City Bank refused to renew a $1,000,000 Paramount-Publix loan. This refusal, executives felt, put the company's entire line of credit amounting to $9,600,000 in jeopardy. A new corporation, without office space, without employees, without stationery, called Film Productions Corporation, issued $10,000,000 worth of promisory notes, which were sold to banks with the twenty-three pictures as collateral. The obligations (also to the banks), totaling $9,600,000, were paid with this $10,000,000.

Austin Keough, head of Paramount's legal department, followed Mr. Kohn to the stand.

"What is the status of Mr. A. C. Blumenthal's claim?" he was asked.

He hesitated a monent, then answered quietly, "It was settled for $36,000." The claim consisted of bonds which had cost A. C. $25,000 and were valued at $7,500 at the time of the settlement."

"You mean you bought off suit with $36,000?"

"We settled the suit," Mr. Keough corrected. He then went on to explain that the company at first intended to fight the action. When A. C. Blumenthal threatened to ask for receivership, it was decided that to settle at a figure agreeable to him might be wiser. Mr. Keough did not add, especially since A. C. had solved the mystery of the twenty-three features.

"Why were the records removed from the files of the court?"

"We thought other bondholders might see the figures and start suit." But, Mr. Keough had misjudged the bondholders. The Sidney Kent settlement had already inflamed them.

When bondholders saw the detailed account of salaries and bonuses paid in stock, (except in years when securities were fluctuating too greatly and cash was given) to Adolph Zukor, Jesse Lasky, Sidney Kent, Sam Katz, and others, they cried, "Looting," and demanded the return of more than $23,000,000. In 1929, the year of the stock market collapse, among the bonuses paid were: Zukor $887,500, Lasky $887,500, Kent $710,000, Katz $710,000. Much of the money was gone, some on the stock market, some at poker, some in high living. A large portion was in unattachable funds.

"Why," Mr. Zirn wanted to know, "was a man whose salary amounted to $2,000 a week given $200,000 to break his contract in these precarious times?" The reference was to the Sidney Kent settlement.

Mr. Keough shifted in his seat before he answered, "In the best interests of the company."

Adolph Zukor was among those who had suffered heavy losses. He no longer was able to maintain his palatial New City estate as a private residence. Under the name Mountain View Country Club, he opened it to the public as a hotel and golf course.

As for the demands of the stockholders, instead of a refund, bills covering the first twelve weeks of receivership amounting to $300,000 poured in. One item alone was for $30,000 for Mr. Hilles, who bluntly admitted he knew nothing about motion pictures. Mr. Zukor, with a quarter century of experience, asked $23,000. Elihu Root, Jr., counsel for the trustees was asked to explain the logic of this.

"Mr. Zukor," he said, "did not feel justified in asking more than the reduced salary he had been receiving; while Mr. Hilles had to give time to learn all about the business. He had to sit up nights and do the work, staking his reputation and his fortune. For this," he went on, "Mr. Hilles' fee is moderate." Mr. Root's own fee was $125,000.

Samuel Zirn demanded the removal of the trustees, a removal Judge Manton refused to allow. The judge, however, reduced the total of $300,000 in claims to $258,000, cutting Mr. Root's bill down to $100,000, a cut Elihu Root hotly contested. Hilles received $30,000 for his twelve weeks of study.

The Blue Eagle

IN THE "FINANCIAL READJUSTMENT," FACTORIES across the United States closed. Great masses of the population were without work. "I lost my savings in Cities Service," "Mine went in Insull Securities," became national chants. On Times Square the breadline that passed alongside a truck bearing a huge Hearst poster was a nightly horror to theatre goers. The number of unemployed and underpaid extras on the West Coast became a national scandal. Wages dropped from a minimum of $3 a day to $1.25 a day, and extras were lucky to have an average of one day's work a week.

Franklin Delano Roosevelt, Herbert Hoover's White House successor, in an effort to alleviate the situation fostered the National Recovery Act (NRA). It was to operate on trial for two years. An eagle, its color blue, was selected as the NRA symbol.

To men in motion pictures as to men in all fields, the Blue Eagle became an oracle. The Majors expected it to spread protective wings over their domain. Independent producers were sure the Blue Eagle would set up spheres for them. Small exhibitors spoke of Blue Eagle reforms. "Blind, block booking," they said, "will become a thing of the past."

Everywhere, in windows, on doors, on walls, reproductions of the Blue Eagle appeared, homage to the oracle.

The studios of Hollywood (where high-salaried talent groups had agreed to a fifty per cent cut in salary over an eight-week period) asked Sol A. Rosenblatt, Deputy Code Administrator, voice of the oracle, to incorporate among other items in the NRA code, agency licensing, anti-raiding of talent, and salary control provisions.

328

The stars retaliated with a telegram in which they said, "The motion picture companies have not been bankrupt by salaries to talent, but by purchasing and leasing of theatres at exorbitant prices, caused by the race to power of a few individuals desiring to get a strangle hold on the outlet of the industry, the box office."

At the end of the eight weeks agreed upon, Darryl Zanuck, for nine years chief of production under Jack Warner, asked that his full salary be restored. Warner Brothers refused, and Darryl Zanuck resigned.

Dissatisfaction spread. The industry faced a crisis. Six hundred sixty-five technicians went on strike. All unionized crafts in Hollywood, cameramen, sound men, laboratory technicians, cutters, editors, property men, electricians, followed.

Sol A. Rosenblatt went to Hollywood to straighten out the differences. He was received as only the film capital receives an honored guest. Music greeted him as he stepped off the train. The station was decorated with banners. Celebrities waited on the platform. A parade escorted him to his hotel. Day and night he interviewed executives and talent groups. He held conferences in his five-room hotel suite, over the dinner table, at night clubs. When he left for the east, no one had the courtesy to wish him "God speed."

Hollywood stages went dark. They did not light up until musicians accepted a twenty per cent reduction and George E. Browne, head of IATSE (International All Theatre Stage Employees and Moving Picture Machine Operators of the United States and Canada), agreed to salary cuts for the members of his union ranging up to thirty-five per cent. All studio workers compromised.

The world's most glamorized personalities, its most highly paid employees formed a trade union, the Screen Actors Guild.

Independents, as weary of the oracle as talent groups, engaged Clarence Darrow to interpret the Code. Among other things, he advised them that the "Motion Picture Code appears to have been made by representatives of the large producing companies. The Authority consists of ten members, of whom eight are known to be directly or indirectly connected with the large concerns. The Code Authority seeks to coerce Independent Exhibitors to waive all rights under anti-trust laws by executing unqualified assent to the Code. Under the Code, the Major Companies get absolute control of clearance or zoning of pictures."

With Clarence Darrow as their attorney, Independents instituted suit in which they charged that Sol Rosenblatt had shown persistent bias against Independent Exhibitors, that he refused to give them a fair hearing, that he incorrectly reported the industry was in agreement on the terms of the Code, that he met them with evasion, equivocation, and pettifogging, and that he aligned himself with influences in the industry which were opposed to the best interests of the Independent Exhibitors.

Dr. A. Lawrence Lowell, President Emeritus of Harvard University, invited to become a member of the Code Authority, said he was forced to decline, because blind block booking compelled exhibitors to accept film practically without choice, and the practice continued to exist under the Code.

Sol Rosenblatt issued a statement in which he declared the criticism against him was biased, ".....solely the vicious mouthings and conjecture of a few disgrunted enemies of NRA." He went on to say, "A star or an executive is worth as much as the public can be led to think he is worth," and "there has been only one decision on block booking, and that decision declared this method of selling legal."

Almost as an answer to Mr. Rosenblatt's statement, the Neely-Pettengill Bill, which asked Congress to outlaw blind, block booking, was drafted. During hearings on this bill a crisp exchange of words occurred when the fact became known that a single motion picture executive entertained more than ninety-six Congressmen.

An anonymous pamphlet, entitled What Do You Know About Block-Booking? which defended this system of selling, was circulated widely. The pamphlet was traced to the Hays office.

The industry was back on the battlefield. Without a word of regret Independents and Majors alike took down their pictures of the Blue Eagle, when the United States Supreme Court invalidated the National Recovery Act.

Book Three, Part Two

On The Heels Of Financial Readjustment

(1934 to 1960)

Out Of The Ether

A s if the Majors had not enough to harass them, Upton
Sinclair, writer, with an "Epic" plan to end poverty, emerged
as the Democratic candidate in the 1934 California Gubernatorial
race.

A plan to end poverty terrified Joseph M. Schenck, who proclaimed,
"This man is a Socialist . . . . If he is elected the moving
picture industry must leave California."

Under an order accredited to Louis B. Mayer, all motion picture
personnel who received more than $100 a week were asked to con-
tribute one day's pay toward the campaign fund of Frank Merriam,
Republican nominee. During an address to his writing staff, Mayer
said, "What does Sinclair know about anything? He is just a writer."

Every film worker, especially those in the frightened white collar
class, was told how to vote. Katherine Hepburn, R-K-O star, was
threatened with dismissal if she voted for Sinclair.

Neither the oratory nor the orders of Mr. Schenck or Mr. Mayer
silenced the writer. Mr. Sinclair went right on to explain how he intended to make his "Epic" plan work. C. C. Pettijohn, who at one
time had a fee for placing Republican propaganda and at another
time had a fee for placing the propaganda of the Democrats, was
imported from New York to carry on an anti-Sinclair campaign.
The "Stop-Sinclair" cry bordered on delirium.

Rumors rose that Sinclair was to be advised to drop from the
race by the Democratic National Committee. The rumors apparently
never reached him for he kept right on addressing the people. Frantic
film magnates solicited the support of railroads, automobile author-

ities, and newspapers. Stories were told of the influx of jobless via freight cars, in automobiles, and on foot. A leading Los Angeles newspaper published as a news shot a still taken from a feature film. It was the picture of a bum entering the state in response to Sinclair's invitation.

A conversation between two hoboes headed for "Sinclair's Utopia," in California became a nightly radio feature. Melodramas based on the Inquiring Photographer idea were attached to newsreels. In one a man with shaggy whiskers and a menacing expression was asked by the interviewer, "For whom are you voting?"

"Vy, I am foting for Seenclair," he answered.

"Why are you voting for Mr. Sinclair?"

"Vell, his system voiked vell in Russia, vy can't it voik here?"

Frank F. Merriam, presented as a representative of the American way of life, became California's governor.

While movie magnates were hysterical over politics on the west coast, politicians were hysterical over movie practices on the east coast. The Republican Party charged that Pathé had a contract to release W.P.A. propaganda. Movie executives were labled "Democrat" or "Republican," as if to be either were a crime. Republicans checked newsreel space accorded Democrats; Democrats checked newsreel space accorded Republicans.

Except to lay groundwork for suitable legislation and to assure themselves of friends in strategic spots, most movie executives preferred not to air their political preferences. Newsreels, except under exceptional pressure, gave foot for foot to each of the major parties, taking into consideration that both parties had followers among their customers, the exhibitors. Cutting and additions often took place in local communities. Politicians, unaware how or where bias crept in, kept demanding an inquiry into film practices.

Senator McAdoo, with some knowledge of the industry's workings, recommended a Senatorial investigation along different lines. Why, he wanted to know, were counsel and receiver fees in the Paramount receivership over $3,000,000, the final bill of Mr. Root's firm alone $700,000. Judge Alfred C. Coxe, before whom the bankruptcy hearings had been held, apparently felt that Mr. McAdoo's criticism had some merit. He disallowed fees by Kuhn, Loeb & Company, the bankers, who were accused of making fat profits through tips given them by a member of their firm who helped plan Paramount's reorganization preliminaries, and to Gravath, de Gersdorff, Swaine and Wood, the Kuhn Loeb attorneys.

In addition Judge Coxe ordered the return of $2,150,000 (less than ten per cent of the amount claimed by stockholders) by Adolph Zukor, his son Eugene, Jesse L. Lasky, Sam Katz, Sidney R. Kent, and Jules Brulatour, who had been a Paramount director. They, with others, were alleged to have mismanaged the company's affairs, and to have voted themselves excessive compensation. Their conduct in connection with the trading on the open market by Paramount executives in the company's stock, and the issue and delivery of 139,800 shares of common stock to the corporation's principal officers and directors under a so-called employee's stock purchase plan was questioned.

The refund paved the way for the lifting of receivership. Reorganization plans were placed before Judge Manton in the Federal Circuit Court of Appeals. He reversed the decision of Judge Coxe, and granted fees to Kuhn, Loeb & Company and their attorneys. "The bankers," he said, "deserve a fee. As a result of their reorganization plan, the business has been turned back to the reorganized company with the properties intact, and well integrated, with fixed charges greatly reduced, and on a sound financial basis, and with its goodwill unimpaired."

The reorganized Paramount company, in which the Atlas Corporation, with offices on Wall Street, became a substantial stockholder, was renamed Paramount Pictures, Inc. John E. Otterson became president at a salary of $156,000 a year. As president of Electrical Research, where he had years of experience, he received $50,000 a year. In a pep talk that followed his appointment, Mr. Otterson spoke so highly of Adolph Zukor, Mr. Zukor was asked to serve as chairman of the board and adviser to Mr. Otterson at a salary equal to Mr. Otterson's plus a percentage of profits.

The refund to Paramount stockholders set an example. Loew stockholders sued Louis B. Mayer, Nicholas M. Schenck, J. Robert Rubin, and the estate of Irving Thalberg, who had died, for $19,-000,000. The court approved of the bonuses paid to these executives, but thought a slight error had been made in computing them. To the stockholders $500,000 was returned. The decision absolved the company officials from any connection with the mistake in computation, or any desire to profit wrongfully from it.

At Warners too, stockholders sued. Three Warners and Renraw, Inc. were requested to transfer 100,000 shares of Warner stock to the Warner Corporation.

Judge Manton was embarrassed. Almost immediately, after adopting the Kuhn, Loeb plan, the reorganized Paramount company was in difficulties.

At the request of the board, Joseph P. Kennedy made a two-month survey. He found that the company had "great potentialities but rough sledding. He criticized the high cost of film output and said that waste at the studios should be eliminated. He had no specific changes to suggest. However, John E. Otterson's contract was purchased for $200,000, and Barney Balaban was elected president of Paramount Pictures, Inc.

Kennedy, who was paid $50,000 for his Paramount survey, which stressed extravagance, also acted as financial adviser to Radio Corporation of America. For R-C-A, which paid him $150,000, he drew up a recapitalization plan.

Following his report, R-C-A, for $11,000,000 sold a part of its controlling interest in R-K-O to Floyd B. Odlum, president of the Atlas Corporation. Shortly after the purchase, Mr. Odlum announced that Leo Spitz, a Chicago attorney, would replace Merlin Hall Aylesworth, who went into the newspaper field with the Scripps-Howard organizations.

Although unknown to the general public, Mr. Spitz had a long motion picture record. An old friend of the Balabans and John Hertz, he was a power behind the throne in the labor settlement in Chicago that established the strength of George E. Browne and William Bioff. In that city, Browne and Bioff headed IASTE. On another occasion, Spitz served in an advisory capacity at Paramount.

In this era of realignment, Joseph M. Schenck and Darryl Zanuck formed a corporation which they named Twentieth Century. With the formation of Twentieth Century, Samuel Goldwyn, nicknamed Stormy Petrel, and who through the years released his pictures through various channels, took over the presidency at United Artists. Al Lichtman, in charge of United Artist's sales for more than ten years, moved over to M-G-M as a vice-president.

The formation of Twentieth Century caused a flurry among M-G-M minority stockholders. They wanted to know why Nicholas Schenck and Louis B. Mayer, M-G-M executives, were named stockholders in a competitive company. Subtle as the answer was, they soon had one.

Fox Film, as well as Paramount and R-K-O, was pulling out of the ether. Milton C. Weisman, receiver for Fox Metropolitan Theatres, urged that these "poor little lambs that everybody has nipped at," be turned over to Joseph M. Schenck, who had volunteered a reorganization plan which would guard against further "nipping." Under Joseph Schenck's plan, Spyros Skouras was to have a voice in the management of "these poor little lambs." The money arrangement provided twenty per cent in cash and fifty-five per cent in securities to bondholders.

When Si Fabian, at the time operating a small circuit in upper New York State, came forward with an alternate plan in which he offered note-holders one hundred cents on the dollar, twenty per cent in cash and eighty per cent in debenture bonds, Joseph Schenck revealed a few of his thoughts on the subject. "I would not give forty cents for the Fox Met group," he said, "if the Skourases are not connected with its management. They are the best theatre operators in the business. And I am not speaking merely from observation. I have had experience with these men. On the west coast I am jointly interested with them in Wesco." One policy of the Skourases on taking over was to cut the manager's salary and set a figure of business he was expected to produce. If the manager exceeded the quota set, he was to get a small percentage of the excess amount; also he was to get a percentage of savings in operating costs. A manager was expected to be on the job eighteen hours a day, seven days a week. The turnover in managerial ranks was constant; once in a two-month period, forty-five managers resigned.

Despite Mr. Schenck's argument and the pleas of Milton C. Weisman, receiver, who asked the court not to consider anyone but Mr. Schenck, Judge Julian W. Mack reserved decision until Mr. Schenck raised his bid, so that the bondholders received as much under his plan as under Si Fabian's.

A full merger of Twentieth Century and Fox Film followed the Joseph Schenck acquisition of Fox Metropolitan Theatres.

In the new line up Sidney Kent was given a seven year contract as president. Joseph Schenck, also with a seven year contract, became chairman of the board. Darryl Francis Zanuck became vice-president and chief of production. Spyros Skouras, with desks allotted to his entourage, was placed in charge of theatre operations.

In whispers, mention was made that certain Twentieth Century stockholders profited by the deal, and that A. C. Blumenthal, an old friend of Joe Schenck, with whom he jointly purchased a Florida estate and with whom he shared a hotel apartment in New York for purposes of entertainment, was to get a commission for acting as intermediary.

This is the part A. C. played. William Rhinelander Stewart, whom he knew, introduced him to Winthrop Aldrich, who in turn introduced him to a Chase National vice-president. A. C. then brought Joseph Schenck and Darryl Zanuck downtown. Chase National Securities still was trying to dispose of the Fox issue which John W. Pope had wired his customers not to purchase. Fox Film had just passed another dividend, and the company's losses were reported to be exceedingly heavy. After the foundation was laid by Schenck and Zanuck, Sidney Kent was brought into the conferences. The fee to A. C. for these introductions was $1,000,000.

Under the salary arrangements Sidney Kent was to get $180,000 a year provided National Theatres, at a salary to be agreed upon, also engaged his services. In the event National Theatres did not, he was to get an additional $25,000. Zanuck was to get $260,000, and Schenck $130,000. All were to receive bonuses, be allowed expense accounts, and the right to purchase stock at a "price."

Minority stockholders charged conspiracy. Also resenting the contract was Winnie Sheehan, who had become known as "the man no one could find." Perhaps one reason he was difficult to locate was because the Harriman Bank was trying to serve him in a $6,800,000 suit, claiming Sheehan's mismanagement had caused losses to the bank. Other Wall Streeters complained that he kept two studios in operation when one would do on the west coast. In his own complaint, Sheehan said that when he gave up nursing his liver to return to active duty, Sidney Kent had promised to keep him up to date on all financial transactions. And there he was up to his neck in production, thousands of miles from New York, completely unaware of the big doings in the east. He did not think this was playing cricket!

Dissatisfaction! Sidney Kent knew how to meet it. The balance of Sheehan's contract was purchased for $360,000.

Incidentals disposed of, a stockholders meeting was called. Sidney Kent, reputed to be America's best salesman, was the main speaker.

He explained the why and wherefore of the amalgamation; he spoke of his aims and of his nobility.

When he was asked to take over the presidency of the company, he said, he night have written his own ticket, but now, because of a "stale law which precludes the officer of a company from receiving company stock unless it is paid for," he has relinquished his claim to 50,000 shares, which were to have been given him as a bonus.

"Had I known," he said, "the internal mess within this company, I would not have taken on the job. But all I saw was the balance sheet. Internal troubles are not visible there."

"Neither Fox nor the Twentieth Century needed capital," he went on. "Both had good credit ratings and could raise whatever they needed. It's just that the name of Fox smelled. We thought it might be a serious detriment to the company's goodwill, and we seriously considered omitting it from the name of the new company. Fox Film was lucky to get the Twentieth Century. My main consideration now is man power. It was only to get the man power of Twentieth Century that Fox united with it. Darryl Zanuck is worth $5,000 a week and more. He and Joseph Schenck are man power insurance."

When applause subsided, Joseph Schenck rose to say that Twentieth Century-Fox was lucky to have Sidney Kent, "who could earn more money elsewhere."

Darryl Zanuck, at a press interview, had a modest moment. Without his press agent, he said, he did not think he would be as great a man.

The Panay Incident

THE DOWNTOWN "SQUEEZE" WHICH HAD UNSEATED so many old timers finally caught up with Carl Laemmle. Erpi, now securely rooted in the motion picture field, let Robert Cochrane run Universal for a while, and then turned it over to Nate Blumberg, formerly on R-K-O's staff.

Retired, Carl Laemmle found time heavy on his hands. To fill his days he entertained a great deal. Something of the "Imp" remained, and his guests were subjected to a strange performance. He had a cabinet composed of many small drawers. Each drawer was filled with false teeth.

"See these!" he would say, as he opened first one drawer, then another. "They are the works of men with exaggerated opinions of themselves. For years I tried to get a set of teeth that fit. No matter how highly reccommended the dentist I still had trouble. At last I hit upon an idea. Whenever I met a dentist I made him a proposition. 'Give me a set of teeth that fit,' I would say, 'and I will give you a thousand dollars. Give me a pair that doesn't fit, and you get nothing.' Now, just listen to these teeth rattle." With that he demonstrated set after set.

Although he poked fun at his store teeth, Carl Laemmle was not happy. He missed his business, and he wondered, when he was gone, if his children would ably assume the responsibility of his vast estate.

Time also had altered the position of William Randolph Hearst. Warners had removed Marion Davies from the payroll. Cosmopolitan scripts were so antiquated, no one would buy them. Hearst newspapers were heavily in debt; so were his magazines. Furnishings from St. Dorat's Castle; armor collected all over Europe; Babylonian, Egyptian, Chinese, Greek, Roman, and Celtic art treasures; English, French and Italian furniture; rare books; a Benvenuto Cellini bowl; paintings from the collection of Empress Eugenie; a complete monastery bought at Sacramenia, Spain, transported to the United States, and stored in a Bronx warehouse, went on the auction block. Of the 230,000 acres at San Simeon, 165,000 were sold. Hearst moved into Marion Davies' forty room bungalow by the sea. Stockholders charged that Hearst Consolidated Publications was guilty of using money raised by the sale of stock for other Hearst ventures and that the corporation was insolvent from its inception. It seemed his mother's prophecy, that he would die broke, had come true. News Of The Day (the name given to Hearst Metrotone News when movie audiences hissed off the screen anything with Hearst on the title), a corporation Hearst regarded too insignificant for his personal attention, was the only Hearst organization operating in the black.

The newsreel did more than keep Hearst in spending money. It brought him credit for one of the most spectacular scoops in the history of the business. In 1937, when the Japanese bombed the United States Gunboat Panay on the Yangtze River near Nanking, two cameramen were on board, Norman Alley, who represented Universal, and Eric Mayell, who represented Fox Movietone and News Of The Day. (Under certain circumstances newsreels pool their cameramen.)

Alley telegraphed a description of his shots to his home office. They sounded so thrilling, Charlie Ford, Universal editor, volunteered to show the pictures to various government departments in Washington, before exhibiting them to the public. The film was widely advertised, and theatre owners were advised that Universal would issue a two reeler on the first act of Japanese aggression.

On the staff of News Of The Day was a writer named Paul Alley. Mike Clofine, editor of the reel, rushed Paul Alley to California to await the Mayell negative. As soon as it arrived Paul Alley scored (added a voice to) the Panay subject. Meanwhile the Norman Alley film went to Washington. Thus movie audiences, few of whom distinguished Paul from Norman, saw pictures of the miniature Pearl Harbor as soon as, or sooner than, government officials.

Incensed that Universal wanted to pass off a newsreel subject as

a two reeler, delivered late at that, many independents switched their
contracts from Universal to News Of The Day. Charlie Ford switched from news to feature productions.

The Panay incident was the forerunner of a series of event which
stimulated interest in news. By the time World War II was under
way, circulation figures on newspapers throughout the country soared.
Hearst had outlived the fear created by the words of his mother,
"William, you will die broke," and moved back into the 65,000
acres left of the original 230,000 acres of his feudal barony of San
Simeon, which had been dark for over three years.

"He Don't Eat No Lunch.
He Eats Apples."

DARK YEARS HAD COME TO AN END. Business was on the upgrade. Labor, though peevish, was under control. Receivers no longer issued orders. The industry had come through bad times with eight Majors intact: Loew's Incorporated (Metro-Goldwyn-Mayer); Twentieth Century-Fox Film Corporation; Paramount Pictures, Inc.; Warner Brothers Pictures, Inc.; Radio-Keith-Orpheum Corporation; Columbia Pictures Company, Inc.; Universal Pictures Company, Inc.; United Artists Corporation.

In the depression the line-up had shifted. Paramount lost the lead. Columbia, with a special, inexpensively produced, "It Happened One Night," and the notable production, "Lost Horizon," emerged a major. Despite the Twentieth Century-Fox merger, Loew's Inc., with assets of over $150,000,000 was the big company of the industry.

As a mark of its importance the company paid its chief of production, Louis B. Mayer, the highest salary paid to any individual in the United States. For six successive years, Louis B. Mayer received a salary larger than that paid to any railroad baron, to any steel baron, to any telephone baron. He was paid a salary greater than that paid to George Washington Hill, who, through his representative Benjamin Hampton, once dangled $100,000,000 over motion picture heads. He received a salary ten times greater than that paid to the Chief Executive of the United States of America. For the year 1937, his salary and bonus totaled $1,296,503.

His throne room harmonized with his salary. It was high ceilinged, spacious. Its walls were of white leather. His desk, also white, was crescent in shape. On it stood a white telephone. Under it was a series

343

of buzzers. The desk was placed before a huge window. Mayer's chair was constructed to make him appear taller. Anyone who visited him crossed the length of the room to reach the crescent. Venetian blinds, set off by heavy draperies, regulated the light so that he might study the expressions of his visitors. The face of Louis B. Mayer was in a shadow.

Louis B. Mayer was, at last, sovereign of the motion picture empire. He rose to his position. His executive secretary was Mrs. Ida Koverman, who had served his friend Herbert Hoover while he was President of the United States. At regular intervals Mayer called his employees together and delivered a speech. He became famous as a rider of horses. His stable enjoyed a national reputation. He learned the rhumba and other modern dances. Newspaper columnists wrote of his grace. Young girls were flattered to have him as a partner; he danced so well!

Top man though he was, his friend Joseph M. Schenck, brother of his partner Nick Schenck, had the honor to act as spokesman for the big companies in labor matters. A day came, however, when the business of negotiating with labor leaders became so ticklish, Joe Schenck wished the honor were not his.

The difficulties of Joe Schenck, who first made money in a drug store, became disasters when the United States Treasury Department failed to understand a transaction with a union leader which involved $100,000.

One morning in June of 1937, Joseph Schenck rang for his secretary, Ruth Nolander. When Miss Nolander entered the office, Mr. Schenck was talking to one William Bioff. A stack of thousand dollar bills was on the desk. Without saying anything to Miss Nolander, Mr. Schenck counted the bills. They numbered a hundred. After the counting he placed them in an envelope which he sealed. With the sealed envelope he walked into the outer office. Miss Nolander followed. There, in the presence of Miss Nolander and the bookkeeping staff, Joseph Schenck placed the sealed envelope in a safe. A few days later he removed the envelope, counted the bills, and placed them in his pocket. Through a medium never divulged, the United States Collector of Internal Revenue heard the story. The department assumed that Joseph M. Schenck had received $100,000, which he had failed to report as income. An investigation of his records followed. The department never proved the charge; however, its investigation unravelled a few intricacies of high finance.

Schenck was a meticulous man. He insisted on vouchers for every expenditure; at his home, vouchers were made out for twenty-five cent aspirins. When a secretary submitted a bill for groceries, she noted on which days he had entertained. If he were away on a trip, detailed reports were submitted to him of all expenses incurred during his absence. A record of those guests, among them Groucho Marx, prodigal in the use of towels, was kept. He scrutinized every bill no matter how insignificant the amount.

Analysis of his income tax records showed that his deductions consisted of poker losses, holidays at resort hotels, parties where he entertained men who had retired from business and gambling companions. One week-end, when at a cost of $400 he entertained a young woman whom he signed up as a $50 a week star, was recorded. His deductions included the cost of his automobile, his yacht, his laundry, a mattress for his sister-in-law, and transportation of his masseur from New York to California.

In addition to his motion picture holdings, Joseph Schenck was a substantial stockholder in several other businesses. He was a director of the Bank of America. He had an interest in a race track with the corporate name of Compania Mexicana del Agua Caliente. A Mexican law enacted in 1937 affected Schenck's holdings in that corporation. Previously Schenck had commissioned his $52,000 a year bookkeeper, Joseph Moskowitz, to find for tax purposes some sizeable deduction to offset the tremendous profits he had made on his motion picture investments. The Mexican law provided an excellent opportunity.

Schenck sold his Agua Caliente holdings for $50,000 to a director named Roland West, who paid $15,000 in cash supplied by Schenck. To cover the balance West gave Schenck a $35,000. note.

In spite of records which made all these things clear, checks which totaled $38,000 all made out to cash, remained unaccounted for on his books. And the $100,000 cash item still puzzled Internal Revenue agents.

A further investigation disclosed that in June of 1937, Schenck borrowed $100,000 from the Bank of America. A few days later he appeared at the bank with a four or six pound grocery bag. It contained $100,000 in currency. For the first time in the history of the bank a director showed up with a grocery bag filled with money to repay a loan.

The Treasury Department was not satisfied. Something more was behind the $100,000, and the Department wanted to know what it was.

In September of 1938 one Jeff Kibre, a studio craftsman, "for and on behalf on the Motion Picture Technicians Committee," filed a complaint with the National Labor Relations Board in which he charged that William Bioff, while acting for George E. Browne, president of the International Alliance of Stage and Theatrical Employees, accepted a $100,000 bribe from Joseph M. Schenck. The purpose of the bribe, according to Mr. Kibre, was to balk collective bargaining. His complaint asserted that the money was paid for the purpose of bringing 35,000 workers, over whom Bioff had jurisdiction, under the control and dominance of the Hays organization, and that since January 2, 1936, Bioff had been in the pay of producers while purporting to act as the official representative of the union head. The complaint further alleged that the producers, through a purported closed shop agreement, simulated a process of collective bargaining under the Wagner act, but that actually they dealt with their own paid agents, Bioff and Browne, who refused to bargain with the employees.

Insofar as the $100,000 was concerned Kibre, like the Treasury, could not prove the accusation, but in the investigation that followed his complaint a story of betrayal, a story of company controlled unions, unfolded.

It began in Chicago in 1922. In that year William Bioff, then an underling of the gangster Al Capone was sentenced to serve six months in jail for pandering. He did not serve the sentence. The reason remains among items unexplained.

Little is known of Bioff's activities during the next ten years. In 1932, while trying to organize the kosher butchers of Chicago, he met George E. Browne, business agent for the stage hands Chicago Local 2 IATSE, who had a side line, the organizing of chicken dealers.

The pudgy Browne liked the short muscular Bioff. He liked to sit and drink beer with him. He valued Bioff's philosophy. He admired his physical strength. He suggested that they work together.

Out of a membership of over 400 in the IATSE local, 250 were unemployed. Browne, with Bioff as his assistant, set up a soup kitchen where meals were served to working members for thirty-five cents and to unemployed brethren free.

The soup kitchen was famous throughout Chicago. Celebrities, politicians, society folk dropped in for meals. They paid anywhere from twenty to fifty dollars for the hospitality.

Early in 1934, Browne, accompanied by Bioff, called on Barney Balaban, whose lawyer was Mr. Spitz. Browne asked Balaban to restore a pay cut taken out of IATSE salaries five years before, in 1929. Mr. Balaban said he would gladly do it. One hitch existed. If he restored IATSE pay cuts, other unions would ask similar restorations. That would be costly.

Browne and Bioff pleaded for their men. They told of the dire conditions existing in the union. They asked Mr. Balaban to look at the soup kitchen they had been compelled to open. "It cost $7,000 a year to operate."

Mr. Balaban offered to pay the $7,000 a year.

"You might as well make your contribution $50,000."

After several conferences, Mr. Balaban agreed to $20,000. No further talks of a restoration of pay cuts to union members were held.

Twenty thousand dollars at one clip pleased the two Bs so much they decided to celebrate. They went to a gambling resort owned by Nick Circella, alias Nick Dean, an old associate of Bioff's in the Capone gang. Browne drank beer. Bioff drank a more potent liquid. Three hundred dollars were spent.

A few days later Browne received a caller, Frank Rio, also of the old Capone gang. Rio wanted to know whether Bioff had muscled Browne. Browne assured Rio that Bioff had not, that Bioff was his assistant.

Rio called on Bioff. "The syndicate wants fifty per cent or else," he said.

The syndicate received fifty per cent.

Business was good. Chicago theatre owners were persuaded to pay over $100,000 to avoid a lot of trouble for themselves. And Chicago was the only city in the country that had one man in most projection booths. All other cities had two men in every booth. Two men in each booth would have cost Chicago theatre men about $500,000 more a year.

As long as the income remained under $100,000, the syndicate was satisfied with fifty per cent. When it reached $100,000, a new arrangement was worked out. Bioff and Browne received one third, the syndicate two thirds.

As in any well regulated organization, meetings were held. The first meeting was called to order in the home of a man who in 1932 was Chicago's Chief Inspector of Morals. Frank Nitto, who held together the remnants of the Capone gang, presided. Besides Bioff, eight former members of the gang were present, among them, Nitto, Frank Rio, Louis (Lefty Louis) Campagna, and Paul (The Waiter) De Lucia, Browne also was present. An IATSE presidential election, scheduled for June of 1934, was discussed. The election was to be held in Louisville. Browne, who had run for that office in 1932, informed his partners that his weak spots were New York City, New Jersey, Cleveland, and St. Louis.

At a second meeting, in addition to those who attended the first, were Lepke Buchalter of New York, Longey Zwillman of New Jersey, Al Palizzi of Cleveland, and Johnny Dougherty of St. Louis.

Lepke was given a message for Lucky Luciano, his New York boss. "Local 306 (New York) is to vote for Browne." Local 306 had once been headed by Sam Kaplan, who had bettered the salaries and working conditions of the membership, whose life had been threatened, who finally was sentenced to jail on the testimony of theatre owners supported by three union members. Later other members stated they had been afraid to come to Kaplan's support.

The group that had met in Chicago gathered at the Louisville race track. They carried white walking sticks and mingled with the delegates. In one syllable words and gestures made with the walking sticks they made known their choice. Browne was elected without opposition, without violence.

Following Browne's election a bit of "cleaning up" took place in Chicago. Thomas E. Malloy, business agent of Chicago's Local 110 of IATSE, was murdered. According to rumor, he had failed to share his spoils with the "syndicate." Fred Blacker, nicknamed Bugs because he made a habit of throwing bed-bugs into theatres of non-paying movie men, met a violent death. Clyde Osterberg, who defied union opinion by attempting to organize apprentice motion picture operators, was slain.

The president of IATSE left for New York. Bioff was still his assistant. Nick Circella was chosen to see that they did not stray from the straight and narrow path of the gang.

Nick would not let the two men out of his sight. He attended meetings with them. He ate with them. He drank with them. One afternoon he drank too much and fell asleep. Relieved, Browne and Bioff let him sleep on while they went out to keep an appointment with Pat Casey, labor representative for Hollywood producers. They did not consider Circella refined enough to introduce to such a "high class gentleman as Casey."

Circella was furious when he awoke and insisted that Bioff accompany him to see John Rosselli, who worked for Casey as an undercover labor investigator. Rosselli confirmed Bioff's claim that he had talked to Casey about a plan for IATSE to regain union jurisdiction over Hollywood workers which they had lost in a strike in 1933.

Bioff went to Hollywood as Browne's representative. His first move was to try to build up IATSE membership among movie production employees on the west coast. Paramount Pictures provided his opportunity. That corporation ordered two cameramen to resign from the union. In retaliation Bioff called a projectionist's strike. Chicago was chosen as the scene. Four hundred theatres darkened. Theatre owners, who had paid over $100,000 to avoid trouble, protested. The union explained it had no desire to harm its friends. It only wanted to prove its power. And it did. Within a short time IATSE had jurisdiction over most of the technical workers in the Hollywood studios.

With his newly acquired strength, William Bioff, representative of George E. Browne, president of IATSE, called on Joseph M. Schenck, president of the Association of Motion Picture Producers. That meeting was the first of a series with Mr. Schenck and other top film executives. Whatever else transpired, no provisions were made to increase wages until late in the 1930's, when it seemed unwise to attempt to hold them down to depression year levels. Members of IATSE received increases up to thirty per cent. To this raise Bioff attributed his downfall. He said that his persecution began when, "against terrific odds," he obtained the last of three ten per cent increases.

Whatever the reason, out of the blue he was requested to return to Chicago to serve the sentence which had been imposed upon him in 1922 for, to use his expression, "a youthful indiscretion" (pandering). For some time he resisted extradition, but as Westbrook Pegler, a newspaper columnist, and others exposed his association with Chicago's underworld (without exposing his "friendship" with motion picture executives), he agreed to return to his native city. On April 15, 1940, he entered Bridewell Jail.

To a reporter he said, "When you're the head of twenty-seven unions in a powerful industry, it's likely that someone is out to get you. I've gotten thirty per cent wage increases for about 30,000 workers. That's why I'm here. Who is interested in bringing up that eighteen-year-old case? But they won. I'm here."

On September 20, 1940, his term served with time off for good behavior, he left prison to resume his job as Hollywood representative of the president of IATSE. Before the car that called for him at the prison gate drove off he thrust a typewritten statement out of the window to newsmen who had come to talk to him. "I hope," it read, "that those who are responsible for my incarceration are satisfied. I have paid my pound of flesh to society, and I want everybody responsible directly or indirectly to know that I have no malice or ill-feeling against any group or anyone." In prison he had gained five pounds, which he soon lost.

During his incarceration the Treasury Department took a bold step in connection with the $100,000 item, which in the meantime had become known as the $100,000 loan, the $100,000 fee, the $100,000 bribe, and the money in the grocery bag. Joseph M. Schenck and his $52,000 a year bookkeeper, Joseph H. Moskowitz, were under indictment. Mathias F. Correa, Assistant Attorney General, had charge of the prosecution.

Silently, dark faced, fifty-eight-year-old Joseph M. Schenck sat beside his forty-year old codefendant and heard Mr. Correa tell the jury, "There are three phases to this crime. One: deductions based on alleged losses incurred in stock deals. Actually, the sales were spurious and made only for the record, while off the record maneuvers nullified the transactions. Two: there were business expenses that were so all inclusive that in 1937, Schenck declared that it cost him $89,000 to earn $117,000. Three: in 1937, there was a mysterious transaction concerning a $100,000 loan to William Bioff, California movie union leader."

Then Mr. Correa revealed that government agents, in an effort to uncover the story behind the $100,000 mystery, discovered how Schenck fretted about household expenses; how he changed his cook three times in one month; how his corporation paid his barber $10 a week to keep him well shaved; how he purchased a new wheel for his Rolls Royce, and furnished at a cost of $7,179.91 an apartment for a young woman and charged these items to business expenses;

how he put up $40,000 so a brother of Joseph Moskowitz, a $7,500 a year employee, might purchase stock to make some money; how he "cleaned-up" in betting on the presidential election of 1936; how he refused to accept anything but cash when he won, yet always paid by check when he lost; how he rented his Hollywood mansion to two brothers, who operated it as a gambling house; how he transferred his Agua Calienta stock to Roland West solely for the purpose of tax deductions.

A. C. Blumenthal, who had an off-stage part in most of the industry's important courtroom scenes, was wanted on-stage this time. He was located as a resident of Mexico City. The United States Government served him with a subpoena, and at the same time provided him with traveling expenses for a trip from Mexico City to New York. Even so, A. C. did not return to testify. Instead he sent affidavits from six Mexican physicians. Each affidavit listed a different illness. On only one thing did all six physicians agree, a trip to New York would be fatal to their patient.

Neither the Government nor Schenck's attorneys made an attempt to call Harry Kadis, the income tax inspector who had approved the Schenck returns. On this inspector's recommendation, Twentieth Century-Fox had once engaged as an actress a girl by the name of Else Valentine. Neither was the fact brought to light at this trial nor at any other time that talent and musicians often were sent free of charge by large motion picture outfits to entertain at parties given by or for people in the Internal Revenue Department.

Schenck's attorneys called a long series of character witnesses. Among them was Will Hays, who had not heard that Schenck had associated with William Bioff; Charles Chaplin, who had been associated with Schenck at United Artists, and the two gamblers to whom Schenck had leased his Hollywood mansion. (Eventually, Chaplin, himself, was forced to flee the United States, when certain politicians pinned the Communist label on this man who had become a multimillionaire through the sale of his films around the world. Oxford University eventually awarded the comedian an honorary degree for his contribution to the performing arts.)

"The term character witness is a misnomer," Mr. Correa declared. "What these witnesses testify to is not character, but reputation, merely reputation. Character is what you are. Reputation is what people say about it."

On April 24, 1941, Joseph M. Schenck was found guilty on two counts. He was sentenced to three years at Danbury prison and fined $20,000. Joseph H. Moskowitz was found guilty on one count. His sentence was for a year and a day. His fine was $10,000.

During Schenck's incarceration his business associates did everything possible to make life bearable for him. On one occasion a special newsreel story was made at the penitentiary, and the film presented as a gift to the warden. Schenck, on his part was a model prisoner. Although he had nothing to say about the $100,000, he readily testified for the Government when it brought suit against Browne and Bioff. In appreciation his sentence was reduced.

The Schenck scandal became a thing of the past. He had paid his debt to society not only by serving a prison term but by testifying against two corporation-controlled labor leaders, Browne and Bioff. Like Schenck, they were indicted because the Government wanted to solve the $100,000 mystery. As in the action against Schenck, who had been convicted on an income tax evasion charge, the $100,000 was mentioned only incidentally in the Browne and Bioff case. Mr. Correa, in charge of the trial, accused them of engaging in a film-union extortion racket.

"I never extorted a dime from anybody," Mr. Bioff declared as he surrendered to a United States marshal in California. He was brought to New York for trial.

Bioff was extremely reticent when reporters asked him about the indictment, but he freely discussed the Hollywood labor situation. "The unions on the West Coast are infested with Communism. We expelled eighteen members during the last four years on charges that they were members of the Communist Party. We eliminate them as fast as we can. Our position won't allow anything to stand in the way of the defense (meaning World War II) program.

Judge J. C. Knox was unimpressed by Bioff's patriotism. On his arrival in New York, Bioff was warned by the Judge, who released him under $50,000 bond, that "You will be jailed if any prospective government witness is molested in any way, shape, or form."

During the course of the trial Mr. Correa disclosed to what extent theatre projectionists, studio cameramen, laboratory workers, sound technicians, electricians, property men, special effects men, and animating men were at the mercy of their corporation-controlled leaders. Through threats of strikes and through strikes, *the syndicate* collected fabulous sums of money from corporate heads. Through an assessment of two per cent of weekly wages levied against union members it collected, perhaps, as much as $6,500,000 annually.

Film executives called to testify described several of the meetings with the spokesman for IATSE. The meetings were held in various cities, usually in hotel bedrooms.

Nicholas M. Schenck related a conversation he had with Bioff. "Browne introduced him on April 14, 1936. We devoted a few minutes to pleasantries, and then Bioff said,

'Now look, I'll tell you why I'm here. I want you to know that I am boss. I elected Mr. Browne, and I want $2,000,000 from the movie industry.'

"I told him he was crazy, but it made no impression on him.

'That's what it has to be,' he said, 'and you have to come through with it.'

"When I tried to show him the folly of this, he said,

'Stop this nonsense. It will cost you a lot more if you don't do it.' "

Two days later the union executives met with the movie executives, and drew up the film industry's "basic agreement."

According to Nicholas Schenck, "The meeting was a lovely one until Bioff got me aside and said,

'Now look. I thought the matter over and maybe $2,000,000 is a little too much. It's too hard to get. I decided that I'll take a million.'

"Again I told Bioff he was crazy, but agreed he was to get some money. It was to be $50,000 a year from each of the larger companies, and $25,000 from the smaller ones."

Nicholas Schenck described how he had taken a little bundle to a room in the Waldorf Astoria and placed it on a bed. Bioff picked it up. He asked Browne to count it. Schenck stood by the window smoking, looking out over the city. Then Sidney Kent came in. He likewise placed a little bundle on the bed. Schenck said each bundle contained $50,000. A year later Nicholas Schenck placed another bundle on another bed.

At this point a defense attorney pointed out that Nicholas Schenck had expressed surprise at being asked for money in 1936, whereas the cash settlement of a strike had occurred in 1935.

"I am terribly surprised when anybody asks for $2,000,000 worth," he answered. When asked why he had not complained to

Federal or State authorities, he said that a fear of strikes kept him silent.

Mr. Bernstein, treasurer of Loew's (one of the men who had received the stock bonus that had riled Arthur Loew), testified that he recovered the money from the company for Mr. Nicholas Schenck by persuading executives of the organization to raise the amount of their vouchers for expenses. Some vouchers were entirely fictitious, others merely raised. Mr. Bernstein considered payments to Bioff legitimate business expenses.

A package from Paramount was delivered to Bioff at the Bismark Hotel in Chicago. A $50,000 payment by R-K-O also came to light. As a result of this payment, a ten-year contract was drawn up in which members of Local 306 received $1.86 an hour instead of $2.12 an hour.

Harry Warner admitted that he had paid $20,000 in December of 1937, and $80,000 in January of 1938, "because I was afraid of bodily harm." He also admitted that with his wife and friends he visited Bioff's San Fernado Valley farm, and that he called his host Willie, "because it was good business to keep on friendly terms with Bioff." Warner also padded expense vouchers.

Hugh J. Strong, former detective, who described himself as supervisor of personnel and confidential assistant to Sidney Kent, explained that it was impossible for Mr. Kent to appear in court in person because he was suffering from coronary thrombosis. He described Kent as a heavy contributor. He thought the amount might have been $550,000. He too told of trips to hotels with packages. Once, he said, he accompanied Mr. Kent to the Warwick Hotel. There the executive turned over a package of money to a bell captain who met them in the lobby. On another occasion Mr. Kent went alone and delivered an envelope containing money. William C. Michel, executive vice-president of Twentieth Century-Fox, said that he raised $93,392 of the company's funds under instructions from Kent. The money was turned over to Kent.

More subtle arrangements for payment were worked out by Louis B. Mayer. In 1937, Loew's bought its raw film through Jules E. Brulatour, who represented the Eastman Kodak Company. Smith & Aller, Ltd., agent for the du Pont Company, wanted the Loew business. Louis B. Mayer and Nicholas M. Schenck, president of Loew's, finally agreed to divert the business to them if a way might be found to let Bioff share in the sales agency's commission. This was arranged and Bioff's brother-in-law, Norman Nelson, acted as subagent for the agency.

As Wesley Smith tells the story, "He was supposed to get the orders for raw film, but did not do so. Like his successor, Harry Beatty (unidentified), he just collected the checks. Beatty's checks totaled $159,025, bringing the total for the two men to $236,474." Wesley Smith admitted that Bioff had a complaint to match his own. "By the time I split with the boys," Bioff had told him, "it is peanuts."

The defense insisted that all monies received were "commissions" not "extortions," and that in any case they were made more than three years before the investigation and therefore outlawed.

Bioff, speaking in his own behalf, said that the money was used to fight a "sandbagging" which the industry was getting through legislation. He said that he flew back and forth between California and New York gathering up over a million dollars which he delivered to Joe and Nick Schenck. He said that on one occasion Joe told him that fighting the industry's battles was a thankless job, and Nick cautioned him against imagining that either of the brothers derived any good from the million dollars. He told how he and Joe sat around for hours eating apples together.

At this point Mr. Correa asked him if he didn't mean that he and the producer often lunched together.

"Naw, he don't eat no lunch. He eats apples. I had apples with him."

The meager diet did not win the jury's sympathy. On November 6, 1941, he and Browne were found guilty of extorting $1,200,000 from film executives. Bioff was given a ten-year sentence, Browne was sentenced to eight years.

Still, the $100,000 remained unexplained.

In a talkative mood in his cell, Bioff told a reporter, who asked him where he got the nerve to ask Barney Balaban for $50,000 "I reckoned I might as well kill a sheep as a lamb."

"What kind of an animal did you consider Mr. Balaban to be?" the reporter asked.

"He turned out to be a lamb."

"A lamb that gave you $20,000."

"We didn't get it all. The soup kitchen got a few cases of canned goods outta it."

"This was after you received a gold honorary membership card from the IATSE local in gratitude for beneficences?"

"Yeh, diamond studded."

"Is it true," the reporter asked, "that Browne drank one hundred bottles of imported beer each day?"

A smile crossed his bitter, weary face. "If you won't hold me to it, it might of been 101; it might of been 70."

In the confines of a prison cell Bioff and Browne wanted to prove their patriotism. They pleaded for an opportunity to get out to fight the Japs. They'd do anything the army would let them do. Mr. Correa had other ideas. With their cooperation he convicted the rest of the syndicate, and then turned to a case that involved George Skouras.

Once Bioff's former pals were safely tucked away and what he said had little consequence, Bioff unburdened himself. "I lied and lied and lied," he said. And then he explained the $100,000 mystery.

As a result of his extortion activities Bioff had acquired about $100,000. He wanted to buy a ranch with the money, but was afraid to arouse the suspicions of the income tax authorities. In his efforts to hide his newly acquired wealth he asked Joe Schenck to lend him $100,000 as a friend. Both realized such a loan would seem suspicious, so Schenck arranged to have his nephew hand the money to Bioff. Bioff gave the nephew a note for it. A real estate dealer advised Bioff that the ranch he was interested in was not worth the price asked. Bioff returned the $100,000 cash to Schenck. The nephew failed to cancel the records on the note. In the eyes of a bookkeeper it appeared that Schenck had derived an income of $100,000 from a deal.

Consequently, an unneeded loan led to the conviction and imprisonment of Schenck, who supplied information that contributed to the conviction and imprisonment of Bioff and Browne, who, in turn, supplied information that contributed to the indictment of eight boys from Chicago.

The Movies and the Law

THROUGHOUT THE BIOFF AND BROWNE TRIAL George Skouras verged
on a nervous breakdown. When he drove into New York from
his home on the shore of Long Island Sound in Westchester County,
he kept as far as possible from all other vehicles on the highway.
A pistol remained handy in the door pocket of his car. He fretted
about being followed. His brother Charlie came East during this
period, and the Skourases, known as the silent, mysterious brothers,
congregated at Spyros' house in Westchester on Long Island Sound.
Their meetings were anything but silent. Charlie constantly teased
George, asking him how he intended to spend his time in jail; Spyros
screamed at Charlie for saying things such as this. Bitter, silly words
passed from brother to brother. Sometimes they were loud enough to
be heard by guests sunning themselves at the water's edge. Much of
what was said seemed senseless, and friends said the Skourases had
gone "nuts," especially since their behavior and arguments seemed
not to reconcile with an unusual award that had been given to
Charlie. Now president of Fox West Coast Theatres, a company for
which he once had acted as trustee in bankruptcy, Charlie was
presented with a diamond studded union card by the International
Alliance of Theatrical Stage Employees as a token of friendship that
existed between capital and labor.

The incarcerated Bioff had spells of talkativeness. In such a mood
he eventually threw light on the George Skouras mystery as he
previously had done on the $100,000 mystery. The story he related
he thought humorous.

"Before I went to prison," he said, "Sol Rosenblatt, former N.R.A.
administrator, got in touch with me. He said George Skouras was in

357

a kind of trouble. I went up to Rosenblatt's office to meet him."

"Well, Mr. Skouras, what's your problem?" I asked. "Skouras explained that he operated a chain of movie houses very similar to the Frisch Rintzler chain. They showed the same pictures at the same time, dealt with the same banks. But there was a difference Skouras found embarrassing. The booth members of my union cost Skouras $60,000 more a year than they cost his competitor. Skouras said the bankers called him on the carpet because of this extravagance. He said something had to be done to put his theatres on a comparable basis. If I would do it it would be worth $50,000 to me.

".I wasn't well acquainted with Skouras, but Rosenblatt guaranteed that I would be paid if I solved the situation. So I went to work. I called up the heads of the Frisch Rintzler circuit, and increased their scale $60,000 a year. You see, I struck a bargain with Mr. Skouras to put the chains on a comparable basis, and I did. Mr. Rosenblatt gave me seventy-five per cent of $25,000."

"Did the other twenty-five per cent go to Sol Rosenblatt?" he was asked.

"That was his fee," Bioff answered.

One cynical story followed another. Judge Martin J. Manton ruled the Circuit Court of Appeals, where he had served as a judge for twenty-two years. His bench, which had taken on the appearance of an absolute monarch's throne, suddenly loosened at the joints, when on January 27,1939, the New York World-Telegram accused him of engaging in business activities. While Manton insisted his business transactions had no relation to his judicial conduct, George Washington Hill, the $100,000,000 dangler, and other American Tobacco officers were charged with bribery in a suit by minority stockholders for the return of $2,672,507. Manton conceded he had borrowed a total of $664,000, of which $250,000 had been advanced by the American Tobacco group. Harry Warner, the film magnate, did not deny lending Manton large sums. Found guilty, Manton was sentenced to serve two years at Northeastern Penitentiary, Lewisburg, Pa. Although erect and stern-faced as usual, tears fell behind the rimless glasses of the ruddy-faced sixty-year old judge as he entered the prison to be fingerprinted, photographed, and bathed. His velvet-collared overcoat and well-tailored suit were exchanged for coarse gray prison garb. After thirty days in quarantine, he was set to clerical jobs.

The downfall of one is apt to bring that of others. Manton's bagman received a nine-month sentence. The lawyer who had represented Mr. Hill was disbarred. And a second revelation in the George Skouras case of nerves came to light. George was indicted. During the receivership of the Fox Corporation, the charge stated, he had conspired to bribe Manton to win approval of an agreement by the receivers to let him have the leasehold on the Academy of Music, a movie house on Fourteenth Street in New York. This leasehold deprived the Fox Corporation of some $1,500,000 in profits. As in so many courtroom scenes the name of A. C. Blumenthal appeared among the list of characters. His role was to be that of a witness against George Skouras. The action was postponed when the prosecutor, Mathias F. Correa, chief assistant to United States Attorney John T. Cahill, signed up to serve his country in a war capacity and placed the Skouras case among unfinished business to be pigeonholed until peace returned. George too sought to prove himself a patriot. He installed booths for the sale of War Bonds in his theatres. He volunteered to get war pictures of Greece, and with two cameramen departed for Cairo. There he remained until Greece was liberated; then he and the cameramen went into Greece, where they photographed ruins and devastation. To date nothing further has been heard of the indictment.

Among the criminal charges of the period were the narcotic story involving the Eliopoulos brothers, told earlier in this history, and the Pennsylvania story, where "good boys" had been given $1,000 bills. Among the "good boys" were state senators. At least $100,000 had been paid for favorable legislation.

The year 1941 found William Fox in trouble again. In 1936, he had filed a petition in bankruptcy with United States Circuit Judge J. Warren Davis, retired in 1939 after thirty-nine years on the bench. With Davis and Morgan S. Kaufman, a lawyer and federal referee in bankruptcy, Fox was indicted in 1941, in Philadelphia on a charge of conspiring to obstruct justice through bribery. Nineteen overt acts were listed. Fox pleaded guilty and admitted he had lent $10,000 to a cousin of Judge Davis and had given Kaufman $15,000 as an unsecured loan for the judge, for which he had received the judge's thanks. Neither loan had ever been repaid, nor had he ever received interest. He related that he also had met Davis in the hallway of a mid-city building in Philadelphia one wintry evening and had passed him a newspaper which had $12,500 hidden in its folds. Some of the bills, which proved to be marked, were traced to the account of Judge Davis's daughter, Mrs. Mary Firestone, in a Florida bank. In October of 1941, Fox, on the verge of collapse from a chronic ailment, was found guilty, sentenced to one year in prison, and fined $3,000. Kaufman was disbarred. Judge Davis was found innocent and continued to receive pay as a retired judge. Fox tried to reopen his case. How could he be guilty if Davis were innocent? Nevertheless, prison gates closed behind him. After serving his term, Fox joined his wife in Los Angeles, where together they operated a machine shop to produce a special type of camera suitable for army and navy use.

In another court room scene, Errol Flynn, who was being sued by a former wife for alimony payments and by Myron Selznick for commissions, informed the judge that as a film hero he required $14,595 a month to live. The judge informed him $12,000 should be sufficient. In an out-of-court scene, Flynn appeared in a night-club brawl. He rushed up to the table of Jimmy Fidler, writer for motion picture fan publications, shouting, "You are no good," and reached to pull Fidler from his chair. Mrs. Fidler, coming to her husband's rescue with a fork, stabbed the actor's ear. The cause of the fight was not mentioned, but Fidler, when interviewed, did say that previously he had refused $2,500 which had been offered him to give a favorable review to The Prisoner of Zenda, a movie in which Flynn starred.

Meanwhile in Europe, Hitler entered Prague, crossed the French border, accepted the surrender of Yugoslavia. Joseph P. Kennedy, his film career behind him, was the United States Ambassador to England. "We can do business with Hitler," Kennedy announced. He retired as ambassador, returned to the United States, and became a landlord. At the time building space was exceedingly scarce because only vitally necessary structures received construction permits. The Joseph P. Kennedy name appeared in the newspapers of this period as a rent-gouger. Rent control had not yet become a law; he left the courts with his humor, his profanity, and his wealth unimpaired. Conversely, Harry Warner and others, who had remained in the film business and who had produced some anti-Hitler movies, were forced to defend warmonger charges. Wendell L. Willkie, 1940's defeated presidential candidate, was appointed the movie industry's general counsel and came to the rescue of the producers.

Ironically, the United States Division of Information of the Office of Emergency Management called the same producers derelict in the crisis and accused them of producing pictures simply for entertainment instead of recognizing that ". . . . . . .the movies could be a perfect medium for keeping the public well informed, and a well-informed public is America's first line of security."

After the December 1941 attack on Pearl Harbor, although the use of film footage was restricted by the government, the industry was classified as essential, and Hollywood informed it might get as tough as it wished with Germany, Italy, and Japan. The green light did not still fears that duplicated those suffered during World War I, when producers felt the public came to the movies to be entertained and would soon tire of war stories.

Harassments stemmed in all directions. Thurman Arnold, United States Attorney General, in the largest anti-trust suit filed by the United States Government against the industry, characterized the business as ". . . an industrial dictatorship and distinctly un-American." Mr. Arnold charged that concentration of industrial power is a tax on the public and a threat to democracy. He held that a situation had developed in which there was no room for an opportunity for free, healthy competition. The old fight against monopoly and block booking was on.

The industry engaged James Roosevelt, son of the United States President, to fill a post on the West Coast. Some of the highest paid lawyers in the United States were employed to fight the Government.

Ralph H. Harris, for Twentieth Century-Fox, said, "Some injustices or occasional instances of unfair discrimination might have occurred, but I never yet heard even the Government claim that, given a free hand, it would regiment our society into Utopia."

Nicholas Schenck was hurt. He said, "I would consider it the worst kind of a crime for a group of companies to get together to prevent another company from doing business." He added he did not believe that such a situation could arise in the motion picture business.

Sidney Kent issued a statement in which he backed block booking as a stable sales method for exhibitors and followed up with a letter in which he called a halt ". . .to bickering and name calling, which has led us no where. Let us look at our problems less selfishly. Have we not been our own worst enemies. There is no exhibitor, no distributor, no producer, no individual in any capacity whatever, who is not worse off today because of the path we had taken than he would have been had we continued to fight our problems among ourselves. No one in the industry can escape the results of ill-advised legislation once it is put into the hopper. Let us stop, look, and listen before it is too late."

He, as well as those who heard the letter read, failed to comprehend they already were too late! The "ill-advised" legislation went into effect. Arnold did not get all the things he asked for, but to sell pictures in greater blocks than five became illegal.

Samuel Goldwyn hailed the change. "It is a blessing," he said, "to have block booking abolished." In film circles he was called traitor, one who bit the hand that fed him.

This was Sidney Kent's last battle. Ill, he failed rapidly, and on March 19, 1942 he died. Spyros Skouras was elected president of Twentieth Century-Fox to succeed him, and Wendell Willkie, the famous lawyer, was elected chairman of the board to replace Joseph Schenck. Schenck, whose sentence had been reduced to one year and a day when he aided in the conviction of Willie Bioff, was released after serving four months and five days. Several years before he had lauded the abilities of Spyros Skouras; Spyros now returned the compliment. "We are happy to have been able," he said, "to prevail upon Mr. Schenck to head our production activities. There is hardly an important progressive step in the industry in which he has not been actively associated. His acceptance is our assurance that the high production standards set by Twentieth Century-Fox will be maintained. Mr. Schenck always has been recognized as a power behind the throne in Hollywood matters generally as well as in the operation of the Fox Company." Whereupon Schenck signed a seven-year contract calling for a weekly salary of $2,500 and became head of production at the Twentieth Century-Fox West Coast studios.

Television

W HEN WORLD WAR II FINALLY ENDED, film men were not as concerned about the type of pictures to be produced as they were about whether to produce pictures at all. Would television rob them of their investments? Would an economic depression come with peace? On August 28, 1946, while film officials worried, Variety announced: "Film Industry's Fattest Six Months In History." Net earnings had dwarfed those of 1945, which had been a peak year. The higher earnings were explained: the Treasury Department's removal of excess profits levies, the opening of additional markets abroad, the upward spiral in film rentals, increased admission prices. Film executives continued to worry, but Wall Street sources said movie issues might be expected to climb and classified ". . . .film industry stocks as 100% stable and not as a luxury" inasmuch as ". . . .the poor man's entertainment must now be recognized as a basic necessity of life in this country." At the box office the "poor man" paid up to $3.50 for a seat.

Industry leaders were earning more than ever. On July 30, 1946, Ralph Hendershot, World-Telegram and Sun columnist, wrote:

> Four executives of Twentieth Century-Fox apparently did pretty well for themselves two years ago when they bought a twenty per cent interest in National Theatres Corp., a subsidiary, for $565,000. Now National proposes to buy the stock back for $7,415,000. The profit will amount to $6,850,000. And even after payment of long-term capital gains taxes, the net profit will amount

363

to more than $5,000,000.

Stockholders have been asked to vote on the proposed purchase on August 20. If past experiences count for anything, they will give it the green light. The deal has an angle. The Transamerica Corp. made an offer of the same price, according to the company's proxy solicitation, so stockholders are more or less over a barrel on the proposition.

One man — Charles P. Skouras — will get the bulk of the easy money. His share for an investment of $353,135 will be $4,634,375. Since his salary has averaged $235,003.39 for each of the last five years, he has been able to build up quite a barricade against the proverbial wolf, which may be just outside his door.

. . . . .Uncle Sam took quite a toll of Mr. Skouras' salary during those war years, of course, and the stock deal was set up, apparently to offset these sacrifices. That $4,634,375 should go a long way toward paying off any debts he may have incurred in meeting his living expenses during that trying period, even if he were obliged to pay black-market prices at times.

Mr. Skouras, no doubt, always will be grateful to the late Wendell L. Willkie for his part in making the deal possible. Mr. Willkie was chairman of the Fox board at the time. This is supposed to be one of the little jobs he helped do in his spare time.

In addition to his $4,634,375 profit, Charles P. Skouras was top United States' earner. His salary and bonuses for the year came to $985,300. Loew's Incorporated established a pension plan, a $200,000 yearly retirement salary for top executives. Other corporations provided their executives with profit participation and stock option opportunities.

In spite of the earnings' zoom, satisfactory retirement provisions, stock options, and the confidence of Wall Street, film men continued to prepare for the day when the market's bottom might drop out. Emphasis was placed on technical achievements. New devices were sought to act as hypodermic needles to stimulate the public. Twentieth Century-Fox financed a giant color screen being developed at the

University of Zurich in Switzerland. R-K-O unveiled a new theatre screen, the same size as the old, but which gave the illusion of much wider range, and promised a surprise with an anamorphic lens capable of showing films in five different aspects. Third dimensional films, especially on a wide screen, were seen as a key to future enchantment. When told of the various devices, a spokesman for the resigned exhibitors said, "Here we go again. No matter what new gimmick they put out, there's always something new we have to buy. It's a field day for the equipment people."

During this period of pessimistic prosperity, the labor question again proved embarrassing. At an investigation conducted by the National Relations Board, B. B. Kahane, chairman of the Labor Committee of the Motion Picture Producers' Association, admitted a policy which continued to favor and coddle the IATSE in an effort to keep unions, which remained independent of corporation control, in line. Mr. Kahane revealed how IATSE brought in scabs to replace regular workers and how these scabs were kept on the payroll during unneeded periods, simply to keep them happy. Willie Bioff and George Browne were allowed a day out of prison to explain at one session just how strikes were suppressed and how IATSE helped corporations maintain low wage scales and poor union conditions.

Other situations also embarrassed the industry. Variety reported that Metro subsidized three book publishers and sent scouts into the hinterland to obtain works, on which Metro would have a first look and an exclusive for thirty days. A top ranking United States State Department attache returned from four years in Europe and declared that American producers didn't fully grasp the political power of the medium they controlled. He said, "Hollywood product, if properly selected for export could meet optimistic response. Rulers of various nations, other than those within the Russian orbit, are fully cognizant of the role American pictures play in instilling the virtues of democracy. Distribution must be selective to take full advantage of this market. Films such as Grapes of Wrath and Tobacco Road must be avoided." The New York World-Telegram and Sun, in a series of articles, stated that Oscars were a Hollywood headache because phony voting created ill will. And then, on October 13, 1948, the New York City newspaper informed its readers:

Film Industry At Lowest
Financial Ebb In History

. . .Strangely enough movie theatres are doing a healthy
business, only slightly below last year. . .
. . .Movies still cost too much to make. . .
The pinch is on in Hollywood, and it's hitting a lot of
people hard. For every three persons working in the studios
in 1940 there are now two.

Thus fears of a recession appeared justified. Theatres were transformed into garages, roller-skating rinks, laundries, dry-cleaning es-
tablishments, museums. Producers blamed television with its night
showings of sport events, exhibitors placed full blame for the slack
on bad and expensive pictures.

For all the blame placed on it, television came forth as the show
business savior. Barney Balaban, president of Paramount Pictures,
one of the few who from the start believed the infant prodigy might
become the hero of the entertainment world, had a well-established
television broadcasting studio in Chicago. He envisioned the Tele-
meter Electronic theatre-in-the-home, that is "pay as you view"
television without commericals. The system, which, according to Mr.
Balaban, operates on cable lines without requiring Federal Com-
munications Commission approval and without need for residual
fees to Hollywood guilds and crafts, had already been tested in Eto-
bicoke, a Toronto, Canada suburb. Feature films were presented,
some after all theatrical runs, some simutaneously with second theatrical runs at a price of one dollar for each showing. Si Fabian
wired a theatre circuit for TV showings. Mr. Fabian envisioned the
day when the public, disenchanted with home TV programs, would
flock to the theatre to see live shows — video performances of boxing
matches, ball games, operas, ballets, dramas. As this history closes
he waits only for a perfected projection apparatus to carry through
his plan, strongly believing that home television cannot compete
with that in a theatre because the figures on a small screen have
not the appeal of beauty or grandeur to be found in the greater-
than-life size figures on a giant screen. Producers, who once had
resented television, began to obtain important revenue by selling
old-time features to the erstwhile competitor. Eventually Variety re-

ported, "Hollywood To Go Steady With TV."

While this love affair progressed, in other parts of the world where television was looked upon as an American phenomenon, newly opened movie houses were requesting films. In the United States, Drive-in theatres, originally known as passion pits with pictures, began to flourish when families, sometimes with small children asleep in the back of the car, sought entertainment while out on a summer's evening for a breath of air.

The Drive-ins, as well as all other movie show places, suffered from the radical changes the industry had undergone. Block booking already had been abolished and, early in 1951, a thirteen-year battle with the Department of Justice was lost by the Majors when they entered into consent decrees and production and theatre units were divorced. The divorce accomplished, the Justice Department lost interest in the movie game. For the first time in fourteen years it functioned without a picture specialist, all future cases to be split up in routine fashion.

The divorcement brought about realignment. Spyros Skouras became president of Twentieth Century-Fox, a producing corporation; George Skouras became president of theatre units which operated under various names. Si Fabian returned as a big time theatre operator, becoming president of the Stanley-Warner Corporation, a theatre chain with which he had been associated twenty-three years before. For a brief period, Arthur Loew headed the circuit founded by his father, but he soon resigned the presidency to let others carry on a proxy battle for control. Howard Hughes, multimillionaire plane builder and oil operator, who had bought a controlling interest in R-K-O in the spring of 1948 from the Atlas Company controlled by Floyd Odlum, sold his interest in the theatre division in November of 1953 to Albert A. List, a textile king.

The maneuvers of Howard Hughes in the R-K-O Picture Corporation, the producing unit, were unfathomable. In minority stockholder suits he was charged with placing various actresses under contract at "exorbitant prices" and failing to use them in pictures; reckless spending; using the corporation to satisfy his whims as if he were the sole owner; causing shareholders to suffer losses while he made deals profitable to himself. Although he promised to embark on full-scale production, little or no films were in prospect at the studio. His releases were almost all made by independents, several of whom he financed. He sold old releases to television users while theatres cried for product. He sold an option on his controlling interest and repurchased it at a profit. He entered into a battle for control of the stock with Floyd Odlum, a feud which was costly to the corporation. In the midst of this fight Walt Disney, who released through R-K-O, withdrew his product and ended a 17-year association. In a guessing game, while a guest at the Tom O'Neil palatial estate at Palm Beach, Florida, Hughes answered alternately "Yes" and "No" when questioned about a merger of R-K-O Pictures Corporation and the Atlas Corporation, of which Floyd Odlum was president.

A controlling interest in R-K-O Pictures, which had been reduced to a corporate shell, appeared as a prize to one who possessed the wizardry to decipher benefits under certain Internal Revenue considerations. Having lost money for years, it had a capital loss carry-over of $20,000,000. Thus, a purchaser might realize profits in that amount and they would be free of federal taxes. Tom O'Neil, who headed General Tire & Rubber Company and controlled the Mutual Broadcasting System, captured the R-K-O Pictures Corporation and merged it with another company he owned, General Teleradio. Teleradio Pictures, Inc., which became the formal corporate name of the merged companies, sold the R-K-O picture library for television use. The studios went to the Desilu Productions, manufacturers of television shows, and R-K-O, one of the Majors, passed from existence.

Theatre owners despaired. Another source of pictures was gone. More movie show places operated than ever in history, and each one was hungry for product. Nevertheless studio activities remained curtailed. Employment of production workers was slashed, some lots closed down completely, others abondoned the movies and turned out television westerns, mysteries, crime thrillers, etc. Warner Bros., which became the owner of the largest newsfilm stock library, when in 1947 it absorbed Pathé News with subjects dating back to 1898, "dumped" the newsreel. Twentieth Century-Fox planted wells to drill for oil on its property. The Loew people organized a corporation dedicated to the building of gigantic hotels. By the late fifties, practically the only movies produced were on a grand scale for release at high rentals to luxury houses with special screens. Variety dubbed these so-called quality films "Blue Chip Pix."

Desperate theatre owners petitioned for the right to produce. To date the government has remained adamant; the theatre-producer divorce is irrevocable. The arrangement achieved by the Skourases, whereby one brother was permitted to operate a producing unit and another brother a theatre unit, has been denied other families in the industry. Wistful exhibitors watch producers release to TV competitors old subjects that might attract audiences into movie show places. And so, exhibitors continue the old cry, "Whatever anti-trust or other legislation is passed, we are the losers."

These new battles between producers and exhibitors are reminiscent of those that were held before the producer became producer-exhibitor or during the period producers were bringing theatres into their organizations. While these battles raged, Spyros Skouras traveled into Russia, Greece, Japan, and other parts of the world to promote the name Twentieth Century-Fox. He had become an honored citizen, feted at a $100 a plate dinner at the Waldorf-Astoria, New York City, as a great humanitarian and American.

In the new era, columnists, whose stories formerly treated casting, parties, fashions, and gossip of filmland's Who's Who in a glamorized world became economists who devoted their space to liquidations, property values, corporate structures and difficulties. When in the late fifties they reported that Wall Street was bullish on motion picture shares because earnings were higher, they explained that the increase came from the unloading of assets such as sound stages and props as well as old features, and from diversification. Stanley-Warner had a corset, brassiere, and pharmaceutical subsidiary; Twentieth Century-Fox had productive oil wells; hotels were falling under Loew's aegis. Music records, aluminum pistons, coal, textiles, uranium, rubber, warehousing, real estate, etc., aided the profit showing. For years stock and bond surveys had carried a column headed "Motion Pictures." In 1959 motion picture securities fell into a category headed "Recreation," which also analyzed the shares of bowling, boating, radio companies, and the like, or the securities were listed among the industrials. America's Fourth Industry lost identity and glamor, but it achieved Empire in diversification.

In their infancy, the movies appeared as an ogre that might devour the reading public. For years the press resisted mentioning them. Once its fears were overcome, the press discovered in motion pictures not merely lively news items but a substantial source of revenue. For over half a century as Variety might have said, "They went steady."

Then, on July 12, 1960, Paul N. Lazarus, Jr., vice-president of Columbia Pictures, appeared before the Newspaper Advertising Executive Association in San Francisco and reproached his hosts for providing TV with fascinating news items and neglecting motion pictures that for over half a century had provided the papers with "juicy" material.

While many in various parts of the world watched to determine if the lights in Hollywood would dim to a degree that another film center might claim the title Motion Picture Capital, shadows fell on the other side of the American continent. Darkness enveloped the world's most ornate movie palace, the Roxy Theatre, in New York City. Its marble columns, coruscating chandeliers, bronze doors, elaborate costumes, heavy curtains and carpets, its massive organ, air conditioning equipment which also made ice for skating, and other mechanisms were offered as a gift to anyone who would cart them away. Two youths loaded the library of music scores, which contained arrangements of Handel's The Messiah, Victor Herbert's operetta The Princess Pat, Gilbert and Sullivan's H. M. S. Pinafore, onto two trucks and drove to Roslyn, Long Island, where they produced open-air band concerts. Everything else was spurned as too gargantuan. The Cathedral of Motion Pictures and most of its fittings, assembled at a cost between $10,000,000 and $12,000,000, transformed into rubble under the torches of a wrecking crew. In the ruins echoes of the triumphant march of Harley Lyman Clarke and Winfield Sheehan are mute.

Throne after throne has tottered, but not that of the movie queen. At her whim, the king who had crowned her might abdicate; a public educated to adore her keeps her place secure. Thus, when the set for production of the super-super, the "Blue-Chip Pic" Cleopatra was erected in an Italian rather than a Hollywood studio to keep costs down, Elizabeth Taylor, the star selected for the role of the Egyptian charmer, appeared whenever she felt in the mood to do so. The director's great worry was how to lure her onto the set on schedule to finish the picture within a reasonable time. When this, and other of her monkeyshines, skyrocketed costs of this super-super into $30,000,000, Spyros Skouras assured Twentieth Century-Fox stockholders that Cleopatra eventually would procure a handsome profit, and then reluctantly vacated the chair at the head of the corporation's table.

Making pictures on a stream-line basis for block booking had faded with other practices into the past. Super-specials seemed to be the only type worth time in an industry de-glamorized by "cease and desist." From the time block booking had been introduced it had created situations as dramatic and often more acrimonious than any on the screen. With block booking irrevocable outlawed, threatre managers, the very men who had fought to destroy that way of bargaining, would have welcomed an oportunity to engage in a package deal which contained inferior films as well as some of the so-called classics. Movie houses, that had swelled into the greatest number in history despite TV competition, were starving for films; to make matters worse many old time productions were unavailable because they had been transferred from the theatre to the television screen. In the younger field, old time sales pep revived. Blocks of pictures were offered with the old unsavory flavor — several lemons had to be contracted for in order to get a picture with a sweeter taste. But, individualism no longer meant "anything goes." At one time, a salesman, although he may have used tactics frowned on by everyone except a distributor (tactics that even in the old days brought him into the courts) was confident that he could stall any adverse decision for years, until the decision had become ineffectual. On November 5, 1962 all that was changed. The Supreme Court, only twenty days after the TV block booking case was argued on October 16, 1962, and less than two years after the lower court had rendered its decision on December 2, 1960, ruled that a motion picture distributor might not demand that any TV station buy a package of films to get the ones it wants. However, one thing the court said may reanimate a salesman's spirits: if a distributor lists the price of each picture individually, he may offer films in packages and briefly defer licensing a single picture to one station if a deal is in negotiation with a competitive station for a package.

As this work is being made ready for press, a deal is being closed for the sale of the Paramount Building on Times Square, the "crossroads of the world." Located in the skyscraper is the 3,650-seat movie palace, which occupies the equivalent of five stories and was the pride of Adolph Zukor's career. The showplace is dark, its seats are to be torn out, its luxurious furnishings and props are to be sold. But memories of its glories persist. Here, the "hot bands" of Glenn Miller, Harry James, Benny Goodman, the Dorsey Brothers stirred patrons to rise from comfortable mohair chairs and dance in the aisles. Here, the rock-'n-roll of Alan Freed, the oily songs of Frank Sinatra roused bobby-soxers to shriek and cry. The now silent auditorium once rang with the jokes of Jerry Lewis and Bob Hope, the crooning of Bing Crosby, the sophistication of Dean Martin. In its golden age, frenzied teen-age fans lined up in the streets before dawn and formed queues that extended around the large square block. Marks of those who tried to knock down the doors can still be seen. The scribbled sign pasted to the glass of the box-office, "Closed until further notice," is fraying. Of all the "Deluxe" theatres which enriched their film shows with elaborate stage presentation, only the Music Hall at Rockefeller Center continues to prosper. The purchaser of the Paramount, bowing to the age of science, has announced this Zukor monument to motion picture art is to be transformed into display space for the exhibition of machine-produced articles.

Nineteen sixty-five. William Fox, Louis B. Mayer, Harry Warner, Adolph Zukor, Charles and George Skouras are dead. Of the old-line czars only the voice of Spyros Skouras is heard, but, within the industry, his words have diminished influence. His more important statements at this time are addressed to members of the United States Government, which he desires to have as a partner in a fleet of freighters that can be loaded mechanically. And the movies themselves? They seem to have fulfilled the destiny Edison first envisioned for them. He conceived action pictures as illustrations for sound recordings that were played on his phonograph. Now, as more and more old and new films find their way to television screens, they, in a sense, illustrate a sound device, the radio.

BIBLIOGRAPHY

BOOKS AND ARTICLES

ADAM, THOMAS R. *Motion Pictures in Adult Education*. New York: American Association for Adult Education, 1940.

ADLER, MORTIMER J. *Art and Prudence*. New York: Longmans, Green & Company, 1937.

ALLIGHAN, GARRY. *Romance of Talkies*. London: C. Stacey Ltd., 1929.

ARNOLD, THURMAN. *The Bottlenecks of Business*. New York: Reynal & Hitchcock, 1940.

_____. *The Folklore of Capitalism*. New Haven: Yale University Press, 1937.

BALABAN, CARRIE. *Continuous Performance*. New York, Putnam Publishing Company, 1942.

BARDECHE, MAURICE, AND ROBERT BRASILLACH. *History of Motion Pictures*. New York: W. W. Norton & Company, 1938.

BERTRAND, DANIEL, W. DUANE EVANS, AND E. L. BLANCHARD. *The Motion Picture Industry*. Washington: Government Printing Office, 1941.

BETTS, ERNEST. *Heraclitus, or The Future of Films*. London: K. Paul, Trench, Trubner & Company, 1928.

BLUMER, HERBERT. *Movies and Conduct*. New York: Macmillan Company, 1933.

CROY, HOMER. *How Motion Pictures Are Made*. New York: Harper & Bros. 1918.

DALE, EDGAR. *The Content of Motion Pictures*. New York: Macmillan Company, 1935.

DAVY, CHARLES. *Footnotes to the Films*. New York: Oxford University Press, 1937.

DE MILLE, WILLIAM C. *Hollywood Saga*. New York: E. P. Dutton & Company, 1939.

DOYLE, GEORGE RALPH. *Twenty-five Years of Film*. London: The Meter Press, 1936.

DRINKWATER, JOHN. *Life and Adventures of Carl Laemmle*. New York: Putnam Publishing Company, 1953.

ELLIOTT, W. F. *Sound-recording for Films*. London: Pitman, Ltd., 1937.

ENCYCLOPEDIA BRITANNICA. *Photography*, a series of articles in the eleventh edition. England, 1910.

_____. *The Theatre and Motion Pictures*, a selection of articles from the fourteenth edition. New York, 1933

ERNST, MORRIS L. *Censored*. New York: J. Cape & H. Smith, 1930.

_____. *The First Freedom*. New York: MacMillan Company, 1946.

Film Daily Cavalcade. New York: Barnes Printing Co., 1939.

FLETCHER, JOHN GOULD. *The Crisis of the Film*. Seattle: University of Washington Chapbooks, 1929.

FLOHERTY, JOHN JOSEPH. *Moviemakers*. Garden City: Doubleday, Doran & Company, 1935.

FLETCHER, JOHN GOULD. *The Crisis of the Film*. Seattle: University of Washington Chapbooks, 1929.

FLOHERTY, JOHN JOSEPH. *Moviemakers*. Garden City: Doubleday, Doran & Company, 1935.

FORMAN, HENRY JAMES. *Our Movie Made Children*. New York: Macmillan Company, 1934.

FOWLER, GENE. *Father Goose*. New York: Covici, Friede & Company, 1934.

FOX, CHARLES DONALD. *Mirrors of Hollywood*. New York: Charles Renard Corp., 1925.

FRANKLIN, HAROLD B. *Motion Picture Theatre Management*. New York: Doran & Company, 1927.

GOLDEN, NATHAN D. *Motion Picture Markets*. Washington: U. S. Foreign & Domestic Bureau, 1944.

GOLDWYN, SAMUEL. *Behind the Screen*. New York: George H. Doran Company, 1923.

GRAU, ROBERT. *Businessman in Amusement World*. New York: Broadway Publishing Company, 1910.

_____. *The Stage in the Twentieth Century*. New York: Broadway Publishing Company, 1912.

_____. *The Theatre of Science*. New York: Broadway Publishing Company, 1914.

GREEN, FITZHUGH. *Film Finds Its Tongue*. New York: G. P. Putnam's Sons, 1929.

HAMPTON, BENJAMIN BOWLES. *A History of the Movies*. New York: Covici, Friede & Company, 1931.

HAYS, WILL. *See and Hear*. New York: Motion Picture Producers & Distributors Assn., 1929.

HEPWORTH, CECIL M. *Came the Dawn*. London: Phoenix House, 1951
_____. *Animated Photography*. London: Hazell, Watson & Viney, Ltd., 1900

HEURRON, F. L. *Block Booking*. Rome: Article in the International Review of Educational Cinematography, 1932.

HOLSTIUS, E. NILS. *Hollywood Through the Backdoor*. New York: Longman's Green & Company, 1937.

HOPPER, HEDDA. *From Under My Hat*. New York: Doubleday & Company, 1952.

HOPWOOD, HENRY V. *Living Pictures*. London: The Hatton Press, Ltd., 1915.

HUETTIG, MAE D. *Economic Control of the Motion Picture Industry*, Philadelphia: University of Pennsylvania Press, 1944.

HULFISH, DAVID S. *Motion Picture Work*. New York: American Technical Society, 1915.

HUNTER, WILLIAM. *Scrutiny of Cinema*. London: Wishart & Company, 1932.

IRWIN, WILL. *The House That Shadows Built*. Garden City: Doubleday, Doran & Company, 1928.

JACOBS, LEWIS. *The Rise of American Film*. New York: Harcourt, Brace & Company, 1941.

JOHNSTON, ALVA. *The Great Goldwyn*. New York: Random House, 1937.

KAHN, GORDON. *Hollywood on Trial*. New York: Boni & Gaer, 1948.

KLINGENDER, F. D. AND STUART LEGG. *Money Behind the Screen*. London: Lawrence & Wishart, 1937.

KNEPPER, MAX. *Sodom and Gomorrah*. Los Angeles: End of Poverty League, 1935.

LANE, TAMAR. *What's Wrong with the Movies*. Los Angeles: The Waverly Company, 1923.

LEJEUNE, CAROLINE A. Cinema. London: Alexander Maclehose, 1931.

LEWIS, HOWARD T. *Cases on the Motion Picture Industry*. New York: McGraw-Hill, 1930.

_____. *The Motion Picture Industry*. New York: D. Van Nostrand Co., Inc., 1933.

LINDSAY, VACHEL. *The Art of the Moving Picture.* New York: Macmillan Company, 1922.

LOVELL, HUGH AND TASILE CARTER. *Collective Bargaining.* University of California Institute of Industrial Relations, 1955.

LUBSCHEZ, BEN. J. *The Story of Motion Pictures.* New York: Reeland Publishing Company, Inc., 1920.

MARCHETTI, ROGER. *Law of the Stage, Screen, and Radio.* San Francisco: Suttonhouse, 1936.

MAYER, ARTHUR. *Merely Colossal.* New York: Simon & Schuster, 1953.

MAYER, ARTHUR AND RICHARD GRIFFITH. *The Movies.* New York: Simon & Schuster, 1957.

McKECHNIE, SAMUEL. *Popular Entertainments Through the Ages.* London: Samuel Loew, Marston, 1932.

MESGUICH, F. *Tours de Maniville.* Paris: B. Grasset, 1933.

MESSELL, RUDOLPH. *This Film Business.* London: E. Benn, Ltd., 1928.

METCALFE, LYNE S. *How To Use Talking Pictures In Business.* New York: Harper & Bros., 1938.

MOLEY, RAYMOND. *The Hays Office.* New York: Bobbs-Merrill Company, 1945.

MOMAND, A. B. *The Hays Office and the N.R.A.* Oklahoma: Shawnee Press, 1935.

MOTION PICTURE ASSOCIATION OF AMERICA (Motion Picture Producers & Distributors of America, Inc.). *A Code to Govern the Making of Motion Pictures.* Washington, 1955.

_____. *A Code Adopted February,* 1930. New York, 1937.

_____. *A Collection of Publications on Motion Pictures.* New York, 1922-25.

_____. *Drive-in Theatres in United States.* New York, 1948.

_____. *Film Facts.* New York, 1938.

_____. *Report of the President,* New York, 1930, 1933, 1934, 1935, 1936, 1937, 1938, 1939, 1940, 1941, 1942, 1943, 1944, 1945, 1952, 1955.

MYERS, ABRAM F. *Manual of Arbitration Under the Motion Picture Consent Decree.* Washington: Allied States Assn. of Motion Picture Exhibitors, 1941.

NICOLL, ALLARDYCE. *Film and Theatre.* New York: Thomas Y. Crowell Company, 1936.

Nizer, Louis. *New Court of Industry*. New York: Longacre Press, 1935.

Palmer, Edwin O. *History of Hollywood*. Hollywood: Arthur H. Crawston, 1937.

Parsons, Louella O. *The Gay Illiterates*. Garden City: Doubleday, Doran & Company, 1944.

Peden, Charles. *Newsreel Man*. Garden City: Doubleday, Doran & Company, 1932.

Perlman, William J. *Movies on Trial*. New York: The Macmillan Company, 1936.

Pettijohn, Charles Clyde. *Brief in Opposition to the Enactment of H. R. 6097*. Washington: House Committee on Interstate & Foreign Commerce, 1934.

_____. *The Motion Picture*. New York, 1923.

Quigley, Martin, Jr. *Magic Shadows*. Washington: Georgetown University Press, 1948.

Ramsaye, Terry. *A Million and One Nights*. New York: Simon & Schuster, Inc., 1926.

Reichenbach, Harry and David Freedman. *Phantom Fame*. New York: Simon & Schuster, Inc., 1931.

Ross, Murray. *Stars and Strikes*. New York: Columbia University Press, 1941.

Rosten, Leo Calvin. *Hollywood, the Movie Colony*. New York: Harcourt, Brace & Company, 1941.

Rotha, Paul. *Documentary Film*. New York: W. W. Norton, 1939.
_____. *Films Till Now*. New York: J. Cape & H. Smith, 1930.
_____. *Movie Parade*. New York: The Studio Publications, 1936.

Schmidt, George (and others). *The Film*. London: Falcon Press, 1948.

Seabury, William Marsten. *Motion Picture Problems*. New York: Avondale Press, 1929.

Seldes, Gilbert. *The Great Audience*. New York: Viking Press, 1950.
_____. *An Hour with the Movies and the Talkies*. Philadelphia: Lippincott Company, 1929.
_____. *The Movies Come from America*. New York: Scribner's Sons, 1937.
_____. *The Seven Lively Arts*. New York: Harper and Brothers, 1924.

Silverberg, Herbert T. *Televising Old Films*. Silverberg, 1952.

SINCLAIR, UPTON. *Upton Sinclair Presents William Fox*. Los Angeles: The Author, 1933.

SPOTTISWOODE, RAYMOND J. *A Grammar of the Film*. London: Faber, Ltd., 1935.

STEVENSON, EDWARD F. *Motion Pictures in Advertising and Selling*. New York: The Stirling Press, 1929.

STRONG ELECTRIC COMPANY. *Then and Now*. Toledo, 1940 (?).

TALBOT, FREDERICK A. *Moving Pictures*. Philadelphia: Lippincott Company, 1923.

TROTTA, V. AND C. LEWIS. *Screen Personalities*. New York: Grosset & Dunlap, 1933.

VAN ZILE, EDWARD S. *That Marvel—The Movie*. New York: G. P. Putnam's Sons, 1923.

WARREN, LOW. *The Film Game*. London: T. W. Laurie, 1937.

WHITNEY, SIMON W. *Antitrust Policies*. New York: Twentieth Century Fund, 1952.

WOOD, LESLIE. *The Miracle of the Movies*. London: Burke, Ltd., 1947.
_____. *Romance of the Movies*. London: W. Heinemann, Ltd., 1937.

WRIGLEY, MAURICE JACKSON. *The Cinema*. London: Grafton & Company, 1939

_____. *The Film*. London: Grafton & Company, 1922.

ZUKOR, ADOLPH. *The Public Is Never Wrong*. New York: Putnam Publishing Company, 1953.

NEWSPAPERS AND PERIODICALS

Artcraft Advance, Artcraft Pictures Corp., New York, 1917.
Atlanta Newspapers.
Billboard, New York City, 1894-
The Biograph, Biograph Company, New York, 1914-1915.
Biograph Programs, Biograph Company, New York, 1916.
Boston Newspapers.
Box Office, Kansas City, 1932-1933.
Box Office Barometer, Kansas City, 1944-1946
Business Week, New York, 1953-
Chicago Tribune.

Christian Science Monitor, Boston.
Collier's Weekly, New York 1905-1953.
Current Opinion, New York, 1888-1925.
Dallas Newspapers.
Duquesnes Film News, Pittsburgh, 1912.
Eclair Bulletin, Eclair Film Company, New York, 1914.
Edison Kinetogram, Edison Corp., Orange, N.J., 1901-1916.
Educational Film Magazine, New York, 1919-1922.
Essanay News, Essanay Company, Chicago, 1915.
Everybody's Magazine, New York, 1899-1929.
The Exhibitor (Later New York State Exhibitor), New York, 1939-54.
Exhibitors Herald, Chicago, 1926-28.
Exhibitors' Times (Later Motion Picture News), New York, 1913.
Exhibitor's Trade Review (Later Motion Picture Daily), New York, 1916-31.
Feature Movie Magazine, Chicago, 1915.
Film Daily (Formerly Wid's Film and Film Folk), New York 1915-
Film Renter, London, 1922-1927.
Fox Film News, Fox Film Corp., New York, 1916.
General Bronze Corp., New York, Circular 1953.
Goldwyn Pictures, Goldwyn Pictures Corp., New York, 1916.
Harper's Magazine (Formerly Harper's Weekly), New York, 1892-
Harrison's Forecaster, New York, 1931-
Harrison's Reports, New York, 1919-1931.
Hollywood Reporter, Hollywood, 1934-1952.
In Equity 6796, 6928, 8289.
Kalem Kalendar, Kalem Company, New York, 1913-1915.
Kansas City Star.
Leslie's Weekly, 1855-1922.
Life Magazine, Chicago, 1936-
Literary Digest, New York, 1890-1938.
Los Angeles Times.
Lubin Bulletin, Lubin Manufacturing Company, Philadelphia, 1916.
Motion Picture Daily (Formerly Exhibitor's Trade Review),
       New York, 1916-1931.
Motion Picture Herald (Formerly Views and Film Index),
       New York, 1911-1931.
Motion Picture News (Absorbed Exhibitors' Times and Motion Picture
       Herald), New York, 1909-1930.
Motion Picture World (Moving Picture World), New York, 1907-1936.

Moving Picture Stories, New York, 1913-1929.

National Board of Review Magazine, New York, 1926-1949.

New Orleans Newspapers.

New Theatre, New York, 1934-1937.

New York Clipper (Absorbed by Variety), New York, 1900-1924.

New York Dramatic Mirror, New York, 1900-1922.

New York Newspapers:

    New York *Herald* (Merged with the Tribune).

    New York *Journal.*

    New York *Morning Telegraph.*

    New York *Sun* (Merged with World and Telegram).

    New York *Telegram* (Merged with Sun and World).

    New York *Times.*

    New York *Tribune* (Merged with Herald).

    New York *World* (Merged with Sun and Telegram).

New York Public Library Form p 411, April 14, 1939.

Paris Herald.

Paramount Progress, Paramount Pictures Corp., New York, 1928-1932.

Paste Pot and Shears, Selig Polyscope Co., Chicago, 1915.

Photoplay Review, Philadelphia, 1915.

Photoplay World, New York, 1917-1920.

Picture Progress, New York, 1915-1917.

Popular Mechanics, Chicago, 1903.

Saturday Evening Post, Philadelphia, 1876-

Scientific American, New York, 1876-

The Screamer, Los Angeles, 1916-1917.

Selig Monthly Herald, Selig-Polyscope Corp., Chicago, 1915.

Show World, Chicago, 1906-1911.

Spirit of the Times, New York, 1873-1902.

System, Chicago, 1928-1935.

Triangle News, Triangle Film Corp., New York, 1916-1918.

Variety (Absorbed New York Clipper), New York, 1905-

Views and Film Index (Later Motion Picture Herald),
    New York, 1907-1911.

Woman's Home Companion, New York, 1899-1957.

World Film News, London, 1936-1938.

World's Work, New York, 1914.

YEARBOOKS

Film Daily Year Book of Motion Pictures, Jack Alicoate,
     Editor. New York.
International Motion Picture Annual, Terry Ramsaye, Editor. New York.
Kinematograph Year Book (Handbook of Kinematography),
     E. T. Heron, Editor, London.
Screen World Annual, Daniel Blum, Editor. New York

INDEX

(Because of the frequency with which corporate names changed, popular names often appear throughout this book and in the following list.)